3 2044 011 138 880

WATERGATE
AND
AFTERWARD

**Recent Titles in
Contributions in Political Science**

WITHDRAWN

Watergate and Afterward

THE LEGACY OF RICHARD M. NIXON

EDITED BY

Leon Friedman

AND

William F. Levantrosser

Prepared under the auspices of
Hofstra University

Contributions in Political Science,
Number 274

GREENWOOD PRESS
Westport, Connecticut • London

E 856 .W38 1992

Watergate and afterward

AMY 1969-0/1

RECEIVED

OCT 2 0 1992

Kennedy School
Library

Library of Congress Cataloging-in-Publication Data

Watergate and afterward : the legacy of Richard M. Nixon / edited by
Leon Friedman and William F. Levantrosser ; prepared under the
auspices of Hofstra University.
      p.   cm.—(Contributions in political science, ISSN 0147–1066 ;
no. 274)
    Papers from the Hofstra Presidential Conference on Richard M.
Nixon held at Hofstra University, Nov. 19–21, 1987.
    Includes bibliographical references and index.
    ISBN 0–313–27781–8 (alk. paper)
    1. Nixon, Richard M. (Richard Milhous), 1913–   —Influence—
Congresses.   2. United States—Politics and government—1969–1974—
Congresses.   3. Executive power—United States—History—20th
century—Congresses.   I. Friedman, Leon.   II. Levantrosser, William
F.   III. Hofstra University.   IV. Hofstra Presidential Conference on
Richard M. Nixon (1987 : Hofstra University)   V. Series.
E856.W38   1992
973.924'092—dc20   90–20677

British Library Cataloguing in Publication Data is available.

Copyright © 1992 by Hofstra University

All rights reserved. No portion of this book may be
reproduced, by any process or technique, without the
express written consent of the publisher.

Library of Congress Catalog Card Number: 90–20677
ISBN: 0–313–27781–8
ISSN: 0147–1066

First published in 1992

Greenwood Press, 88 Post Road West, Westport, CT 06881
An imprint of Greenwood Publishing Group, Inc.

Printed in the United States of America

The paper used in this book complies with the
Permanent Paper Standard issued by the National
Information Standards Organization (Z39.48–1984).

10   9   8   7   6   5   4   3   2   1

WITHDRAWN

Contents

DISCUSSANTS:

DISCUSSANTS:

DISCUSSANTS:

Preface

This volume of papers and proceedings from the Hofstra Presidential Conference on Richard M. Nixon examines the darker sides of the Nixon Presidency—the Watergate controversy, his impeachment, his alleged misuse of governmental power for political ends, and his administration's obsession with secrecy and the control of information.

Whatever else will be said about the accomplishments of the Nixon Administration—in terms of its opening of relations with China, its domestic initiatives, including the passing of new environmental laws and welfare modifications, and so forth—the fact remains that the Watergate scandal and the forced resignation from office of a sitting president marks the Nixon Presidency off from every other reign in our history. The governmental accomplishments of the Nixon Administration are described in companion volumes to this one. However, it seems appropriate to present what would be called the dark years of the Nixon period in a single volume.

Included in this volume are a final assessment of the Nixon Presidency by a group of biographers who have written about the man and his politics. In addition, various administration figures and outside historians appraise his accomplishments and failures in light of the scandals of the time. The question still remains whether the constitutional crisis created by Watergate ultimately outweighs the list of achievements under Nixon's rule.

In planning the conference we sought both papers and discussants to examine these contrasting impressions. The participants included scholars, journalists, and people who served in the Nixon Administration. We wanted to make the panels as comprehensive in scope and as extensive in depth as possible to create the optimum environment for the free exchange of ideas. In a few instances we realized that a comfortable time frame would not afford the opportunity to balance views on one panel, so another panel devoted exclusively to opposing views was established. When papers were presented, the discussants had already read them so they were able to evaluate them and add their own observations. The discussions have been edited to make them compatible with a written format, but the flow of thought has been preserved as much as possible. Audio cassettes were made of all panels for distribution to those who desired to purchase them, and C-Span televised about half the panels nationally. As a matter of record, in order to avoid confusion, John Ehrlichman participated in the conference but not in this book.

This book would not have been possible without the assistance of many people. We would like to thank all who prepared papers and those who served as discussants. A special word of thanks goes to Frank Zarb, Hofstra alumnus and Chairman of the Board of Trustees at the time of the conference, for his help in recruiting many of the participants who had worked in the Nixon Administration. We are grateful to James Hastings and his staff at the National Archives for acquainting us with the documents of the Nixon Presidency and the researchers using them. We also thank the staff of the Hofstra University Cultural Center, capably directed by Natalie Datlof and Alexej Ugrinksy, for coordinating many of the details and arrangements of the conference along with Athelene A. Collins, Marilyn Seidman, and Laura J. Tringone. We are especially grateful to Jessica Richter for the various tasks connected with shepherding the pages of the manuscript to the publisher.

Part I

Watergate and the Abuse of Presidential Power

The Nixon Administration will always be known for the Watergate scandal and Nixon's forced resignation from office. Foreign observers were always baffled by the uproar that such a "third-rate" burglary produced, and the young Americans who were not alive when the controversy grew into a political hurricane are still unclear about exactly what happened and still have difficulty understanding how it could lead to the loss of the presidency. Why did certain paid members of the Committee to Re-Elect the President (CREEP) plan and carry out a burglary in the Democratic National Committee headquarters in the Watergate, and after they were caught, who took what actions to insure that the Nixon Administration would not be blamed for what occurred?

For the first time in a public forum, Reverend Jeb Stuart Magruder, one of the insiders, describes what the break-in was supposed to accomplish, in an exchange with author J. Anthony Lukas, who has written an important study of the original events. One of the key prosecutors, Earl J. Silbert, tells how the government approached the case, and Stanley I. Kutler emphasizes the important moral and political principles involved.

David R. Simon describes the political reactions to Watergate, and Nancy Kassop writes on Nixon's attempt to remove the first Watergate special prosecutor, Archibald Cox, and the firestorm that followed, which laid the basis for impeachment.

Other panels dealt with additional abuses of the time. Alan F. Westin describes different efforts by the Nixon Administration to uncover information about political opponents, and Michael A. Genovese discusses the politicization of the Justice Department. Responses by Charles W. Colson, who was in the White House at the time, and from John Shattuck, an important American Civil Liberties (ACLU) lawyer who participated in the events, round out the discussion.

The attempted expansion of presidential power is further discussed in a paper by Howard Ball on the constitutional confrontation in the Supreme Court over the Nixon tapes in *United States v. Nixon* and Philip Lacovara, one of the lawyers in that case. The dark side of the Nixon years is further examined in a panel on the protest movement, with participants such as Tom Hayden, David J. Garrow, and Sanford Gottlieb describing how the government attempted to sabotage the protest movement and how the dissenters affected the political currents of the time.

The Nixon Administration's concern with secrecy and control over governmental information is examined in the context of the Pentagon Papers case in a paper by John Kincaid and in the context of the assertion of presidential privilege, in Mark J. Rozell's paper. Important press figures of the time, including Tom Brokaw of NBC, Howard Simons of the *Washington Post*, and Victor Navasky of *The Nation* debate these issues with Ronald L. Ziegler and Gerald L. Warren of the White House press office.

Finally, the impeachment proceedings are reexamined. Two papers by Dagmar S. Hamilton and Terry Sullivan describe the specific charges against the president and the political coalitions that formed in Congress around them. Three key members of the House Judiciary Committee reenact their original roles: John Doar, the chief counsel for the committee, and two important members of the committee who were on opposite sides, Elizabeth Holtzman and Judge Charles E. Wiggins, debate the issues pro and con.

WATERGATE REEXAMINED

Watergate and the Nixon Presidency: A Comparative Ideological Analysis

DAVID R. SIMON

The Watergate scandal that toppled the Nixon Presidency involved virtually every type of political deviance. These included (1) excessive secrecy, lying, and "dirty campaign tricks," political repression and violations of civil rights, (2) "the fix"—accepting campaign contributions in return for personal favors, (3) acts that resulted in personal financial gain for the politicos involved, and (4) possible violations of the president's war-making powers. These divisions are arbitrary; they are meant only to categorize what in reality are many interrelated acts of either questionable ethical conduct or outright criminality (e.g., bribery, perjury, obstruction of justice, forgery, burglary, and possible income tax code violations, to list some of the most frequently mentioned.

I have elsewhere provided a more detailed analysis of the nature of the political deviance that comprised the Watergate break-in and its accompanying "horrors."[1] What is of equal interest as well concerns the various reactions by policymakers, ideologues, and social critics to the most serious scandal since Teapot Dome. This paper constitutes a case study analyzing various ideological reactions to Watergate. It is based on a representative sample of some 800 articles and books written between 1972 and 1976 by elite social critics.[2]

Methodologically, this study is based on an item unit content analysis of the document ideologies in American intellectual life, the categories, sample, and other methodological considerations of which I have explained elsewhere in detail.[3] The categories utilized in this analysis concern conservative, liberal, and socialist views of the causes, solutions, and predicted consequences to society (should solutions advocated not be placed into effect). The significance of the findings therein are also explored.

THE CONSERVATIVE VIEW

One must realize that the conservative community was initially stunned by the Watergate scandal. Many conservatives supported Richard Nixon in 1972, and some had even been his advisers. It should not surprise us that the initial reaction included descriptions like "frightening" and "madness."[4] Following the initial reaction, the specter of mass politics was used to explain the increased political activity of the 1960s and 1970s (riots and demonstrations) as well as the Nixon Administration's reactions to such behavior.

Specifically, the 1960s witnessed what some conservatives consider a "revolution of rising entitlements"; expectations in America became hedonistic, "concerned with consumption and pleasure, and lack of any moral underpinning. . . . [T]he promise of equality ha[d] been transformed into a revolution of rising entitlements—claims on government to implement an array of newly defined and vastly expanded social rights."[5]

Consistent with conservative ideology, which fears anarchy above all, Watergate is typically depicted as an attempt to restrain potentially undemocratic masses from engaging in status politics. On the other hand, some conservative analysts claimed that the scandal was itself not an extremist reaction, but actually constituted an improvement over "witch-hunts" of the past. Watergate is an "improvement" over previous scandals primarily because the Watergate horrors were perpetrated covertly, in the dark of the night, whereas in the 1920s, the illegal activities of the government were carried out in the open, and apparently with the overwhelming approval of the American people. In the Nixon Administration, by contrast, the most elaborate operation was the cover-up, which is itself a measure of the restraining power of the cosmopolitan climate not only within the administration but in the nation at large—that is, in the growing cosmopolitanization of the American people.[6]

This growing cosmopolitanism among Americans in general is due to precisely those secondary institutions that were to integrate the anomic and antidemocratic masses into the society, especially education. Nixon's cosmopolitan character had largely been shaped by his experiences in colleges and his stint in cosmopolitan New York as a well-paid lawyer. Similarly, Americans in general have become better educated; from 1920 to 1970, the proportion of the college-education population increased from 8 percent to nearly 50 percent, and college professors now number over one-half million, now constituting a separate occupational group.[7] This view of Watergate, like conservative analyses in general, holds that deviance by elites does not constitute a major source of societal concern; it is mass deviance that necessitates cause for alarm. This theme is likewise manifest in the conservative solution (policy proposals) coming in reaction to Watergate.

THE CONSERVATIVE SOLUTION

Viewing Watergate as, in part, the fault of anomic masses invading elite domains and as a restrained form of status political backlash, the conservative solution to such political deviance involves no great reforms. For the masses, theirs is an impassioned plea for restraint (noninvolvement in politics), even if such actions are legal. Alexander Bickel, of Yale Law School, has spoken of Watergate from the context of the civil disobedience that took place during the 1960s against the Vietnam War:

Like the law itself, civil disobedience is habit forming and the habit it forms is destructive of the legal order. Disobedience, even if legitimate in every other way, must not be allowed to become epidemic. Individuals are under a duty to ration themselves, to assess occasions in terms of their relative importance.[8]

Conservatives also recommend that nonelite groups participate less in politics in general. Such is S. F. Huntington's cure for the disease of democracy that he calls the democratic distemper: "The entire operation of a democratic political system usually requires some measure of apathy and noninvolvement on the part of some individuals and groups."[9] Noninvolvement is viewed as a necessity, lest the system become overloaded with demands of the masses, and, hence, present the danger of undermining the authority of elites. Moreover, no reform measures are thought necessary because the scandal (1) was an improvement over previous undemocratic episodes, and (2) the self-correcting aspects of the system performed successfully because the scandal was brought out into the open and fully investigated, and wrongdoers were punished.[10] For conservatives, the emphasis is clearly on the dangers of lack of mass restraint.

CONSERVATIVE OUTCOMES: THE DANGERS OF ANARCHY

Anarchy on the part of the masses is viewed with such alarm by conservatives that even too much education is deemed dangerous where nonelites are concerned.

The electorate in general has grown more cosmopolitan largely because of education, but education has also helped to create more ideological fervor at both ends of the political spectrum. According to a study by Everett Ladd, college-educated Republicans are more ideologically conservative than less educated party partisans. And abundant data indicate that well-educated ideologists are the most likely of all to be active in party affairs and to vote in primary elections.[11]

The prospect, then, is for a *possible* continuation of the cosmopolitan withdrawal from national politics and an increase in political extremism, and perhaps restraint.

Should the disenfranchised not practice the politics of restraining, Huntington warns of the *decline of America*, both internally and externally *as a world power*. Governing under distemper, he claims, makes it impossible for government to constrain citizens in any way. Wage and price control cannot be instituted; the new special interest groups will continue to bend government to suit their purposes; youth no longer will submit to being drafted into the military. Weakened at home, democratic leaders will find it harder to negotiate with dictators abroad. Friendly countries will be tempted to minimize their trade exports in order to keep prices down at home. Within each country so weakened, there will be an appeal for high, protective tariffs against imported goods. Worst of all, should a "real crisis" occur, government will be in no position to ask citizens to sacrifice living standards or lives.[12]

THE LIBERALS AND WATERGATE: CAUSES

For liberals the first horror of Watergate was that the totalitarian state they so much fear was (in their view) brought dangerously close to reality as an almost direct result of an institutional arrangement that they had originally championed. The verdict on this score comes from innumerable sources; the presidency has become imperial (king-like) in character:

> There is no question that the Presidency has got out of control and badly needs a new definition and restraint.[13]

> What got us into the horrors of Watergate is unbridled Presidential power.[14]

> Watergate is a natural outgrowth of liberal Democratic policy: the development of a strong presidency relying on implied powers to get things done that might be politically awkward otherwise. . . . [T]his has been an attempt to extend the power of the government over the rights of the individual, but . . . neither conservatives—who should be most outraged—nor liberals who had a great deal to do with the situation—have recognized the situation for what it is.[15]

While this may describe the problem of centralization of power in general terms, it does very little to explain how Watergate came about.

The theory shared among liberals is that the president surrounded himself with assistants who acted to insulate him from the outside world. This insulation was accompanied by some rather general commands from the president, which were carried out in unscrupulous ways. Having acquired immense power in the directing of foreign policy, an attempt was now made to consolidate that portion of the executive bureaucracy responsible for domestic affairs.[16] Motivated by a wish to rid themselves of liberals and other "enemies," especially within the federal bureaucracy, H. R. Haldeman and John Erhlichman set out to concentrate the power usually found at the cabinet level in the White House. The result was an "aborted [failed] revolution,"[17] but it was typical of a tactic used in Nazi Germany setting up a duplicate bureaucracy, thereby making the original bureaucracy (usually infiltrated with spies) obsolete. This was begun by firing virtually all original members of the Nixon Cabinet at the beginning of the second Nixon Administration. The Watergate break-in itself was simply an outgrowth of an overall plan of getting rid of political enemies. The plan for the supercabinet also included a scheme to incorporate the power of intelligence agencies, especially the Central Intelligence Agency (CIA) and the Federal Bureau of Investigation (FBI), in the White House (Executive Office of the President).[18] This attempt at consolidation of what the Nixon staff perceived as an unruly federal bureaucracy, together with the enemy's list, burglaries, agent provocateurs, and so forth, has become the liberal blueprint for the emergence of a totalitarian state in America.

Moreover, liberals are not heartened by those who view Watergate as proof that the system works. In the first place, it was nothing short of a minor miracle that the whole initial affair was uncovered and the cover-up foiled: "No claim that 'the system worked' could be made during the actual Watergate wrongdoings. *Nothing* had worked to block the various subversions at their inception, and *nothing* had worked to impede them once underway."[19]

LIBERAL SOLUTIONS

The liberal solution proposals arising from the Watergate scandal are based on the premise of reform. Campaign financing laws based on federal funding of presidential election from tax receipts; more use of the initiative, referendum, and recall of public officials; and a prohibition against CIA covert operations were all proposed by various commentators. Many of these reforms were adopted. Unfortunately, space limitations make a full discussion of them impossible. Those interested in a fuller treatment of the reforms arising out of this era may consult one of a number of extant sources.[20]

LIBERAL OUTCOMES: 1984

Despite the reforms arising from Watergate, liberals in general remain cynical concerning the notion that the mere revelation of the scandal could restore America's moral climate to one of decency.

The American people's betrayal of their most basic principles—liberty and justice for all—has touched, and probably corrupted, every one of us and every part of our society. The response so far is discouraging, for it suggests that corruption in the highest officials in the country has prompted the public at large not to angrily repudiate them but to sympathetically identify with them. If profound corruption in our leaders merely reflects profound corruption in the rest of us, we clearly have no reason to be [confident] about our future.[21]

Liberals claim that the public was largely cynical about politics before the scandal. Some like to point out that opinion began to shift against Nixon only when it was revealed that he might be doing things that personally affected the "people in the street": opening their mail, auditing their taxes, inflating their food prices by doing political favors, and the like.

An important part of the liberal notion that the public sympathetically identified with the Watergate horrors concerns, not what wrong was done, but the *style* in which the acts were committed. The fact was that Haldeman and crew were public relations men, and this had important consequences:

There is the atmosphere of—shall we say Madison Avenue?—in which those in power view government as a giant public relations enterprise. This view assumes that policies are to be argued not on principle but on the merits of their packaging, as it were, that everyone and everything can be manipulated, never mind what methods are used, never mind how the products turn out. Just as political campaigns are turned over now to public-relations firms, so great issues of war and peace, of wealth and commonwealth, are to be decided not on their merits but through the manipulation of public opinion polls or the purveying of false information even by the President, who himself appears and sounds more and more like head of a giant public relations firm.[22]

A final factor was the inability to control the special interest groups who were involved in many of the attempts to "fix" ongoing investigations within government government. About all these factors, liberals are anything but optimistic:

Our theoretical perspectives leads us to predict more such extralegal uses of power. This means not only more Watergates, but more lying in official statistics; more manipulation of fronts through political tricks; more secret taxation by using Newspeak [lying] to name taxes "insurance" . . . and more secret leaks by newspapers and television aimed at destroying political enemies. . . . [In the long run] . . . [t]yrannical power will be wrapped in democratic forms—indeed in the glorification of these democratic forms. This will be all the more possible because . . . such tyranny will have to be based in good part on the power of the mass media: Television will trumpet the revival of the Great American Democracy. . . . The drive toward centralized executive [presidential] power will continue, and with it will come a new form of democratic tyranny. . . . This new democratic tyranny will be a comfortable tyranny in which the masses are paid off with liberal reforms such as guaranteed incomes and health "insurance." . . . [O]ur massive interest groups, from Big Business and Big Labor to Big Agriculture and Big Welfare, will continue to demand their government pay-offs, while denouncing both the rip-offs of other groups and the Big Government their effective demands have created.[23]

This prediction of course is predicated on the belief that the masses will not become aware of such dangers in time to act, while big interest groups may recognize that they are the ones who are creating the big government they complain about so much; and that they will cut back on their immediate demands for payoffs, thus enabling more democracy to be restored. However, as J. Douglas and many other liberals say, they are not optimistic about such prospects because "the times do not justify it."

THE SOCIALISTS AND WATERGATE: LEGITIMATION CRISIS

It may not be too exaggerated to state that many radicals are very dubious concerning the nature of the character of elites. As Herbert Marcuse has said:

"Today, the old problem of the judgment of governing groups is complicated by a clinical problem. Modern elites tend increasingly to be recruited from psychopaths of various kinds."[24] Along with this proposition goes another claiming that elite deviance is built into the very context of capitalist politics.

This context is the present state of American capitalism. It seems that it cannot function, cannot grow any more without the use of illegal, illegitimate means, without the practice of violence in the various branches of the material and intellectual culture. . . . Today's conglomerates and multinational corporations would, by their very structure, exercise conspiratorial and illegitimate power. The difference between the Mafia and legitimate business becomes blurred. The purveyors of violence, as entertainment or as part of the job to be done, find sympathetic response among the underlying population whose character they have shaped.[25]

The only difference about Watergate, radicals claim, was that the repression usually reserved for anticapitalist radicals was visited upon the Democrats, bona fide members of the power elite. Moreover, Nixon was ousted because of the legitimation crisis of the capitalist state. Watergate was not only a conflict between factions of the ruling class; the scandal created a serious problem of legitimation for the ruling class as a whole, which was then linked to Nixon's growing inability to deal with the structural problems.[26]

Thus, as the Watergate scandal unfolded and it was revealed that Nixon had not done anything that other presidents had not also done, such revelations might turn Watergate into a questioning (by the masses) of the entire political system. The polls reflected a loss of confidence in government, and "there was widespread awareness of the system's moral bankruptcy, of the extent to which people are no longer the source of sovereignty of the state but simply the object of manipulation by elites."[27]

Some radicals believe that Nixon plumbers might have sabotaged the airplane flight of Dorothy Hunt (Howard Hunt's wife) and stolen (from her purse) secret Watergate-related files. Others believe that Nixon aides might have hired Arthur Bremmer to assassinate George Wallace. Still others see a tangled web of intrigue that includes the cover-up of President John Kennedy's assassination in Dallas in 1963, drug smuggling in Vietnam by the CIA, Teamster investments, and Syndicate real estate deals with which Nixon and his friend Bebe Rebozzo have been involved. For such believers, the investigation and ouster of Nixon was itself a cover-up designed to convince the public that the system had worked and that its relegitimation was possible.

SOLUTION AND OUTCOMES: MORE WATERGATES

Socialist commentators feel that solutions to the problems arising from Watergate are simply not resolvable under the present structure of political economy. The basic problem, claim socialists, remains the great inequalities of wealth and power characteristic of monopoly capitalism.[28]

Consistent with the dialectic outlook, socialists believe that the solution to the problem of Watergate and the legitimation crisis of late capitalism is really more scandal. Further scandal would cause further questioning of the legitimacy of the political economy, and ultimately, changes in a socialistic direction. Without further scandal, the result could be a continuation of the centralization of executive power, staffed by personnel from economic rulers who will make policy at the behest of big business,[29] perhaps ultimately resulting in a sort of "friendly fascism" characterized by a repression of the rights of dissidents, Orwellean newspeak, and "big brother" invasions of privacy, as well as Huxlean psychosexual gratification via sexual and chemical stimulation.[30]

Consistent with contemporary socialist thought, then, there are no guarantees that the objective and subjective conditions necessary for the Marxian dialect to socialism will take place. Of all the ideological groups studied, however, the socialists seem the least pessimistic of the three regarding the long-term consequences of the scandal.

WATERGATE AND INTELLECTUAL IDEOLOGIES

As an exercise in the sociology of knowledge, this chapter is not so much about the acts that comprised the Watergate scandal as it is about the reactions of the dominant groups of intellectual ideologues that characterized the Nixon era. The analysis is important not only for its study of the scandal that brought down a president but for assessing shifts in the American ideological landscape as well. Such shifts may perhaps be measured by assessing the degree to which an ideological group is optimistic or pessimistic concerning the future of a given issue.

In the case of Watergate, conservatives and liberals seem to raise the most alarm, but for diametrically opposed reasons. The conservatives have traditionally feared an anarchy by nonelites that would overwhelm elite authority and institutions, culminating in a dictatorship of either the right or the left.[31] Liberals, for their part, have become so cynical about the possibility of progressive reform and so fearful of the imposition of an Orwellean state on the masses by elites that liberalism as an ideology has all but lost its initial enlightenment-based optimism.

Socialists, who were originally the target of repression by governmental elites, remain cautiously and dialectically optimistic concerning the realization of their goals. Perhaps the ideological legacy of the Nixon Presidency was threefold. First, it prepared the groundwork for a further shift to the right among former liberal and leftist intellectuals now referred to commonly as neoconservatives.[32] Second, it resulted in further pessimism and cynicism among liberals; and third, the Nixon excesses and abuses gave radicals a chance to say "we told you so" to their ideological rivals.

Finally, Watergate and Iran/Contragate need to be compared for their effects on the political and ideological climates of their respective times. A comparative study of the writings of the same social critics writing in both eras would serve as a valuable guide to the future of both ideology and policy formation in American politics.

THE IMPACT OF WATERGATE ON THE PRESIDENCY

Watergate has had a profound impact on the nature of political ethics, campaign financing, and foreign policy; as just about everyone who has written on these subjects attests. The real question, however, is what that impact has been, and this is a matter of intense debate between conservative, liberal, and radical social critics; especially in light of the Iran/Contragate affair. Again, we look at each of these views seriatum and in brief fashion.

The Conservative View

Conservatives continue to be upset about the threat to elite authority and power posed by the post-Watergate view of morality. In the shadow of Iran/Contragate, the "Guns of Watergate," as Leonard Garment terms them, have given rise to prosecutorial politics, wherein elites must now make information public in ways not required of them before Watergate.[33] This has meant a renewed muckraking among the press, increased congressional oversight of the FBI and CIA, more stringent ethics codes (e.g., Hamilton Jordon's battle against accusations of cocaine use), and an era of hyperscandal under Ronald Reagan (e.g., Richard Allen, Donovan, and Burford-Lavelle). Thus, today there are seven independent counsels carrying on investigations. Special counsel investigations and the threat thereof now make lying in politics necessary, and this conspires to keep good people out of government.

In addition, argues Garment, all this has given rise to an era of flank covering, the increase of secrecy, and an increased likelihood of criminal acts due to failure to disclose. Finally, "What did you know and when did you know it?" has now become a key question in American politics, and real policy issues are becoming obscured by a lack of responsible inquiry, to which the Tower Commission is a notable exception.

These sentiments have also been echoed by L. G. Crovitz.[34] The law is now filled with such a great assortment of crimes that it is merely a matter of pinpointing the person and proceeding to pin something on him or her. As a result, presidents no longer dare to exercise the full authority placed in them by Congress, especially in foreign policy. Moreover, claims Crovitz, Congress has continually eroded presidential authority by passing a series of unconstitutional laws, including the legislative veto, the War Powers Resolution, the Boland Amendment, certain aspects of the Gramm-Rudman Act, and, especially, the post-Watergate special counsel law, allowing for the selection of a special prosecutor by a three-judge panel when it is suspected that a high-ranking official has committed a crime. In short, conservatives fear an erosion of the imperial presidency, and with it a potential rise of practices that they claim are anti-democratic.

The Liberal Position

Watergate, *The New Yorker* claims, has given rise to a smoking gun mentality. Under Reagan the question of presidential accountability has become one of whether the president is responsible for the illegal acts of his aides and closest appointees, resulting in the subversion of the constitution for the sake of plausible deniability.[35] Other liberals, like Bill Moyers, Alan Westin, and Theodore Draper, view Watergate as a continuation of the activities of the secret government that comprises the national security state.[36] Reagan's National Security Council amounted to an equivalent of Nixon's "Plumbers." The only real lesson that seems to have carried over from Watergate to Iran/Contragate was the notion of destroying the evidence. Otherwise, both scandals manifest the same contempt for Congress, the law, and the truth. The new twist in Iran/Contragate was the unprecedented use of military personnel, who blindly followed orders, resulting in ever more secrecy and executive control of foreign policy in the name of anticommunism, national security, and presidential authorization via the finding. Except in the Iran/Contragate case, the president signed the finding after the sale of arms to Iran and kept his finding hidden from Congress.

The Radical View

While liberals see similarities between Watergate and Iran/Contragate, radicals tend to find a direct link between the two scandals. The central figures in Iran/Contragate appear as a sort of distorted testimonial to C. Wright Mills's contention regarding a "military metaphysic" and preparation for World War III. Thus, the principal players in the Iran/Contragate drama constitute a cabal frustrated by the American loss in Vietnam and the decline of covert operations since Watergate and the Senate Intelligence Committee hearings of the mid-1970s.[37] Headquartered in the National Security Council (NSC), John Poindexter, Oliver North, James McFarland, and their military colleagues represent the largest collection of military personnel ever assembled within that particular organ of government.

The selling of arms to Iran and the diversion of funds from such sales to the Nicaraguan Contras was accomplished by the setting up of a private supply operation using a company owned by retired Air Force general Richard Secord. Secord's National Management Corporation had also been involved in other covert operations besides Iran/Contragate, including logistical support for the military elite's Delta Force commandos and certain short-term airlift operations.[38]

In fact, radicals claim, the Iran/Contra operation methodology may have been conceived by Secord, a Vietnam veteran, during a meeting on Special Operations held in 1983 at the Georgetown University National Strategy Information Center.

That meeting was attended by a number of CIA and military officials (including Oliver North) and Secord associate Ted Schackley (himself later involved in Contra aid shipments). Present also was Carl Channel, a former motel owner and aide to Oliver North in raising money for candidates supporting administration policy in Central America.[39] At the Georgetown meeting, Secord spoke of the need to circumvent Congress and the bureaucracy in setting up covert operations, and argued that the NSC would be a likely place to attempt such circumvention. Secord had originally argued this in a master's thesis written at the Naval War College, and the proceedings of the 1983 Georgetown meeting, now in their second edition by the U.S. Government Printing Office, contain a description of the plan.[40] Thus, radicals view Iran/Contragate as emerging directly from frustration felt over reforms passed as a result of the Watergate scandals.

Some radicals, moreover, claim that a confluence of interests among an unusual set of allies, including international narcotics smugglers, "former" CIA agents and ex-military officers, Central American death squad leaders, ex-Nazi Klaus Barbie, and organized crime figures now form a shadow CIA of which both Watergate and Iran/Contragate were a part. There is also the claim that the Reagan administration accepted illegal campaign contributions from certain repressive foreign governments, much like the Nixon administration did during the Vietnam War.[41] Radicals view Watergate as having set the stage for further corruption and repression on the part of the U.S. capitalist elite both at home and abroad.

Campaign Financing and Watergate

Aside from the issue of continued illegal covert operations in the post-Watergate era, another major debate related to the Watergate legacy concerns the impact of election financing reforms. One outgrowth of Watergate was the Federal Election Campaign Act of 1971 (amended 1974). Briefly, the act provided for the establishment of a six member Federal Election Commission (FEC) to administer election laws; amended the Internal Revenue Code to provide financing of presidential elections at virtually all stages of the election process; established spending ceilings on campaigns for all federal offices; prohibited domestic cash contributions in excess of $100 and prohibited all foreign contributions; limited independent expenditures on behalf of individual candidates, and, most important, set a limit of $1,000 per candidate per portion of the election cycle per individual (with a $25,000 cumulative ceiling). Moreover, political action committees (PACs) were restricted to contributions of $5,000 per candidate per portion of an election cycle and an unlimited aggregate amount per candidate. This final provision has virtually guaranteed that PACs now dominate the American election financing process, and the election financing debate, as a result, has become ipso facto a debate about the influence of political action committees and their influence in American politics.

CAMPAIGN FINANCING

The Conservative View

The election financing reforms that came out of the Watergate era have given rise to the political action committees, and there is much debate among different ideological schools concerning their influence. Conservatives have, by and large, supported PACs, arguing that they have resulted in various benefits for the democratic process. Ann Matasar has summarized this perspective:[42]

1. [PACs] provide legitimate organized interest representation for individuals.
2. PACs enable candidates without personal wealth or partisan support or both to seek office and have a chance of winning. This . . . opens up the democratic process for more diverse citizen participation.
3. Corporate PACs and the rules that govern them (e.g., disclosure requirements) have brought corporate political involvement into the light for all to see. This adds legitimacy to corporate political activity and increases public faith in our political system.
4. PACs enhance debate and competitions of ideas in politics by raising issues (e.g., free enterprise) that are otherwise ignored by political parties.
5. Corporate PACs have helped to balance the overwhelming political power of organized labor.

The Liberal View

Liberals have been quite critical of the role of PACs in the electoral process. They claim that PACs have had the following negative consequences:

1. Corporate PACs foster legalized corruption. This occurs because lawmakers become dependent on them as an easily available course for obtaining substantial sums of money to finance increasingly expensive campaigns and to provide an improved chance of winning. . . .
2. Corporate PACs as well as PACs in general have catalyzed and benefited from the decline of political parties and the diluted representation of constituents by their legislators. Thus PACs have stimulated voter apathy by undermining the party organizations which had traditionally educated voters and brought them to the polls and by making the citizenry cynical regarding the importance of voting for members of Congress.
3. Corporate PACs as well as PACs in general undermine the democratic process and exacerbate the decline in national unity regarding economic and ideological issues by strengthening smaller, specialized interests which work in opposition to the larger public interest and by drowning out the voice of the individual who cannot compete with concentrated wealth.
4. Corporate PAC financial support of candidates buys access and thus influence. Incumbents, in particular, benefit from this system; therefore, they have a self-interest in maintaining the status quo.

5. Corporate PACs provide corporations with an indirect conduit for channeling corporate funds into federal election campaigns, thus bypassing the intent, if not the wording, of the laws prohibiting direct corporate financial involvement.[43]

Radicals view the financing reforms of the Watergate era as being undone by political action committees and rich candidates. Thus, the Federal Election Campaign Act of 1971 ostensibly outlawed influence peddling. However, it was passed by Congress only after the inclusion of enough loopholes to ensure the continued unhindered funding of Democratic and Republican candidates by their traditional capitalist-class sponsors.

While outlawing huge direct contributions from corporations, other vested interests, and wealthy individuals, the act and subsequent court decisions still allow huge, direct contributions from the same sources to political action committees. The PACs can legally dispense no more than $5,000 to a candidate per campaign—but there are hundreds of PACs and many of them share the same corporate sponsors and thus dispense funds to the same politicians.

The act also allows wealthy presidential candidates unlimited spending on their own campaigns should they choose to forgo the funding of campaigns.[44]

Ironically, the issue of campaign financing may have been involved in both Watergate and Iran/Contragate. In Watergate, it was the South Vietnamese government that may have donated to the 1972 Nixon campaign, ostensibly to insure continuation of the war that was supposedly being Vietnamized. In Iran/Contragate, speculation persists by radicals that right-wing governments from Taiwan to Central America may have donated illegally to either or both of the Reagan campaigns in order to insure that the United States would undertake anticommunist covert operations and military aid to right-wing governments.

WATERGATE, THE PRESIDENCY, AND THE SOCIAL CRITICS

With the exception of the conservative view of PACs, there is consensus among social critics of the left, center, and right that Watergate has had a negative (read undemocratic) effect on the presidency and the political process. Conservatives continue to point to challenges to elite authority and legitimacy and the potential anarchical effects of intrusions into the domain of the executive branch, especially in foreign policy. Both liberals and radicals point to the growth of a shadow government loaded with unsavory characters and exempt from all the usual checks and balances of the democratic process as envisioned by the Constitution's originators. Radicals continue to point to a government of, by, and for the ruling class and its multinational corporate interests. There are notably few other issues over which social critics contend wherein such a consensus has been achieved.

Second, it is no small irony that after thousands of articles, books, and numerous official investigations, there remain questions about why the Watergate

break-ins took place initially, and even why President Nixon submitted to resignation (rather than facing an impeachment process). Concerning the break-ins,
most observers feel that the Nixon White House wanted to know if Larry O'Brien
knew of the $100,000 paid to Nixon associate Bebe Rebozo by Howard Hughes.
O'Brien had been Hughes's Washington representative for a year, and was in a
position to know about such dealings. Moreover, a loan from Hughes had hurt
Nixon in his 1960 campaign against John F. Kennedy, or at least Nixon thought
the loan had cost him the election.[45]

However, there are writers, such as Jim Hougan, who claim that the Watergate
burglars had actually tapped no phones and that the actual tap on the phone of
Spencer Oliver had been planted by someone else, possibly Alfred Baldwin, an
associate of Watergate burglar James McCord, in order to listen to Oliver's
conversations. Allegedly, Oliver's secretary, Ida Wells, was introducing visiting
Democrats to call girls who were part of a Columbia Plaza Apartment ring being
run by Washington attorney Philip Bailey, who was arrested in 1972 for running
that organization. Among the clients were supposedly a White House lawyer
who enjoyed being horsewhipped and a congressional executive secretary who
engaged in zoophilia, voyeurism, and other sexual aberrations. The second Watergate break-in took place following Bailey's arrest, perhaps to find out if
O'Brien knew of any derogatory information on the Republicans resulting from
the ring in question.[46]

Moreover, there is some speculation that the entire call girl ring may have
been a CIA operation, as were the taps on the Democrats' phones. Indeed,
Hougan believes that James McCord actually sabotaged the break-in by the Nixon
Plumbers by having a bogus tap placed on Larry O'Brien's phone. Moreover,
McCord came into possession of the key to and certain files in Ida Wells's desk,
files allegedly containing a list of the call girl ring clients.

All this speculation is of interest because it demonstrates a central feature of
Watergate's impact on the presidency; namely, the extent of CIA activity in
presidential and congressional politics either before or after Watergate. Moreover, the impact of the scandal itself on such domestic operations remains unknown. So long as this is the case, Watergate's full impact on the presidency
remains clouded. What does seem clear from Iran/Contragate is that some of
these operations were transferred to the National Security Council.

There are also the questions raised by Renata Adler concerning the possibility
of Nixon's acceptance of secret campaign contributions from the South Vietnamese government in 1972 in return for prolonging the Vietnam War.[47] If true,
such contributions would indicate a scandal far worse than anything revealed in
Watergate because such contributions constitute a return of American foreign
aid dollars as a bribe of an American president in exchange for prolonging a
war that ended up taking over 58,000 American lives.

Finally, the theories concerning the motives behind the Watergate break-in
and Nixon's actual motives for resigning from office serve to point up what is
to date the lasting effect of Watergate on the American political culture. What

conservatives decry as the decline in respect for authority, liberals term the crisis of confidence in American politics, and socialists label the legitimation crisis of capitalism has never really been reversed.[48] The Iran-Contra scandal, as well as the resignation of well over a hundred high-level Reagan appointees, has merely served to reinforce a deeply held public suspicion of political elites in American society. It remains to be assessed just how much lack of voting in elections, how much nonelite and elite crime and corruption, and how much tax avoidance and evasion are motivated by scandals on high. However, the public opinion polls have never risen to their pre-Watergate levels concerning confidence in both political and economic elites, and it is this legacy of alienation that may constitute the most negative and enduring impact of Watergate on the American political landscape.

NOTES

1. See David R. Simon and D. S. Eitzen, *Elite Deviance*, 2d ed. (Newton, Mass.: Allyn and Bacon, 1986), especially chapters 6 and 8; and David Simon, *Watergate as a Social Problem* (Unpublished paper presented at the 1976 meeting of the Society for the Study of Social Problems).

2. See Charles Kadushin, *The American Intellectual Elite* (Boston: Little, Brown, 1974); and David Simon, "The Ideologies of American Social Critics," *Journal of Communication* 27 (Summer 1977): 40–50.

3. David Simon, "Teaching Ideology in the Classroom: An Exercise in Item Unit Content Analysis," *Teaching Political Science* (July 1981): 561–565.

4. Irving Kristol, "Nightmare of Watergate," *The Wall Street Journal*, May 17, 1973, p. 20.

5. Daniel Bell, "The Revolution of Rising Entitlements," *Fortune*, April 1975, p. 98.

6. S. M. Lipset and E. Raab, "An Appointment with Watergate," *Commentary* 36 (September 1973): 43.

7. Ibid., pp. 42–43.

8. A. Bickel, "Watergate and the Legal Order," *Commentary* 57 (January 1974): 24.

9. S. F. Huntington, "The Democratic Distemper," *The Public Interest* 39 (Spring 1975): 10.

10. "Where Do We Go from Here?" *National Review*, November 9, 1973, p. 3.

11. Lipset and Raab, "An Appointment with Watergate," p. 43.

12. Huntington, "Democratic Distemper," pp. 30–31.

13. A. Schlesinger, "How to Save the Presidency," *The Wall Street Journal*, June 1, 1973, p. 10. See also A. Schlesinger, *The Imperial Presidency* (Boston: Houghton Mifflin, 1973), esp. pp. 377–419.

14. J. Gardner, "The Colonies Will Overcome," *The New York Times*, May 16, 1973, reprinted in *Current* 147–157, no. 153 (July 1973): 19–21.

15. T. Wicker, "Is the Restoration of Public Confidence Possible?" in *Crisis in Confidence: The Impact of Watergate*, ed. D. Harward (Boston: Little, Brown, 1974).

16. Archibald Cox, "Ends," *The New York Times Magazine*, May 19, 1974, pp. 19–28.

17. Hans Morganthau, "The Aborted Nixon Revolution," *The New Republic*, August 11, 1973, pp. 17–19.

18. R. Sherrill, *Why They Call It Politics* (New York: Harcourt, Brace, Jovanovich, 1974), pp. 16–17.

19. M. Mintz and J. Cohen, *Power, Inc.* (New York: Viking, 1976).

20. See, for example, D. Harward, *Crisis in Confidence*.

21. "Talk of the Town," *The New Yorker*, August 10, 1973, p. 20.

22. H. Commager, "The Constitution After Watergate," *Current* 16, 158–168, no. 166 (October 1974): 16.

23. J. Douglas, "Watergate: Harbinger of the American Prince," in *Official Deviance*, ed. J. Douglas and J. Johnson (Philadelphia: Lippincott, 1977), pp. 112–120.

24. H. Marcuse, "Watergate: When Law and Morality Stand in the Way," *New York Times*, June 27, 1973, p. 39.

25. N. Chomsky, "Watergate: A Skeptical View," *The New York Review of Books*, September 20, 1973, p. 3.

26. S. F. Bay Area Kapitalistate Group, "Watergate, or the 19th Brumaire of Richard Nixon," *Kapitalistate*, Spring 1975, p. 3.

27. B. Brown, "Watergate: Business as Usual," *Liberation*, July–August 1974, p. 16.

28. M. Harrington, "Watergate: On Politics and Money," *Dissent* 20 (Summer 1973): 278.

29. See I. Howe, "Watergate: The Z Connection," *Dissent* 20 (Summer 1973): pp. 275–277, for such a prediction. See, in this regard, S. Weisman, ed., *Big Brother and the Holding Company* (Palo Alto, Calif.: Ramparts Press, 1974).

30. B. Gross, *Friendly Fascism* (New York: Liveright, 1980).

31. See William Kornhauser, *The Politics of Mass Society* (New York: The Free Press, 1959).

32. P. Steinfels, *The Neoconservatives* (New York: Simon and Schuster, 1981).

33. Leonard Garment, "The Guns of Watergate," *Commentary* 83 (April 1987): 15–23.

34. L. Crovitz, "Crime, the Constitution, and the Iran-Contra Affair," *Commentary* 84 (October 1987): 23–31.

35. "Notes and Comment," *The New Yorker*, July 27, 1987, p. 21.

36. Bill Moyers, "The Secret Government," *Public Broadcasting System* (aired November 4, 1987). See also "Deja Vu All Over Again," *The Nation*, December 5, 1987, p. 680; Theodore Draper, "The Iran Contra Affair: An Autopsy," *The New York Review of Books*, December 17, 1987, pp. 67–77; and I. Fredman, "The Presidential Follies," *American Heritage*, September/October, 1987, pp. 38–43, for various descriptions of similarities between Watergate and Contragate.

37. Peter Scott, "Beyond Irangate," *Crime and Social Justice* 6 (Summer 1987): 24–46.

38. J. Conason and J. Waas, "Contragate: Judgement Days," *Village Voice*, July 28, 1987, pp. 15, 18.

39. J. Morley, "Ollie's Blueprint," *The New Republic*, May 25, 1987, pp. 16–18.

40. Ibid., p. 16.

41. For a complete analysis of this viewpoint, see David Simon, *Character Structure*

and Organizational Behavior: America Scandalized, paper presented at the 1987 Meeting of the Society for the Study of Social Problems, August 14–17, Chicago, Illinois.

42. Ann B. Matasar, *Corporate PACs and Federal Campaign Financing Laws: Use or Abuse of Power* (New York: Quorum Books, 1987), p. 4.

43. Ibid., p. 3.

44. Ann B. Matasar, *The People*, November 3, 1987, p. 3.

45. See J. Anthony Lukas, ''A New Explanation of Watergate,'' *The New York Times Book Review*, November 11, 1984, p. 7; also see below.

46. Jim Hougan, *Secret Agenda: Watergate, Deep Throat 7 and the CIA* (New York: Random House, 1984).

47. Renata Adler, ''The Search for the Real Nixon Scandal,'' *The Atlantic*, December, 1976, p. 76ff.

48. Simon and Eitzen, *Elite Deviance*, pp. 1–5, for a recent review of opinion poll data on this issue.

2

President Nixon's Dismissal of Special Prosecutor Archibald Cox: An Analysis of the Constitutionality and Legality of an Exercise of Presidential Removal Power

NANCY KASSOP

At his press conference on October 20, 1973, Special Prosecutor Archibald Cox issued the following statement: "Whether we shall continue to be a government of laws and not of men is now for Congress and ultimately the American people to decide." Dramatic? Yes. Hyperbole? No.

At issue here was the very delicate question of a president's power to remove an executive branch official—on its face, a seemingly simple procedure supported by a reasonable expectation of a president that the office of chief executive carries with it the authority to control its subordinates. However, this was no ordinary executive branch official (nor, may it be argued, was this any ordinary chief executive), and the institutional relationship between them was, itself, unique and unprecedented.

It is no mere accident that during the Senate Judiciary Committee's hearings on Judge Robert Bork's nomination to the Supreme Court in the summer of 1987, the American public, once again, has had its collective memory directed back toward President Richard Nixon's dismissal of Special Prosecutor Archibald Cox in October 1973 at the height of the Watergate investigation. This spectacular, pivotal, and profoundly disturbing incident may well capture, in the events of just a few days in history, the very essence of our political system. It illustrates, in microcosm, the best and the worst that our system has to offer, a system that is characterized by the intimate intertwining of law and politics as it strives fitfully to adhere to our most compelling and fundamental norm, that of a government of constitutionally limited powers.

It is precisely that norm of limited government guided by the rule of law that was so flagrantly violated by President Nixon's actions on that memorable Saturday in October. In my analysis, I intend to show that Nixon's dismissal of Cox was not only clearly unconstitutional and illegal but, in addition, represented a much deeper assault on the Constitution in general, in Nixon's willingness to push beyond the boundaries of constitutionally allocated powers and restraints and into the realm of undefined, independent, and fully discretionary executive power.

My analysis will proceed on two levels: (1) first, as an examination of the *constitutional* and *legal* arguments offered by each side in this incident and (2) second, as an explanation of how the *practical* arguments surrounding the dismissal are deeply interwoven among the other two levels of arguments.

To begin, it is first necessary to briefly summarize the actual chain of events leading up to the dismissal. They start with Elliot Richardson's confirmation hearings in May 1973 before the Senate Judiciary Committee on his appointment as attorney general.[1]

A few points figure prominently here:

1. Richardson determined shortly after his nomination that he would appoint a special prosecutor with authority to investigate and prosecute offenses arising out of the Watergate break-in and other related affairs.

2. He agreed to give a veto power to the Senate Judiciary Committee if it did not approve of his choice of special prosecutor or the guidelines of the office.

3. The guidelines for the Office of the Special Prosecutor stipulated that the special prosecutor could only be removed by the attorney general for "extraordinary improprieties."[2]

4. When Richardson was asked by Senator Gene Tunney whether the President would have authority to fire the Special Prosecutor, Richardson responded:

No, the Special Prosecutor is my appointee who, although not technically confirmed by the Senate, would still have been the subject of full opportunity for the Senate to satisfy itself as to his qualifications. And if I were directed to fire him and I refused, and I would refuse in the absence of some overwhelming evidence or cause, then the President's only recourse would be to replace me.[3]

5. In an exchange with Senator Robert Mathias, Richardson agreed to publish the charter of Office of the Special Prosecutor as a Justice Department regulation in the Federal Register so that it would specifically have the force and effect of law.[4]

6. On May 23, Richardson received the unanimous approval of the Senate Judiciary Committee, and within two hours, full Senate confirmation of his nomination to be attorney general. Implicit in this confirmation was the approval by the Senate of Richardson's designation of Archibald Cox as the Watergate Special Prosecutor. (The link between Richardson's confirmation by the Senate Judiciary Committee and the committee's approval of the guidelines of the special prosecutor's office and the appointee himself cannot be overemphasized. This connection is crucial to an understanding of later events.)[5]

7. On July 16, Alexander Butterfield, in testimony before the Senate Watergate Committee, startled the public when he revealed that President Nixon had taped all conversations and phone calls in his office at the White House and at Camp David for the past two years.

8. On July 18, Cox requested eight tapes of presidential conversations and other documents from Nixon for the purpose of gathering evidence of possible wrongdoing for the ongoing criminal investigation. The tapes would provide direct evidence that could prove whether the president and other top administration officials had, in fact, been involved in the planning of the Watergate burglary and the subsequent cover-up, and Cox deemed them crucial to his investigation.

9. Nixon refused to supply the tapes, at which point Cox went to the Federal District Court to obtain a subpoena for them.

10. Nixon refused to comply with the subpoena.

11. In subsequent litigation between Cox and White House attorneys, both the Federal District Court and the Court of Appeals ruled that Nixon must turn over the tapes to Cox.

12. On October 19, Nixon declared that he would not appeal the Court of Appeals ruling to the Supreme Court but, instead, proposed a compromise by which he would personally prepare summaries of the tapes and give them to Senator John Stennis to verify their accuracy. In addition, he ordered the special prosecutor not to make any "further attempts . . . to subpoena still more tapes or other presidential papers of a similar nature."[6]

13. Cox refused to comply with Nixon's proposed compromise and refused to agree to the ban on future access to presidential documents.

14. Within hours, the president ordered Attorney General Richardson to dismiss Cox. Richardson refused and resigned.

15. The president then dispatched Chief of Staff Alexander Haig to order Deputy Attorney General William Ruckelshaus to dismiss Cox. Ruckelshaus refused and drafted a letter of resignation, but was fired before his letter reached the White House.

16. The president then informed Solicitor General Robert Bork that he was now acting attorney general and ordered him to dismiss Cox. Bork complied with the president's order and fired Cox.

17. Two days later, Bork ordered that the Watergate investigation revert back to the Criminal Division of the Justice Department.

18. The following day, Bork issued a Justice Department regulation rescinding the Watergate Special Prosecutor regulation retroactively, effective as of Sunday, October 21.[7]

19. On that same day, Nixon announced that he would abide by the Appeals Court ruling after all, and would turn over the tapes requested by the grand jury.

20. A week later, Bork, with Nixon's approval, appointed Leon Jaworski to replace Cox as special prosecutor, pursuant to a new Justice Department regulation that was virtually identical to the original one with the additional stipulation

that the new special prosecutor could not be fired even for "extraordinary improprieties" except after consultation with leaders of both parties of both houses of Congress.[8]

21. Two weeks later, U.S. District Court Judge Gerhard Gesell ruled in the case of *Nader v. Bork* (a) that Bork had violated a Justice Department regulation that prohibited the firing of Cox "except for extraordinary improprieties," (b) that Bork's order revoking the original regulation establishing the office of special prosecutor was "arbitrary and unreasonable," and, therefore, (c) that the discharge of Cox, on the stated grounds that he was requesting compliance with a court order, was illegal.[9]

Having established these facts, let us now turn to the constitutional and legal arguments in this case. These go directly to the heart of the nature of executive power. More precisely, they can be characterized as a conflict that pits discretionary executive power against constitutionally limited power. The ultimate question here is the following: Is presidential removal power *limited* or *unlimited*? The answer to this question rests on nothing less than the viability of separation of powers as an operative principle in our system of government.

CONSTITUTIONAL ARGUMENTS

The president's position, very simply, maintains that there are two constitutional bases of authority that support an unlimited removal power: (1) the grant of executive power to the president in the opening clause of Article II as a complete grant of authority to the president to take any actions that are inherently "executive" in nature and (2) the "take care" clause, or, more specifically, the assigning to the president the "duty to take care that the laws be faithfully executed," also in Article II.

These two constitutional arguments contain the following two corollaries: (1) the power to remove is incident to the power to appoint, and the power to appoint is inherently executive in nature and (2) if the president has the duty to "take care" and to supervise the execution of the laws by his subordinates, then he must be able to remove those subordinate officers who refuse to carry out his orders.

Taken together, these two constitutional arguments and their corollaries appear to create an impenetrable barrier to any restrictions Congress might want to impose on the president's power to remove executive officers. This was exactly the stated constitutional position presented by President Nixon and Acting Attorney General Bork to justify their removal of Cox.

More specifically, Bork noted at his press conference on October 20 that he also believed that the president has the right to discharge at will any member of the executive branch.[10] He did, however, concede that he did not believe and did not base his decision to dismiss Cox on any such belief that Cox had, *in fact*, committed any "extraordinary improprieties," the sole reason for which Cox could be validly removed.[11] Nor, for that matter, did Bork give *any* substantive reason for discharging Cox in his letter of dismissal to the special prosecutor. Bork's sole stated reason for firing Cox was that he believed that the order from the president to discharge Cox was "final and irrevocable."[12]

The president's reason for firing Cox was that Cox insisted on countermanding the president's decision to deny him access to the tapes and that the Special Prosecutor refused to agree to the president's compromise proposal.[13]

Therefore, in essence, the president and the acting attorney general maintained that there were virtually no limits to the president's power to remove any official within the executive branch. Furthermore, they believed that challenging an order of a president was sufficient cause for the removal of any such officer.

LEGAL ARGUMENTS

These relate specifically to the Justice Department regulation, and consist of the following four positions held by Bork:

1. The attorney general (or one acting in that capacity) has the sole authority under the Justice Department regulation to fire the special prosecutor, and that he acted pursuant to that regulation.[14]

2. Since the special prosecutor is clearly an executive officer and exercised executive functions, he is under the ultimate control of the chief executive.[15]

3. The attorney general is not required to promulgate the departmental regulation establishing guidelines for the Office of the Special Prosecutor, and the limitations in the regulation regarding causes for removal are also voluntary and not constitutionally or statutorily required.[16]

4. The attorney general, in creating the Office of the Special Prosecutor and providing for its functions, can voluntarily abolish the office and the regulation at any time, and can ignore the limitations.[17]

What, then, are the counterarguments to both the constitutional and legal positions underlying an unlimited presidential removal power here? In other words, what are the constitutional and legal arguments for a *limited* presidential removal power?

They start with the same separation of powers concept relied on by defenders of a strong presidential removal power, but here it can be seen that the separation of powers arguments cut both ways. Consider the following argument:

1. Where the president has no power to appoint, the president has no power to remove. In this case, the special prosecutor owed his appointment to the attorney general, not to the president, and, therefore, his removal could only be effected by the attorney general and not this president (a requirement that even Nixon appeared to realize).

2. Supreme Court decisions supporting limits on the president's power have held that (1) heads of departments have the power to control the removal of inferior officers in those instances where Congress has lodged their appointment

in department heads,[18] and (2) "to contend that the obligation imposed on the president to see that the laws be faithfully executed implied a power in the president to forbid their execution [which is exactly the construction Nixon argued here] is a novel construction of the Constitution and entirely inadmissible."[19]

3. If one turns to the nature of the duties executive officers perform, the Supreme Court has characterized these as either "ministerial" or "discretionary."[20] (It may be plausible to assert that Cox possessed the authority to exercise both types of duties.) *Ministerial duties* are those duties that an officer may be legally entitled to perform, even in defiance of a president; moreover, the officer may be forced by judicial process to do so. (Cox was authorized by the Justice Department regulation to challenge the president's assertions of executive privilege. His challenge resulted in two successful federal court rulings granting him the right of access to presidential documents.) *Discretionary duties* are those duties in which a greater latitude of judgment in their exercise is entrusted to the officer. If those duties originated in the president, then the president may exercise control over the officer. However, if they have been delegated by Congress to a subordinate executive officer, that casts an entirely different light of them, leading to vastly different consequences. (Cox's charter left an enormous amount of discretion to him in performance of his duties, but the real question here is whether those duties were delegated by Congress.)

Even Chief Justice William Howard Taft in the more far-reaching Supreme Court decision on presidential removal power, *Myers v. U.S.*, recognized the impropriety of presidential interference in such instances where the executive branch officer's duties were of such a sensitive nature as to preclude any presidential intrusion or control. He wrote: "There may be duties of a quasi-judicial character . . . the discharge of which the president cannot in a particular case properly influence or control."[21] (This appears to characterize very accurately the position of Cox as special prosecutor in this instance.)

An even sharper articulation of this position, and one that appears quite consistent with the character of Cox's duties, comes from the Supreme Court case of *Kendall v. U.S. ex rel. Stokes*:

There are certain political duties imposed upon many officers in the executive departments, the discharge of which is under the direction of the president. But it would be an alarming doctrine that Congress cannot impose upon any executive officer any duty they may think proper, which is not repugnant to any rights secured and protected by the Constitution and, in such cases, the duty and responsibility grow out of and are subject to the control of law, and not to the direction of the president.[22]

Taft went even further in *Myers* when he said: "There may be duties so *peculiarly and specifically* committed to the discretion of a particular officer as to raise a question whether the president may overrule or revise the officer's interpretation of his statutory duty in a particular instance" (emphasis added).[23]

The practical argument enters here in that this extraordinary investigation of

White House aides and the president himself seems to be precisely that kind of duty that is, in Taft's words, "peculiarly and specifically committed to the officer's discretion," and where presidential interference is most clearly inappropriate and inadmissible.

The crowning touch to these arguments comes from no less ardent a proponent of a broad presidential removal power than James Madison himself, who claimed "that the president would be impeachable for the wanton removal of a meritorious officer."[24]

The most respected scholar on the presidency, Edward Corwin, summed up the arguments here in what he described as a "paradox":

While the Constitution permitted Congress to vest duties in executive officers in performance of which they were to exercise their own independent judgment, at the same time, it permitted the president to guillotine such officers for exercising the very discretion which Congress had the right to require![25]

Once again, the parallels to Cox can be clearly seen here, for it is precisely the operationalization of the independence and discretion that Congress was so insistent on insuring for the special prosecutor that provoked Nixon's negative response.

4. The strongest arguments, however, against an unlimited presidential removal power come from a 1936 Supreme Court decision, *Humphrey's Executor v. U.S.*, in which the Court very simply set down three criteria for determining whether the president, in any situation, has the power to remove.[26] These criteria are, first, *nature of function of office*—which, in this case, is investigatory and prosecutorial; and, second, *character of the office*—which here is utterly unique and unprecedented. The charter of the special prosecutor authorized him to investigate and prosecute offenses against the United States arising out of the unauthorized entry at the Watergate and all other offenses arising out of the 1972 presidential election, and allegations involving the president, members of the White House staff, and presidential appointees.[27]

Most pointedly, the charter authorized the special prosecutor to determine whether to contest the assertion of executive privilege—which is exactly what Cox was doing when he was fired. The argument can be made with force here that because of the exceptionally sensitive nature of the investigation, involving the highest executive-branch officials, including the president, the office demanded a degree of discretion that should have put the special prosecutor beyond presidential power to interfere. The third criterion is *the intent of Congress*—which seems to provide the most compelling argument here:

- that the special prosecutor should be utterly independent of the president;
- that it was made very clear at Richardson's confirmation hearings that the president was to be precluded from exercising control over the special prosecutor;[28] and
- that Richardson's confirmation by the Senate Judiciary Committee was outrightly con-

ditioned on Senate approval of the appointment and the charter of the special prosecutor.[29]

In focusing specifically on a rebuttal of the *legal arguments* offered by Bork, some answers can be found in Judge Gesell's ruling in *Nader v. Bork*. He ruled on November 14, 1973, that the dismissal was illegal in light of the facts that (1) dismissal could only be for "extraordinary improprieties" and that no one (neither Bork nor Nixon) *ever* claimed that Cox had committed such acts and (2) the ultimate statutory authority to create the office of the special prosecutor resided in Congress, which vested the authority to appoint in the attorney general the power to limit removal.[30] As a result, the federal district court ruled that the special prosecutor served subject to congressional, not presidential, control.[31]

Furthermore, the district court ruled that the Justice Department regulation had the force of law and was legally binding, and as such, could not be willfully abrogated. Specifically, it cited Supreme Court precedents striking down executive department discharges of department members where those discharges were inconsistent with the department's own regulations concerning dismissals.[32]

Finally, the court noted that the special prosecutor was *not* discharged for the only reason for which discharge was permitted, but, rather, was discharged for specifically exercising the duties that he had been authorized by the charter to perform.[33]

The basic foundation on which both the constitutional and legal counterarguments rest is one that may at first glance appear questionable and vulnerable to attack, but can ultimately be validated when considered against the dramatic backdrop of this extraordinary period in history and the critical nature of the stakes involved, for these arguments go directly to the heart of determining where the ultimate and initial authority to appoint the special prosecutor resides.

It is here that the entire issue of presidential removal power begins to crystallize when juxtaposed against a competing congressional power to regulate appointments and removals. It is also here that the constitutional and legal arguments bump up against the practical arguments, and the two thus become wedded to each other.

Although Congress clearly does not possess the power to appoint or remove, it is directly authorized by the Constitution to regulate those processes. Therefore, when Congress chooses to vest the appointment power in the courts or in department heads, the ultimate responsibility for establishing conditions for removal still remains with Congress and does not automatically pass to the appointer except under terms provided by law. Where Congress makes clear that an office is to be free from presidential control and interference, it may establish, by law, specific and exclusive causes for removal that limit the president or any other appointer.

The monkey wrench here, at least superficially, is that the special prosecutor guidelines were not enacted into law by an act of Congress but, rather, were promulgated by the attorney general as a Justice Department regulation. However, they were established by the attorney general *precisely* because Congress insisted on a special prosecutor and conditioned Richardson's confirmation on its satisfactory creation. Second, the Justice Department regulation outlining the office, functions, and sole condition for removal was duly considered and *implicitly approved* by the Senate. Third, both the Federal District Court and, later, the U.S. Supreme Court in *U.S. v. Nixon*, declared that the regulation had the force of law.[34]

Therefore, even though Congress did not *technically* establish by law the special prosecutor's office, it nevertheless was an intimate participant in the creation of this office and in the securing through the removal clause in the regulation a guarantee of independence from the president.

Another argument that responds critically to Nixon's and Bork's contention that the president may fire anyone in the executive branch is that if this proposition is true, and if a president could fire a subordinate officer over the head of a department, such authority would make a mockery of the principle of separation of powers and the power of Congress to vest appointments in governmental bodies other than the president.

What is becoming apparent here is the full extent of Nixon and Bork's theory of an unlimited, fully discretionary, executive removal power. The ramifications of such a power are staggering and subversive; moreover, subverting the law is exactly what Nixon was attempting to do by firing Cox. By asserting such an unlimited power, the country witnessed a president who did not "take care that the laws be faithfully executed," but instead attempted to insure that the "law" emanating from the Justice Department regulation was thwarted, and in addition obstructed the administration of the criminal laws that Cox was charged, by regulation, to administer. By removing Cox, Nixon placed in jeopardy the entire Watergate prosecution, and, by extension, outraged the country into wondering whether the alleged criminals would ever be brought to justice.

This brings us back full circle to where we began, with the notion that the firing of the special prosecutor, although one small act, symbolized to the country the arrogance and disregard for the rule of law of a president who, when faced with the decision, chose unlimited presidential power over constitutionally limited power.

Finally, the ultimate test to which presidential actions are subjected is that of a determination of legitimacy. Legitimacy is determined by the expression of support (or a lack thereof) for a president's action as evidenced through public consensus, congressional response and, where applicable, judicial response.

Without a doubt, the case can easily be made here for a nationwide consensus that Nixon's actions were very clearly illegitimate. The public responded overwhelmingly in what has been characterized as a "firestorm" of public shock and criticism; Congress responded by calls from eighty-four members to invoke the impeachment process, on one front, and to enact its own special prosecutor legislation, on another, in order to insure even greater congressional control over the charter of a new special prosecutor; moreover, the federal district court ruling in *Nader v. Bork* supplied a judicial ruling of the illegality of the firing.

However, it is important not to lose sight of the larger perspective here: though the case can be made, forcefully, I think, for the technical determinations of unconstitutionality and illegality of the firing, it seems to me that the fundamental indictment of Nixon and Bork's action rests on the far more elemental and frightening grounds of corruption of the entire basis of our constitutional system through a willingness to elevate unlimited presidential power over the whole notion of separation of powers.

NOTES

1. This chronology was complied from two sources: *Watergate: Chronology of a Crisis* (Washington, D.C.: Congressional Quarterly, 1973), vols. 1 and 2; and *The End of a Presidency* (New York: The New York Times Company and Bantam Books, 1974), pp. 204–234.

2. 38 F.R. 14688 (June 4, 1973).

3. U.S. Congress, Senate, *Hearings Before the Senate Committee on the Judiciary on the Nomination of Elliot Richardson to be Attorney General*, 93rd Cong., 1st Sess., 1973, p. 72.

4. Ibid., pp. 200–201.

5. In the federal district court case of *Nader v. Bork*, plaintiffs Ralph Nader, members of Congress Bella Abzug and Jerome Waldie, and Senator Frank Moss argued strongly that there was an intimate and absolute connection between Richardson's confirmation and Senate approval of the Office of the Special Prosecutor. They stated the following in Plaintiff's Memorandum in Support of Preliminary Injunction, p. 21:

There can be little doubt that the confirmation of Elliot Richardson was contingent upon establishment of a truly independent prosecutor. Senator Hart [in Judiciary Committee hearings on Richardson's nomination] stated, "until we have an agreement on the ground rules establishing the independence of this Special Prosecutor, we ought not to move to confirmation." Mr. Richardson stated at the start of the hearings that the Senate should "concur" in the selection of the Special Prosecutor. Thus, even though, technically, the only confirmation was that of Mr. Richardson, it can hardly be disputed that the Senate also specifically approved the appointment of Mr. Cox as Special Prosecutor.

6. Letter from Richard Nixon to Elliot Richardson, Oct. 19, 1973, as reprinted in *Congressional Quarterly Weekly Reports*, Oct. 27, 1973, pp. 2848–2849.

7. 38 F.R. 19466 (Oct. 23, 1973).

8. 38 F.R. 30738 (Nov. 9, 1973).

9. *Nader v. Bork* 366 F. Supp. 104 (1973).

10. Transcript of Press Conference of Acting Attorney General Bork and Henry Petersen, assistant attorney general in charge of criminal division, Oct. 24, 1973.

11. *Nader v. Bork*, Plaintiff's Memorandum in Support of Preliminary Injunction, pp. 25–26. Plaintiffs stated the following: "At his October 24 press conference, the defendant never suggested that Mr. Cox had violated the regulation but stated that he wrote the letter [to discharge Cox] because 'the decision of the President to discharge Mr. Cox was final and irrevocable.' "

12. Ibid.; Oct. 24, 1973, Press Conference of Acting Attorney General Bork and Henry Petersen.

13. Letter from Richard Nixon to Solicitor General Bork, Oct. 20, 1973, as reprinted in *Congressional Quarterly Weekly Reports*, Oct. 27, 1973, p. 2850.

14. *Nader v. Bork*, Defendant's Brief in Opposition to Plaintiff's Motion for Preliminary Injunction (filed Nov. 8, 1973), p. 11.

15. Ibid., p. 12.

16. Ibid., pp. 13–14.

17. Ibid., pp. 13–14.

18. *U.S. v. Perkins* 116 U.S. 483 (1886).

19. *Kendall v. U.S. ex rel. Stokes* 12 Pet. 524 (1838).

20. Edward S. Corwin, *The President: Office and Powers* (New York: New York University Press, 1957), pp. 92–93.

21. *Myers v. U.S.* 272 U.S. 52 (1926).

22. 12 Pet. 524 (1838).

23. 252 U.S. 52 (1926).

24. As quoted by Raoul Berger, "Was Cox Fired Illegally?" *The Washington Star*, Nov. 4, 1973, p. B-3.

25. Corwin, *The President*, pp. 89–90.

26. *Humphreys' Executor v. U.S.* 295 U.S. 602 (1935).

27. 38 F.R. 14688 (June 4, 1973).

28. U.S. Congress, *Hearings on the Nomination of Elliot Richardson*.

29. See note 5.

30. 366 F. Supp. 104 (1973).

31. Ibid.

32. Ibid.

33. Ibid.

34. *U.S. v. Nixon* 418 U.S. 683 (1974).

Discussant: Stanley I. Kutler

Has Richard Nixon succeeded in the ultimate cover-up? Have the former president and his men, aided and abetted by revisionist historians, managed to reduce Watergate to a mere blip in his presidency? In his recent book, *1999: Victory Without War*, the former president wrote to describe the leadership we need to give us "victory" over Russian determinism, Chinese inscrutability, and Japanese cleverness. But such leadership, Nixon stated, had no need for "a morality of duty," which he dismissed as an altogether inadequate "standard for a great people." Nixon's remark is but a lame attempt to obscure Watergate. Clearly, his Watergate experience taught him nothing about American traditions and the expectations people have of their leaders. A "morality of duty" very much preoccupied the minds of the Framers of the Constitution.

John Ehrlichman, who coincidentally served as President Nixon's domestic adviser (as well as his link to the "Plumbers"), likewise has labored strenuously to deflect attention from Watergate and instead has called for an "archeological disinterment . . . and rediscovery of Nixon's creditable domestic achievements." Ehrlichman wrote that Watergate consumed only the "tiniest" percentage of Nixon's presidency. But for twenty-six of the sixty-seven months of the Nixon presidency, Watergate both hung like a Sword of Damocles and acted as an obsession for the president and many of his aides.

Scholars must find their own course; neither Richard Nixon nor John Ehrlichman should set our agenda. Why, then, the tendency to deemphasize Watergate and relegate it to so small a portion of this conference and others? Participants here, as they have elsewhere, will explore a rich variety of Nixonia. We will fruitlessly (and tiresomely) debate whether Richard Nixon was a liberal or a conservative. We will talk about welfare, and environmental, foreign, defense, monetary, and racial policies, among others. At one recent Nixon conference, more than twenty persons offered their views of the Nixon White House, Nixon and the economy, the press, the Congress, the cabinet, foreign and defense policy, and history's judgment of Richard Nixon—conveniently rendered by his chief speech writer. But no John Dean—a shabby hero, to be sure—has participated to offer *his* views at these conferences; and no congressmen, including leaders of Nixon's own party, who experienced crass betrayal and deceit by their president, have participated; and no congressmen, Republican or Southern Democrats, who formed part of what they called the "fragile coalition" and who voted to impeach the president, have been asked to give us their assessment of events; and the judges and prosecutors who had intimate knowledge of the Nixon Administration and its sordid record of criminality seem rather invisible.

In short, Watergate at times seems to be an "un-event." Revisionism—choreographed by Richard Nixon himself, beginning with his resignation speech

on August 8, 1974—has been riding high, determined, it seems, to equate
Watergate to such peccadillos as the Teapot Dome scandal of Warren Harding's
time or the Star Route Frauds of Ulysses S. Grant's Administration, or—even
worse—to be contemptuously dismissed, as Henry Kissinger has done at this
conference, as an "American extravaganza."

The movie is *Sleeper*; the scene is the year 2073. Some people are watching
old tapes of Richard Nixon:

Dr.: Some of us have a theory that he might once have been President of the United
States, but that he did something horrendous. So that all records—everything was wiped
out about him. There is nothing in the history books, there are no pictures on stamps,
on money. . . .

Woody Allen: He actually was President of the United States but I know whenever he
used to leave the White House, the Secret Service would count the silverware.

That was in the context of the Watergate affair and Richard Nixon's subsequent
resignation. Nixon remains, to some extent, still a comical figure, still an object
of derision. Every Nixon resurrection is accompanied by a wave of cartoons and
jokes, sometimes quite savage. He plays well for laughs in Peoria and Middle
America, not just the Washington Beltway. But Woody Allen's other line from
Sleeper has a frightening reality about it. We are, to some extent, in danger of
forgetting—not forgetting Richard Nixon, but forgetting what he did and what
he symbolized to his contemporaries. History, after all, is not just what the
present wishes to make of the past for its own purposes. Present-mindedness
has an alphabet of sins. Historians must judge the past by the standards of that
past, not their own, and certainly not those imposed by the actors themselves.

Nearly twelve years after Richard Nixon resigned in disgrace from the presidency, *Newsweek* magazine magically proclaimed the former president "rehabilitated." Yet, several weeks earlier, that same publication noted that Nixon
had defiantly offered Watergate's most enduring lesson: "Just destroy all the
tapes." On the tenth anniversary of Nixon's resignation, one scholar argued that
Nixon's Family Assistance Program (FAP) had more significance than Watergate—clearly faithful to Ehrlichman's reasoning—while another described Watergate as only a "dim and distant curiosity" that eventually would be seen as
"a relatively insignificant event." Worse yet, perhaps, we run the danger of
trivializing Watergate. Imagine: The "Today" show interviews Gordon Liddy
for *his* views on the Soviet Union.

Revisionism perhaps is as certain as death and taxes. But the Nixon revisionism
has inflicted a collective, national amnesia on historians, the media, and our
political leadership regarding Watergate. Watergate at times seems to get lost
in the mists of history, an odd fate for an event that consumed and convulsed
the nation, and tested the constitutional and political system as it had not been
tested since the Civil War.

Nixon's "Struggle for History"—let's call it his "Final Crisis"—at times has succeeded in obliterating the memory and meaning of Watergate. But un-foreseen dangers lurk everywhere for him. The Iran-Contra affair has—to quote one bit of unforgettable Watergatese—rendered some of the above ''inopera-tive.'' Despite the Herculean efforts of the former President and Many of (though not All) His Men, Watergate resonates, and the nation remembers. Richard Nixon commands our attention precisely because of his indissoluble links to Watergate, a connection indelibly engraved on our history. Will our high school texts a century from now debate the merits of Nixon's FAP? Whether he was a liberal or a conservative? Whether he brought great men into government? No, the opening line undoubtedly will begin: ''Richard Nixon, the first president to resign because of scandals. . . . '' Nixon's achievements will get their due, as different generations evaluate them, favorably or unfavorably, but they probably never will rival Watergate for historical attention.

''Extravaganza'' indeed; it is not every president who has stood in danger of impeachment and been named the first unindicted coconspirator. Neither Nixon nor we can escape Watergate. That history demands our serious attention. It was neither trivial nor insignificant. It raised important, painful questions about Amer-ican political behavior and the American political system, questions buried deep in the structure of American life. Watergate was a very special moment in modern political and cultural history that confronted those problems—successfully or unsuccessfully, directly or passively, honestly or conveniently: Those are valid judgments yet to be made. But the questions are inescapable. That is the sig-nificance of Watergate.

History is above all the discipline of context. The Age of Watergate is not bounded by a burglary and a resignation. Instead, it is rooted in a decade-long melange of events and personalities. Watergate was the last act in the intense political melodrama that haunted the American stage, beginning with John F. Kennedy's assassination in 1963. War and unprecedented social protest about the war and about complex problems in American life followed, and eventually culminated in Watergate. To that extent, Richard Nixon was the last casualty of those events. And ''Watergate'' goes beyond—with an impact that we only can begin measuring through a plethora of legislation (campaign financing, ethics in government, and privacy in banking regulations), foreign policy considerations (the Vietnam War, the War Powers Act, Detente, and Iran-Contra), on insti-tutions (FBI, CIA, and IRS), and on the nature of the presidency and the quality of interinstitutional relations. All this makes Watergate a serious matter for historical inquiry. If not, then truly the dictum applies: The only thing we learn from history is that we forget it.

As he campaigns to control his history, Richard Nixon has struggled mightily for the soul of history and for the souls of historians. Historians *ought* to worry about theirs. Shall we pass on to our heirs and successors a history that strains to rationalize alleged goods versus perceived evils—some rationalized nobility of purpose versus documented examples of greed and abuse of power—some rationalization that ''everyone does it'' versus vindictive abuses of official power to punish imagined political enemies? Good there may well be in the history of this administration; and it need not be interred. But we indeed risk our souls if we ignore Watergate and thereby produce "un-history."

Richard Nixon said (in one of his numerous "farewell addresses") that he had resigned because he lost his "political base." In other words, he resigned because of "politics," an especially odious concept in American life. But Richard Nixon lost his political base because he had lied—he lied repeatedly to his friends, advisers, and supporters, in and out of government, and he lied to the nation. His deceit was intended to obscure overwhelming evidence that he *had* abused power and that he *had* obstructed justice. The actions of the president and his men were serious. More than seventy persons were convicted or offered guilty pleas as a consequence of the Age of Watergate. These included a vice president, several Cabinet officers, two Oval Office aides, and numerous presidential assistants. Revisionism, to be whole, must produce more than pardons at the bar of history; it must produce the necessary exculpatory evidence.

Egil Krogh, who had served the president with an unlawful break-in of a psychiatrist's office, among what he described as "other things" illegal, admitted that his work "as official Government action, . . . struck at the heart of what the Government was established to protect, which is the individual rights of each individual." His mission was not designed to protect national security but to gain material to discredit Daniel Ellsberg, who had "leaked" the Pentagon Papers. Charles Colson similarly admitted that "the official threats" to individual rights were wrong and had to be stopped. Watergate was no trivial matter. Indeed, it may have been a close call.

Richard Nixon cannot be separated from Watergate, however valiant his own efforts and those of his friends and media trendsetters. He discovered that the nation would tolerate an imperial president, but not an imperious one—and most of all, a president who regarded himself above the law, and broke it. Nearly two hundred years of the American Constitution—and centuries of prior experience that is woven into our constitutional fabric—have dictated limitations and restraints on power. However necessarily powerful the presidency must be in this fragile, dangerous world of the twentieth century, however indispensable presidents seem to be to the nation's security and well-being, those taught traditions of constitutionalism, with both limitations on power and the Rule of Law, count for something.

The Watergate War eloquently testifies to the seriousness of our commitment to that Rule of Law. We are a nation of laws, not men; a nation of orderly means and processes, not burglars or vigilantes—that is the stuff of American constitutionalism. Men are not angels, James Madison once wrote; presumably, he also had presidents in mind. Consequently, we have wisely fenced them in with a Constitution and the Rule of Law. As E. P. Thompson has written: Rulers cannot impose a Rule of Law on the ruled unless they themselves will submit to it.

Watergate—the generic word, not just a third-rate burglary—diminished the moral level of political life, the authority of the presidency, and the credibility and efficacy of government itself. In the wake of the Vietnam War, with social peace so fragile, so precarious, that fact colors whatever positive contributions Richard Nixon may have made. He diminished the system; he also diminished himself. That spot will not out.

President Nixon, his supporters, and the would-be revisionists, have claimed that he did not behave differently than other presidents. The long answer to that is that "*not* everyone did it." The short answer is that it is beside the point. Nixon and those supporters contend that he was an unfortunate victim of time and place, and deserves consideration entirely apart from Watergate. Still, Watergate happened, and he was found culpable. That has not, and cannot, change.

Discussant: J. Anthony Lukas

I found both essays provocative. I agree with Professor Simon that there are some striking similarities between Watergate and Irangate, even perhaps with Alan Westin that it is Watergate II, but I think I find as many dissimilarities as similarities. I was struck by Professor Ambrose's enormously sophisticated analysis of the differences between Ike and Dick. I would like to hear him when he gets further along in his Nixon biography on the differences between Ron and Dick. I suspect that they are great. I found Professor Kassop's essay persuasive and very tightly argued. I would have enjoyed a colloquy between her and Professor Robert Bork.

But I must confess that I'm less comfortable in my role as academic discussant than I am as reporter, which I've been for three decades. And my presence on the podium today with Jeb Stuart Magruder and Earl Silbert frankly stirs my reportorial juices. So I think that perhaps the best contribution I can make today is to ask two questions—one of Mr. Magruder and one of Mr. Silbert. They will be slightly discursive, but I intend them as genuine questions for which I hope we might be lucky enough to get actual answers.

Watergate has become a generic term, spreading its limbs around a host of illegal and improper and dubious activities from the White House's efforts to refresh the recollection of Dita Beard and the ITT matter to the illegal campaign contributions raised from the dairy industry. And later, of course, due principally to the strenuous efforts of Bill Safire, the term has almost lost its meaning. It's been transformed into "Billygate" and "Lancegate" and now into Irangate and Contragate. But I think we ought to remember that originally it had a very specific meaning. It referred to two break-ins, both at the headquarters of the Democratic National Committee in the Watergate complex, the first on May 27, 1972, the second on June 16th, 1972.

I agree with Professor Simon that one of the astonishing facts about this whole affair is that a decade and a half later, after prodigious testimony, litigation, journalistic examination, and scholarly exegesis, we still cannot say with any certainty why those burglaries were carried out, what they were meant to accomplish, and what in fact they did accomplish. I was fascinated yesterday to hear Chuck Colson say that he couldn't understand why anyone would break into the Democratic National Committee, which was "utterly irrelevant"—his words—to the conduct of the campaign.

Now we have a rare opportunity to clarify this question, because we have on the platform one of a tiny handful of men who must surely know the answer to this question. Mr. Magruder is looking at Mr. Silbert. I am looking at Mr. Magruder. Mr. Magruder, as deputy director of the Committee to Re-Elect the President, was certainly a key link between the political figures in the Nixon Administration, principally Bob Haldeman and John Mitchell, on the one hand,

and the operational types, Gordon Liddy, Howard Hunt, and their Cuban troops, on the other. Indeed, according to Mr. Liddy, it was Jeb Magruder who gave him his marching orders for the second Watergate burglary on June 12.

In Mr. Liddy's book, he recalls a critical June 12 conversation with Mr. Magruder. Let me hasten to add, because I'm sure Mr. Magruder will note this also, that Gordon Liddy is perhaps not the most reliable source on all these matters since, as I recall, he once threatened to rip Mr. Magruder's arm off and beat him to death with it, so there was no love lost between the two men, and Mr. Liddy may be slightly distorting history. Nonetheless, in his book he says:

Mr. Magruder swung his left arm back behind him and brought it forward forcibly, and said "I want to know what O'Brien's got right here." At the word "here," he slapped the lower part of his desk, the place where he kept his derogatory information on the Democrats. The purpose of the second Watergate break-in was to find out what O'Brien had of a derogatory nature about us, not for us to get something on him or the Democrats.

Now, of course, if Mr. Liddy is correct, that would go some of the way toward answering Mr. Colson's question. Mr. Colson is saying, "They didn't have anything in the Democratic National Committee that could tell us anything about how the Democrats were going to run the campaign because the Democratic National Committee was irrelevant to the campaign." Mr. Liddy is saying, "That's not what they were after, Chuck. They were after what Mr. O'Brien knew about the Nixon White House."

Mr. Liddy's account, when I read it several years ago, intrigued me because it tended to support my little pet theory about the roots of Watergate, which Professor Simon has briefly alluded to. It's not mine originally. I think that it probably ought to be attributed to Terry Lenzner, an energetic, resourceful, and I think imaginative—perhaps too imaginative—counsel for the Ervin Committee. But I had long talks with Mr. Lenzner about this theory. Gradually I came to adopt it as my own, and let me very briefly summarize it for you. Then I would like to add it as a corollary to my question to Mr. Magruder: Namely, what was the motive for the Watergate burglary?

Briefly, it is my belief that the roots of the burglary—at least the second Watergate burglary—lay in the convoluted, decades-long relationship between Richard Nixon and Howard Hughes. Specifically, I believe the Nixon forces were trying to determine what the Democrats and their allies knew about some very shady dealings between Hughes and Nixon, particularly the famous $100,000 passed through the millionaire and close presidential friend, Charles "Bebe" Rebozo. Secondarily, they have have been trying to dig up some dirt with which to blackmail the Democrats into withholding what O'Brien knew about the Nixon-Hughes relationship until the end of the 1972 campaign. We know, or at least we thought we knew, that two phones had been tapped at the Watergate—one the phone of R. Spencer Oliver, executive director of the Association of State Democratic Chairmen, and two, that of Larry O'Brien's secretary, Fay Abel. Jeb Magruder said in a memo at the time that O'Brien was the Democrats' "most professional political operator" who could be "very difficult in the coming campaign," and that the White House was constantly looking for information which might discredit him. This would give us reason to believe that O'Brien was the principal target. But not a target merely because he was shrewd, but because O'Brien had worked for a substantial period for Howard Hughes through his friend Robert Maheu, and therefore knew a great deal about the Hughes-Nixon relationship.

Now Nixon was incredibly sensitive about the Nixon-Hughes relationship. He felt that Hughes' loan to Donald Nixon for a fast food business which specialized in triple-decker sandwiches called "Nixon Burgers" had helped to defeat him in his 1960 presidential race and in his 1962 race for governor. Nonetheless, their dealings continued—as much because of Hughes' opportuning of Nixon as because of Nixon's solicitation of Hughes. Hughes seems to have funneled some substantial sums into the Nixon campaign coffers. Then Maheu was dismissed, and O'Brien, because he was Maheu's ally, was in turn dismissed. Both then had ample motive to use what they knew of the Nixon-Hughes relationship against Nixon in the 1972 campaign. One could go on spelling this out in great detail. One thinks one knows that the $100,000, which came in two $50,000 segments, later went to pay for a pair of $4,562 diamond-studded earrings which Nixon gave his wife for her sixtieth birthday; some $45,000 in home improvements; and $243 for an Arnold Palmer putting green.

All of these things, which you recall were looked into by the impeachment committee, were ample reason for the president and the president's men to be very deeply concerned about what O'Brien knew about all of this, and I believe that this as much as anything else is an explanation for the second Watergate burglary.

Now if I may quickly get in my question to Earl Silbert. References have been made on several occasions here to an intriguing but very strange book written by Jim Hougan called *Secret Agenda*. I did review it, as Professor Simon says, for the *New York Times*, and it was a very difficult task because Mr. Hougan was in some sense attacking what he called "the received version" of Watergate, and he identified my book *Nightmare: The Underside of the Nixon Years* as one of the central texts of the received version. He had some nice things to say about it, but it's always difficult for a perpetrator of the received version to deal with an announced revisionist.

Nonetheless, I found much of what Mr. Hougan wrote very interesting. I do not go as far as Alan Westin did yesterday in my respect for the book. It is full of intriguing notions, but they are piled one upon another, one unproved assumption supporting another unproved assumption until one ends up with a *tower* of unproved assumptions. Still, I expected the press to spend a great deal of time examining Mr. Hougan's allegations, and have been somewhat disappointed that they haven't.

There is one revelation in the book which struck me as particularly interesting and which would seem to shake our faith in one important strand of the Watergate story, of the received version if you will—namely, that the burglars tapped phones at the Democratic National Committee (DNC).

The story generally accepted at the time, as you will recall, was that James McCord had installed two tapes during the first break-in at the DNC on May 27–28, one on the telephone of Fay Abel, a secretary to Chairman O'Brien, who shared several extensions with him, and a second one on the phone of R. Spencer Oliver of the Association of Democratic State Chairmen. But when James McCord and his associate, Alfred Baldwin, tried to monitor the tape, they couldn't pick up the Abel-O'Brien tap. For the next two weeks, Mr. Baldwin listened in on the Oliver tap, passing summaries of the conversations to G. Gordon Liddy, who was in charge of political espionage for the Committee to Re-Elect, and who indeed, as I recall, passed on some summaries to Mr. Magruder. So Mr. Magruder may be able to shed some light on this one, too.

According to this version, one purpose of the June 16 break-in, the second break-in, was to make the Abel-O'Brien tap operational. But the memoranda which Mr. Hougan obtained under the Freedom of Information Act reveal that well into the autumn of 1972, the FBI laboratory was convinced that neither phone had been tapped by the Watergate burglars. Moreover, the laboratory believed that the tap recovered from Spencer Oliver's phone on September 13 had been placed by someone else, perhaps by the Democrats themselves, well after the burglars' arrest. According to these memoranda, this notion provoked outraged incredulity from Earl Silbert, who was then preparing the Watergate prosecutions. In a September 28 memo to Assistant Attorney General Henry Peterson, Mr. Silbert is said to have argued that the FBI was seeking to justify its own goof in failing to detect the tap during three earlier sweeps. But he recognized that the lab's judgment posed a problem for him. According to the memo included in *Secret Agenda*, he wrote Mr. Peterson, "Obviously we do not want to be put in the position of challenging such testimony of the FBI, particularly its lab, while at the same time relying so heavily on the FBI in general, and the lab in particular, for other important aspects of our proof." A point well taken, I think.

Assuming that these documents are authentic, they pose several intriguing questions with which Mr. Hougan does not grapple. Under the Brady rule, prosecutors are required to turn over to defense attorneys any exculpatory evidence, that is, evidence which would tend to show that a defendant is innocent. Since the Watergate burglars were charged, among other things, with violations of the federal wiretapping laws, those memoranda would certainly appear to be exculpatory. I wondered when I wrote my review whether Mr. Silbert did in fact turn this evidence over to the defense, and if so, why it never surfaced? After I wrote my review, a young reporter named Phil Stanford, writing for the *Columbia Journalism Review*, decided to pursue this. And, according to his piece, he did two things. One, he went to the FBI reading room and satisfied himself that the documents were indeed authentic. And then he went one step further. He reached Wilbur G. Stevens, who was supervisor of the FBI lab during the Watergate period, and confirmed with him (1) that the FBI lab was never able to find a bug at the DNC, and (2) that when one was later discovered after a call from the secretary at the DNC, the FBI considered it a fake. Moreover, Stevens said that today there is "nothing I know of that would have changed [these findings]."

Starting with this revelation about the taps, Mr. Hougan goes on to make an astonishing argument. Namely, if Mr. Baldwin, sitting in the Howard Johnson motel across the street, was not listening to tapped conversations at the Watergate, what was he listening to? What were those Gemstone summaries which were finding their way through Mr. Liddy to Mr. Magruder? Mr. Hougan advances the proposition that what Mr. Baldwin was in fact listening to were conversations about sexual acts which were to be performed by prostitutes in the Columbia Plaza Apartments nearby. And that the sexually loaded conversations, which prosecutors and investigators were astonished to find in summaries of the alleged tap on Spencer Oliver's phone, were not from wiretaps of his phone at all. They were from wiretaps on the Columbia Plaza prostitutes who were indeed in touch with Spencer Oliver's office because people in Oliver's office were setting up assignations for visiting Democratic firemen with the Columbia Plaza prostitutes.

That's the theory. I don't know what to make of it. But I would like to address one question to Mr. Silbert. This information is intriguing to historians and journalists, but also, I would think, to the defendants in the case. When Phil Stanford asked Mr. Silbert whether he had turned this material over to the defendants in the case, he said he had no clear recollection, but he went on to say that the Brady rule is only a "legalism," and that, in any case, the prosecutor is required to turn over this material only if asked to do so by the defense. "And frankly, I just can't say that they asked." When Mr. Stanford wondered how they could ask for it if they didn't know it existed, Mr. Silbert said, "I can see your point." I have great respect for Earl Silbert. I think he did a very important job of work during Watergate, but I wonder if he could clarify that for us.

Thus, having tried to fulfill my role as reporter, I thank you.

Discussant: Reverend Jeb
Stuart Magruder

Well, I feel somewhat like the shill in a poker game. But I will try to answer both those queries. I congratulate Earl because I think Earl bore the brunt of the deceit of Watergate and handled it very well. And I think his summary of Watergate was very accurate. So I do feel somewhat the shill in this position. It reminds me of the story of how the Romans treated the early Christians. In those days, we didn't have a chance to preach on Sunday, we usually preached to the lions in the Coliseum. And on that particular day, the Christian decided that his only salvation was to get down on his knees and begin to pray. And he did so. Lo and behold, he looks up and there is the lion also down on his knees in a position of pray. So the Christian says: "Now we can begin to communicate." The lion says: "Communicate Hell, I'm saying grace."

The past six respondents indicated correctly the basic issues of Watergate. I will get to the answers, at least my answers to these questions, but let's not trivialize Watergate by the details. Watergate and what is occurring today in this country is symptomatic. I think this is a society that is adrift. It's adrift in its own selfishness, it's adrift in its own consumption, it's adrift in its overemphasis on individualism, it's adrift in its inability to be committed to anything.

As a divorced person, I think I can say we can't commit to marriage which has been the institution that has held this society together. Employees can't commit to employers and employers can't commit to employees. And possibly more serious, our political parties cannot commit to any ideals. If we just think of what is occurring in Washington today when the two major parties cannot get to the real issues that face our society, when we're faced with budget deficits and trade deficits, and not one, not one politician is willing to discuss these issues in a meaningful way, as well as other issues like Social Security and other entitlement programs, defense spending, and farm subsidies. As Pogo suggested a long time ago, "I have met the enemy, and he is us." I would suggest that Watergate is only one part of a long string of issues that have created in this society an unwillingness on our part to face the truth.

In 1662, there was a group of Quakers who were in prison because they would not make any oaths. They were in a crowded prison where they had been incarcerated and the warden of the prison said: "Yes, we need you over at another prison. Would you mind moving over there on your own?" So those prisoners left Bridewell Prison and moved to another prison without any guards. So it was that they followed their leader Thomas Elwood and marched unescorted, as criminals, from one prison to another. To an inquisitive spectator, hard put to understand such a sight, Elwood is reported as having said, "We have made a promise, we have given our word, and our word is our keeper."

Now I would like to suggest that if we were following those admonitions today as a society, Watergate would not have occurred, Irangate would not have occurred, Gary Hart's problems would not have occurred, nor would Joe Biden's problem, or Judge Douglas H. Ginsburg's. Now I think as an overview, we need to be aware of what Watergate was. It certainly was a failed burglary. But I want to be honest about what happened here. It was a planned burglary. It was planned because after Gordon Liddy was hired, he was asked by John Dean to develop a number of information-gathering proposals. In January 1972, he had seven proposals which John Mitchell, John Dean, and I thought were preposterous, but at the bottom list of those proposals, was one proposal to do just what occurred. That was, to wiretap Larry O'Brien's phone.

Now I don't want to make excuses for dirty tricks. We engaged in them, and there is a whole series of them that Earl has mentioned, but I do think we should understand that these types of dirty tricks have existed in all campaigns, particularly campaigns at the national level, and have been engaged in by both political parties. It has gone on then and it goes on today. It is wrong now and it was wrong then.

Now if you think of it in that context, the burglary was not that far removed from the other types of dirty tricks that had occurred. It didn't make it right, but it was a natural progression considering the situation we were in.

There was a certain degree of paranoia in the White House, and there was a certain degree of fear about the "enemy," and we dealt with it in many ways. Some of the ways we dealt with it were clearly illegal and unethical. These people were hired at the end of March at the insistence of Bob Haldeman in a phone conversation that he had with John Mitchell and myself. He indicated to us that it was important to get as much information about Larry O'Brien, particularly any information that referred to cash that Howard Hughes had supposedly given to Bebe Rebozo and then possibly given to the president. Therefore, the purpose for the break-in and the wiretapping was to find out what information Larry O'Brien knew so that we would be able to keep it under wraps during the election.

On the Monday after the break-in, I sat down with John Mitchell. He had come back from California and I had the Gemstone Documents with me. These were conversations between Spencer Oliver and others on the telephone. They were not particularly revealing of anything of any importance, nor was anything of importance discussed. So I said to John: "We ought to just cut our losses and get out of this while we can. It is a minor issue right now." Mitchell then went over to the White House and talked, as I understood it, to Haldeman and Erlichman, and came back and said, "Now there are other reasons why we can't do that, we need to keep this under wraps." My understanding of why we had to keep it under wraps was because these same burglars and their leaders, Liddy and Hunt, were the same people who had broken into Daniel Ellsberg's psychiatrist's office. So then we got into this elaborate cover-up that eventually led to the destruction of the Nixon Presidency.

I would like to conclude that I feel we have trivialized democracy in this country. We are getting to the point where the truth is not known by the public. It is getting to the point where we, as a nation, have lost our moral compass. I think the real question that we have to ask as a public is, "How can we as a public live a principled life in an unprincipled age?" Now I don't mean a perfect life but a principled life, and I think until we decide to do that, Watergate is only the first of many events that will occur. I think the panelists are correct when they make the comparison to the Iran-Contra affair in the sense of a lack of understanding of what our democracy has stood for, and I think our democracy stands for a number of things. Let me just indicate them to you as I finish. If we are going to have the kind of democracy that will prevent future Watergates and future Iran-Contra affairs, first we have to pick honesty over dishonesty; secondly, we have to pick justice over injustice; thirdly, we have to pick love over hate; fourthly, I think we have to pick peace over war; and, fifthly, and maybe most importantly, in this context we have to pick truth over self-interest.

Discussant: Earl J. Silbert

Good afternoon. As I think Mr. Lukas could verify from his experience covering the Watergate investigation, I made a practice of almost never talking to the press for two reasons; first, because I thought it was improper for a prosecutor to do that. I was, for those of you who may not know, assigned at the time with others to investigate the Watergate break-in. Second, I frankly found a number of reporters quite unreliable, as is reflected by that excerpt of the conversation that supposedly took place between me and whatever the name of that young man referred to by Mr. Lukas. While I did talk to that young man on the phone, he totally distorted what I said to him.

Turning to the question that Mr. Lukas has posed to me, I should say at the outset that, with the exception of the improprieties by the then-acting director of the FBI—really his exploitation by John Dean—I thought the FBI did a terrific job investigating the Watergate case. There was no request that my colleagues or I made to them during the course of that investigation that they turned down. Sometimes they hesitated, sometimes they queried, but when push came to shove, whatever I wanted, I got. I was therefore bewildered by the official FBI response when a wiretap device was discovered by Spencer Oliver on September 13, 1972, on his telephone at the Democratic National Committee. Mr. Oliver, in fact, was a victim of the Watergate burglary and wiretapping. The break-in was on June 16th. Shortly after the break-in, a number of poorly constructed, hand-made wiretap devices and an oral bugging device were recovered. The FBI did conduct a number of electronic sweeps to see if there were any other bugs in the Democratic National Committee headquarters. They came up with none.

From talking with Alfred Baldwin, that former great FBI agent who was assigned to be a lookout during what Mr. Lukas refers to as the second Watergate break-in, the one on June 16th, he was more interested in a Friday night horror movie than in observing whether or not anyone was coming on the scene to interfere with the burglary and wiretap effort. Mr. Baldwin had overheard conversations on Mr. Oliver's telephone. We assumed he did so through the wiretap devices that we had recovered. These devices operated within the megahertz range that could be picked up on the receiver that Baldwin was using.

On September 13th, after we interviewed Mr. Oliver, he went back to his office and checked his own phone. He found a device on it and reported it. The next thing I knew the FBI had labelled that Watergate II and was conducting a separate investigation to determine what double agent had planted it. Particularly because the device Oliver had recovered operated on a megahertz range closer to the one that Al Baldwin was picking up, I believed that was in fact the device that had been placed on Mr. Oliver's phone back in the first Watergate break-in about May 25th, 26th, or 28th, and that frankly, the FBI had missed it on their sweeps.

As I said, and I want to repeat, the FBI, I thought, did a terrific job on that investigation; certainly the field office and the field agents. But the FBI is a protective institution. It was my view, as reflected in that memorandum referred to by Mr. Lukas, a memorandum I wrote because I thought the idea of assigning an investigation on that bug found on September 13th to a separate agent and labelling it Watergate II was ridiculous. I considered it no more than a bureaucratic, institutional attempt to enable the FBI to overcome the impact of what I considered a goof: The bureau had missed the device on its sweep. It is not necessarily surprising, in my view, that the FBI had missed it. As I understood from having talked with Baldwin, the principal insider available to us then, the Watergate burglars were after political information.

I'd be very interested to hear what Mr. Jeb Magruder has to say about the precise political information that they were after. Spencer Oliver was an unknown to the burglars, according to Mr. Baldwin. When the conversations were first intercepted from one of Spencer Oliver's telephones, McCord and others had to get a directory of who was working at the Democratic National Committee headquarters in order to try to find out who this fellow was. The location of Oliver's office was not anywhere near the office of Larry O'Brien, whom we always understood to be the principal target.

Consequently, when the FBI conducted their sweep back in the very early days after the Watergate break-in, they didn't focus on the part of the office where Spencer Oliver was located. Therefore, they may well have missed that listening device.

Did we disclose the information about this listening device to the defense? The Brady doctrine is a legal doctrine. I don't mean by using that word to undermine its significance. It is an important constitutional doctrine. It requires a prosecutor to turn over information to the defendant that is exculpatory of guilt. It was my judgment at the time, for which I of course take the full responsibility, that the listening device discovered by Mr. Oliver confirmed the guilt of the defendants and in fact was the device placed in late May of 1972 through the conspiratorial efforts in which Mr. McCord and the Cubans, Liddy and Hunt, and whatever others at that time, if any, were involved. Therefore, it was my judgment that not only was the device not exculpatory evidence, it was incriminating and inculpatory, and therefore not disclosable.

I'd like briefly to turn to some remarks that have been made about what we mean when we refer to "Watergate." The term is one that we use on this particular occasion, here and elsewhere, quite indiscriminately. Initially—and remember now you're hearing this from the point of view of a person who in 1972 was assigned to investigate a burglary involving five persons—now, it was not a third-rate burglary. But it was a burglary. It was not a burglary—and this was clear right from the start—to steal money, but to steal information. Also, as was obvious, it had some unusual defendants, not the usual cast of characters that, in a district attorney's office, one finds in a burglary.

There were four expatriate Cubans from Miami, there were two former mid-to high-level officials from the CIA, one of whom also was a mid- to high-level official from the Committee to Re-Elect the President, together with Gordon Liddy. It was a burglary and a wiretap with a whole host of unanswered questions. It's hard now to talk about the break-in case because so much has transpired since. It's difficult to put yourself back at the time when one was faced with the questions: Who is involved? How did this come about? Who is responsible? To where did it lead? But the point I want to emphasize is that during the several months following that break-in and the investigation that went on (though many of the press, having the benefit of hindsight, may disagree with this), Watergate was not a matter of great national interest. It was at most a matter of some interest to the D.C. press and one newspaper in particular. It was not a matter that received a whole lot of attention nationwide. And to this day, if you think about it, in terms of responsibility for the break-in, the burglary, and the wiretap, the liability, at least as established in a court of law, has only been established at a level one rung above Mr. Liddy. That was, of course, Mr. Magruder. No one else with more authority, power, or responsibility has ever been charged or convicted in a court of law of authorizing or participating in that burglary and wiretap.

You might ask, "What is the significance of this?" The significance is that the break-in is not what we talk about or really mean when we now talk about "Watergate," or use the term. When we use the term "Watergate," we are referring to what was going on during the course of the investigation. This is something that has now become part of our lexicon: the cover-up and the obstruction of justice. It is for the cover-up and obstruction of justice that the people with the highest positions in government or former high positions were subsequently indicted and properly convicted. And that extends to the highest levels of the White House, with the evidence unfortunately pointing very dramatically to the involvement of the president himself. When we talk about Watergate, what we're talking about is not primarily the burglary; we're talking about a combination of events: the cash—unbelievable cash flowing into the Committee to Re-Elect the President—and the political skullduggery; not simply the break-in into the Watergate headquarters, but the dirty tricks, the spies, and the enemies' list. We're also really talking about the widespread disrespect for institutions in government, the exploitation by those involved at the highest levels to pervert the proper functioning of the FBI—witness what happened to Pat Gray; the Department of Justice—witness what happened to Henry Peterson; and the constant lying to my colleagues and me down in the United States Attorney's Office; and the exploitation of the CIA. Difficult as it was for us to get anything out of the CIA, its lack of cooperation was attributable in part—and this was an integral part of the cover-up—to eforts from the White House to have the CIA say that certain investigative leads from the break-in were CIA matters and therefore the FBI should not become involved.

So you had an exploitation and perversion of the legitimate functioning of government, an exploitation and perversion that also extended to the criminal justice system operating through the grand jury and those charged with investigating criminal offenses.

That, in my view, is what Watergate really is today. It was the great failure, through an excess of the arrogance of power of the Nixon Administration at its highest levels. It is something that all of us will have to live with forever. Now for those of us that live in Washington, Washington is replete, as I'm sure you'll recognize, with an arrogance of power. It surely extends to those in the highest levels of the executive branch of government. The executive branch, however, doesn't have a monopoly on that arrogance of power. It surely extends to certain members and staff in the legislative halls of Congress. It frankly extends to the news media in Washington as well. But it was that arrogance of power—perhaps in a way stimulated by what Bud Krogh has referred to as a fortress mentality, or certainly a paranoia—but that combination led to the horrendous excesses that resulted in what we now refer to as Watergate—the massive cover-up, the massive obstruction of justice, the utter disrespect for the lawful institutions of government, all of which resulted in the resignation of a president, an unprecedented resignation of a president of the United States and a nightmare for this country. Thank you.

POLITICS AND THE GOVERNMENTAL PROCESS

3

Information, Dissent, and Political Power: Watergate Revisited

ALAN F. WESTIN

My assignment at this excellent Retrospective Conference on the Nixon Presidency is to reflect in 1987 on the meaning and legacy of the Watergate affair. Two sets of events currently before us—the Iran-Contra episode and the observance of the Constitution's Bicentennial—combine to remind us how very timely it is to have this reassessment of Watergate. They provide the twin perspectives from which I want to develop my analysis.

WATERGATE AND THE IRAN-CONTRA AFFAIR

Take the Iran-Contra affair. For those of us who lived through the day-by-day unfolding of the Watergate affair, Iran-Contra is like the faithful remake of a movie classic with a new set of players. During the past year, the American public has learned that the President's Men under Ronald Reagan virtually duplicated the kinds of extralegal activities carried out by the President's Men under Richard Nixon.

- Finding the regular federal agencies too "timid" to carry out the assumed "will" of the president, Reagan's aides created ad hoc and secret operating units to carry out executive policies.
- Unable to use public moneys for their projects, the president's men raised money secretly from private sources in the business and political communities.
- Fearing leaks if they employed well-trained and responsible government professionals to conduct their affairs, the Reagan men turned to adventurers and shadowy soldiers of fortune to do their work.

- Unwilling to accept the limitations of legislation and judicial rules, the president's men spun out novel theories of "executive power" to "justify" their violating legal requirements for presidential action.

- Having set secret projects in motion, the president's men knowingly lied to Congress, the media, and the American public, to keep their covert activities from disclosure.

- Believing that the president's electoral mandate and his administration's dedication to fighting communism justified their "ends," the president's men under Reagan embraced morally questionable means that would evoke deep public revulsion when revealed.

- And, once their covert activities began to unravel and become public knowledge, the president's men resorted once again to the shredding machines and the kinds of cover-up activities that marked obstruction of justice in the Watergate affair.

Given these striking parallels between Watergate and the Iran-Contra affair, one must approach a reexamination of Watergate by asking whether such kinds of executive conduct have become endemic to the management of national policy in the frustrating and troubled international world we now inhabit.[1] Are we condemned to go through new "Watergates" every decade or so? Did we fail to take the proper corrective actions in the post-Watergate era that would have averted Watergate II?

WATERGATE AND THE BICENTENNIAL

The second current event that frames our reconsideration of Watergate is our celebration of the Bicentennial. Throughout this year, we have been refreshing our memories and reconsidering the wisdom of the arrangements that our eighteenth-century Founding Fathers worked out in Philadelphia, and how those original conceptions have been adapted through interpretation, amendments, and governmental practices over two centuries. Three aspects of the Framers' blueprint relate directly to Watergate.

1. By creating our separation of powers system, the Framers opted for a checks-and-balances theory of interinstitutional consensus over the competing idea of unified efficiency. They *knew* that dividing power between Congress and the president invited conflict and struggle, but they consciously preferred that condition over the dangers of the executive abuse of power.

2. The Framers committed the republic to open rather than to secret government. Congressional powers of investigation and appropriation insured that executive-branch policies would be publicly ventilated. Moreover, by guaranteeing freedom of the press by the First Amendment, the Framers insured that an activist and even muck-raking press would be part of the total governmental process.

3. Finally, the Framers committed the American nation to protect the rights of individual citizens and political groups against unreasonable and secret surveillance by the government. In the Fourth Amendment, the Framers protected the people's right to be "secure in their persons, houses, papers, and effects

against unreasonable searches and seizures.'' They required all agents of the executive branch—the police and other investigative authorities—to apply for search warrants from the independent judiciary, to document specific crimes being investigated, and to describe specifically what evidence was sought to be seized or premises to be searched.

Equally important was the First Amendment's relationship to privacy. Though there were no pre–Civil War rulings by the Supreme Court on First Amendment rights, Supreme Court Justice Joseph Story wrote in 1833, in his classic work, *Commentaries on the Constitution of the United States*, that the First Amendment's guarantees of free speech, press, assembly, and religion were intended by the Framers to secure rights of ''private sentiment'' and ''private judgment.'' Similarly, Francis Lieber, a leading commentator on public law in the 1850s, wrote that the First Amendment protected ''freedom of communion.'' He explained that this meant that Americans could form associations and conduct their political activities free from surveillance by ''the spy, the mouchard, the dilater, the informer, and the sycophant'' of police government. In the United States, Lieber noted, government could not put citizens under watch in coffee houses or cabarets, in the offensive manner of ''European police states.''[2]

These three central features of the American constitutional system—separation of powers, open government, and limitations on government surveillance of citizens—were precisely the ''unacceptable limits'' that the Nixon Administration set out to overcome by ''executive action.'' Looking back on Watergate from a Bicentennial perspective, and especially in light of the Iran-Contra affair a decade later, we have to ask whether these constitutional rules are still practical guidelines for governing in the last decades of the twentieth century. Have they become so restrictive, so contrary to the imperatives of national leadership and policy-making, that we ought to modify or limit them? Are we proclaiming legal ideals whose restraints cannot be lived with, and that invite deceptive noncompliance by successive White Houses?

WATERGATE REVISITED: DO WE KNOW WHAT REALLY HAPPENED?

Let us turn now to the historical record of the Watergate affair. In preparation for this conference, I gathered the primary literature written about the Watergate affair between 1973 and 1976, as well as books and memoir material published from 1977 to the present. (A list of the references examined appears at the end of this paper.)

I conclude from this review that—with one exception—we are still, in 1987, operating from the same understanding of the *facts* of the Nixon Administration's illegal activities between 1969 and 1974 that emerged in the Ervin Committee Report (U.S. Congress, 1974) and books like Anthony Lukas's *Nightmare* ([1973] 1976). There are plenty of conflicts over the motivations and justifications for doing these things (see the 1978 Nixon *Memoirs*) or among various Nixon aides as to who did what and why, especially during the "cover-up" period (see the books by Dean, 1976; Ehrlichman, 1982; Haldeman, 1978; Magruder, 1974; and Stans, 1978). There are also some variations in memoirs as to the roles played by different investigating bodies in uncovering the cover-up (see Dash, 1976; Doyle, 1977; Ervin, 1980; Jaworski, 1976; Sirica, 1978; and Thompson, 1975). However, these contemporary and subsequent works share a basically similar account of the illegal actions that make up the "Watergate list."

The one important exception to this consensus is an intriguing book published in 1984 by Jim Hougan, the Washington editor of *Harper's* magazine. Hougan's book is based on Freedom of Information Act access to the Federal Bureau of Investigation (FBI)'s investigative file on Watergate, and extended interviews he did with some well-known and lesser known principals. Hougan's central thesis is that the Central Intelligence Agency (CIA) was far more involved in many facets of the White House illegalities, and especially the break-in at Democratic National Headquarters, than ever came out in the official investigations or in the "received wisdom" of books by Woodward and Bernstein, Lukas ([1973] 1978), the London Sunday *Times*, and others. Hougan's basic propositions are as follows.

1. Howard Hunt and James McCord were planted in the White House as active CIA operatives, reporting to the CIA. Many of the supposedly "bungled" or "unproductive" illegal missions they arranged were actually successful operations whose products were given to the CIA but denied to the White House. Hunt and McCord continually duped G. Gordon Liddy and used his gung-ho proclivities to the CIA's own purpose, which was to collect intelligence on the likely behavior of Nixon, Henry Kissinger, and other key presidential figures.

2. The real target of the break-in during May and June of 1972 was not Democratic party political activities but a prostitute operation for Washington political notables housed in the Columbia Plaza Apartments near Watergate. The taps and bug at Democratic National Headquarters were not, as generally pictured, aimed at Party Chairman Larry O'Brien but were a CIA effort to tap the telephone of Democratic National Committee (DNC) aide R. Spencer Oliver. Since Oliver was often on the road, his telephone was used by a woman employee of the DNC to arrange assignations for visiting Democratic political figures at the Columbia Plaza sex hideaway, and that was the intelligence that CIA operatives McCord and Hunt were after.

3. The combination of the White House's program of illegal break-ins and wiretaps and the simultaneous operations being conducted by the CIA-directed operatives eventually "collided," according to Hougan, and exposure of the White House activity at Democratic Headquarters may even have been deliberately arranged by the CIA team.

4. Once the Watergate break-in was discovered, Hougan believes the CIA's role was never explored thoroughly by the official investigators. They were convinced, correctly, that Nixon had said that the CIA was involved only in an effort to close down the early FBI probe. They also believed that pursuing a

CIA presence would undercut the "presidential responsibility" position that fixed blame on the White House, and eventually forced Nixon's resignation.

I have taken the time to report the Hougan thesis not only because it is the major factual challenge to the "received" version of Nixon White House illegalities, but also to make this observation about it. Whether or not one is convinced by Hougan's evidence about the CIA's infiltration and manipulation of White House operations is not critical to the essential judgment of Watergate. White House officials up to the president approved and furthered a chain of illegal conduct from the break-in at Dr. Lewis Fielding's office to the Watergate Complex break-in. They approved decisions to go ahead with illegal wiretapping; illegal dirty tricks in election campaigns; illegal use of campaign funds; the illegal cover-up of the "Dita Beard" affair; the attempts to misuse Internal Revenue Service (IRS) files to punish political enemies; false reporting of the secret bombings on Cambodia; and then the whole chain of lies, deception, shredding of official papers, and obstruction of justice that became the "cover-up."

In particular, at no time did Attorney General John Mitchell or White House Counsel John Dean reply to the proposals for gross illegalities offered by Tom Charles Huston, G. Gordon Liddy, or Howard Hunt in terms like these: "This Administration does not and will not engage in such plainly illegal and outrageous conduct within the borders of the United States, whatever we may be ready to do on foreign soils, and even if some things like this may have been done by previous administrations." Neither did the president at any point in time from 1969 to 1974 tell his aides, "We can and will conduct this Administration at all times *within the law*." Instead, the wrangles of the Nixon White House were always over the size of budgets for illegal operations; the creation of "deniability"; insuring that no trail could lead back to the White House; where to get the surveillance hardware; and similar, wholly tactical, considerations.

Given that essential truth, nothing that we now call the Watergate affair and our moral judgment of it will change, in terms of presidential responsibility and the subsequent cover-up, even if we learn eventually that the CIA was undercutting the White House Plumbers and using its surveillances to advance the CIA's own intelligence goals.

WATERGATE AND GOVERNMENT INFORMATION ACTIVITIES: THE CENTRAL LESSON

Reflecting on the meaning of Watergate over a decade later, I am struck by the fact that almost all the major improprieties that we group under "Watergate" involve dimensions of government information policy. Consider some examples of this phenomenon:

• The White House felt a compelling need to gather intelligence about political opponents and radical groups that was not available through regular channels or the legal operations of law enforcement agencies, leading to illegal wiretapping and office break-ins.

- The White House sought to use sensitive political information (such as IRS data) about its "enemies" to punish critics improperly through government administrative actions.
- The White House felt it necessary to withhold information from Congress and the public or to lie to them about its "more delicate" activities, such as the Cambodian bombing.
- White House aides deliberately falsified two cables implicating President John F. Kennedy in the 1963 assassination of Premier Diem of South Vietnam, and tried to get a *Life* magazine reporter to run a story based on that forgery.

As these and many other examples suggest, Watergate revolved around information and its role in the formulation and execution of national policies. To return to our earlier framework of the Bicentennial, history may come to see Watergate as a major test of how information is to be gathered and used by executive government, and then how information about executive actions is shared—or withheld—from Congress and the public.

The Framers, of course, knew nothing of wiretaps, bugs, IRS computer files, and similar twentieth-century information tools. However, they understood how often information represents power in governing, and they knew how surveillance and secrecy had been tools of oppression in every repressive regime since antiquity, as Francis Lieber noted in 1853. Therefore, they gave us two constitutional rules relating to information.

1. The executive branch in a constitutional republic should conduct the nation's affairs almost wholly in public, sharing matters of state with Congress and the people. A *temporary* and *limited* period of confidentiality for preparation and negotiation is the only exception to that fundamental principle.

2. Government, and especially the executive branch, should respect the right of citizens and political opponents, including radical dissenters, to be free from government political surveillance. Official investigations using law enforcement means should be directed only at *unlawful acts* and in the forestalling of violent crimes.

The essence of the Watergate affair was that it represented an attempt to turn these two constitutional propositions around. The Nixon Administration was convinced that it had a mandate from the American people to conduct "vital" executive operations in secrecy, deceiving both Congress and the public, at the same time that it mounted covert operations to put domestic political groups under warrantless FBI and White House surveillance.

This was, I submit, a move toward what might be called "totalitarian democracy." Had it succeeded, we would have retained the trappings of democracy—political parties, elections, presidential press conferences, and formal compliance with presidential-congressional amenities. However, by subverting the basic rules of constitutional democracy as to open government and rights of political privacy, we would have taken a giant step toward a concept of government use of information that would ultimately deny and destroy the Constitution's fundamental principles.

In some ways, we can count ourselves fortunate that Watergate I took place in the 1969–1974 period, and also that the domestic scene was not in political turmoil when the Reagan White House engaged in Watergate II, the Iran-Contra operations. The reason is that we are moving inexorably into an era of information-technology and covert-surveillance resources that would make the government computer systems and bugging equipment of the early 1970s look like the Kitty Hawk stage of aircraft development. The tools for collecting and manipulating information are becoming so powerful and the data banks so full and interconnected that one shivers to think what a Huston Plan for the late 1980s would look like. Watergate III, if it happens, and especially if it involves surveillance and actions against domestic protest groups, is likely to involve information weapons far more powerful than what the Nixon Administration had available.

ARE THERE REMEDIES AND PROTECTIONS TO APPLY?

''Never again'' was the message that most Americans thought they heard articulated in Watergate's aftermath. In part, we thought this would be insured by the passage of ''Watergate-based laws'' (such as the Federal Privacy Act of 1974, the Freedom of Information Act (FOIA) Amendments of 1974, campaign reform legislation, and so forth). Partly, we thought it would be furthered by exposures of improper FBI and CIA surveillance activities, through well-publicized investigations that would never have been held but for Watergate. Indeed, in part, many saw the work of the Senate Watergate Committee, the Special Prosecutor's Office, and the court system (from Judge John Sirica's courtroom to the U.S. Supreme Court in the Nixon tapes case) as a kind of political innoculation of a generation. Those who had lived through the ''Watergate horrors,'' we assumed, would not allow elected officials to act in those ways again.

Given the fact of Watergate II—the Iran-Contra affair—did we fail to enact some needed laws, neglect to expose some techniques of covert action, or deliver too weak a therapeutic shock to the American people? How could a nation that was delivered from a slide into totalitarian democracy in the early 1970s ''allow'' this to start again in the mid-1980s?

My answer is that some lessons come hard, and probably must be learned several times. Managing democratic government abroad and at home in our nuclear age creates fierce pressures on presidents to sidestep the pains of democratic leadership and the restraints of compliance with the law. It is so tempting to go from one's deeply felt beliefs concerning the defense of freedom, and one's assumption that the American people share those convictions, to the use of covert operations, domestic surveillance of opponents, and false or deceptive reporting to the public.

Can we forestall such conduct by new laws? I wish that I saw some set of new legislative safeguards to guarantee that the Framers' principles of open government and respect for political dissent were not violated by presidents and their aides. However, if the fifty-five men of Philadelphia were here today, I do not think they would have any such laws in mind, nor would they believe that major new limitations would be good for the executive leadership on which we still depend for the health and progress of the nation.

Rather, I think that the three institutions that eventually exposed and then corrected the wrongdoings of the Nixon Administration, and are at work now doing the same with the Iran-Contra affair, remain our best hope for preserving constitutional government against White House zealots. The three institutions are Congress, the press, and the courts, and perhaps one should add to that the Special Prosecutor's Office. Basically, these institutions have to do their work most of the time by trusting and working cooperatively with the executive as long as it seems that the national consensus concerning ends and means is being observed. However, these institutions must be ever vigilant and move aggressively whenever the behavior of an administration gives indications that it is prepared to bend or evade the law.

This is no easy prescription to administer. It hurts our sense of trust and reliance on shared values to carry on governmental affairs under a cloud of public skepticism and suspicion of elected officials. However, twice in our lifetimes we have seen fundamental principles of the republic violated by presidential administrations, in the name of advancing democracy abroad and protecting it at home. Whatever the administrations that occupy the White House in the future, whether Republican or Democratic, liberal or conservative, they will have to be watched with special vigilance, and their compliance with the rule of law will have to be constantly monitored.

Two hundred years ago the Framers understood this, and gave us an excellent system with which to operate constitutional government. Watergate I and Watergate II are trumpet calls warning us that preserving their blueprint will not be easy. However, in the most pragmatic sense, the lessons of Watergate I and II are that attempts at secret government *will come out*; that the American people *will turn against* any leader who orders or allows this to happen; and that *respect for law* is more powerful in this nation than any program, cause, or leader, no matter how temporarily popular.

NOTES

1. One significant difference, of course, is that the Iran-Contra affair did not involve spying on militant dissenters, attempts to punish political "enemies," and "dirty tricks" against the Democratic Party, as did Watergate. One can only speculate whether the Reagan Administration—had it faced mass protests, leaking of government secrets, and media hostility comparable to that during the Nixon Administration—would have opened up a "home-front" campaign similar to that of the Nixon Administration.

2. Francis Lieber, *On Civil Liberty and Self Government* (1853), pp. viii, 44–47, 71–75, 224. For a detailed discussion of privacy and surveillance in early and contemporary America, see Alan F. Westin, *Privacy and Freedom* (New York: Atheneum, 1967).

REFERENCES

Bernstein, Carl, and Bob Woodward. 1974. *All the President's Men*. New York: Simon and Schuster.

Chester, Lewis, Cal McCrystal, Stephen Aris, and William Shawcross. 1978. *Watergate: The Full Inside Story*. New York: Random House.

Dash, Samuel. 1976. *Chief Counsel: Inside the Ervin Committee*. New York: Random House.

Dean, John W., III. 1976. *Blind Ambition: The White House Years*. New York: Simon and Schuster.

Dobrovir, William A., Joseph D. Gebhardt, Samuel J. Buffone, and Andra H. Oakes. 1973. *The Offenses of Nixon: A Guide for the People of the United States*. New York: The New York Times Book Co.

Donner, Frank J. 1980. *The Age of Surveillance*. New York: Knopf.

Doyle, James. 1977. *Not Above the Law: The Battles of Watergate Prosecutors Cox and Jaworski*. New York: William Morrow.

Drossman, Evan, and Edward W. Knappman, eds. 1974. *Watergate and the White House*. Vol. 2, *July–December 1973*. New York: Facts on File.

Ehrlichman, John. 1982. *Witness to Power: The Nixon Years*. New York: Simon and Schuster.

Ervin, Sam, Jr. 1980. *The Whole Truth: The Watergate Conspiracy*. New York: Random House.

Haldeman, H. R., with Joseph DiMona. 1978. *The Ends of Power*. New York: Quadrangle/The New York Times Book Company.

Harward, Donald W., ed. 1974. *Crisis in Confidence*. Boston: Little, Brown.

Hougan, Jim. 1984. *Secret Agenda: Watergate, Deep Throat and the CIA*. New York: Random House.

Jaworski, Leon. 1976. *The Right and the Power: The Prosecution of Watergate*. New York: Reader's Digest Press.

Knappman, Edward W. 1973. *Watergate and the White House*. Vol. 1, *June 1972–July 1973*. New York: Facts on File.

Knappman, Edward W., and Evan Drossman, eds. 1974. *Watergate and the White House*. Vol. 3, *January/September 1974*. New York: Facts on File.

Liddy, G. Gordon. 1980. *Will: The Autobiography of G. Gordon Liddy*. New York: St. Martin's Press.

Lukas, J. Anthony. [1973] 1976. *Nightmare: The Underside of the Nixon Years*. New York: Viking Press.

McCord, James W., Jr. 1974. *A Piece of Tape*. Rockville, Md.: Washington Media Services.

Magruder, Jeb Stuart. 1974. *An American Life*. New York: Atheneum.

Mankiewicz, Frank. 1973. *Perfectly Clear: Nixon from Whittier to Watergate*. New York: Quadrangle.

Nixon, Richard M. 1978. *RN: The Memoirs of Richard Nixon*. Vol. 2. New York: Grosset and Dunlap.

Osborne, John. 1975. *The Last Nixon Watch*. Washington, D.C.: New Republic.

Powers, Thomas. 1979. *The Man Who Kept the Secrets: Richard Helms and the CIA*. New York: Knopf.

President's Commission on CIA Activities Within the United States. 1975, June. *Report* to the President by the Commission on CIA Activities Within the United States. Washington, D.C.: U.S. Government Printing Office.

Schell, Jonathan. 1976. *The Time of Illusion*. New York: Vintage Books.

Sirica, John J. 1979. *To Set the Record Straight: The Break-in, the Tapes, the Conspirators, the Pardon*. New York: Norton.

Stans, Maurice H. 1978. *The Terrors of Justice*. New York: Everest House.

Sullivan, William, with Bill Brown. 1979. *The Bureau: My Thirty Years in Hoover's FBI*. New York: Norton.

Sussman, Barry. 1974. *The Great Cover-Up*. New York: Thomas Y. Crowell.

Szulc, Tad. 1974. *Compulsive Spy: The Strange Career of E. Howard Hunt*. New York: Viking Press.

Thompson, Fred. D. 1975. *At That Point in Time: The Inside Story of The Senate Watergate Committee*. New York: Quadrangle.

U.S. Congress. Senate. Select Committee. 1974, June. *The Final Report of the Select Committee on Presidential Campaign Activities*. United States Senate. Washington, D.C.: U.S. Government Printing Office.

White, Theodore. 1975. *Breach of Faith: The Fall of Richard Nixon*. New York: Atheneum.

Woodward, Bob, and Carl Bernstein. 1976. *The Final Days*. New York: Simon and Schuster.

4

Richard M. Nixon and the
Politicization of Justice

MICHAEL A. GENOVESE

The word "politics" has several meanings. On the one hand, it is a descriptive term used to describe a profession or type of human activity (e.g., "He is a politician," or "the art of politics"). Used in this descriptive sense, the word politics has no value judgment attached to it. However, politics also has another meaning. In this second sense, politics is used as a dirty word, as in saying: "Oh, that's politics," to describe a disreputable act.

Politics is a necessary and important part, even an indispensable part, of our governmental system. Being political need not mean being dirty or sinister. However, when political behavior crosses the line of legality or appropriateness, the politization becomes unsavory and unacceptable.

Thus, when speaking of politics, we must be cognizant of the word's multiple meanings. We may be speaking of politics as a noble human endeavor, or as an undeleted expletive. In this paper, the politicization of justice leans towards the second definition, and really refers to the over-politicization of justice, the use of the levers of justice for narrow, partisan, personal, and inappropriate purposes: It is the use of politics for personal gain, not to achieve justice.

The politicization of justice is not unique to the Nixon Presidency. Past administrations have used—or attempted to use—law, the courts, and the Justice Department for narrow, selfish, and political purposes. From the early Federalists who attempted to pack the courts with their loyalists prior to Thomas Jefferson assuming the presidency, to the Reagan Administration checking on the "philosophical purity" of potential court appointees, it has been all but impossible to separate politics from the administration of justice.

In point of fact, politics and justice have always been linked together in the

United States. Moreover, while U.S. citizens are guaranteed a variety of procedural safeguards, and although the United States maintains that it is a nation
of laws, not of men, it is men—and now also women—who make decisions,
administer laws, and control the levers of justice. This is not to say that decisions
are made purely on the basis of partisanship or political influence; far from it.
However, one must always remember that in the United States, hardly a political
issue arises that is not translated into a legal issue; and as long as the system of
justice is administered by political appointees, and as long as courts are staffed
by "political" appointees, we must expect that—to an extent—politics will enter
into the system of justice.

Thus, presidents of all political persuasions have, to a greater or lesser extent,
used law and the courts for political purposes. However, in the Nixon years,
the attempted politicization of justice was more carefully orchestrated and cen-
trally planned than at any other time in modern history. During the Nixon
Administration, there was a more or less conscious effort to politicize the levers
of justice. In fact, one can identify it as a *policy* to politicize justice (a policy
being defended as a set of interrelated activities designed to achieve an identifiable
goal). While other presidents politicized the courts or levers of justice on occasion
on a specific issue (for example, Attorney General Robert Kennedy's wiretaps
during the administration of his brother), the Nixon Administration made a more
general, conscious effort to politicize justice.

Nixon himself recognized the political uses of justice when, in his memoirs,
he noted how the levers of justice may have been used against him. He wrote:

Department of Justice files leaked to the *New York Times* in 1972 showed that within
months of his brother's inauguration, Attorney General Robert Kennedy used the Justice
Department to try to develop evidence that would justify bringing criminal charges against
my mother and brother over the matter of the Hughes loan. The probe, according to this
report, cleared members of my family of any wrongdoing. The political motivation behind
this use of a federal agency was manifest. I especially resented the attempt to get at me
through my family. These instances of abuse of the Internal Revenue Service and the
Justice Department for political purposes were typical of the partisan vindictiveness that
pervaded the Kennedy administration.[1]

While this may be an example of the pot calling the kettle black, it can also
serve to help us better understand why Nixon felt justified in using the levers
of justice for political purposes. After all, that's the way the game was played,
and Nixon liked to play "hard ball." He had a deep need to show that he was
tough and not weak, and that if they did it to him, he would do it to them.

The paper will examine how Richard Nixon attempted to manipulate and use
the levers of justice for political ends. It will focus on Nixon's use of the crime
issue in the 1968 campaign, the use of the Justice Department, the politics of
the civil rights issue, the use of the Supreme Court, and the politics of the crime
issue. It will *not* deal with Watergate-related questions of justice.

NIXON CAMPAIGNS FOR THE PRESIDENCY

In the late 1960s, crime, or more specifically the fear of crime and disorder, emerged as one of the central concerns of the American electorate. Campaigning for the presidency, Richard Nixon seized the opportunity to make crime, the Justice Department, and the Supreme Court major campaign issues in the 1968 presidential election.

Blaming the Democratic administration for the rise of crime, Nixon promised to replace the "soft-headed judges" with law-and-order judges who would be "strict constructionists." He also promised to appoint a no-nonsense, get-tough attorney general. "If we are going to restore order and respect for law in this country," Nixon pledged, "there's one place we're going to begin: We're going to have a new Attorney General of the United States of America."[2]

On September 29, 1968, candidate Nixon delivered a half-hour radio address on the issue of crime. In the speech, Nixon said, "Some have said that we are a sick society. We're sick, all right, but not in the way they mean. We are *sick* of what has been allowed to go on in this nation for too long. Under the stewardship of the present Administration, crime and violence . . . have increased ten times faster than population."

After blaming the Democrats for the rise in crime and for failing to deal with the crime problem, Nixon concluded his speech by saying, "Now, what is the responsibility of the Administration of which Hubert Humphrey is a part? Well, it's time for an accounting. Its responsibility is large. It has failed. It has failed in energy, failed in will, failed in purpose."[3]

Nixon also attacked the Warren Court, repeatedly charging that it was guilty of "seriously hamstringing the peace forces" of the United States. In extending the rights of the accused in criminal cases, the Warren Court was believed, by much of the public, to be "pro-criminal." This perception gained momentum as the 1968 campaign approached, and candidate Nixon promised to appoint "tough" justices to the nation's highest court. This combined attack on the courts, the Democrats, and the crime issue, served Nixon well. He became identified as the law-and-order candidate, the man who would appoint a get-tough attorney general and tough judges, and would promote tougher anticrime policies.

NIXON'S JUSTICE DEPARTMENT

If the courts were to serve as part of the new president's plan to turn the nation around, the Justice Department was also to play a significant role in the politicization of justice, for it was through the Justice Department, to be headed by Nixon's friend and former law partner John Mitchell, that the structure and organization of Nixon's plan was to take shape. While remarkably little can be found in Nixon's memoirs (*RN*, 1978) on the Justice Department, its central importance was recognized by Nixon's chief domestic adviser John Ehrlichman, who wrote that Nixon felt the "Justice Department to be a weak link, and [that] the President was determined that it become our strongest."[4]

The Justice Department was to operationalize the Nixon strategy of using the government to achieve political ends in areas such as law and order, civil rights, the Southern strategy, and other policy domains. Moreover, while Attorney General–designate John Mitchell at his confirmation hearings assured Senator Sam Ervin that "my activities in a political nature and of a political nature have ended with the campaign," it is clear that Nixon had a different plan in mind.[5]

Richard Harris wrote that "Mitchell appeared to be turning the Department of Justice into a political mechanism overnight," and in Mitchell's first press conference, he hinted at a broad, political role. A reporter asked, "Mr. Mitchell, because of your closeness to President Nixon during the campaign, it has been speculated that he will seek your advice during this Administration on matters even outside the legal sphere. Would you clarify a little bit on that in detail?" Mitchell answered, "Yes, I will be available to do whatever the President asks me to."[6]

Indeed, Mitchell did a great deal of political work for the president, including working with the National Security Council, working with the Urban Affairs Council, and advising the president in other areas as well. Mitchell's central role in pushing Nixon to invade Cambodia is an example of the broad scope of advice he gave the president. In fact, Mitchell became Nixon's campaign manager in the 1972 race. John Mitchell was indeed a most political attorney general.

In many areas, Mitchell had what Rowland Evans and Robert Novak called an "overpowering influence on the President."[7] Nixon liked, trusted, and relied on his attorney general. In the absence of strong leadership by the president, Mitchell began to take control of a variety of policy issues not normally under the attorney general's authority. This allowed Mitchell to take control of a variety of policy domains in an effort to promote the political interests of the president, always with an eye to the 1972 election.

NIXON AND CIVIL RIGHTS

> Don't look at what we say, but what we do.
>   —Attorney General John N. Mitchell

Richard Nixon entered the presidency in a time of social and political unrest. One element of that unrest was reflected in the civil rights movement, which gained momentum in the late 1950s and emerged as a powerful force in American politics in the 1960s. The movement reflected the demands of black Americans for equal rights and opportunities, and challenged the white power structure in America.

In his memoirs, Nixon commented on this state of affairs in America when he wrote:

Table 4.1
First-Ballot Voting of Southern Delegates at the 1968 Republican Convention

	Total Votes	Nixon	Reagan	Rockefeller
Alabama	26	14	12	0
Florida	34	32	1	1
Georgia	30	21	7	2
Louisiana	26	19	7	0
Mississippi	20	20	0	0
North Carolina	26	9	16	1
South Carolina	22	22	0	0
Tennessee	28	28	0	0
Texas	56	41	15	0
Virginia	24	22	0	2
	292	228	58	6

Source: Paul N. McClosky, Jr., *Truth and Untruth: Political Deceit in America* (New York: Simon and Schuster, 1972), p. 154.

When I came into office in 1969, the black extremists were still riding high. Despite the laws, the money spent on the problem, and the significant progress that had in fact been made, black Americans appeared to be more dissatisfied with their lot at the end of the 1960s than they were at the beginning, and tensions between black and white had never been higher.[8]

While Nixon's comments may be a bit overstated, they did capture the way he perceived the issue at the time. Nixon saw—and attempted to exploit—the white backlash over the progress that had indeed been made by the civil rights movement. Nixon owed his election in part to the forces opposing the civil rights advances, and as Representative Paul N. McClosky, Jr. (R-Calif.) wrote: "In 1968 the workings of our political system had produced a President who owed his nomination and election to a coalition of forces dependent upon the same elements in the Deep South which had for so many years blocked the evolutions of civil rights for black people."[9]

At the Republican convention in 1968, Nixon was challenged for the party's presidential nomination by Ronald Reagan on the right and Nelson Rockefeller on the left. In order to get the 667 delegates necessary to win, Nixon knew he had to get the Southern delegates. As it turned out, of the 292 delegates available from the Southern states, Nixon got 228 votes (see Table 4.1). This allowed Nixon to win the Republican nomination on the first ballot with 692 delegate votes, a bare 25 votes more than necessary. The deep South helped Nixon; he would try to repay them.

In the general election, Nixon won the presidency by an even narrower margin, in part with the help of third-party candidate Governor George Wallace of Alabama, who attracted normally Democratic votes away from Hubert Humphrey and won five Southern states. With Nixon carrying five other Southern states, he was able to squeak by Humphrey with 43.6 percent of the popular vote to Humphrey's 43.2 percent. Nixon received less than 10 percent of the black vote in the 1968 election. The white South had indeed helped Richard Nixon carry the prize of the presidency. How would Nixon repay his debt?

In fact, Nixon had never received the support or votes of blacks in the United States. In his loss to John F. Kennedy in the 1960 presidential election, the 1962 loss to Pat Brown for the California governorship, and even in his 1972 presidential landslide victory, blacks voted overwhelmingly for Nixon's Democratic opponents. Since Nixon neither needed or used the support of blacks to win the presidency, and since there was little likelihood that he would be able to win over black support, it is not surprising that his policies were at best lukewarm to the promotion of civil rights.

Nixon claimed that when he came into office he "was in the unique position of being politically unbeholden to the major pressure group involved," and that he had "more flexibility and freedom to do solely what I thought was the right thing" on civil rights.[10] In fact, however, Nixon owed a great deal to the whites of the deep South. He paid his debt in what became known as the "Southern Strategy."

Eleanor Holmes Norton sees "two civil rights Nixons":

There have been two civil rights Nixons, neither of them ever particularly principled. The more benevolent has moved but only with calculation, taking initiatives where opposition seemed least likely but stopping short when challenged. The other seems to have enjoyed leading a popular retreat as the majority indicated those civil rights gains it could not stomach. Both these Nixons were beholden to the idea of the supremacy of majoritarian preference.[11]

Throughout his early political career, Nixon could be characterized as a moderate on civil rights. He neither actively opposed nor actively worked for their promotion. Moreover, while he was slightly more liberal on civil rights than his congressional constituency and his party, he did not make it a major issue in his early career.

In terms of the "private" Nixon, we get very few glimpses of how he felt about blacks and racial equality. One of the few insiders to reveal how Nixon may have felt is John Ehrlichman who wrote, "Twice in explaining all this [racial equality] to me, Nixon said he believed America's blacks could only marginally benefit from Federal programs because blacks were *genetically inferior* to whites" (emphasis in original).[12] In handwritten notes taken by Chief-of-Staff H. R. Haldeman in a March 5, 1970, meeting with the president, Haldeman noted that "P—has concluded blacks really want tokenism *instead* of results—(based on meeting today with black admin officials)."

Just prior to Nixon's inauguration, six black leaders met with the president-elect to discuss racial problems. Nixon was quoted as telling the group that he would "do more for the underprivileged and more for the Negro than any President has ever done."[13] However, the two civil rights Nixons were not evenly divided, and the president would not keep this promise, for while Nixon could point to several positive steps taken to promote civil rights (moving forward— slowly—on "affirmative action" early in his presidency, developing plans to increase minority participation within the construction trade, the Philadelphia Plan, attempts to eliminate discrimination against women and minorities in college and university hiring, and voluntary councils to promote Southern segregation), overall, the Nixon approach to civil rights was "withdraw and retreat."

If there were two individual Nixons on civil rights, there were two bureaucratic Nixons as well, and this is the key to understanding the evolution of civil rights policy in the Nixon administration. The split within the administration occurred between the Department of Health, Education, and Welfare (HEW) headed by Robert Finch, which was seeking to promote several civil rights reforms and to continue—at a slightly slower pace—the work done by the John F. Kennedy– Lyndon B. Johnson administrations, and the Justice Department headed by John Mitchell, which was seeking to retreat on the civil rights issue while promoting the Southern strategy. In the long run, the HEW crowd was no match for Mitchell at Justice, and the Nixon Administration marched a quick retreat away from the early, meager efforts of HEW at civil rights reform. As early as October 1969, H. R. Haldeman's notes reflect great displeasure with the job being done by Robert Finch at HEW and a growing concern over pressure from Southern Conservatives over school desegregation and the Voting Rights Act. From this point on, the goal within the administration was to get everyone "tracking together" on civil rights. This meant "all moving steadily as one in the same direction, with the same destination in mind, and, hopefully, with an identical map in each tracker's hand."[14] If there were two Nixons on civil rights early in 1969, by late 1970 it was the anti–civil rights side of the Nixon personality that would come to dominate the policy and political agenda.

The bureaucratic battle within the Nixon Administration over control of the civil rights agenda reflected a reversal of sorts from the approach taken during the Kennedy-Johnson years. When Robert F. Kennedy and Ramsey Clark served as attorneys general, it was the Justice Department that spearheaded the civil rights push within the government, while HEW took a back (though supporting) seat. In the Nixon years, the reverse was true. HEW attempted to promote civil rights early on, and Justice blocked these efforts. The Justice Department was no longer to be the driving force to promote civil rights in the United States.

By 1970, when Justice had won control of the civil rights issue, there emerged a marriage of John Mitchell's Southern Strategy to Nixon adviser Daniel P. Moynihan's benign neglect civil rights. The full weight of this marriage crushed HEW's efforts to stay the course on civil rights.

The Southern Strategy was an effort to play up to white Southern voters in an effort to woo them away from the Democratic party. This meant retreating on black civil rights and giving special favors to Southern segregationists. As

Reg Murphy and Hal Gulliver saw it, the Southern Strategy represented "a deal" between Nixon and the Southern segregationists:

The essential Nixon bargain was simply this: I'm president of the United States, I'll find a way to ease up on the federal pressures forcing desegregation. Whatever the exact words or phrasing, this was how the Nixon commitment was understood by Thurmond and other Southern GOP strategists. . . . The Nixon Southern Strategy did not end with his narrow victory in the 1968 presidential election. It became apparent . . . that this was a long-range strategy. Nixon clearly hoped to woo Southern support so ardently that there might once again develop a solid political South—but this time committed as firmly to the Republican party as it once had been to the Democratic party.

It was a cynical strategy, this catering in subtle ways to the segregationist leanings of white Southern voters—yet pretending with high rhetoric that the real aim was simply to treat the South fairly, to let it become part of the nation again.[15]

Benign neglect represented a belief, presented to the president by Daniel Moynihan in a memo written in early 1970:

The time may have come when the issue of race could benefit from a period of "benign neglect." The subject has been too much talked about. The forum has been too much taken over by hysterics, paranoids, and boodlers on all sides. We may need a period in which Negro progress continues and racial rhetoric fades.[16]

While Nixon and Moynihan insisted that this was merely an effort to deflate the hot rhetoric of the race issue, critics saw it as yet another piece of a policy of civil rights retreat. However, as Robert Finch's political star descended, benign neglect and the Southern Strategy fit together as part of the civil rights policy which did indeed mark a backing away from the federal government's affirmative role in promoting civil rights.

The core of the Nixon civil rights policy can be seen in the Southern Strategy and the demands it made on the administration of justice. Nixon knew that, as notes taken by Bob Haldeman in meetings with the president reveal, "There's no political gain in integrating!" On top of that, the President was doubtful that integration was a good idea at that time. As notes taken by Haldeman in an August 4, 1970, meeting with the president reveal, Nixon said:

law does not require integration
not sure integration will work
serious reservations re inter-racial playgrounds
not right for this year—maybe in 10 years.

If Nixon (and, secondarily, the Republican party) was to gain control of the political agenda, not only did he need to win another victory in 1972, he needed to "realign" the political allegiances of the American voting public. Since the

1930s, the public had identified itself with, and usually voted for, the Democratic party. Nixon wanted to move America toward the Republican party, and ideologically, the white conservatives of the South seemed the best place to start. Thus, a Southern Strategy emerged that was designed to favor the whites in the South in hopes of bringing them into the Republican fold. The Southern Strategy was developed in part by Kevin Phillips, who worked for John Mitchell in the Justice Department and later wrote *The Emerging Republican Majority* (1969). This book laid out a blueprint for a realignment of the American voting public toward the Republican party. Nixon was well aware of Phillips's thesis, and attempted to develop policies designed to implement the latter's vision of a New American majority consisting of a combination of the Nixon and George Wallace vote of 1968 along with the social policy conservatives and white ethnics.

On civil rights issue after civil rights issue, the Nixon Administration began to pull the federal government back from an advocacy position to the point where a broader "policy" on civil rights began to emerge. This policy reversal was fully expected by the white South, but while the administration sought to accommodate the demands of Southern segregationists, it found that there were roadblocks in the way of the retreat. They could not change the law, they could not force the courts to reverse themselves, and they could not move the nation away from its legal and moral commitment to civil rights. However, even within these limitations, there were actions that the administration could take that were designed to fulfill its Southern Strategy. One thing that could be done was to limit or control the level of civil rights enforcement. As Haldeman noted in a July 22, 1970, meeting with the president, Nixon ordered "nothing more done in South beyond law requires." Again, on August 4, 1970, in Haldeman's notes of a meeting with the president, we find "only do what law requires—*nothing more*" (emphasis in original).

While administration officials denied that there was a Southern Strategy, an examination of the Nixon presidential papers reveals that indeed this is precisely what motivated the president. In notes taken by John Ehrlichman at a November 28, 1972, meeting with the president, Ehrlichman wrote, "[President]—continue The Southern Strategy." Moreover, Southerners were aware of the strategy, as a Republican state chairman from Georgia, Wiley A. Wasden, Jr., wrote to Nixon's liaison to the South, Harry Dent, in 1969 that "maybe the southern strategy is beginning to work."

The Nixon policy on civil rights emerged piecemeal, but nowhere was it more evident than in the attempt to overthrow the Voting Rights Act of 1965. This act was one of the most effective civil rights laws ever passed, as it promoted voter registration among blacks in the South and began to give the black community some hope for gaining political power. On June 26, 1969, Attorney General John Mitchell testified in Congress against renewal of the Voting Rights Act, and suggested a much weakened bill in its place. Evans and Novak said that this was "by far the most ominous break with civil rights that the administration had yet attempted."[17] In addition, six weeks after taking office, Nixon pulled federal voting registrars out of Mississippi, and the administration began to deliberately underenforce the Voting Rights Act.[18]

On school desegregation, Nixon sought to satisfy the demands of Republican Senator Strom Thurmond of South Carolina, and to withdraw the federal government from its efforts at desegregation. Leon Panetta, former director of HEW's Office for Civil Rights during the early days of the Nixon Administration, recognized the difficulty Nixon had in attempting to reconcile his campaign promises to Thurmond and the South with the need to obey the court decisions on school desegregation, but saw Nixon giving in to the political pressures from Thurmond, political pressures that HEW was seeking to overcome.[19]

Nixon's liaison to the South, Harry Dent, wrote a January 23, 1969, memo to the president in which he stated: "So far as Southern politics is concerned, the Nixon Administration will be judged from the beginning on the manner in which the school desegregation guidelines problem is handled. Other issues are important in the South but are dwarfed somewhat by comparison."

Of course, the demands of the law and the needs of politics could not, at least in this case, be reconciled. Moreover, Nixon gave a clear signal of intent when he fired Leon Panetta in early 1970 and issued a lengthy position paper on school desegregation in which he pledged that "we are not backing away" (from school desegregation), but that the *Wall Street Journal* said signalled "a go-slow approach geared to maximum political mileage."[20]

In point of fact, the Nixon Administration was severely restrained in what it could do to back away from school desegregation by court decisions from *Brown v. Board of Education* in 1954 to two recent court rulings, *Green v. [New Kent] County School Board* (1968), which dealt a blow to Nixon's "freedom-of-choice" option, and *Swann v. Charlotte-Mecklenburg Board of Education* (1971), which set tough requirements on districts with one-race schools. The government sought to overturn these orders, but in the end, the decisions stood. This forced Nixon to back down slightly from his antidesegregation stance, but nonetheless he urged "minimal compliance with the law."[21]

On July 5, 1969, a statement on school desegregation was released by the Justice Department and HEW which began, "This Administration is unequivocally committed to the goal of ending racial discrimination in schools, steadily and speedily in accordance with the law of the land." Later in the statement, however, the administration began to back away from this stance. "This Administration," the report read, "does not intend to continue old procedures that have been controversial and at times inflammatory." The report went on to state that the administration would enforce "realistic administrative procedures, not new guidelines."

How did the South view these new "procedures"? *The Atlanta Journal* wrote, "Door Opened to New Delays"; *The Savannah Morning News* wrote, "Desegregation Deadlines Won't Be Strictly Enforced"; and *The Greenville News* wrote, "Fall Desegregation Deadline Dropped by Administration." Clearly the white

South was pleased. Harry Dent reported in a July 8, 1969, memo to the president that "Southern reaction . . . was good—very good."

On the busing issue, Nixon attempted to make a quick retreat from the court-ordered busing that was the law, and instead in 1972 proposed a moratorium on all busing which, in his own words, "would put an immediate stop to further new busing orders by the federal courts."[22] While the *Brown, Green, Holmes*, and *Swann* decisions stood in his way, Nixon repeatedly sought to enact policies based on his belief, stated in a January 28, 1972, memorandum to John Ehrlichman which said that "This country is not ready at this time for either forcibly integrated housing or forcibly integrated education." Nixon hoped for what he called "a middle course" on school desegregation, but on October 29, 1969, the Supreme Court announced that "The obligation . . . is to terminate dual school systems at once." Nixon delayed, but the Court forced him to reluctantly and slowly comply.

Beginning in 1970, and running through 1972, there was a great deal of discussion within the administration about sponsoring a constitutional amendment to prevent forced busing. At first the issue was promoted by Harry Dent and opposed by HEW and Robert Finch's assistant Len Garment. Later, in 1971, John Ehrlichman pushed for an antibusing amendment, in part, as a May 19, 1972, memo revealed, to smoke out the Democratic presidential candidates. Notes by H. R. Haldeman of a February 27, 1970, meeting with the president, Haldeman, and Ehrlichman, contained the following:

move fast on Constit. amendment re schools
shld bite bullet now & bite it hard
if it's racism—so be it.

Murphy and Gulliver describe Nixon as a "reluctant integrationist." Forced by the Courts to move ahead on desegregation, Nixon nonetheless used the issue to pursue his Southern Strategy and ingratiate himself to the white segregationists of the South. As Murphy and Gulliver noted:

The terrible cruelty of the Nixon administration's indecision on school desegregation was that it gave direct encouragement to those white Southerners *least* reconciled to the ending of an era. . . . [Moreover], there was a much larger group of troubled white Southerners, men and women who were frustrated and uneasy at the rapid pace of social change over the past decade. They had come to believe that such change was inevitable. . . . But Richard Nixon, thirty-seventh president of the United States, gave them reason to hope . . . that at the very least the *direction* of change could be somewhat altered, . . . that quite possibly, for instance, some form of token integration might satisfy the laws and the courts. Had not Nixon said that the federal government should get out of the business of trying to run local school districts? . . .

The victims of Nixon's calculated catering to Southern segregationist sentiment were, often as not, the responsible white citizens who had tried honestly to obey the law. The law had not changed, nor had the court decisions on the HEW guidelines. But Nixon managed to let many white Southerners suddenly *believe* that things had changed.[23]

Another area of concern centered around the fair housing issue. Early in his first term, Nixon's Housing and Urban Development Secretary George Romney told the Civil Rights Commission that his goal was to create "open communities" and to increase "housing options for low income and minority families." However, as was the case with Robert Finch at HEW, Romney's good intentions were quickly dashed by the White House, which had a slightly different, less ambitious plan in mind.

While the policy reversal was not nearly as dramatic in housing as in other areas; and while the administration did proceed to threaten some local communities with federal funding cutoffs if they failed to comply with housing laws, and did sue the city of Black Jack, Mississippi, over zoning improprieties; the overall pattern on housing was again one of backing away from the aggressive pursuit of civil rights and moving toward a more "benign" approach.

An area where Nixon seemed to take a constructive role was in "black capitalism," or as it later became known, "minority business enterprise." Nixon felt that this was an area where he could satisfy some of the demands of the black community while not alienating whites, especially in the South.

In the 1968 campaign, candidate Nixon endorsed efforts by the government to promote black capitalism, and the reaction was generally favorable. Nixon had found a policy that served many needs: It fit into his philosophy of government, helped blacks, and did not seem to anger whites. On March 5, 1969, President Nixon announced the signing of Executive Order 11456, which created a new agency, the Office of Minority Business Enterprise (OMBE), within the Department of Commerce. With the signing of this order, Nixon announced,

I have often made the point that to foster the economic status and the pride of members of our minority groups, we must seek to involve them more fully in our private enterprise system. . . . Involvement in business has always been a major route toward participation in the mainstream of American life. Our aim is to open that route to potentially successful persons who have not had access to it before.[24]

OMBE would have the power to coordinate all existing federal efforts at promoting minority enterprise (116 programs within 21 departments and agencies), and would, in Nixon's words, "be the focal point of the Administration's efforts to assist the establishment of new minority enterprises and expansion of existing ones." Unfortunately, the OMBE was not to have any funds to give financial assistance to minority business, but was only to serve as a coordinating agency. In this way, it generated a great deal of good publicity at a very low cost.

Once again, however, the early efforts of the administration gave way to the demands of the Southern Strategy, and by 1971, the president had all but forgotten minority business enterprise as an issue. As with other civil rights issues, the administration turned away from promoting minority issues, and by late 1971, Nixon had prepared virtually no constructive plan for promoting civil rights or minority economic development. Arthur Blaustein and Geoffrey Faux summed up the results of Nixon's black capitalism efforts as of 1972:

1. There was no overall, coherent private sector strategy.
2. Corporate involvement in and financial institution support of economic development had been largely devoted to advertising and public relations.
3. Private sector coalitions and volunteer advisory/support groups had been overpublicized and underproductive.
4. Business leaders had yet to perceive the full dimensions of economic development as a multifaceted, community issue.
5. The business establishment was still unwilling to encourage the development of new institutions (such as CDCs) for the minority (poor) community that might one day demand interaction on the basis of real equality.
6. Time was running out. Those minority and community leaders who were at least willing to give the private sector a change—as Max Ways said back in 1968, "Business is the one important segment of society Negroes today do not regard with suspicion"—were becoming more distrustful of the business community and were under increasing pressures from their own constituencies to deliver concrete projects.[25]

What did the short-lived efforts at black capitalism accomplish? Very little. As was the case with other efforts by the Nixon administration in the area of civil rights, there was never a concerted institutional drive to accomplish very much, nor was there the leadership from the president to move the machinery of government and the American people behind the issue.

Overall, the Nixon policy on civil rights unfolded piecemeal through bureaucratic infighting, the law, campaign rhetoric, political needs, and public relations imperatives. It was not a well-thought-out, carefully crafted package of programs and initiatives that fit together tightly, but a randomly organized forcing together of ideas and programs on which only periodic attention was focused.

What little was attempted in support of civil rights was only luke-warmly proposed, and even that support was often withdrawn in midstream. In the end, the Nixon civil rights policy was best summed up in November 1971 in a report by Father Theodore Hesburgh, chairman of the U.S. Civil Rights Commission, who wrote, "The President's posture . . . has not been such as to provide the clear affirmative policy direction necessary to assure that the full weight of the federal government will be behind the fight to secure equal rights for all minorities."[26]

Eleanor Holmes Norton summed up the Nixon civil rights policy in comparison to other presidents:

Examined in the traditional areas of civil rights concern—employment, education, and housing—the Nixon record fails the test of the times, the test by which previous presidents have been judged. History has tended to evaluate each chief executive's civil rights record in the light of historic circumstances, a kind standard indeed. What did the time allow for? How well did the president brave majority opposition? Truman and Kennedy, for example, have received reasonably high marks not because they achieved very much, but because they moved in the face of clear opposition on the country's toughest issue. But Nixon took virtually no risks at a time when aggressive action to enforce equal rights was easily possible for the first time in our history. He chose the opposite course—totally to politicize an issue which, because it affects a disfavored minority, cannot survive a uniformly political approach. Given the country's past history, the majority cannot be depended upon benignly by itself to undertake to chart a proper course to relieve the country's minorities of discrimination. Richard Nixon has chosen other areas in which to be remembered kindly by history. And he seems to have done so knowing exactly what he was doing.[27]

NIXON AND THE SUPREME COURT

As a politician of great skill and insight, Richard Nixon saw in 1968 a hot campaign issue: the Supreme Court. The liberal/activist Warren Court was under siege from the right, and a significant segment of the public, fearing the rise of crime, looked to the Supreme Court as one of the problems. Nixon campaigned hard on this issue, promising to name "strict constructionists" to the Court. Nixon wanted judges who would strictly and objectively interpret the Constitution; and not "make laws." The Warren Court had, according to Nixon, gone soft on crime. As he said at different times during the campaign:

The *Miranda* and *Escobedo* decisions of the High Court have had the effect of seriously hamstringing the peace forces in our society and strengthening the criminal forces. . . .

The barbed wire of legalisms that a majority of one of the Supreme Court has erected to protect a suspect from invasion of his rights has effectively shielded hundreds of criminals from punishment as provided in the prior laws.

Let us always respect, as I do, our courts and those who serve on them. But let us also recognize that some of our courts in their decisions have gone too far in weakening the peace forces as against the criminal forces in this country and we must act to restore the balance.[28]

Attacking the Court became good politics. As America grew more and more fearful of street crime, as urban unrest and riots made the headlines, and as the campuses exploded with protest, Nixon seized the issue and put much of the blame on the Courts. In the short span of a single year (1967–1968) the Gallup poll revealed a dramatic 9 percent decline in the popularity of the Supreme Court. As James F. Simon wrote: "Richard Nixon sensed the tense national mood and suspected that the public was willing to have the Supreme Court shoulder part of the blame. By campaign time, Nixon was convinced that the Court was politically vulnerable and he would act shrewdly on that knowledge."[29] Nixon appears to have been attracted to the "attack the Warren Court" strategy for two reasons: (1) ideology (Nixon was by inclination and design a law-and-order

Table 4.2
Federal Judgeships as Political Patronage

President	Party	Percentage
Cleveland	Democratic	97.3%
B. Harrison	Republican	87.9
McKinley	Republican	95.7
T. Roosevelt	Republican	95.8
Taft	Republican	82.2
Wilson	Democratic	98.6
Harding	Republican	97.7
Coolidge	Republican	94.1
Hoover	Republican	85.7
F.D. Roosevelt	Democratic	96.4
Truman	Democratic	93.1
Eisenhower	Republican	95.1
Kennedy	Democratic	90.9
L.B. Johnson	Democratic	95.2
Nixon	Republican	93.7
Ford	Republican	81.2
Carter	Democratic	94.1
Reagan	Republican	97.0 (as of 1983)

Source: Henry J. Abraham, "Reflections on the Recruitment, Nomination, and Confirmation Process to the Federal Bench" (unpublished paper presented at conference, The Federal Courts, 1980, American Enterprise Institute for Public Policy Research, October 1, 1980); Sheldon Goldman, "Carter's Judicial Appointments: A Lasting Legacy," *Judicature* 64 (March 1981): 344; Sheldon Goldman, "Reagan's Judicial Appointments at Mid-Term: Shaping the Bench in His Own Image," *Judicature* 66 (March 1983): 334.

advocate) and (2) politics (it would help him get elected, and fit into his broader scheme of a Southern Strategy). Moreover, since the Court was powerless to fight back, it became an even more attractive target.

In his six years in office, Richard Nixon had the opportunity to appoint four justices (including the chief justice) to the Supreme Court. Being one vote short of a majority gave Nixon the opportunity to remake the Court in his own political and philosophical image. Nixon, like most presidents, used his power to appoint justices as a way of promoting his political and philosophical goals. While Nixon's appointment of federal judges was no more partisan than most (see Table 4.2), he did pay especially close attention to the political nature of his Supreme Court appointments.

Nixon's first opportunity to recast the composition of the Court came with the appointment of Warren E. Burger as chief justice. Burger was a Nixon discovery who had a long record of activism in the Republican party and who fit the Nixon model: strict law-and-order judge, conservative, and a critic of the Warren Court.

Burger was easily confirmed by the Senate, and the search then went on to fill the seat being vacated by Abe Fortas.

The Fortas seat opened up after some behind-the-scenes maneuvering by John Mitchell and Nixon, who presented Chief Justice Warren with information about some questionable financial dealing by Fortas. Rather than face the charges against him, Fortas resigned his seat on the Court. Nixon used this opening to send a signal to the South. His appointee would be a Southern conservative who would be seen as an early installment in the Southern Strategy, but whom to chose?

Attorney General Mitchell suggested, and President Nixon accepted, Clement F. Haynsworth as the nominee for associate justice. Haynsworth, a fifty-seven-year-old lawyer from Greenville, South Carolina, was then serving as chief judge of the Fourth Circuit Court of Appeals. Initially, he seemed an ideal choice, but upon further investigation, serious problems emerged.

It should be noted that some Democrats in the Senate were predisposed to find fault with Haynsworth due to displeasure over the way the Nixon team had pressured Abe Fortas into resigning from the Court, and also due to the unnecessary and ill-fated threats of impeachment against Justice William O. Douglas.

This, coupled with several serious charges against Haynsworth, promised a battle over Nixon's first Southern nominee to the Supreme Court. Haynsworth was somewhat vulnerable on the issue of race, and Joseph L. Raub, Jr., counsel for the Leadership Conference in Civil Rights, called him a "hard-core segregationist." Labor also had problems with the nominee, with AFL-CIO President George Meany calling him "antilabor." However, it was questions of Haynsworth's judicial ethics based on several questionable decisions made by Haynsworth that may have benefited him financially that placed the nomination in deep trouble. The charge of conflict of interest in several cases was leveled against Haynsworth. The charges were serious, and needed to be answered. However, the Nixon administration so botched their effort to defend Haynsworth that even the charges of questionable legitimacy "appeared" to be true. Clark R. Mollenhoff, who was charged eventually with orchestrating the Haynsworth defense for Nixon, wrote that "the Administration's handling of the Haynsworth case . . . demonstrated to me that Nixon's White House team captains were rank amateurs in the operation of government. Through arrogance, superficiality, ignorance, and ethical insensitivity they could destroy the very people they hoped to use to their political advantage."[30]

The Judiciary Committee of the Senate approved the nomination by a 10–7 vote. However, when the nomination reached the floor of the Senate, it was clear that things had gone from bad to worse. The Nixon forces could not hold the line. On November 21, the Senate rejected the Haynsworth nomination by a 55–45 vote, with 17 Republicans voting against the president's choice.

Nixon was, to put it mildly, outraged. However, he would stay the course and appoint another Southerner to the Court. His commitment to the Southern

Strategy was unshakable, and three months later, Nixon nominated G. Harrold Carswell to the Supreme Court.

Carswell, an activist in the Republican party in Florida, was a U.S. attorney, a district judge for the northern district of Florida, and at the time of his nomination to the Supreme Court, a U.S. court of appeals judge for the Fifth Circuit. Even his supporters had difficulty defending Carswell as a man deserving of a seat on the Supreme Court. He was, in the words of Evans and Novak, "not a first-class judge or, as the Senate became convinced after full study of the record, even a first-class man."[31] Some of Nixon's critics thought that the Carswell nomination was a deliberate insult, offered after the Haynsworth defeat, in the belief that the Senate would *never* reject two nominations in a row.

At first it appeared as if the Senate would unenthusiastically but overwhelmingly consent to the nomination. However, problems arose that began to threaten the status of the Carswell nomination: There was a 1948 speech in which Carswell proclaimed:

I am a Southerner by ancestry, birth, training, inclination, belief, and practice. I believe that segregation of the races is proper and the only practical and correct way of life in our states. I have always so believed and I shall always so act. . . . I yield to no man as a fellow-candidate, as a fellow-citizen, in the firm, vigorous belief in the principles of white supremacy, and I shall always be so governed.

Moreover, there was his involvement in the transfer of a golf course from municipal to private control in an effort to evade a Supreme Court integration ruling; his misrepresentation of his own involvement in that matter; an unusually high rate of reversal of his judicial decisions (approximately 60 percent) by higher courts; and the failure of many of his colleagues on the Fifth Judicial Circuit to endorse him. These among other charges spelled trouble for the nomination. Perhaps the final humiliation, though, came in an effort to defend Carswell. Senator Roman Hruska (R-Nebr.), arguing against Carswell's critics, defended the judge's competence by arguing that "even if he were mediocre, there are a lot of mediocre judges and people and lawyers. They are entitled to a little representation, aren't they and a little chance? We can't have all Brandeises and Frankfurters and Cardozos and stuff like that there."[32] These problems, coupled with repeated Nixon administration blunders, led to the full Senate rejecting the Carswell nomination by a 51–45 vote.[33]

Amazingly, a president had been turned down twice in a row on Supreme Court nominations. This had never happened in U.S. history, and the president took it personally. Nixon's response—which he himself characterized as "cold and reasoned anger"—was harsh.

I have reluctantly concluded, with the Senate presently constituted, I cannot successfully nominate to the Supreme Court any federal appellate judge from the South who believes as I do in the strict construction of the Constitution. . . .

Judges Carswell and Haynsworth have endured with admirable dignity vicious assaults on their intelligence, their honesty and their character. They have been falsely charged with being racist. But when all the hypocrisy is stripped away, the real issue was their philosophy of strict construction of the Constitution, a philosophy that I share—and the fact that they had the misfortune of being born in the South. After the rejection of Judge Carswell and Judge Haynsworth, this conclusion is inescapable. . . .

With yesterday's action, the Senate has said that no Southern federal appellate judge who believes in a strict interpretation of the Constitution can be elevated to the Supreme Court. As long as the Senate is constituted the way it is today, I will not nominate another Southerner and let him be subjected to the kind of malicious character assassination accorded both Judges Haynsworth and Carswell. . . .

I understand the bitter feeling of millions of Americans who live in the South about the act of regional discrimination that took place in the Senate yesterday. They have my assurance that the day will come when men like Judges Carswell and Haynsworth can and will sit on the high Court.[34]

Even in losing, however, Nixon may have gained something. By fighting so hard ''for the South,'' Nixon displayed his loyalty to them, and furthered the cause of the Southern Strategy. Nixon *and* the South were victims; together they would march ahead.

Nixon still had a Supreme Court seat to fill, and he turned to an old friend of the chief justice, Harry A. Blackmun (he was the best man at Warren Burger's wedding). A Republican activist, Blackmun was on the U.S. Court of Appeals at the time of his nomination. He was a conservative, but not an extremist, and was confirmed by the Senate 94–0.

President Nixon soon had two more chances to fill Supreme Court vacancies, and he chose Lewis Powell, Jr., and William Rehnquist. In filling the Rehnquist seat, the president originally favored appointing a woman, California Court of Appeals Judge Mildred L. Lillie (a conservative Democrat and a Catholic) to the seat, but Chief Justice Warren Burger hinted that a woman on the Court was unacceptable to him, and Nixon backed away. Tennessee Senator Howard Baker was offered a seat on the Court, but turned down an appointment. Powell, of Virginia, was a Southerner with a distinguished career in the law, serving as, among other things, president of the American Bar Association; Rehnquist was an assistant attorney general in the Nixon Administration, and was extremely conservative. Both were easily confirmed. Now, it truly was the ''Nixon Court.''

Having nominated four of the nine Supreme Court justices, Richard Nixon had, in effect, a Court majority, needing only one of the remaining five Justice's votes to attain a majority. Did the Nixon Court perform as Nixon had hoped and anticipated?

While the Nixon Court did not quickly overturn all the Warren Court decisions, it did begin a slow, measured retreat away from some of the policies of the Warren Court. A type of ''gradual withdrawal'' characterized the Nixon/Burger approach: a more lax attitude on charges of discrimination; a belief that capital punishment is not ''cruel and unusual,'' less sympathy to labor, less sympathy to the rights of accused person, less sympathy to demands of the poor, less sympathy to civil liberties and the rights of the press, more concern with the sanctity of property rights, and—perhaps surprisingly—some support of women's rights. In short, while the Nixon/Burger Court retreated from the policies of the Warren Court, it did so slowly and cautiously.

NIXON AND CRIME

Before 1968, crime and "law and order" were not significant issues in presidential campaigns. Normally considered within the domain of state and local governments, crime became one of the chief campaign themes for Richard Nixon in the 1968 race.

The law-and-order issue did not rise in a vacuum. The urban riots of the mid-1960s, rising crime rates, campus unrest, and other symptoms lifted crime to a national concern on which Richard Nixon ran in the 1968 campaign. Nixon had to seize the law-and-order plan because George Wallace was using that issue to promote his independent bid for the presidency, and Nixon feared that his own natural constituency would be drawn by the Wallace appeal. After Nixon was elected, he had to convert campaign rhetoric into policy.

Nixon's law-and-order policy emerged—as was true of so many domestic concerns to which he gave only secondary consideration—piecemeal and gradually. In 1969, the president spent a great deal of time on the crime issue, but became frustrated by the limited options available to him. In early 1970, Nixon ordered Haldeman to "do something on crime *now*" (emphasis in original). However, the President did not know *what* to do. In 1970, the Domestic Council, headed by John Ehrlichman, was given responsibility for lending coherence to the disparate parts of the Nixon law-and-order policy. Ehrlichman, with the help of his assistant Egil "Bud" Krogh, and always with the input of Attorney General John Mitchell, put together an anticrime package which, while not explicitly, consisted of four parts: *policy, politics, limits*, and *symbols*.

The federal government could do little on the crime issue nationally, so they focused on the District of Columbia. The Nixon District of Columbia anticrime policy consisted of a variety of "get-tough" proposals designed to give police greater freedom and power. It contained provisions that empowered judges to jail criminal suspects ("preventive detention") for 60 days before trial; allowed police to break into houses without producing a search warrant ("no-knock"); and other "get-tough" approaches.

Senator Sam Ervin (D-N.C.) denounced the plan as a "blueprint for a police state" and called it a "repressive, nearsighted, intolerant, unfair, and vindictive legislative proposal."[35] Beyond the D.C. plan, the Nixon Administration waged a high-visibility campaign against organized crime. While this program got headlines, it did not produce very significant results.

The public relations offensive on crime became a central concern in 1970, as revealed in March 10 notes taken by Haldeman of a meeting with the president,

Attorney General John Mitchell, Ehrlichman, and Haldeman himself, and held in the Executive Office Building. Haldeman's notes read:

problem is not what we do—but the appearance
  not getting the points we should on crime
Agnew can lead on this
  should take strong position as crime fighter but can't do as his views—must be Admin.
shld have Mitchell do like J. Edgar used to
  no one else in Admin can put on this play tough SOB role—as crime fighter
time to go on real crusade—not just do good
  put all PR effort we can into this area need to make asset of Mitchell's toughness
should do more on TV, speeches, etc.
VP & others shld build up Mitchell
  and our appts—Attys, Judges, etc.

Nixon also stepped up the war on drugs. The Nixon Administration felt that if the flow of narcotics into the United States could be decreased, street crime would also drop. Led by Bud Krogh, efforts increased in this area (for example, the Special Action Office for Drug Abuse Prevention and the Office of Drug Abuse Law Enforcement), but in spite of the effort, the results were disappointing. While an internal memo written by Egil Krogh admitted that "nothing really was accomplished," these efforts did generate a great deal of favorable publicity for the administration.[36] The pattern of devising policies for their favorable press as a way to boost the image of Nixon as tough on crime replaced substantive policy as a means of reducing crime.

The politics of Nixon's crime policy, like the policy itself, became a way to make it appear as if Nixon were trying to act, but now, the political strategy was an effort to shift blame away from Nixon and onto the Democrats who controlled Congress. An internal memo by Egil Krogh, written in July 1970 and entitled *Crime Control and Law Enforcement, Current Status: Political Position for the 1970 Elections*, stated that "the Administration position in the crime field depends on our ability to shift blame for crime bills inaction to Congress."[37] This policy failed when the Congress, afraid of appearing soft on crime, passed Nixon's bill.

There were only limited successes on the policy front, so the administration pursued extensive efforts on the political front, reflecting the recognition by the administration that there was not a great deal it could do about crime. It was a local issue, and the federal government, short of giving money and aid, was severely limited in what it could accomplish. This led Nixon to rely on dramatic gestures and symbolic leadership in the crime area. Nixon would talk tough, make dramatic speeches, and propose strict legislation, primarily for the impact on symbolic power these actions could achieve. As Edward Jay Epstein noted:

In retrospect the "law and order" campaign seemed to have had a much more marked effect on public opinion than on crime in America. It etched on the public consciousness the image of an unmerciful "law and order" administration (later turned by political critics into a Frankenstein's monster of repression). The campaign of 1972 began with the same foreknowledge that the federal government lacked the power significantly to affect unorganized crime, and it ended with the recognition that at best the Administration could achieve "visibility" for its efforts through symbolic action.[38]

Despite the campaign rhetoric, Nixon never developed a thought-out, coherent anticrime program, in part because there was little the federal government could do in the area and in part because Nixon quickly became distracted by other issues, and symbol replaced substance in the crime area. "Law and order" was a theme used to give the appearance of toughness, but there was no policy of substance to put meat on the bones of a legitimate anticrime program.

CONCLUSION

If by "policy" one means a more or less related set of actions designed to achieve a goal or purpose, then indeed it could be said that Richard Nixon had a policy to politicize justice. Beginning with the 1968 campaign themes of law and order, through the political use of the Justice Department, to the civil rights and crime policies and the use of the Supreme Court, a pattern of politicization emerges.

Nixon used these issues not so much to achieve substantive policy results, but primarily for symbolic, political purposes. The Southern Strategy is perhaps the most glaring example of this: the use of the levers of law and justice to achieve broad partisan/political results.

In this respect, was Nixon any different from other presidents? While it is true that all presidents will, to a degree, politicize justice, the Nixon effort led by John Mitchell was more conscious, more explicit, and more ambitious than that of other presidents. Nixon's was truly a "policy" of politicizing justice for partisan purposes.

All this is not to say that President Nixon was not concerned with crime or the other issues mentioned. However, Richard Nixon, as his administration moved ahead, became so concerned with other issues ("big" issues such as the war in Vietnam and U.S.-Soviet relations) that the domestic agenda was put on the back burner. Nixon felt that the domestic area could, in effect, run itself. He had to orchestrate the grand design for peace. He thus gave progressively less and less attention to domestic policy, and in this way, the domestic area went from an arena for problem solving to an avenue from which to seek political mileage.

NOTES

1. Richard M. Nixon, *RN: The Memoirs of Richard Nixon* (New York: Grosset and Dunlap, 1978), p. 247.

2. Quoted in Richard Harris, *Justice* (New York: Dutton, 1970), p. 14.

3. Ibid., p. 28.

4. John Ehrlichman, *Witness to Power: The Nixon Years* (New York: Simon and Schuster, 1982), p. 168.

5. Quoted in Harris, *Justice*, p. 131.

6. Ibid., p. 150.

7. Rowland Evans, Jr., and Robert Novak, *Nixon in the White House: The Frustration of Power* (New York: Vintage Books, 1971), p. 142.

8. Richard M. Nixon, *RN* (New York: Grosset and Dunlop, 1978), p. 435.

9. Paul N. McClosky, Jr., *Truth and Untruth: Political Deceit in America* (New York: Simon and Schuster, 1972), pp. 152–153.

10. Nixon, *RN*, p. 435.

11. Eleanor Holmes Norton, "Civil Rights: Working Backward," in *What Nixon Is Doing to Us*, ed. Alan Gartner, et al. (New York: Harrow Books/Harper and Row, 1973), p. 204.

12. Ehrlichman, *Witness*, p. 223.

13. Quoted in Evans and Novak, *Nixon in the White House*, p. 134.

14. Leon Panetta and Peter Gall, *Bring Us Together* (Philadelphia: Lippincott, 1971), p. 165.

15. Reg Murphy and Hall Gulliver, *The Southern Strategy* (New York: Scribner's, 1971), pp. 2–3.

16. Memo quoted in Nixon, *RN*, p. 437.

17. Evans and Novak, *Nixon in the White House*, p. 150.

18. See McClosky, *Truth and Untruth*, pp. 152–172.

19. Panetta and Gall, *Bring Us Together*.

20. Quoted in McClosky, *Truth and Untruth*, p. 158.

21. See ibid., p. 160.

22. Presidential Message sent to Congress, 3/17/72.

23. Murphy and Gulliver, *Southern Strategy*, pp. 66–67.

24. See Arthur I. Blaustein and Geoffrey Faux, *The Star-Spangled Hustle: The Story of a Nixon Promise* (Garden City, N.Y.: Anchor Books, 1972), p. 130.

25. Ibid., pp. 212–213.

26. Quoted in McClosky, *Truth and Untruth*, p. 151.

27. Norton, "Civil Rights," p. 215.

28. Quoted in McClosky, "Truth and Untruth," p. 189.

29. James F. Simon, *In His Own Image: The Supreme Court in Richard Nixon's America* (New York: McKay, 1974), p. 18.

30. Clark R. Mollenhoff, *Game Plan for Disaster* (New York: Norton, 1976), p. 56.

31. Evans and Novak, *Nixon in the White House*, p. 164.

32. Quoted in Richard Harris, *Decision* (New York: Dutton, 1971), pp. 23, 110.

33. See ibid., p. 192.

34. Quoted in Evans and Novak, *Nixon in the White House*, pp. 170–171.

35. Sam Ervin, *Preserving the Constitution* (Charlottesville, Va.: Michie, 1984), p. 277.

36. See Edward Jay Epstein, "The Krogh File—The Politics of 'Law and Order,' " *Public Interest*, Spring 1975.

37. Ibid.

38. Ibid.

Moderator: Monroe H. Freedman

Our first commentator, Charles W. Colson, is a fascinating man. His biographical sketch includes some ordinary and some impressive things. A law degree in 1959, a law partnership, service as assistant to the assistant secretary of the Navy, administrative assistant to Senator Leverell Saltonstall, and then he ascends to special counsel to the President of the United States. I remember Mr. Colson best, perhaps, from a quote. And if it is a misattribution, I hope he will correct me. The quote was, "I would walk over my grandmother for Richard Nixon." Those are the words of a man that's thought of as much in his capacity as a former Marine Corps captain than anything else. Then we have a Charles Colson who is the founder of Prison Fellowship Ministries, Prison Fellowship Inc., and who served as the president of that organization and now is the chairman of the Board of Prison Fellowship Ministries. In between, of course, Mr. Colson spent seven months in prison, out of his sentence of one to three years, on a guilty plea of having disseminated derogatory information into the press with regard to Daniel Ellsberg. The Mr. Colson who is speaking to us today is characterized better by two other quotes. One is what he has to say about prisons:

Prisons are rotten holes in America as well as most of the countries I've visited. My first night in prison was a horror, with helpless feelings of being separated from family, of men crowded together, yet so desperately alone, of guards shining flashlights in my face every two hours, of the stale odors of open urinals filling the air, and violence too. My life was threatened my very first week.

And the second quote:

I came out of prison wanting to forget prisons and never go near the places again. The stench was in my nostrils, I threw away the set of clothes that had been locked up in a prison locker because it smelled like that prison. But I found when I got home from prison that I just couldn't forget the men that were there. No one really cared that much about them; it's a leper community in America. I ended up convinced that this is what God wanted me to do with my life.

So we have an extremely complex man who will speak to us next, and I look forward with anticipation to hearing Charles Colson.

Discussant: Charles W. Colson

Thank you very much Professor Freedman. After that introduction I think I'd really rather talk about prison than the Nixon years, but that's not my assignment today. I have to take it as a matter of personal privilege to respond to the grandmother remark; however, I hope it doesn't come out of my ten minutes. But I never said that I would run over my own grandmother. In 1971 a *Wall Street Journal* front page profile piece was done about me entitled "Nixon's Hatchet Man." I didn't give them an interview because I didn't want publicity. So they interviewed somebody who'd worked for me in the United States Senate, and the person they'd interviewed, unnamed, gave some very glowing statements about me, but then said, "Be careful, Chuck Colson's so tough he would run over his own grandmother." A month later, the *Washington Star* picked it up as a quote, saying a month ago Chuck Colson had boasted he would run over his own grandmother. I called all my friends in the Washington press corps, both of them, and attempted to correct the record, but now it was too late and by the 1972 campaign, there were grandmother organizations formed to protest. Certain things become legend when they're in print, and it's very hard to live them down. My mother was never happy that I talked that way about my father's mother.

As Professor Freedman's introduction indicated, I was not a newcomer in the politics of the Nixon Administration. I'd been around the business a little while in Washington, and I do have to say that there is nothing that I can recall that we invented in the Nixon years, though we might have refined the art somewhat. But politics itself is not really a dirty business; because people have political motives, you might think, listening to Professor Genovese, that that makes them automatically sinister and suspect. Politics is what makes the wheels of government turn in a free society. That's what happens in democracy: We elect people; they have to get 50 percent of the vote plus one in order to serve in office and 50 percent of the vote plus one to stay in office. So politics is an inevitable part of the process of government, and the two can't be separated. The question is whether you discharge them responsibly, honestly, openly, and consistent with the law, which obviously in the case of Watergate, we did not do.

I want to begin today with Professor Westin's remarks and then move to Professor Genovese's and attempt to put some things in perspective if I may.

I graduated from a law school that Professor Freedman taught at, George Washington Law School. I earned a juris doctor. When those degrees were earned, my specialty happened to be in constitutional law. I believe as much in the intent of the Framers, I suspect, as anybody who graduated from that law school or took his oath as a lawyer or went into the White House and did so with a great sense of idealism. So we didn't go in to pervert the intent of the Founding Fathers. I do appreciate what Professor Westin said about the intent inadvertently being frustrated. But I think you have to understand just a little bit of the setting of the Nixon years in order to understand why that happened. And for me, the pivotal point was the release of the Pentagon Papers. When this happened, the ground rules began to change. This happened over a weekend, on a Sunday, and I can remember that Monday in the White House being in several meetings with both Dr. [Henry] Kissinger and the president. I can remember, whether justified or not, the genuine alarm that at least both men conveyed about the release of the Pentagon Papers, the unauthorized exposure of those documents. As a matter of fact, I remember Dr. Kissinger saying that this could undermine our war effort completely, our effort to get out of Vietnam. I can remember the fear that that it would undermine the China initiative which was then known to just a few of the president's aides. We did know that that National Security Study Memorandum number one was in the hands of a member of Congress who called to tell us. We had intelligence, later disputed, that a copy of the Pentagon Papers had been delivered to the Soviet embassy and to the Soviet delegation at the United Nations. There was great fear about other papers that Dr. [Daniel] Ellsberg had access to, whether they too might be disclosed.

We should now realize that if you took the dates of the Pentagon Paper controversy and overlaid them against the secret negotiations going on between Dr. Kissinger and Le Duc Tho for the ending of the war in North Vietnam, any reasonable person would conclude that the particular dates involved in July of 1971 were very, very sensitive dates in terms of those secret negotiations, when Dr. Kissinger was shuttling back and forth to Paris in an effort to try and bring peaceable solutions to the very unpleasant, unhappy war going on in Vietnam. Whether we were rightly concerned about security or whether that was a pretext, I would have to say, in hindsight, that people could draw contrary conclusions, but I can tell you as someone sitting in the room, feeling the intensity and vibrations and the expressions by Kissinger and Nixon both, that nobody had any question but that there were serious security violations involved in the release of those papers. At least that is what those in charge both believed, and that argument was made to the Supreme Court in the Pentagon Papers case when several documents were presented in camera, showing the names of agents compromised. We subsequently learned that one of the things that one of the Pentagon Papers disclosed—we knew it at the time and could not say so—was that we were intercepting conversations in automobiles inside the Kremlin. That later came out about two years ago, that was finally disclosed, but that was revealed in the Pentagon Papers, and when we went to the Supreme Court we made that point to them, but very few people in the White House did know about it.

Things from that point on unraveled. Actually, if you look at the Nixon presidency in perspective, on how power was ultimately abused leading to Watergate, one would have to start with the Huston plan, which was clearly an extralegal proposal involving extralegal means, and was rightly rejected by the head of the FBI, officials at the so-called "politicized Justice Department" rejected it, but it left a certain frustration with Mr. Nixon. I can remember one night in the summer of 1971 when he expressed to Bob Haldeman his great frustration; Bob Haldeman and the president and I were sitting alone in the president's Oval Office when he expressed enormous frustration that there was no way to get back stolen government documents, and he turned to Bob and said, "Whatever happened to that plan that we had that we would have some people here who could do those jobs for us that no one else would do?"

I've always felt that that was the beginning of the Plumbers. The Plumbers subsequently got out of control. One of the great mysteries of Watergate to me— and with all the documentation and all of the investigations that have gone on over the years—I still have trouble understanding why someone broke into the Democratic National Committee looking for information about what was going on in the Democratic National Committee. I've been in politics long enough to realize that what went on in the Democratic National Committee was utterly irrelevant to the campaign. The candidate wouldn't care what was going on in the Democratic National Committee, the candidate was going to be Senator [Edmund] Muskie or was going to be Hubert Humphrey or was going to be George McGovern, but in any case what was going on in the Democratic National Committee was utterly irrelevant. So I think that, as has been mentioned, there is a fascinating theory advanced by Jim Hougan in his book which has been referred to by Professor Westin, and I don't believe it's entirely irrelevant. I happen to be one of those people—I wish I had time to tell you—who read the entire CIA file, because it was made available to me by Fred Buzhardt, one of Mr. Nixon's counsels during Watergate. I read it, as a matter of fact, and made a copy and then surrendered it to the Watergate prosecutors after I pleaded guilty and before I went to prison. I read the file in its entirety. The CIA knew things going on in the Watergate before any of us in the White House knew about them. Is it relevant? No, we still broke the law, so in one sense it is not relevant. But it is relevant if we didn't know why the law was being broken and a cover-up was entered into because an activity had been launched by an agency of the government that we were unaware of and therefore were perhaps backed into a cover-up.

Still, Mr. Nixon could have done exactly what Mr. Westin said, and said: "I don't want the law violated, I want the truth disclosed," and it would have been the end of it. So we don't lose our sense of responsibility because of that, but I certainly think we lack an effective motive of why Watergate took place, which to this day we do not know. The people convicted of having ordered it say they did not, and no one has given a plausible explanation of why people went in and did what they did. But I think the forces which brought it about were set in motion by the Plumbers and by the release of the Pentagon Papers. That was to me the pivotal moment in the Nixon years—when we crossed the line—and I don't say this to defend what happened, we crossed the line with at least what were believed to be justifiable reasons at that time. The secret bombing of Cambodia, which Professor Westin also mentioned, is a whole other subject which no conference of this sort could possibly avoid dealing with and that is, that a president always has to tell the truth. Ted Koppel in a recent interview in *Newsweek* said, "Of course, a President can't always tell the truth," and I would not selectively take the secret bombing of Cambodia which is somewhat a discredited chapter in history. Also consider whether you should have told the truth when Henry Kissinger was in Pakistan on his way to China and got a "cold" because that was the only way he could throw the press off his trail while the Chinese were sending a plan E to bring him to Peking, to Beijing; or consider how Secretary [George] Shultz defended disinformation, that unpleasant term that we used in connection with the Libyan propaganda campaign in the Reagan years: Shultz, quoting Winston Churchill, said, "The truth is so precious that it must be defended by a bodyguard of lies." There are times when government simply can't tell the truth and cannot make full disclosures in the nuclear age. I, spending my life as I do in Christian service, have some difficulties with this, and yet looking back through the Bible I see that Rahab, the harlot, is considered one of the heroes in the hall of fame in the Bible (Heb. 11), and she of course lied to protect Israeli spies as they entered into the promised land. There are cases in government going back at least as far as Rahab the harlot where lying is justified to prevent a much greater evil, and that's not situational ethics.

My time is up, but just let me say one thing if I may. Professor Genovese's premise, I believe, is flawed. His premise is that because Mr. Nixon did not aggressively pursue the civil rights policies of the prior administration, that he, with some sinister connotations, was politicizing government. Professor Genovese might have had a different interpretation of how best to accomplish the goals of desegregation in the South. I notice your paper is conspicuously silent on the question of the councils which Mr. Nixon set up, the voluntary councils of community leaders throughout all the Southern states which I've heard a number of scholars, none of whom are cited in your footnotes, refer to as making more progress, genuine progress, in desegregation than the laws that were being bitterly resisted at the time. So it is at least conceivable, and in a conference like this, the possibilities should be at least entertained, that Mr. Nixon might have felt that he could have accomplished more by quiet diplomacy in the South, making work the laws that were then on the books, than by zealously trying to bring more laws into effect, and I think one could come to that conclusion without believing that there was an improper politicization of the Justice Department. If we say that the Justice Department was more politicized by the Nixon Administration than any other time in history—well, if he were here, Bobby Kennedy might take some offense at that statement.

Discussant: John Shattuck

What was the central problem of the Nixon Presidency from the standpoint of civil liberties? Was it Richard Nixon? That was how a majority of the House Judiciary Committee saw it, and they were probably speaking for a majority of the Congress. Was it a problem of the "imperial presidency" taking over powers of the other branches of government? That's certainly the way a lot of scholarly opinion has looked at the crisis of the Nixon White House, and no doubt there is much truth to be found there. Was it a problem brought on by covert manipulation of power to suppress dissent, as Alan Westin sees it, or the "politicization" of justice, as Michael Genovese describes it? No doubt it was all these things. But I believe the problem lies much deeper, and it affects not only the presidency of Richard Nixon but also those that came before and after him. It is also a problem that has grown, not diminished, since Nixon left office.

Nixon himself hinted at it in a court deposition I had the privilege of taking in Morton Halperin's wiretap lawsuit in 1976. Halperin had been the victim of a twenty-one-month warrantless wiretap on his home telephone during and after the time he served as an aide on the National Security Council staff in 1969. The Halperin tap was part of a much larger secret White House investigation of leaks which became the prototype for Watergate. When I questioned Nixon about the wiretap program, here's how he answered:

In America, we have the blessings of security and freedom. What we were trying to do with this program was to maintain security with the least possible infringement upon freedom. It is not always possible to do so. . . . The use of electronic surveillance to enable the United States to conduct a responsible foreign policy, to get all the options and to get the best possible advice and to get the communication with people abroad that we need to have—I believe that for those fundamental reasons this kind of activity was not only right, but from the standpoint of the security of this country, I think it was legally right.

Nixon's view of national security had a profound impact on the people who worked for him. In June 1974, for example, one of the many dramas of Watergate was played out in a Los Angeles courtroom when Egil Krogh, chief of the White House Plumbers, was sentenced for perjury in connection with the burglary of Daniel Ellsberg's psychiatrist. Before imposing sentence, the judge asked Mr. Krogh whether he wished to make any final statement for the record. What he said was both moving and profoundly disturbing:

I see now . . . the effect that the term "national security" had on my judgment. The very words served to block critical analysis. It seemed at least presumptuous if not unpatriotic to inquire into just what the significance of national security was. . . . The discrediting of Dr. Ellsberg, which today strikes me as repulsive and an inconceivable national security goal, at the time would have appeared a means to diminish any influence he might have had in mobilizing opposition to the course of ending the Vietnam War that had been set by the President. Freedom of the President to pursue his planned course was the ultimate national security objective.

The underlying crisis in the Nixon presidency was a crisis of national security, and it was a crisis that began long before Watergate.

At the end of World War II, the United States emerged from its traditional peacetime isolation and became an active and frequent intervener in international conflicts. The Cold War that prompted this fundamental policy shift appeared to require a permanent place for many of the temporary institutions and powers of wartime mobilization. Just as the executive agencies that had grown up in response to the Depression became a permanent feature in the political landscape during the New Deal, so the security policies and intelligence community that grew out of World War II became a permanent feature of the postwar era. Within a few years, Truman and Eisenhower had created a secrecy classification system, imposed loyalty and security investigations on government employees, and required members of the Communist party and other "subversive organizations" in the United States to register with the government. The impact of these developments on civil liberties reaffirmed Madison's warning to Jefferson in 1798 that "perhaps it is a universal truth that the loss of liberty at home is to be charged to provisions against danger, real or pretended, from abroad."

Deep involvement in foreign political and military affairs became the dominant feature of postwar American policy. The consequences for the structure of government in the United States were profound. An interventionist foreign policy served to diminish the power of Congress and to increase the power of the executive branch, and the growth of the executive branch had an increasingly distorting effect on the Constitution. The premise of the Founders that Congress makes the laws and the executive carries them out was seen more and more as a major obstacle by presidents seeking to shape world events to their view of national security. Under the Constitution, of course, it is the Congress, not the president, that has the power to declare war and raise armies, and has the final say in the making of treaties. But these arrangements were swept aside as an unnecessary hindrance to presidential intervention in a long series of foreign conflicts—Berlin, Greece, Iran, Lebanon, Guatemala, the Congo, Cuba, the Dominican Republic, Vietnam, Laos, Cambodia, Chile, Angola, El Salvador, Nicaragua—a list that extends to virtually every corner of the world. Hanging over each of these conflicts, of course, has been the confrontation between the United States and the Soviet Union, and the nuclear balance of terror that has dominated American defense and foreign policies since 1945.

This, then, is the national security framework within which postwar presidents have sought "the freedom to pursue [their] planned courses of action," as Mr. [Egil] Krogh so eloquently put it. To make up for their lack of constitutional authority to act so freely, every president since Truman has relied on two doctrines to justify executive initiatives to protect national security: inherent presidential power and congressional ratification of that power. Taken together, they provide a new law of national security within which presidents have felt justified in acting outside the Constitution.

In the case of inherent power, repeated presidential acts of warrantless wiretapping or covert manipulation of foreign governments are said to validate claims of presidential authority to perform these acts. The Supreme Court rejected the theory of inherent presidential power in its 1952 decision in the Steel Seizure case, when President Truman sought to nationalize the steel industry. But Justice Robert Jackson's frequently cited concurring opinion in that case left the door open to future presidents by recognizing a gray area where the president may act in the absence of express constitutional authority, unless and until the Congress tells him to stop.

In the case of congressional ratification, military or intelligence initiatives by the executive branch, even if secret, are said to be approved by Congress when it votes general appropriations, as in the case of the secret bombing in Cambodia in 1969 or clandestine efforts to overthrow the government of Chile in 1973. Broad language in congressional statutes, such as the provisions in the National Security Act of 1947 giving the CIA director power to "protect intelligence sources and methods," is also said to ratify programs of doubtful constitutionality, such as the CIA's requirement that former employees submit manuscripts for prepublication censorship.

These doctrines of expanded presidential authority have become the major building blocks of national security policy. They are also major roadblocks for the Constitution.

For our purposes, the chief legacy of the Nixon years was a vast expansion of the concept of national security. It is true that out of the national trauma that accompanied the Nixon impeachment proceedings there emerged a consensus that abuses of presidential power had to be contained by law. This consensus was articulated by a unanimous Supreme Court in the White House tapes decision, which served as Nixon's exit papers in July 1974: "Many decisions of this Court have unequivocally reaffirmed . . . that it is the province and duty of the judicial branch to say what the law is. . . . We conclude that . . . the [president's] generalized assertion of executive privilege must yield to the demonstrated, specific need for evidence in a pending criminal trial."

But the rule of law has little force if the law can be bent by claims of security. Another passage from [Warren] Burger's opinion in the tapes case reminds us that the consensus about Nixon's abuse of power never touched his claims about security.

Here is what the Court said: "The President does not place his claim of privilege on the ground that [the tapes] are military or diplomatic secrets. As to these areas . . . the courts have traditionally shown the utmost deference to presidential responsibilities."

The result of this deference is that today we have greater secrecy, more censorship, a CIA with broader authority, an FBI with fewer restraints, and a National Security Agency with greater power than we have ever had in our history. And all of these developments have taken place in the shadow of the Nixon presidency, after we thought we had struck down the abuses that produced Watergate.

What is most disturbing about all of this is that we seem to have drifted into a sort of permanent state of national emergency that has no immediate context. We do not know what the emergency is, how long it will last, or what its impact is on our system of liberty. In fact, we do not even think of ourselves as living in a state of emergency. On the contrary, we believe that such things happen only in other countries—mostly Third World—and could never happen here.

But take an example close to home. In October 1970, Prime Minister [Pierre] Trudeau went on Canadian television and declared a "state of insurrection" throughout Canada, based on the kidnapping of a Canadian minister and a British consul by Quebec separatists. Trudeau invoked the Canadian War Measures Act, and authorized the national police to conduct predawn roundups of French Canadians suspected of associating with the separatists. Trudeau's emergency decree had the effect of temporarily suspending the Canadian Bill of Rights.

Could it happen here? In truth, it happens all too often, but we are never likely to hear such a dramatic announcement as Trudeau's. Why not? Because our concept of national security is flexible enough to accommodate almost any necessity. In 1971, Nixon's attorney general, Richard Kleindienst, commented on Trudeau's declaration of emergency by stating:

It could not happen here under any circumstances. We wouldn't suspend the Bill of Rights even if the whole Cabinet, the Chief Justice and the Speaker of House were kidnapped. . . . We wouldn't have to because our existing laws—together with our surveillance and intelligence apparatus, which is the best in the world—are sufficient to cope with any situation. . . . There is enough play at the joints of our . . . law, enough flexibility, so that if we really felt that we had to pick up leaders of a violent uprising, we could. We would find something to charge them with and we would hold them that way for a while.

That, of course, is exactly what the Nixon Justice Department did when it rounded up twelve thousand people in the streets of Washington during the May Day antiwar demonstrations in 1971. Although these mass arrests were later condemned by federal courts as unconstitutional, they were an awesome display of raw executive power to define and declare emergencies and suspend the Constitution. Comparing the Canadian and American approaches to national security, the Canadian Attorney General, John Turner, made an ironic comment after Trudeau had lifted his emergency decree: "In a certain sense, he said, it is a credit to the civil liberties of a country that it has to invoke extraordinary powers to cope with a real emergency. Some countries have these powers at their disposal all the time."

Is the United States such a country? Without clearly defining what we mean by national security, we have turned it into a sort of magic wand to ward off any evil that might befall us as a nation. Listen to how this magic wand is perceived by the Reagan Administration, in the words of a former National Security Advisor, Richard Allen:

In the 1980s "national security" is in itself an all-encompassing term too often narrowly construed as having to do only with foreign policy and defense matters. In reality, it must include virtually every facet of international activity, including [but not limited to] foreign affairs, defense, intelligence, research and development policy, outer space, international economic and trade policy, and reaching deeply into the domains of the Departments of Commerce and Agriculture. In a word, "national security" must reflect the entire presidential perspective.

It is disturbing, but hardly surprising, that the Reagan Administration has turned the CIA loose under an executive order that allows it to spy on Americans and conduct "covert actions" inside the United States, created a presumption that most government information about foreign or military affairs can be withheld from the public, mounted a campaign for official censorship of scientific research, and accused the critics of its foreign policy of promoting Soviet propaganda.

There is a simple question that we must ask ourselves as we look at all these developments and the long history of presidential maneuvers that preceded them: Where does the Constitution fit in? National security is what protects us from our adversaries, but the Constitution and the Bill of Rights are what distinguish us from them. Have we allowed our view of security to blur our principal distinguishing features as a nation? "Liberty lies in the hearts of the people," Judge Learned Hand said in a famous wartime speech delivered in 1943. "When it dies there, no constitution, no law, no court can save it." Judge Hand echoed the warnings of the drafters of the Bill of Rights that, in the words of Thomas Paine, "Those who expect to reap the blessings of freedom must always undergo the fatigue of supporting it."

SEPARATION OF POWERS

5

United States v. Nixon Reexamined: The United States Supreme Court's Self-Imposed "Duty" to Come to Judgment on the Question of Executive Privilege

HOWARD BALL

On Friday, May 31, 1974, the Justices of the U.S. Supreme Court met in conference to discuss whether to grant an expedited hearing in the case of *United States v. Nixon*.[1] On May 20, 1974, U.S. District Court Judge John Sirica ordered President Richard M. Nixon to surrender sixty-four tapes to the special prosecutor in the criminal trial of seven of Nixon's former White House staff members. On May 24, 1974, Nixon's lawyers filed an appeal in the U.S. Court of Appeals challenging the Sirica order. That same day, Leon Jaworski, the special prosecutor, took the extraordinary step of seeking Rule 20 review by the Court before the Court of Appeals decided the questions of law.

Rule 20 states that "a writ of certiorari to review a case pending in a court of appeals, before judgment is given in such court, will be granted only upon a showing that the case is of such imperative public importance as to justify the deviation from normal appellate processes and to require immediate settlement in this court."[2] This was a "real gamble," yet, after conferring with his staff, Jaworski decided to make the request.[3] Wrote Jaworski: "It would be a drastic step and, if the strategem failed, our case would be set back seriously. I decided the move had to be made."[4]

One week later, in the Court's Friday conference session, the justices voted to grant the expedited request for certiorari. At the beginning of the discussion, most of the justices, including Chief Justice Warren E. Burger, Potter Stewart, Byron White, and William O. Douglas, "strongly opposed taking the case."[5] However, preliminary views and votes were changed during the course of the extended discussion in conference, wrote Justice William J. Brennan, Jr., "on the ground [that] every other institution has delayed and we have the duty to our institution and to the public not to be one of these."[6] In the end, only justices Harry Blackmun and Byron White were recorded, on Brennan's and Douglas's docket sheets, as having voted to deny expedited certiorari in the case of *U.S. v. Nixon*.

Justice Douglas recollected, in his autobiography published in 1980, that "there seemed to be a feeling that the Court had a 'duty' to step in and clarify the Watergate mess."[7] Both Brennan and Douglas have used the phrase "duty" to describe the compulsion of the Supreme Court majority in 1974 to hear and resolve the *Nixon* litigation in an expedited fashion.

The purpose of this essay is to reexamine, through an analysis of the papers of two justices, William J. Brennan, Jr., and William O. Douglas, this self-imposed duty of the Court, in a unanimous decision, to quickly come to closure on the controversial litigation. This unanimous ruling of the Supreme Court "provides a good . . . example of the justices working toward an institutional decision and opinion."[8]

The first part of this paper will briefly examine what became known as the Watergate scandal, which began in the summer of 1972. The second part will view the Supreme Court in 1974; that is, its personnae, its processes, and its politics. The following four sections will analyze the activities of the Court in the case of *U.S. v. Nixon*, from May 24, 1974 (when the president's lawyers and Jaworski filed their appeals with, respectively, the Court of Appeals and the U.S. Supreme Court) to July 24, 1974 (when the Supreme Court announced its unanimous judgment in the case). The next section will critically examine the Court's view of executive privilege as it was enunciated in *U.S. v. Nixon*, and the final part will present a conclusion.

THE WATERGATE SCANDAL

Democratic Party National Headquarters, housed in the Watergate complex in Washington, D.C., was the scene, on the evening of June 17, 1972, of a break-in by five persons in order to plant electronic bugging devices.[9] Caught, these "Plumbers" were quickly traced to the White House and, shortly thereafter, John Mitchell, Nixon's close adviser (and formerly the U.S. attorney general), resigned as chair of the Committee to Re-Elect the President. The trial of the five led to further revelations about White House involvement in the break-in and, evidently, to further cover-ups by the White House.

Although the president made an effort to end the Watergate discussion in the spring of 1973 by dismissing his chief advisers and other staff persons; namely, H. R. Haldeman, John Ehrlichman, John Dean, and Richard Klein-dienst; the issue continued to attract international attention with the televised sessions of the Senate Select Committee on Presidential Activities of 1972, chaired by Senator Sam Ervin (D-N.C.). During these televised hearings, on July 16, 1973, Alexander Butterfield, a former Haldeman assistant, revealed that the president had taped all conversations in the Oval Office and the Executive Office Building.

With that revelation, both the Ervin Committee and the recently appointed Watergate special prosecutor, Archibald Cox, sought the tapes. Nixon refused to turn them over. For the president, the basic position was that these conversations were absolutely privileged; there is an inherent executive privilege and power, protected in the constitutional system of separation of powers, to withhold such confidential information and material.

Undaunted, Cox, working with a federal grand jury charged with determining whether additional criminal activities were associated with the Watergate break-in, went into federal court for permission to review a selected number (eight) of the tapes. He used the subpoena power of the federal courts, Rule 17(c) of the Federal Rules of Criminal Procedure. Rule 17(c) sets standards that have to be met before a subpoena can be issued for relevant and admissible information.

On August 29, 1973, Sirica ordered Nixon to turn over the tapes to the federal judge for in camera inspection. The federal judge concluded that the court had jurisdiction and that the matter was justifiable, that is, capable of resolution by the judiciary. While the privilege has developed over the centuries, it is not absolute, and can be negated by a legitimate claim of a grand jury to all papers and other testimony that sheds light on its investigations into alleged criminal activity.

Nixon chose not to comply, and instead appealed the Sirica ruling to the U.S. Court of Appeals in the District of Columbia. The court heard the case *en banc* and, on October 12, 1973, upheld the Sirica order. The result was the infamous "Saturday night massacre" in which Archibald Cox was fired by Acting Attorney General Robert Bork (Elliot Richardson and William Ruckelshaus had both resigned rather than fire the Watergate special prosecutor) because Cox had refused to accept a Nixon compromise on the tapes. As a consequence of these stunning events over a weekend, the president's lawyers capitulated and agreed to turn the tapes over to Judge Sirica.

In March 1974, the grand jury, led by the new Watergate special prosecutor, Leon Jaworski, on the basis of a review of portions of six of the tapes released by the president in the fall of 1973, handed down indictments against seven persons. Jaworski then had the task of preparing a criminal case before a jury trial in September 1974. In that effort, the Watergate special prosecutor, in April 1974, went before Federal Judge Sirica and requested the additional sixty-four tapes. The president's attorneys reargued the presidential privilege, intrabranch dispute issues. In late May, Sirica ordered the president to turn the tapes over to him for an in camera inspection. Appeal was made to the Court of Appeals and, on May 24, Jaworski's drastic step was taken: bypassing the Court of Appeals by asking the Supreme Court to grant certiorari under expedited review as permitted in Rule 20.

THE U.S. SUPREME COURT IN 1974: PERSONAE, PROCESSES, AND POLITICS

The Personae

The 1973 term of the Court was the second full term of the nine-person "Burger" Court.[10] President Nixon, in his first term, 1969–1972, had appointed four men to the U.S. Supreme Court: Chief Justice Warren Burger had been appointed and confirmed in 1969, Associate Justice Harry Blackmun in 1970, and justices Lewis Powell and William Rehnquist in 1972. Partly because there were four new justices on for such a relatively brief time, the Court was a fractionalized one in the 1973 term. Of the 144 decisions announced during that term, a majority of them were split 5–4 or 6–3 decisions. On constitutional decisions, the conservative Nixon quartet plus Justice Byron White (85 percent) and Justice Potter Stewart (82 percent) voted as a bloc and had successfully frustrated the other court group. The "liberal" bloc, consisting of justices William O. Douglas, William J. Brennan, Jr., and Thurgood Marshall voted as a bloc 74 percent of the time on these constitutional issues—and lost on most of them.[11] It would take a truly exceptional case or "challenge" to unite such a widely diverse and fragmented group of justices.

It was clear that one of the liberal justices, William O. Douglas, did not like Richard M. Nixon. In May 1973, more than a year before the Watergate litigation came to the Court, Douglas was asking friends of his—for example, Palmer Hoyt (former owner of the *Denver Post*), James M. Carter (a sitting U.S. Court of Appeals judge for the Ninth Circuit), and, through Judge Carter, Roger Kent (a prominent San Francisco attorney)—for information about Nixon in "order to get to the bottom of the story that some of RMN's aides [H. R. Haldeman, Maurice Stans, Murray Chotiner, and Herbert Kalmbach among others], were prosecuted in a state court in California as a result of conduct in the 1962 campaign in which Pat Brown won. . . . I have been hearing about it for days, but from no one who knows firsthand."[12] The contacts quickly responded to the Douglas inquiry by providing him with data that showed that, to use Douglas's language, "Our Hero [Nixon] was not the victim of unsuspected associates. He knew his way around without help."[13] Given that President Nixon and his attorney general, Mitchell, were very instrumental in encouraging impeachment proceedings in Congress against Douglas in 1970 through their man in the House of Representatives, Gerald Ford (R-Mich.), it is easy to see why Douglas did not have a great affection for the president.[14]

Sitting on the Court in May 1974 was a Roosevelt appointee, two Eisenhower appointees, a Kennedy appointee, a Johnson appointee, and four Nixon appointees. There were, in this grouping, three recognized "liberal" justices, three "conservative" justices, and three "moderate" or swing justices. In short, the ideological divisions on the Court at the time of the Jaworski gambit strongly suggested that, at best, there would be a very fragmented and divided court ruling—if it took the case at all on an expedited basis—on the merits.

Certainly, the president's lawyers expected such an outcome; they thought that the Rule 20 certiorari petition would be denied.[15] Even Jaworski, the Watergate special prosecutor, and Philip Lacovara, the counsel to the special prosecutor, "thought that it would be 5–3 with William O. Douglas writing the majority opinion."[16] (One commentary on the Watergate did note, however, that when the Court voted to hear the case in an expedient fashion, "Fred Buzhardt [Nixon's attorney] and Al Haig [Nixon's Chief of Staff] knew that as soon as the Court bypassed the Appeals Court, they were fairly certain the President would lose.")[17]

The Process

"The business of the Court," said Potter Stewart, "is to give institutional opinions for its decisions."[18] The opinion of the Supreme Court is the vehicle through which the Supreme Court expresses its institutional decision. The process of decision making; that is, arriving at consensus on particular opinions at the Supreme Court, can be understood by viewing it as two distinct phases of Court work: the group and the individual phases. Group activities include oral argument and the conference sessions.

The conference session is the heart of the judicial decision-making process. It is in these sessions that initial questions of jurisdiction and justiciability are raised, and where, after oral argument is heard, the justices discuss their views on the litigation and then take their initial vote on the outcome of the case before them. During the term of the Court, from the first Monday in October until early July, there will be twenty to twenty-three Wednesday (afternoon) and Friday sessions, coinciding with the weeks the Court schedules oral argument.

"The most important work of the Supreme Court . . . occurs behind the scenes, particularly at the Conference Session, where the Justices discuss and vote on cases."[19] It is in that setting that the "mettle of a justice is tested, for here he must meet his colleagues in the rough and tumble of free discussion."[20] In the *Nixon* case, the conference sessions were critically important in the initial judgment to grant expedited certiorari under Rule 20 and in the subsequent group discussion on the substantive issue of executive privilege. Although there were a number of justices who were opposed to bringing the case up to the Court under Rule 20, once it was in the Court, they participated fully and quite effectively. As Justice Hugo Black once noted, the jurisdictional vote "is not the equivalent of a final vote on the merits."[21]

The vote taken in conference is not the final, binding vote. After the conference session, there are a great many interactions between the justices, and this leads to the occasional switch. There is a fluidity of judicial choice in Supreme Court decision making.[22] Persuaded by arguments in conference, a justice will move in one direction. After conversations with some of his or her brethren and after reading or writing one of the opinions that will circulate for each case, he or she may begin to move in the opposite direction. Justice Brennan has said, ''I have had to convert more than one of my proposed majority opinions into a dissent before the final opinion was announced. I have also, however, had the satisfying experience of rewriting a dissent as a majority opinion of the Court.''[23] Black summed up this phenomenon when he wrote: ''My votes at conference are never final. They are tentative and I am always ready to change the vote if I reach the conclusion that my vote was wrong.''[24]

The individual phase of the judicial decision-making process is the lonely time spent by each justice as he or she reviews the briefs, oral arguments, and memos prepared by the clerks for the justice's review, in order to either write an opinion or to respond to one circulated to the brethren by some of the other justices. (For example, in the *Nixon* case, justices Powell, Douglas, Brennan, Stewart, and White wrote separate opinions or portions of opinions and circulated these to their colleagues.) A great deal of craftsmanship enters into the development of a quality opinion; it is the expression of collegial thinking on a number of important issues. In order to hold the majority, the drafter has to be sure that the opinion meets with the approval of the rest of the group. ''Opinions for the Court,'' wrote a scholar, ''are not statements of a particular justice's jurisprudence. Rather, they are negotiated documents forged from ideological divisions within the Court.''[25]

During this individual phase, communication exchanges take place among the justices through drafts and through the exchange of ''Memorandum to the Conference'' notes. Justice Blackmun, for example, wrote that

a Memorandum to the Conference does have impact, for it sets forth in specific language the concerns entertained by the author. In some respects, it is better than general observations made orally at conference. And they tend to fill in the gap occasioned by the lack of time for extended conferences or one-on-one conversations. By a Memorandum . . . , all nine are brought into the discussion.[26]

Additionally, the Court's process of arriving at decisions in cases does not give the justice the luxury of reviewing and reflecting on a single case of importance to the exclusion of all others. Justices are reviewing, reflecting on, and writing on a number of cases at the same time. For example, when the Court met in conference on July 23, 1974, the day before the *Nixon* opinion was announced, Burger's Memo to the Conference had an attachment: the Agenda for that conference. In addition to the discussion of Nixon, there were four other opinions circulating that would be discussed (including the important bussing case, *Milliken v. Bradley*, which was decided a day after *Nixon*), two holds that had to be discussed, and six petitions that had to be acted on by the justices in that conference.[27]

It is clear that ''deciding the merits of those few cases taxes the individual powers of the justices and their capacity for compromise."[28] Examining the bargaining process among the justices during the last thirteen days of the Nixon negotiations clearly illustrates the fluidity of judicial choice. The process is a complex, time-consuming one that demands intense commitment to the issues by the jurists contemplating the facts and the law. Moreover, the "votes are tentative until an opinion announcing the Court's decision is handed down."[29] In *Nixon*, four days before the opinion was read in open court by the chief justice, Douglas was circulating his *eighth* draft of a separate concurring opinion. Justice White, barely two days prior to the announcement, was informing (and threatening) the chief that he would write a separate opinion if Burger did not change a portion of the executive privilege segment of the Burger draft opinion that was circulating.

That the Court moved so quickly on such an important constitutional case while it was continuing to review and resolve other important statutory and constitutional questions was a credit to the resolve of the justices. It was due in great part to their collective commitment to the belief, raised by Brennan in the first conference session on May 31, 1974, that it was the institution's "duty" to clarify the Watergate "mess." This clarification by the Court was not, however, accomplished without difficulty.

Politics and Courts

Beyond doubt, the Watergate issue was the all-consuming political and moral dilemma of 1973–1974. It is extraordinarily clear, reviewing the papers of the justices, that they were very aware of the politics of the Watergate litigation and of the potential impact a definitive institutional judgment of the Court would have on the resolution of that dilemma. (Interestingly, Douglas, the justice Jaworski and Lacovara thought might write the opinion for the Court, believed initially that the motion for expedited certiorari under Rule 20 should be denied because, in part, the issue was "political" and therefore nonjusticiable.) The Court's decision to bypass the Court of Appeals, under the guidelines of Rule 20, was a "crucial" timing judgment.[30]

The Court's "headlong rush" into the controversy was a critical factor in the ultimate resolution of the societal and constitutional crisis.[31] The opinion of the Court in *U.S. v. Nixon*, said one scholar, "represents nothing less than a bold and stunningly successful instance of judicial activism."[32] From Judge Sirica's perspective, by not acting as quickly as it did, the Court "would have delayed the cover-up trial perhaps into 1975 and would certainly have left the crippled president in office well beyond the time when he was able to govern effectively."[33] While there was some concern about expediting the case, thereby bypassing the Court of Appeals, the majority of the justices moved to expedite the litigation in order to, as Douglas wrote in his autobiography, "clarify the Watergate mess." The concern expressed by some of the justices in the May 31, 1974, conference was reminiscent of the dissenting opinions in *U.S. v. New*

York Times and Washington Post (1971), the "Pentagon Papers" case. Burger, Blackmun, and John M. Harlan, Jr., wrote dissenting opinions that, generally, reflected their views that "these cases have been conducted in unseemly haste. . . . Prompt judicial action does not mean unjudicial haste. . . . The Court has been almost irresponsibly feverish in dealing with these cases."[34] Burger's concern was pervasive and voiced in conference, when he said to his colleagues, "No judge on any of the cases knows the whole facts" and until the complete facts are in, "he is unable to vote on the merits." John M. Harlan, Jr., also in the conference meeting, thought that the "judicial process has been made a travesty—it has been panicky and hurried . . . [and] judicial review has been very, very limited."[35]

U.S. V. NIXON IN THE SUPREME COURT: GAINING ACCESS TO THE SUPREME COURT, MAY 1974

On March 1, 1974, H. R. Haldeman and six others (John Mitchell, John Ehrlichman, Gordon Strachan, Robert Mardian, Kenneth Parkinson, and Charles Colson) were indicted by a federal grand jury. The Special Prosecutor's Office had then to turn to developing the case for the forthcoming (scheduled for September 9, 1974) criminal trial, *U.S. v. Mitchell, et al.* (DC Crim. No. 74–110), and requested that the federal court issue a subpoena to the president of the United States. If issued, it would direct Nixon to produce tape recordings and documents relating to sixty-four conversations between Nixon and his advisers. On April 18, Judge Sirica issued the subpoena pursuant to Rule 17(c) of the Federal Rules of Criminal Procedure.

On May 1, 1974, James St. Clair, the president's new counsel, filed a Special Appearance and Motion to Quash the subpoena.[36] He argued that the materials sought were "within the constitutional privilege of the President to refuse to disclose confidential information when disclosure would be contrary to the public interest."[37] In addition, St. Clair argued that the matter was an internal controversy not subject to judicial scrutiny. (He also moved, on May 11, for an order of the court expunging the grand jury's naming of Nixon as an unindicted coconspirator in the upcoming criminal trial.)

On May 20, Sirica denied both motions and ordered Nixon to produce the sixty-four tapes. The federal judge found that Jaworski met the requirements of Rule 17(c) and that the prosecutors' submissions constituted a prima facie showing adequate to rebut the confidentiality privilege raised by the president. Four days later, St. Clair filed notice of appeal in the U.S. District Court and docketed the appeal in the Court of Appeals for the District of Columbia Circuit. Jaworski, that same day, May 24, then took the "drastic step" of requesting a writ of certiorari from the U.S. Supreme Court before judgment of the Court of Appeals.[38]

The next day, May 25, Chief Justice Burger, after a conversation with justices Potter Stewart and Lewis Powell, wrote a note to his colleagues. While concerned about the Court being "pressured or rushed by news media or anyone else, nevertheless, the case is one of obvious importance and time factors are important," he stated. He indicated that he would "canvass all the members of the Court to secure reactions with the idea of having the Clerk call Mr. St. Clair and suggest that the Court would like to have his response if at all possible by next Thursday ... so as to enable the Court to begin its consideration of the petition."[39] A conference was set for May 31, in order for the Supreme Court to respond to Jaworski's petition and the president's response.

Three days before the scheduled conference, Justice William H. Rehnquist wrote to Burger. While he believed in "having a full court decide important questions of constitutional law," he regretted that he "must disqualify [him]self from participation." It was not based on his "previous relationship with the named parties in the case before [him]" but because "this litigation" was an "offshoot of *U.S. v. Mitchell*, a pending criminal prosecution in the District Court." Because of his "varying degrees of close professional association with three of the named defendants in that action, . . . it seem[ed] to [him] that there [was] no doubt as to [his] proper course."[40]

On May 30, a day before the conference, James B. Gingy, clerk of the Court, at Burger's request, prepared and circulated a detailed nine-page Memorandum for the Conference.[41] It framed six threshold issues for the eight justices:

1. Did Jaworski have standing to seek a petition for certiorari before judgment under Rule 20?

2. Did Jaworski, as an "agent" of the executive branch, have the authority to conduct and argue a case before the Court?

3. Was Judge Sirica's order an appealable one?

4. How had the phrase in Rule 20, namely, "imperative public importance," been interpreted by the Court?

5. Did the District Court correctly apply Rule 17c of the *Federal Rules of Civil Procedure* (*FRCP*)? Was executive privilege a power, or could the district court interpose and make judgment on that constitutional question?

6. Was the court of appeals decision in *Nixon v. Sirica* (1973) a controlling decision regarding the question of executive privilege?

This very timely memo framed the May 31 conference discussion of the justices. The threshold issues were appealability (the jurisdiction of the Court), intrabranch nature of the dispute—thought by Sirica to be an "absurd and insulting" claim of the president—(the "justiciability" issue), and the question of prosecutorial and judicial compliance with the standards inherent in Rule 17c of the *FRCP*.[42] Inexorably, these questions led to the overarching substantive question associated with the separation of powers concept: executive privilege.

On May 31, the eight justices met in conference to review the petition for an expedited writ of certiorari. Interestingly, the initial vote to grant, based on the Brennan and Douglas docket files, was negative. According to Brennan's records,

Brennan and, to a much lesser extent, Marshall were early supporters of an expedited certiorari grant. However, justices Blackmun, White, Powell, Stewart, Douglas, and Burger were not. At conference end, Powell, Douglas, Stewart, and Burger switched their votes, and the final tally in conference was 6–2 to grant the expedited petition for certiorari.[43]

Initially, Justice Douglas "strongly opposed taking the case." He felt that the court of appeals "would quickly affirm the District Court and we could quickly deny certiorari. We should deny it because the legislative and constitutional issues were frivolous and, as they involved impeachment, were political."[44] Brennan's notes indicated that Douglas wanted the case to remain at the court of appeals, and that Douglas believed that "it would be shocking to withhold exculpatory material that would free men." Although he "prefer[red] not to bypass," Douglas did say, according to Brennan, that he would "acquiesce if the Court grants."[45]

Blackmun, according to Brennan's notes, believed that "a six-month delay in a criminal case [was] no irreparable injury. . . . It [might] be an unpopular decision but I'd deny."[46] Stewart also voiced some misgivings and thought that "a criminal trial [could] be put off without real damage." He did not see this litigation "qualifying" under Rule 20. White, too, was reluctant to "bypass" the court of appeals because "Jaworski's application [did not] really demonstrate immediate need."[47] According to Brennan, White then stated that the expedited appeal was "just a transparent attempt to have an impact on [the] impeachment proceeding. I don't think we should let ourselves be used that way." White clearly "preferred to deny."[48]

Justice Powell felt the same way. On the merits of the case, Powell was "inclined to say [that Nixon] can't claim privilege to keep material from defense"; however, procedurally, Powell "would expedite any appeal from the Court of Appeals but not under Rule 20."[49]

According to the Brennan docket notes, Marshall commented that he did not "see why we should go to the Court of Appeals,"[50] while Burger essentially focused on the substantive issue of executive privilege.[51]

Brennan, however, "felt strongly that we should take the cases," wrote Douglas. Evidently, after a while, "so did Marshall."[52] Further, Douglas recalled, Brennan stated that if the Court declined to hear the *Nixon* case, "he would write in dissent." As the discussion continued, there "developed an opinion in the minds of Stewart, Blackmun and Powell that the [case] should be taken."[53]

Evidently, the feeling grew among five of the justices—Brennan, Marshall, Powell, Stewart, and Douglas (joined strategically at the end of the discussion by Burger)—"that the Court had a 'duty' to step in and clarify the Watergate mess."[54] Brennan saw the case as one that, "in the context of the times, called for the kind of opinion we had in 1958 with *Cooper v. Aaron*."[55] His views, clearly enunciated, brought Brennan's hesitant brethren to his view that it was the Court's "duty to our institution and to the public not to delay" hearing the case.[56]

The final vote in the May 31 conference was 6–2; Blackmun and White continued to believe that Rule 20 should not be employed to grant certiorari. Brennan's arguments, however, convinced Powell, Stewart, and Marshall and Douglas. Burger joined with the majority in order to be able to write the opinion of the Court in *U.S. v. Nixon*. Later that day, the Supreme Court's Journal noted (without acknowledging the split vote) that the petition for writ of certiorari to the Court of Appeals and motion for an expedited schedule was "granted." The Order established dates for the filing of briefs (by July 1), oral argument (July 8) and also noted that Rehnquist did not participate in the proceedings.

Once the writ of certiorari was granted, the lawyers for the parties to the dispute began to prepare their briefs for presentation to the Court. The justices, too, began to seriously review the threshold and substantive issues and, with their law clerks, began to develop tentative answers to the constitutional issues.

Further, a flurry of additional appeals in early June led to a modified Court order in mid-June. On June 3, Lacovara, counsel to the Watergate special prosecutor, wrote to the clerk of the court "requesting instructions on how to proceed with two aspects of this case": (1) printing of materials from the sealed files and (2) briefing and arguing a legal issue that "turns inextricably upon information currently under seal."[57]

Evidently, according to the counsel, the sealed materials contained information that "in our judgment [was] necessary to the Court's informed decision on the executive privilege question." Under Sirica's May 13 order, their office was "not permitted to disclose this information to anyone."[58]

On June 4, in response to the Lacovara letter, the justices were instructed by Burger that the "sealed" materials were in the Court vault and were "available to any justice. We should be prepared to resolve those questions," wrote Burger, "at the Friday conference."[59] (Prior to that conference, *The Washington Post* and the *Star* had leaked portions of the sealed material that had been delivered to the House Committee on Impeachment. The leaked data indicated that Nixon had been named by the grand jury as an unindicted coconspirator.) On June 10, Jaworski and St. Clair submitted a joint motion requesting the Court to unseal the record. However, on June 11, six defendants wrote a memo "respectfully objecting to the release of the sealed materials to anyone except the defendants' counsel."[60]

The June 15 conference adopted the Stewart response to the new appeals: The Court denied the motion to unseal except for an extract that had already been leaked, and framed two additional questions for the parties to brief and argue.[61]

By mid-June 1974, the justices of the Supreme Court, a very mixed small group, which had been together as a full court only since the appointment and confirmation of justices Powell and Rehnquist in 1972, and with four of them appointed by Richard M. Nixon, had from May 31 to June 15:

• granted certiorari in an expedited fashion,
• raised fundamental threshold constitutional questions about the separation of powers, and
• drawn together in an institutional "duty" to resolve the "Watergate mess."

The next stage, prior to the oral argument scheduled for July 8, was for the justices to review the briefs and prepare their responses to the very important legal and political questions raised in the case of *U.S. v. Nixon*.

THE JUSTICES PONDER THE LEGAL AND POLITICAL ISSUES: JUNE 1974

While Justice Rehnquist was busily engaged in arranging seating for the oral argument session scheduled for July 8, the other justices were engaged in the creative task of reviewing the submitted briefs and developing their tentative responses to the key issues of jurisdiction, justiciability and executive privilege.[62] The fluidity of judicial choice was well underway.

Jaworski's main brief focused on these questions: Who invokes executive privilege—is it the president, or does a "federal court determine itself if executive privilege is properly invoked in a criminal proceeding?" Is the president subject to a judicial order directing compliance with a subpoena calling for production of evidence? Does a generalized claim of executive privilege outweigh the specific need for evidence in a pending criminal trial? Was the subpoena issued correctly? St. Clair's main brief made the following points: Did the judiciary have jurisdiction to review the Sirica order and to intervene "in an internal dispute of a co-equal branch?" Can the Court substitute its judgment for that of the president? Can it enforce a subpoena against a president? Had the prosecutor made the necessary showing required to obtain materials under Rule 17(c), *FRCP*?[63]

Concerned about the time factor, the justices were eager to share their thoughts with the others, and so the process of circulating drafts and developing a consensus began after the June 15 conference session ended. In that conference they had agreed that "exchanges of memoranda would be welcomed."[64] On July 5, Justice Douglas circulated the first of many draft opinions (eight) written by him and by his brethren in the *Nixon* case. It was a lengthy, thirty-page note that focused on the major issues. "I enclose herewith an explanatory memorandum in the *Nixon* cases which I prepared to expedite my own resolution of the main issues," he wrote to his colleagues.[65]

The Douglas opinion focused on four issues:

1. appealability (it was appealable);

2. justiciability (Jaworski did have standing because he was ultimately an appointee with authority derived directly from Congress. Douglas believed that Archibald Cox, Jaworski's predecessor, had been fired illegally by acting Attorney General Robert Bork because that office "was established explicitly to be an independent agency in response to the public demand for a prosecutor who was not subject to the direction of the President whose activities are intertwined with the investigation which need be conducted.");[66]

3. executive privilege (which was not involved at all; "to allow . . . [the President] to

conceal from a court information which may be critical to the fairness of a trial of named defendants would be a monstrous affront to the rule of law under which we live.''[67] In his eighth version, circulated on July 20, Douglas wrote that it was a ''travesty to think of this case in terms of the so-called executive privilege. Every citizen, high or low, has a right of privacy and confidentiality concerning his conversations except as they be reached by process for use in a civil or criminal trial. This present controversy is a prelude to a serious criminal trial. In that setting it stands on no higher a footing than does a subpoena issued against members of the Mafia.'');[68] and

4. the question of whether the Grand Jury was justified in naming Nixon as an unindicted coconspirator (a nonjusticiable issue; ''Beyond question, that issue is a 'political' issue, not a justiciable one.'').[69]

The strongly worded memo of Douglas was followed, on July 6, by a draft opinion written by Powell. In contrast to Douglas's memo urging a rejection of the executive privilege argument, Powell's draft was very deferential to the president on that issue. After briefly outlining reasons why he believed the Court had jurisdiction and stating that there was a justiciable case, he turned to executive privilege and ''standards and procedures governing the exercise of judicial authority to order the president to comply with a subpoena.''[70]

''[My] views and conclusions stated are tentative and subject, of course, to oral argument and our discussion at conference,''[71] he wrote. Moreover, defining the ''precise contours of the separation of powers concept is a task for the Courts,'' stated Powell.[72] However, the Supreme Court has to note that because ''the interest in confidentiality pertains to the President's effective exercise of his executive powers, it is nevertheless constitutionally based.''[73] Brennan, in his margin notes on the Powell draft opinion, wrote that ''we need not decide in this case whether the confidentiality interest has a constitutional or common law source.''[74] In this light, Powell wrote that ''absent compelling justification, competing societal interests, the courts cannot presume to order the President to produce confidential materials.''[75] Moreover, Powell clearly stated that ''nothing in the concept of separation of powers . . . compels the conclusion that . . . the decision whether to sacrifice confidentiality in a particular case is singularly committed exclusively to [Nixon's] discretion and cannot be reviewed or overridden by the judicial branch.''

Powell's discussion of the procedures and standards for judicial determination of whether there was ''compelling justification'' in the case followed.[76] The Sirica action was a good initial starting point. If the president argued that the release of the subpoenaed materials ''would prove injurious to the public interest, he may invoke executive privilege.''[77] At this point, a court ''must require a special showing from the moving party.'' Jaworski had to show the necessity of the subpoenaed materials ''to the ends of justice.''[78] If the showing was made, then an order must issue for the president to produce the subpoenaed materials.

A few days later, on July 8, 1974, justices Brennan and Stewart circulated their memos on the case. Brennan's was the shorter of the two, and was in direct response to Powell's circulation. "Although greatly impressed by Lewis' analysis in his memorandum, . . . I think his Part IV [executive privilege] requires some expansion and I am taking the liberty of circulating the attached in the hope that it may serve to focus that problem in our conference discussion."[79]

Brennan argued that Rule 17(c) was adequate to protect the president "from unnecessary interference or harassment." In cases involving the president, "appellate review, in deference to the comity properly accorded a coordinate branch of government, should be particularly meticulous to insure that the standards of Rule 17(c) have been correctly applied."[80] Brennan summarized his position by stating that Nixon should "transmit directly to the District Court those materials for which no specific claim of privilege limited to national defense, foreign relations or domestic security is made."[81]

Potter Stewart's memo was a more reflective essay. Stewart addressed the question of court jurisdiction and justiciability. He rejected St. Clair's suggestions that it was an internal dispute, and that the issue was a nonjusticiable political issue. For Stewart, Jaworski was an employee appointed under congressional guidelines and could not be dismissed by Nixon.[82]

That same day, the case was argued before the justices. For the prosecution, Jaworski raised the basic constitutional question when he asked, "Who is the arbiter of what the Constitution says?" St. Clair's arguments before the Court contained a categorical defense of absolute presidential immunity from every kind of criminal investigation unless the president decided that "in the public interest" the requested data could be turned over to a prosecutor. An active eight-person Supreme Court interrupted the lawyers numerous times. Jaworski recalled that he was interrupted 115 times during his presentation before the Court. For the special prosecutor, the heart of the matter was the issue of separation of powers:

Now enmeshed in almost 500 pages of briefs, when boiled down, this case really presents one fundamental issue. Who is to be the arbiter of what the Constitution says? . . . In refusing to produce the evidence sought by a subpoena . . . in the criminal trial of the seven defendants—among them former chief aides and devotees—the President invokes the provisions of the Constitution. . . . In his public statements, as we all know, the President has embraced the Constitution as offering him support for his refusal to supply the subpoenaed tapes. Now the President may be right in how he reads the Constitution, but he may also be wrong. And, if he is wrong, who is there to tell him so? And if there is no one, then the President, of course, is free to pursue his course of erroneous interpretations. What then becomes of our constitutional form of government?"[83]

This was a major question that went to the very "heart of our basic constitutional systems," and to which the justices returned time and again over the course of the *Nixon* decision process.[84] St. Clair was also asked many questions—over two hundred in the course of the first hour of argument—by the justices. Given his starting point that the president was the absolute, final determiner of the use of executive privilege and that the federal judiciary could not interpose without violating the separation of powers, this was not surprising. His view that the President was not subject to the processes of the law "unless he so determines he would give evidence," was at odds with the justices.[85] For St. Clair the matter was outside the jurisdiction of the federal courts, and a non-justiciable, intrabranch dispute as well.

In the July 9, 1974, Conference Session, convened a day after the oral arguments, the justices unanimously voted that there was jurisdiction to hear the case, that it was a justiciable case, that Rule 17(c) was correctly applied, and that executive privilege did not bar the courts from ordering the president to turn over the requested tapes for an in camera court inspection. On the unindicted coconspirator issue, the justices voted without dissent to dismiss the petition as improvidently granted.[86] There was "no political question" in either impending impeachment or otherwise. "No reason to stay our hand," wrote Brennan.[87] He indicated that Justice Douglas proposed that the Court "dismiss as improvidently granted" the unindicted coconspirator issue because it was not relevant to the issue of discovery, and was, insofar as it was relevant to Watergate, a political question.[88] Furthermore, from Brennan's notes, it is clear that Chief Justice Burger did most of the talking. Burger viewed that case as falling within the Court's jurisdiction, saw it as a "justiciable" case of controversy, felt that Rule 17(c) was appropriate, and distinguished executive privilege from presidential privilege. Presidential privilege, said Burger, "was qualified privilege limited to official duties." Who decides, he asked, "when it is no longer crucial?" Burger also noted that "conduct outside Article II (executive power) is not covered [under presidential privilege]."

The conference ended with strong consensus on all the legal issues raised in the briefs and oral arguments by counsel. In addition, the four justices—Douglas, Powell, Brennan, and Stewart—who had circulated memos prior to the conference session, had greatly aided in the framing and answering of the legal questions: *Appealable*, Yes (8–0); *Justiciable*, Yes (8–0); *Rule 17(c) Appropriately Applied*, Yes (8–0); *Executive Privilege Not Applicable in This Case*, Yes (8–0). Brennan wanted the Court to develop an opinion signed by all as was done by the Court in *Cooper v. Aaron (1958)*, and although he "went around to see everyone and tried to sell that idea, . . . it was a complete failure. Nobody agreed, not one."[89]

According to tradition, Chief Justice Burger took the opinion. It was now his responsibility to write a most historic opinion involving a major concept of our constitutional system, the separation of powers.

THE SUPREME COURT SEEKS AGREEMENT ON THE RATIONALE FOR ITS VOTE IN *U.S. v. NIXON*: JULY 1974

While the chief justice was given the awesome task of writing the opinion for the Court, and although the justices had rejected Brennan's *Cooper* suggestions, the reality, seen before the July 9, 1974, Conference Session, was the opinion of an eight-person group, extremely involved in the creation of the *U.S. v. Nixon* opinion. An undated "opinion outline" in the Brennan file indicates that at least seven of the eight justices had a hand in the crafting of the opinion. According to the Brennan note, the breakdown went as follows: Blackmun, Facts; Douglas, Appealability; Brennan/Burger, Justiciability; White, Rule 17(c); Burger/Powell with Stewart revisions, Executive Privilege; Powell with Brennan revisions, Standards Met before in camera Inspection; Brennan, Court's Judgment and Order.[90]

This involvement by the justices in the successful effort to create "institutional unanimity" took place between July 10 and July 23, 1974. The justices and their clerks worked throughout the week and on weekends in Washington and elsewhere—Douglas in Goose Prairie, Washington, and Brennan in Nantucket, Massachusetts—to quickly write, review, and modify drafts of portions of the opinion. There was extreme pressure placed on Burger by his brethren to get the drafts circulated.

Indeed, Burger wrote to his colleagues on July 10, 1974, that he would "not await a complete draft but will send sections as they are ready." He ended his note by writing what turned out to be an understated truth: "The enclosed material is not intended to be final and I will welcome—indeed I invite—your suggestions." ("More later!" was handwritten on the letter by Burger.)[91]

Although the justices had, in the July 9, 1974, Conference Session, voted unanimously on each contested issue, the next phase of opinion writing was a complex, critical and sensitive one. Poorly crafted opinions written by justices had led to breakdowns of majorities, switches of votes to the point that dissents become majority or plurality opinions of the Court (or vice versa), multiple opinions in a case, and so forth. The justices were obviously aware of these possibilities, and were all mindful of Counsel to the Special Prosecutor Lacovara's plea in the final moments of oral argument that the Court provide the president and the country with a "definitive," that is, unitary, judgment against the president.[92]

A review of the Brennan and Douglas docket sheets and notes on the litigation reveals the following pattern of judicial interaction in the creation of the *U.S. v. Nixon* opinion (Table 5.1). Clearly, Burger was involved in the drafting of each segment of *U.S. v. Nixon*. Equally clear is the fact that his colleagues, in almost every segment of the opinion, either preceded him in the drafting of the section or substantively modified the language and direction that Burger had taken. Not until July 20, 1974, barely four days before the judgment and order of the Court were announced, was a complete draft circulated by the chief.[93]

The "Facts" Section

On July 11, 1974, Burger wrote a memo to his colleagues: "I have received various memos in response to preliminary and partial sections circulated. . . . I think it is unrealistic to consider a Monday, July 15, announcement. The case

Table 5.1
Judicial Interaction in the Creation of the *U.S. v. Nixon* Opinion

Area	Drafters	Responses
I. FACTS	WEB-7/10	HAB draft
		WJB to WEB, 7/12: HAB draft is excellent
		PS to WEB, 7/12: " " " good
		TM to WEB, 7/15: " " " O.K.
II. APPEALABILITY	WOD-7/5	PS, 7/8, 7/11, supports w/modifications
(Jurisdiction)	WEB-7/10	LP,7/11, supports PS modifications
		WOD,7/11, " " " "
		TM,7/15, " " " "
III. INTRA-BRANCH	WOD-7/5	WJB, mod. of WOD, 7/10
(Justiciability)	WEB-7/10	WOD,7/11,7/12; prefers WJB mod.
		to WEB mod.
		TM,7/15, to WEB: likes WJB version
IV. APPLICABILITY	WJB-7/10	WOD,7/11, likes
OF RULE 17(c)	LP-7/8	
	LP-7/12	WJB,7/15, supports LP 7/12 rewrite
	WEB-7/10	WOD,7/12, cannot support
		BW,7/12, to WEB, offers to draft sub.
		PS,7/12, support WJB or WEB
	BW-7/13	WJB,7/15,support BW version
		TM,7/15, " " "
		WOD,7/15, " " "
		(BW,7/13 incorporated into final opinion)
V. EXECUTIVE PRIVILEGE		LP-7/8
		WOD,7/11, supports
		TM,7/15, "
	WEB-7/15,/17	PS,7/17, offers to draft sub.
		TM,7/18, responds
		BW,7/18, "
	PS-7/17	TM,7/18. likes

is too important to 'rush' unduly although it is in fact receiving priority treatment."[94] As expressed in that memo, although he felt that the Court "could meet an end-of-the-week announcement, i.e., July 19 or thereabouts," the unabated flow of memos from Burger's colleagues pushed the date of Court announcement back to July 24. Indeed, so hectic were the intra-Court memos on the Burger drafts in *Nixon* that on July 15 he wrote another memo: "My effort to accommodate everyone by sending out 'first drafts' is not working out. I do not contemplate sending out any more material until it is *ready*."[95]

Revision of Burger drafts included his "fact" segment, the introductory portion of the opinion. Justice Douglas's law clerk, in a July 10 memo, indicated that there were "several factual inaccuracies (or at least ambiguities) in the statement of facts."[96] (Douglas, on July 11, wrote the chief a short note enumerating the errors.) On July 12, Burger received a memo from his close friend, Harry Blackmun. Since Burger had asked for recommendations and suggestions, Blackmun wrote, "Accordingly, I take the liberty of suggesting herewith a revised statement of facts and submit it to you for your consideration."[97] Given his concern about the impact of this suggested revision on his friend from Minnesota, Blackmun quickly added, "Please believe me when I say that I do this in a spirit of cooperation and not of criticism. I am fully aware of the pressures that presently beset all of us."[98] Burger also received notes from Brennan and Stewart that same day, and from Thurgood Marshall on July 15, supporting the Blackmun version of the Statement of Facts. Blackmun's ideas were subsequently included in the final Statement of Facts in *U.S. v. Nixon*.

The "Appealability" Issue: Did the Supreme Court Have Jurisdiction to Hear *U.S. v. Nixon*?

Justice Douglas's clerk indicated to his boss that Burger's section on jurisdiction "basically tracks very closely the appealability portion of the draft you initially circulated, although the phrasing is changed (often for the worse) in many instances."[99] (The justices had unanimously agreed on July 9 that the case was appealable, and, on July 10, Burger had circulated his draft on appealability.) Paralleling the comments of the law clerks, justices Stewart and Powell, on July 11, wrote "with all due respect," urging the chief to incorporate Douglas's draft "into the Court opinion." Douglas himself wrote Burger a note on July 11: "Stewart's [and Powell's] proposal meets with my approval and it might be more acceptable to the brethren than the early preliminary draft which you circulated."[100] On July 17, Thurgood Marshall told Burger that he too supported Stewart's suggestion that Douglas's comments be incorporated into the final draft. Douglas's views were made the basis of the appealability section of the Opinion.[101]

The Intrabranch, Justiciability Segment

On July 10 Brennan sent Burger a draft of the justiciability segment. Brennan was very concerned about Burger's feelings on being bombarded with drafts of the various segments by most of the brethren. After noting that his draft "tracks your oral analysis yesterday of the issue [at the conference]," he wrote the chief:[102]

Needless to say insofar as its incorporation, or any part of it, furthers your preparation of the opinion I freely deed it to you in fee simple absolute. I don't think I presume in saying that that is also the thought of the brethren who have sent you memos on this and other issues. I think Lewis, Potter, and Bill Douglas (I borrowed some of the attached from Bill's memo) have written out some particularly persuasive views.

Brennan wrote on his copy of the draft that it was "agreed to by BRW, PS & WJB but not circulated pending Chief's revised section."[103]

Essentially, the Brennan draft—supported by Stewart (who could "equally cheerfully" support the chief's version) and White,[104] by Douglas on July 11 and 12 (after he read Burger's draft); and, on July 17, "unreservedly" by Thurgood Marshall[105]—rejected the president's "first and broadest contention" that the federal courts were without power to review the claim of privilege once Nixon asserted it. Balancing the president's second argument that, as a matter of constitutional law, "the [generalized] privilege he has asserted must prevail over the subpoena *duces tecum* in this case," against the need "for disclosure to demands demonstrably material to a criminal prosecution," Brennan wrote that Nixon "may be ordered . . . to produce the requested materials."[106]

Burger's July 11 version, left largely unchanged in the final opinion, took aim at Nixon's intrabranch dispute argument in noting jurisdiction. It was a narrower statement than the Brennan version and, by and large, was the one that was left in the final version of *U.S. v. Nixon*.[107]

Satisfying the Requirements of Rule 17(c)

Burger, reflecting the vote in conference, concluded that the Supreme Court was "unwilling to conclude that the District Court's evaluation of the Special Prosecutor's showing [of relevancy, specificity, and admissibility] under Rule 17(c) was clearly erroneous."[108]

Brennan, on July 10, supported by Douglas (on July 11), suggested to Burger that the Rule 17(c) section include a note indicating that Sirica concluded that Jaworski had satisfied Rule 17(c) "but also . . . had demonstrated a need sufficiently compelling to rebut the President's privilege."[109] However, on July 12, Douglas, taking a harder view of Brennan's statement, concluded that the "compelling need" language was inappropriate in a situation where a president "discussing crimes to be committed and/or crimes already committed with and/or by him or by his orders, stands no higher than the mafia with respect to those confidences.''[110]

In addition, justices Powell and White sent separate draft versions of a Rule 17(c) segment to the brethren. Powell's, sent on July 12, tried to develop a Rule 17(c) interpretation that all the brethren could accept regarding the ''standard to be met in overcoming the privilege.'' He reminded the Chief that ''some of us emphasized that a President of the United States . . . must be entitled to a *higher level* of protection against disclosures than a citizen possessing no privilege who is charged with crime or who may be a witness in a criminal case.''[111] Powell was convinced that the Court should not avoid this important issue, and rewrote his earlier draft to underscore Sirica's ''compelling need'' criterion in addition to Rule 17(c).[112]

Justice White's circulation, also on July 12 (a revision recirculated a day later), focused on the issue of the relevancy and admissibility of the tapes.[113] (Douglas, on July 12 and 19,[114] Brennan on July 15,[115] Stewart on July 15,[116] and Thurgood Marshall on July 17,[117] all wrote to the chief stating their agreement with the White modification of Rule 17(c) segment.) He focused on the president's contentions that: (1) Jaworski failed to satisfy the requirements of Rule 17(c), and (2) regardless of this fact, the subpoenaed materials may be withheld in the president's ''absolute discretion pursuant to an executive privilege, which is extended to him by the Constitution and is beyond review by the courts.''[118]

For White, beyond a doubt the special prosecutor had, consistent with Rule 17(c), established the relevancy and admissibility of the evidence held by Nixon. ''On the basis of the record before us, we find no basis for disturbing this conclusion,'' wrote White in his draft.[119] The memo, however, contrary to Powell's 17(c) proposal, *did not* incorporate the ''compelling need'' language of the Powell and other Rule 17(c) drafts. White merely said, addressing the fact that Nixon was a party to the suit, that ''appellate review, in deference to a coordinate branch of government, should be particularly meticulous to ensure that the standards of Rule 17(c) have been correctly applied.''[120] White concluded that the Court was ''fully persuaded'' that Sirica's denial of Nixon's motion to quash was consistent with Rule 17(c).[121]

As finally written in the Burger opinion, Part III, Rule 17(c), was the White draft. The very deferential language of the Powell draft was not incorporated. Instead, the opinion spoke solely to the value of the standard inherent in Rule 17(c) itself. Burger's use of a colleague's draft was most dramatically evident in this segment of *U.S. v. Nixon*.

The Substantive Issue: "Executive Privilege"

Even before Burger circulated, on July 15, his first ''very rough draft'' (and only to Douglas, who was off to Goose Prairie, Washington), Douglas was writing to the chief that the Court need not ''reach the decision of whether [executive privilege] is based on the Constitution."[122] Also on July 15, White wrote to Burger about executive privilege. While he initially agreed with Powell's earlier memo that the privilege is "rooted in the Constitution"; White cautioned, however, that "shielding a conspiracy in the making or in the process of execution carries the privilege too far."[123]

On July 17, just one week before the final opinion was announced, Burger sent a draft of the "executive privilege" section, in "rough form," to his colleagues to "expedite" the court's "undertaking."[124] It contained a few glaring errors of constitutional law and, almost immediately, on July 17, Justice Stewart sent him a memo noting these and offering a new Section A. On July 18, Brennan and Marshall wrote to Burger indicating that they liked his section *with* the Stewart addition.

Burger had crafted a five-part privilege section. Part A examined the location of the privilege—in common law and statutes and in the Constitution—and focused on the question of reviewability of a claim of privilege. Part B reviewed Nixon's claims of *absolute* privilege. Burger noted that the president argued that the claim rested on two grounds: (1) Article II, Executive Powers, and the "supremacy of each branch within its own assigned area of constitutional duties"; and (2) the Separation of Powers doctrine which, according to the president, provides each coordinate branch independence in its own sphere and thus insulated the president from honoring the subpoena request. Burger rejected the *absolutist* contention: Separation of powers, without more, cannot sustain an absolute, unqualified presidential privilege of immunity. Part C focused on the need to "resolve the competing interests [of the Executive and the Judiciary] in a manner that preserves the essential functions of each." While for the first time acknowledging a presumptive executive privilege in the Constitution, Burger noted that it could not override the necessity of a subpoena to secure evidence in a pending criminal trial. Parts D and E noted that the trial judge did not commit error in ordering the inspection of materials in camera.[125]

Stewart's memo to Burger, a "Dear Chief" letter dated July 17, was sharp, stating that there must be an "unambiguous response" to the president's argument that "he alone has the power to decide the question of privilege and that the Judicial Branch has no role to play."[126] He asked that his draft of a new Section A be considered by the brethren.

In his draft, Stewart continued the sharp language. The judiciary "unreservedly reject[ed] the claim" that the president alone, "by a simple assertion of privilege," had an *unreviewable power* to decide not to deliver the subpoenaed documents and tapes to the U.S. District Court. "Under the Constitution," Stewart wrote, "it is only the Judicial Branch that is *ultimately* empowered to determine questions of law." Arguing that no man could be a judge in his own case, Stewart wrote that "the existence and scope of presidential privilege is thus a judicial question for the Judicial Branch alone to decide."[127]

On July 18, an evidently chagrined Byron White wrote to Burger.[128] While not wishing to "complicate a difficult task or to increase [his] labors," and while not objecting to Stewart's change, White "submit[ted] some comments for the Chief's review.[129] "The Court does not have to rely on the 'inherent' Article III judicial authority to deal with the review of presidential privilege in this case." The Constitution already provides, he wrote,

for the enforcement of the laws, and the Special Prosecutor is enforcing criminal laws passed by Congress. The Due Process Clause provides for fair trial, the 6th Amendment provides for compulsory processes for witnesses, and the United States is constitutionally required not to withhold exculpatory materials from defendants in criminal cases. *I doubt, therefore, that we need discover or fashion any inherent powers in the judiciary to overcome an executive privilege which is not expressly provided for but which we also fashion today.*[130] (Emphasis added)

White concluded by again voicing his concerns about a too-broad judicial deference to the use of executive privilege, and referred to the enhanced "compelling need" standard in the Burger draft:

You are suggesting that there is a dimension to overcoming the privilege beyond the showing of relevance and admissibility. This makes far too much of the general privilege rooted in the need for confidentiality, and it is not my understanding of the conference vote. . . . Relevance and admissibility themselves provide whatever compelling need must be shown.[131]

He closed his note with a threat: "Perhaps none of these matters is of earth-shattering importance, but it is likely that I shall write separately if your draft becomes the opinion of the Court."[132]

Burger incorporated the commandatory language of Stewart into Part A of the Privilege section. He did not use White's language, and White did not write a separate concurring opinion in *U.S. v. Nixon.*

THE SUPREME COURT REACHES AGREEMENT ON THE FINAL VERSION OF *U.S. v. NIXON*: JULY 20–JULY 24, 1974

On Saturday, July 20, Burger sent two memos to his seven colleagues. One was attached to the complete draft of the proposed opinion. "This is the first opportunity I (or anyone) have had to see the entire product." While there would "inevitably" be "rough spots," Burger felt that it was unnecessary and unproductive to have a "full scale conference."[133]

The other memo he sent was marked *"Personal"* and was a note of thanks to his colleagues:

I have appreciated the helpful suggestions given in this case, some privately and some by general circulation. From the outset we were unanimous on the core issues; . . . I have tried to keep the opinion as straightforward as the basic issues. . . . I have tried to [follow] the restraint and tone of the *Burr* [*U.S. v. Burr*, 25 Fed.Cas. 187 (1807)] pattern. The more restrained and even the tone of the opinion the greater will be the force of the holding—or so it seems to me. . . . Whatever problems anyone has can best be resolved by discussing them "across the table." As to each individual's views, . . . I will stand ready for any discussion today, Sunday, and thereafter.[134]

Coincidentally, on Saturday, July 20, Stewart, Marshall, and White were in the building when the printed draft of the Burger proposed opinion was circulated. After individually reviewing the draft they met with Burger that day to "convey these suggestions."[135] Stewart was "delegated" to redraft Burger's IV(C)— Executive Privilege (the "Presumptive Privilege") section.[136]

On Monday, July 22, two days before the opinion was announced from the bench, Stewart sent a memo to Douglas, Brennan, Blackmun, and Powell (the four justices who were not in the building on Saturday). Attached to the memo was a draft of IV(C) which, said the justice, "embodies the views of Byron, Thurgood and me, and we have submitted it to the Chief Justice this morning. As of now, Byron, Thurgood, and I are prepared to join the proposed opinion, if the recasting of IV(C) is acceptable to the Chief Justice."[137] In a postscript, Stewart noted that "as you will observe, the enclosed draft borrows generously from the draft of the Chief Justice as well as Lewis Powell's earlier memorandum."[138]

The essence of Potter Stewart's amendment was to attempt clarification of the character of executive privilege. Privilege, wrote Stewart, "is fundamental to the operation of government and is inextricably rooted in separation of powers under the Constitution."[139] It is also, wrote the justice, "constitutionally based." However, given the very strong core value of the fair administration of criminal justice, a "balance" must be struck between the "generalized assertion" of privilege and the "demonstrated, specific need for evidence in a pending criminal trial."[140] In that balancing process, the federal courts must rule that the generalized privilege must yield to the Rule of Law.

Burger's response was quickly forthcoming. "I assure you that I will work on it promptly with the hope to accommodate those who wish to get away this week."[141] The chief believed that the two drafts could be "accommodated and harmonized and, indeed, [did] not assume it was intended that [he] cast aside several weeks' work and take this circulation as a total substitute."[142]

While Burger was redrafting his opinion for circulation the following day (Tuesday, July 23), Douglas's law clerk, on July 22, conveyed a message to the justice from one of Justice Brennan's law clerks:

Brennan is very much in agreement with the enclosed memo from . . . Stewart regarding [Burger's] latest circulation in the *Nixon* case. Apparently there are five Justices who are in agreement on the position in the memo from . . . Stewart. Mr. Justice Brennan would like to speak with you about the circulation from [Burger and Stewart]."[143]

(That day, one of Douglas's clerks indicated to Douglas that the eighth draft of his opinion would be circulated to Burger the same day.)

On Tuesday, July 23, Lewis Powell sent some IV(C) suggestions to his colleagues. At this late date Powell was still urging great deference to the presidential office. "Normally," he wrote, "a President by virtue of his control of the Executive Branch is in a position to determine whether the greater public interest lies in preserving confidentiality with respect to certain evidence or in making it available for the prosecution of an accused person."[144] Another of Powell's suggestions was to add the following: "It is the manifest duty of the Courts to vindicate those guarantees and to do so it is essential that all relevant evidence be produced unless *inadmissible because of an applicable privilege or for other valid reasons*" (emphasis added).[145]

A comment on Douglas's copy of Powell's suggestions, by the senior justice, stated: "Riders prepared by LP and objected to by WOD with vigor—and dropped by LP.—WOD"[146] Burger carefully avoided the problem by writing Powell on July 23 that he was accepting them "subject always to the views of the four!"[147] Powell dropped the suggestions.

Burger, on July 23, one day before the public announcement, wrote two memos to the brethren; one was attached to a revised IV(C).[148] The second was the second draft of the opinion labeled "NOT PROOFREAD." He wrote, "Immediately on having seven 'joins' I will order a full print—obviously with corrections and changes, if any. I suggest that if we need to meet it should be approximately one-half hour after delivery of this draft. Regards, WEB. P.S. This can be ready by 10:00 A.M. Wed."[149]

Douglas immediately wrote a memo agreeing with the opinion. "I think the opinion is ready to go and I hope we hand it down tomorrow at 10 A.M."[150] He recommended that a "rather full oral announcement . . . be made." Douglas seconded the call for a conference "today—Tuesday, July 23rd."[151] Burger heard from others, received "joins" from them and, in a final memo, called a conference for 1:30 P.M. "The bell will be rung at 1:25."[152]

On Tuesday, July 24, 1974, at 11:00 A.M., Chief Justice Warren E. Burger read a prepared thirteen-page "rather full oral announcement" in the case of *U.S. v. Nixon* summarizing the thirty-one-page opinion written by the brethren.

AN ANALYSIS OF THE COURT'S EFFORTS TO RESPOND TO THE ISSUES RAISED IN *U.S. v. NIXON*

Special Prosecutor Jaworski argued, before the justices at the oral argument and in his written briefs, that executive privilege was not in the Constitution. At best, he admitted, it was a common-law privilege, but it did not have the status and standing of a constitutional principle. His arguments did not prevail in the case. Justice William O. Douglas was quite concerned about the direction his colleagues were taking regarding executive privilege. He believed that it was a "travesty to think of the case in terms of executive privilege." In a letter to Powell, with a copy to the Conference, he urged his brethren to view the privilege in more modest terms for, in his estimate, it was not a "constitutionally based" principle. Further, as the requested information involved questions of criminal conspiracy, it was not a true Article II case. Douglas was unsuccessful.[153] His friend and colleague, William J. Brennan, was just as unsuccessful. Brennan, like Douglas, encouraged his brethren to downplay the issue of whether the executive privilege was constitutionally based or was, instead, based on the common law. He believed that the issue need not be decided. However, like Douglas, he was not able to persuade his colleagues on the bench.

So, too, was Justice White unsuccessful. He was, for a brief period of time, the most critical of the majority's position that the executive privilege was a constitutionally rooted power of the president. As he wrote to the chief justice, on July 22, he was very concerned about the court fashioning out of whole cloth an inherent constitutional power of executive privilege: "I doubt . . . that we need discover or fashion any inherent powers in the judiciary to overcome an executive privilege which is not expressly provided for but which we also fashion today." The Jaworski, Douglas, Brennan and White view of executive privilege—that it was essentially a question that was not necessary for the court to "reach"— did not find a majority in the 1974 Supreme Court.

Chief Justice Burger, who had dissented in the 1971 "Pentagon Papers" case (in which the federal courts restricted the powers of the president to withhold news from the media), was very committed to the maintenance of a constitutionally based executive privilege. Although he was forced to accept modifications in his *Nixon* opinion in order to forge an institutional statement of the Supreme Court, the executive privilege segment was only modestly changed. The chief justice refused to cave in to White's short-lived threat, and correctly guessed that Douglas would not have his separate opinion published. Burger could not accept any further weakening of the executive branch, and refused to amend the executive privilege segment to constrict presidential behavior. Thus, the Court majority, with the silent acquiescence of Douglas, Brennan, and White, stood firm and held, "for the first time," that the president's claim of executive privilege is "fundamental to the operation of government and inextricably rooted in the separation of powers under the Constitution."[154]

Relying on a few judicial opinions, chiefly *U.S. v. Burr* (1807), Burger's opinion lacked any detailed reference to the available historical research on the subject of executive privilege.[155] As Laurence Tribe noted, "Whatever may be the correct resolution of the historical debate, it is unfortunate that the Court paid it no heed."[156] Certainly, Burger did not examine the intent of the Framers of the Constitution on this question of executive privilege, nor did he refer to any scholarly texts that analyzed the constitutional issue. Had he done so, he would have found that "executive privilege is mentioned neither in the Constitution nor in the Constitutional debates."[157] (For example, Raoul Berger's book on the subject concludes that the claim of the president that he has the constitutional authority to withhold information from the Congress or the federal courts is simply not based on the historical record.)[158]

The Rule of Law calls for appropriate information, which must be relevant and admissible, in order for there to be the fair administration of justice. The president cannot unilaterally, given the clear intent of the Framers, refuse to provide information that has been correctly requested by coordinate branches of the national government. Article II, as written in 1787, did not contain the inherent power of executive privilege.[159] The powers of the executive were carefully enumerated by James Madison and others. "Certain powers must be given to the President," wrote Madison, but his power "should be confined and defined."[160] Given these views of the Founding Fathers, it is "incongruous" to think that they would extend the executive power beyond the confined and defined execution of the laws.[161]

Burger, for the Court majority, however, was very interested in invoking the concept of executive privilege "to justify withholding evidence and other communicative materials from the legislative and judicial branches."[162] As his earlier dissent in the "Pentagon Papers" opinion indicates, the chief justice was clearly concerned about maintaining a broad-based power of the president to withhold information from the media, from Congress, and from the courts.[163] Philosophically, his views were quite like the views of his associate on the bench who excused himself from participation and discussion of the *Nixon* case: William H. Rehnquist. (In 1971, then Assistant Attorney General Rehnquist and a member of the Nixon Justice Department, he told a Senate committee that while the "President's authority to withhold information is not an unbridled one, it necessarily requires the exercise of his judgment [as to whether the disclosure] would be harmful to the national interest.")[164] The Court itself, after *Nixon*, in such cases as *Nixon v. Fitzgerald* (1982),[165] *Snepp v. U.S.* (1980),[166] *Haig v. Agee* (1981),[167] and *Weinberger v. Catholic Action of Hawaii* (1984),[168] moved to expand presidential powers and prerogatives. It was as if the justices, after *U.S. v. U.S. District Court* (1972) and the *U.S. v. Nixon* litigation, felt compelled to show an enhanced deference to the executive branch.[169]

Until the 1974 judicial creation of the constitutionally based executive privilege claim made in *Nixon*, presidential claims of that "inherent right to withhold ha[d] been rare and the instances of congressional acquiescence ha[d] been infrequent."[170] However, the Burger language in *Nixon* had immediate precedential impact. In the opinion, Burger correctly and ironically noted that "no case of the Court . . . has extended this high degree of [judicial] deference to a President's generalized interest in confidentiality. Nowhere in the Constitution . . . is there any explicit reference to a privilege of confidentiality, yet to the extent this interest relates to the effective discharge of a President's powers, it is constitutionally based." In *U.S. v. Nixon*, the Supreme Court gave its "imprimatur to this executive right to withhold certain information and accorded it constitutional dimension."[171]

Nixon's reaction was interesting. "I was gratified," he said immediately after reviewing the opinion with his counsel on July 24, "to note that the Court reaffirmed both the validity and the importance of the principle of executive privilege, the principle I had sought to maintain."[172] However, the Court did so in a dangerous manner, for the basic ramification of the now-established inherent constitutional executive privilege is the creation of an extremely "nebulous," boundless description of presidential executive power.[173]

In developing its institutional response to the serious constitutional questions raised in *U.S. v. Nixon*, the Court directed its attention to the concept of separation of powers. Although there was serious disagreement among the justices regarding executive privilege, there was unanimity among the eight jurists regarding the role of the federal judiciary in defining the parameters of the political system. For the eight justices, the Supreme Court was, as Potter Stewart wrote in the drafting of *Nixon*, the "ultimate interpreter" of the Constitution.

Rejecting the president's mechanical assertion that the separation of powers deliberately created insulated, fragmented centers of countervailing power immune from review by the coordinate branches, the Supreme Court stated in *U.S. v. Nixon* that the concept of separation of powers did not preclude judicial review of the presidential claim of privilege and immunity.[174] Contrary to the St. Clair argument that the president was the sole interpreter of the Article II powers, the Supreme Court reaffirmed its interpretive responsibility, consistent with Article II, to say what the law meant (*Marbury v. Madison*, 1803).[175] As Justice Powell wrote in his July 6 draft to his brethren, judicial review by the Supreme Court defines the "contours" of the doctrine of separation of powers, including the definition and use of the concept of executive privilege.

In defining the contours of separation of powers in *U.S. v. Nixon*, however, the Court majority showed great deference to a coordinate branch. In so acting, five justices set aside the pleas of three of their brethren. Justices Brennan, Douglas, and White thought it unnecessary and unwise to decide the question of the nature and dimension of the executive privilege conception. More than likely, they ran out of time, and probably energy, in their efforts to persuade their colleagues that the Court should not be strengthening the presidency through the judicial creation of the inherent power of executive privilege.

CONCLUSION

Alan Westin has written that *U.S. v. Nixon* was "one of the most predictable rulings in the history of American constitutional law. The political situation was not only hospitable to a ruling against the President but almost irresistably pressing for it."[176] While the issue's "delicacy . . . might have counseled restraint, deliberate speed rather than majestic instancy," the justices chose to act with dispatch to fulfill their "duty" to end the Watergate crisis.[177]

However credible or noble that action of the Court might have been at the time, the simple truth is that in their commitment to come to judgment quickly, the eight justices accepted the arguments of the Nixon attorneys that executive privilege was constitutionally based. It would have been enough for the Court to have ended the crisis; the justices did not have to create a broad constitutional executive privilege. The precedent, however, has been established. While there

was some discussion about executive privilege, there should have been a great
deal more reflection and analysis by the judges before the judicial creation of
the constitutional privilege. (Between May 31 and July 24, 1974, there were
many strongly held views expressed—and modified—by the brethren, except
for the executive privilege principle.) The Court ended the 1974 presidential
crisis of Watergate, but by employing judicial review to define the contours of
Article II, it may well have set the stage for future constitutional crises.

NOTES

1. *United States v. Nixon*, 418 U.S. 683 (1974).
2. In Robert L. Stern and Eugene Gressman, *Supreme Court Practice*, 5th ed.
(Washington, D.C.: Bureau of National Affairs Press, 1978), p. 1085.
3. Bob Woodward and Carl Bernstein, *The Final Days* (New York: Simon and
Schuster, 1976), p. 261.
4. Leon Jaworski, *The Right and the Power: The Prosecution of Watergate* (New
York: Readers Digest Press, 1976), p. 148.
5. William O. Douglas, *The Court Years, 1939–1975* (New York: Random House,
1980), p. 139.
6. Docket Book, 1973 Term, Box 423, Brennan Papers, Library of Congress,
Washington, D.C.
7. Douglas, *Court Years*, p. 140.
8. David M. O'Brien, *Storm Center: The Supreme Court in American Politics* (New
York: Norton, 1986), p. 215.
9. Data in this segment from *Congressional Quarterly*, "Watergate: Chronology of
a Crisis" (Washington, D.C.: Congressional Quarterly Press, 1975).
10. See, generally, Vincent Blasi, *The Burger Court* (New Haven: Yale University
Press, 1984).
11. Paul A. Freund, Foreword: "On Presidential Privilege," *Harvard Law Review*
88 (November 1974).
12. William O. Douglas to Palmer Hoyt, May 3, 1973, Box 1659, Douglas Papers,
Library of Congress, Washington, D.C.
13. William O. Douglas to Roger Kent, February 4, 1974, Box 1659, Douglas Papers,
Library of Congress, Washington, D.C.
14. See Melvin Urofsky, *The Douglas Letters* (Bethesda, Md.: Adler and Adler,
1987), pp. 384–413, for interesting materials surrounding the 1970 impeachment effort
led in the House by Congressman Gerald Ford.
15. Generally, see Woodward and Bernstein, *Final Days*.
16. Ibid., p. 262.
17. Ibid.
18. Quoted in O'Brien, *Storm Center*, p. 214.
19. Bernard Schwartz, *The Unpublished Opinions of the Warren Court* (New York:
Oxford University Press, 1986), p. 7.
20. Loren Beth, *Politics, the Constitution and the Supreme Court* (New York: Row,
Peterson, 1962), p. 41.
21. Hugo L. Black to Howard Ball, January 31, 1969.

22. J. W. Howard "On the Fluidity of Judicial Choice," *American Political Science Review* 62 (March 1968).

23. William J. Brennan, "Inside View of the High Court," *The New York Times Magazine*, October 6, 1963, p. 22.

24. Hugo L. Black to Howard Ball, January 31, 1969.

25. O'Brien, *Storm Center*, p. 215.

26. Harry A. Blackmun to Howard Ball, November 26, 1986.

27. Memorandum to the Conference (MTTC), July 23, 1974, Box 329, Brennan Papers, Library of Congress, Washington, D.C.

28. O'Brien, *Storm Center*, p. 213.

29. Howard Ball, *Courts and Politics*, 2d. ed. (Englewood Cliffs, N.J.: Prentice-Hall, 1987), p. 215.

30. Blasi, *Burger Court*, p. 200.

31. Ibid.

32. Ibid., p. 201.

33. John J. Sirica, *To Set the Record Straight* (New York: Norton, 1979), pp. 224–225.

34. *United States v. New York Times and Washington Post*, 403 U.S. 713 (1971).

35. Douglas Conference Notes, June 26, 1971, Box 1519, Douglas Papers, Library of Congress, Washington, D.C.

36. James St. Clair took over when Charles A. Wright left after problems were uncovered when Nixon began releasing the eight tapes ordered released by Sirica in August 1973.

37. *Congressional Quarterly*, "Watergate," p. 619.

38. Jaworski, *Right*, p. 148.

39. MTTC, May 25, 1974, Box 329, Brennan Papers, Library of Congress, Washington, D.C.

40. William Rehnquist to Warren Burger, Box 329, Brennan Papers, Library of Congress, Washington, D.C.

41. MTTC, May 30, 1974, Box 1659, Douglas Papers, Library of Congress, Washington, D.C.

42. Sirica, *Record*, p. 224.

43. See appendices A and B.

44. Douglas, *Court Years*, pp. 139–140.

45. Docket Book, 1973 Term, Box 423, Brennan Papers, Library of Congress, Washington, D.C.

46. Ibid.

47. Ibid.

48. Ibid.

49. Ibid.

50. Ibid.

51. Ibid.

52. Douglas, *Court Years*, pp. 139–140.

53. Ibid., p. 140.

54. Ibid.

55. William J. Brennan, quoted in Jeffrey T. Leeds, "A Life on the Court," *The New York Times Sunday Magazine*, October 5, 1986, p. 25. *Cooper v. Aaron*, 358 U.S. 1 (1958), was an important civil rights case involving a fundamental challenge to federal

judicial authority by the governor of Arkansas. The opinion forcefully reminded the state officials that federal courts had ordered the integration of the Little Rock high school and that, in a federal system, federal action had to prevail over state action. It was a unique, powerful opinion because all nine justices affixed their names to the statement by the Court.

56. Docket Book, 1973 Term, Box 423, Brennan Papers, Library of Congress, Washington, D.C.

57. Philip A. Lacovara to Michael Rodak, June 3, 1974, Box 329, Brennan Papers, Library of Congress, Washiington, D.C.

58. Ibid.

59. MTTC, June 4, 1974, Box 329, Brennan Papers, Library of Congress, Washington, D.C.

60. Defense Attorneys to Michael Rodak, June 11, 1974, Box 1659, Douglas Papers, Library of Congress, Washington, D.C.

61. MTTC, June 14, 1974, Box 329, Brennan Papers, Library of Congress, Washington, D.C.

62. See Rehnquist's MTTC, June 11 and June 24, 1974, Box 1659, Douglas Papers, Library of Congress, Washington, D.C.

63. Briefs reprinted in Leon Friedman, ed., *U.S. v. Nixon* (New York: Chelsea House, 1974), pp. 209–317, 320–426.

64. MTTC, July 6, 1974, Box 329, Brennan Papers, Library of Congress, Washington, D.C.

65. MTTC, July 5, 1974, Box 1659, Douglas Papers, Library of Congress, Washington, D.C.

66. Ibid.

67. Ibid.

68. MTTC, July 20, 1974, Box 1659, Douglas Papers, Library of Congress, Washington, D.C.

69. MTTC, July 5, 1974, Box 1659, Douglas Papers, Library of Congress, Washington, D.C.

70. MTTC, July 6, 1974, Box 329, Brennan Papers, Library of Congress, Washington, D.C.

71. Ibid.

72. Ibid.

73. Ibid.

74. Ibid.

75. Ibid.

76. Ibid.

77. Ibid.

78. Ibid.

79. MTTC, July 8, 1974, Box 329, Brennan Papers, Library of Congress, Washington, D.C.

80. Ibid.

81. Ibid.

82. MTTC, July 8, 1974, Box 1659, Douglas Papers, Library of Congress, Washington, D.C.

83. Oral Argument in Friedman, *Nixon*, pp. 528–529.

84. Ibid., p. 529.

85. Ibid., p. 549.

86. Docket Book, 1973 Term, Conference Notes, July 9, 1974, boxes 329 and 423, Brennan Papers. See also Box 1627, Douglas Papers, Library of Congress, Washington, D.C.

87. Ibid.

88. Ibid.

89. Quoted in Leeds, "A Life," p. 75.

90. Note, Box 329, Brennan Papers, Library of Congress, Washington, D.C.

91. MTTC, July 10, 1974, Box 329, Brennan Papers, Library of Congress, Washington, D.C.

92. Lacovara oral argument, in Friedman, *Nixon*, 594.

93. MTTC, July 20, 1974, Box 329, Brennan Papers, Library of Congress, Washington, D.C.

94. MTTC, July 11, 1974, Douglas Papers, Box 1659, Library of Congress, Washington, D.C.

95. MTTC, July 15, 1974, Douglas Papers, Box 1659, Library of Congress, Washington, D.C.

96. DK to William O. Douglas, July 10, 1974, Box 1659, Douglas Papers, Library of Congress, Washington, D.C.

97. Harry Blackmun to Warren Burger, July 12, 1974, Box 329, Brennan Papers, Library of Congress, Washington, D.C.

98. Ibid.

99. DK to William O. Douglas (memo), July 10, 1974, Box 1659, Douglas Papers, Library of Congress, Washington, D.C.

100. William O. Douglas to Warren Burger, July 11, 1974, Box 1659, Douglas Papers, Library of Congress, Washington, D.C.

101. Thurgood Marshall to Warren Burger, July 17, 1974, Box 1659, Douglas Papers, Library of Congress, Washington, D.C.

102. William Brennan to Warren Burger, July 10, 1974, Box 329, Brennan Papers, Library of Congress, Washington, D.C.

103. Ibid.

104. Potter Stewart to Warren Burger, July 11, 1974; Bryon White to Warren Burger, July 11, 1974, Box 1659, Douglas Papers, Library of Congress, Washington, D.C.

105. Thurgood Marshall to Warren Burger, July 17, 1974, Box 1659, Douglas Papers, Library of Congress, Washington, D.C.

106. MTTC, July 10, 1974, Box 329, Brennan Papers, Library of Congress, Washington, D.C.

107. See *United States v. Nixon*, 418 U.S. 683 (1974).

108. MTTC, July 11, 1974, Draft 5, Box 329, Brennan Papers, Library of Congress, Washington, D.C.

109. William Brennan to Warren Burger, July 10, 1974, Box 329, Brennan Papers, Library of Congress, Washington, D.C.

110. William O. Douglas to Warren Burger, July 12, 1974, Box 1659, Douglas Papers, Library of Congress, Washington, D.C.

111. Lewis Powell to Warren Burger, July 12, 1974, Box 329, Brennan Papers, Library of Congress, Washington, D.C.

112. Ibid.

113. Byron White to Warren Burger, July 12, 1974, Box 329, Brennan Papers, Library of Congress, Washington, D.C.

114. William O. Douglas to Warren Burger, July 12 and 19, 1974, Box 1659, Douglas Papers, Library of Congress, Washington, D.C.

115. William Brennan to Warren Burger, July 15, 1974, Box 329, Brennan Papers, Library of Congress, Washington, D.C.

116. Potter Stewart to Warren Burger, July 15, 1974, Brennan Papers, Library of Congress, Washington, D.C.

117. Thurgood Marshall to Warren Burger, July 17, 1974, Box 329, Brennan Papers, Library of Congress, Washington, D.C.

118. Byron White to Warren Burger, July 12, 1974, Box 329, Brennan Papers, Library of Congress, Washington, D.C.

119. Ibid.

120. Ibid.

121. Ibid.

122. MTTC, July 15, 1974, Box 1659, Douglas Papers, Library of Congress, Washington, D.C.

123. Byron White to Warren Burger, July 15, 1974, Box 329, Brennan Papers, Library of Congress, Washington, D.C.

124. MTTC, July 17, 1974, Box 329, Brennan Papers, Library of Congress, Washington, D.C.

125. Ibid.

126. Potter Stewart to Warren Burger, July 17, 1974, Box 329, Brennan Papers, Library of Congress, Washington, D.C. Stewart pointed out that Burger probably "completely misinterpreted" the St. Clair brief and oral argument when Burger wrote (3): "Although the President's counsel asserts that the privilege of confidentiality of presidential communications is absolute *he does not challenge the authority of this Court to interpret the law.*" William Brennan noted another seeming error in the Burger draft (7) when Burger wrote: "The right of privacy of every citizen to the confidentiality of his conversations, private papers and records has been accorded a high place in our concept of liberty *although it is not expressed in the Constitution.*" Brennan circled the underlined words and wrote, in the margin, "4th Amendment?"

127. Ibid.

128. Byron White to Warren Burger, July 18, 1974, Bos 329, Brennan Papers, Library of Congress, Washington, D.C.

129. Ibid.

130. Ibid.

131. Ibid.

132. Ibid.

133. MTTC, July 20, 1974, Box 1659, Douglas Papers, Library of Congress, Washington, D.C.

134. Ibid.

135. Memo to William O. Douglas, William Brennan, Harry Blackmun, and Lewis Powell, July 22, 1974, Box 1659, Douglas Papers, Library of Congress, Washington, D.C.

136. Ibid.

137. Ibid.

138. Ibid.

139. Ibid.

140. Ibid.

141. MTTC, July 22, 1974, Box 1659, Douglas Papers, Library of Congress, Washington, D.C.

142. Ibid.

143. AA to William Douglas (memo), July 22, 1974, Box 1659, Douglas Papers, Library of Congress, Washington, D.C.

144. MTTC, July 23, 1974, Box 1659, Douglas Papers, Library of Congress, Washington, D.C.

145. Ibid.

146. Ibid.

147. Warren Burger to Lewis Powell, July 23, 1974, Box 329, Brennan Papers, Library of Congress, Washington, D.C.

148. MTTC, July 23, 1974, Box 329, Brennan Papers, Library of Congress, Washington, D.C.

149. Ibid.

150. William Douglas to Warren Burger, July 23, 1974, Box 1659, Douglas Papers, Library of Congress, Washington, D.C.

151. Ibid.

152. MTTC, July 23, 1974, Box 1659, Douglas Papers, Library of Congress, Washington, D.C.

153. William Douglas rarely tried to persuade his colleagues on cases and controversies before the Court. However, on the issue of executive privilege, he was especially active: this clearly came out in letters written to Lewis Powell and Warren Burger. In a July 11, 1974, letter to Powell, Douglas pleaded with his colleague, since the group was torn between the privilege being a common law or a constitutionally grounded privilege, to "reserve making a decision on it as it is a question not necessary for us to reach on the facts of this case." In a July 12, 1974, letter to Burger, Douglas wrote:

I don't think it is necessary to reach the decision of whether this [executive privilege] is based on the Constitution. The office of the President as I read the Constitution is to execute the laws faithfully. A conspiracy to violate the laws or a conspiracy to protect people who have violated the law cannot be brought under Article 2 of the Constitution. . . . On the basis of the showing so far, conversations relating to law violations are impossible to bring within the scope of Article 2 obligations. (Box 1659, Douglas Papers, Library of Congress, Washington, D.C.)

154. Jethro Lieberman, *Milestones* (St. Paul: West, 1976), p. 392.

155. Anne Y. Shields, "The Supreme Court Under Pressure," *St. Johns Law Review* 57 (1983): 759.

156. Laurence H. Tribe, *American Constitutional Law* (Mineola, N.Y.: Foundation Press, 1978), p. 202 n. 4.

157. Ibid., p. 202.

158. Raoul Berger, *Executive Privilege: A Constitutional Myth* (New York: Bantam/ Harvard University Press, 1974).

159. Ibid.

160. Quoted in ibid., p. 66.

161. Ibid.

162. Jean M. D'Ovidio, "Executive Privilege," *University of Richmond Law Review* 18 (1983): 203.

163. *United States v. New York Times and Washington Post*, 403 U.S. 713 (1971); also see Douglas Conference Notes, June 26, 1971, Box 1519, Douglas Papers, Library of Congress, Washington, D.C.

164. Quoted in Berger, *Executive Privilege*, p. 9.

165. *Nixon v. Fitzgerald*, 102 S.Ct. 2690 (1982).

166. *Snepp v. United States*, 444 U.S. 507 (1980).

167. *Haig v. Agee*, 453 U.S. 280 (1981).

168. *Weinberger v. Catholic Action of Hawaii*, 454 U.S. 139 (1981).

169. *United States v. U. S. District Court*, 407 U.S. 297 (1972).

170. Berger, *Executive Privilege*.

171. Tribe, *Constitutional Law*, p. 202.

172. *Congressional Quarterly*, "Watergate," 719.

173. Shields, "Supreme Court," 760.

174. Tribe, *Constitutional Law*, p. 2.

175. *Marbury v. Madison*, 5 U.S. 137 (1803). Chief Justice John Marshall wrote: "It is emphatically the province and duty of the judicial department to say what the law is."

176. In Friedman, *Nixon*, p. xiii.

177. Freund, "Presidential Privilege," p. 14.

Discussant: Philip Lacovara

Thank you and good morning. Among the various images that I have had of Richard Nixon over the years, none of them had portrayed him in the zoot suits of the conventional mafiosi, so I was intrigued to see that Justice [William] Douglas was using that kind of imagery during the debates on how to formulate an opinion in the Nixon tapes case. Professor Ball quoted Alan Westin's comment that the Nixon tapes decision was one of the most predictable in recent American jurisprudence. With the benefit and luxury of hindsight, that may be true. We know now that the Court did rule unanimously. We do know what the evidence showed; we do know that the president resigned shortly after the evidence became available to the House Judiciary Committee. I can remember mornings, afternoons, and evenings of wrenching and anguishing debate, however, not only with Leon Jaworski, but even earlier with Archibald Cox, no mean constitutional scholar in his own right; and I can assure you that they did not have the degree of confidence that Professor Westin now is able to ascribe to this controversy.

As Professor Ball noted, we tried to tally up the votes when this controversy was provoked the first time with the grand jury subpoena that led ultimately to the Saturday night massacre when President Nixon ordered Cox not to enforce the court order. We did that in approving the subpoena in order to decide whether to take on the president's refusal to turn over the evidence. We did some soul searching and some vote counting, and we came up with a reasonable degree of confidence that we could get a 5–3 decision, that's a 1 vote margin obviously, since a 4–4 decision would have had not only no precedental effect, but also, and perhaps more importantly for the political context in which this dispute arose, would have given President Nixon quite ample foundation to say, as he had threatened to say, that in the absence of a so-called "definitive ruling" from the Supreme Court, he had as much say about what the Constitution meant in defining his powers as did the justices. Even a 5–3 decision would have left the president with some elbow room to claim that he was not beholden to the court, and was not obliged to subordinate his view as chief executive to the views of others on this delicate issue of executive privilege. A 4–4 decision of course would have been utterly meaningless, and probably would have set back the effort to investigate high crimes in high office.

Professor Ball quite appropriately touched on some of the preliminary procedural judgments that we had to make in deciding whether to go to the Supreme Court, to put the controversy before the Court in an extraordinary fashion, and that was by seeking Supreme Court review before the intermediate court of appeals ever had the opportunity to pass upon the decision.

One prefatory note on that judgment: The case that got to the Supreme Court was not in my view the strongest context in which to litigate the issue of executive privilege against President Nixon and his counsel. The earlier case involving a grand jury subpoena was in our view the best context in which to present the Supreme Court with the question whether the courts may override a claim of executive privilege interposed by the president. The case that went to the Supreme Court, as Professor Ball noted, involved in effect a trial subpoena issued by a prosecutor in order to help him improve his case against the Watergate cover-up defendants, who were then the objects of a grand jury indictment. The grand jury case, however, in our view would have been a stronger one, despite the implications of some of the internal debates to which Professor Ball has rather amazingly been able to obtain access. Most lawyers who consider themselves well connected in Washington did not know these papers were available—not only the Douglas papers but also Justice [William] Brennan's papers.

One of the subjects of the discussion among the justices concerned the argument that it was unthinkable that potentially exculpatory evidence could be withheld from a criminal trial. That, however, missed the mark at the stage at which the Nixon tapes case actually got to the Supreme Court, because the subpoena that was at issue there was the subpoena issued by the prosecutor to obtain additional evidence beyond what had already been gathered for the grand jury process.

As you well know, the courts feel rather comfortable rejecting claims by prosecutors that they need to get in extra evidence to establish a conviction. The Fourth Amendment indeed is designed in some measure to exclude evidence that might be very useful in showing that someone is guilty of a crime. The privilege against self-incrimination under the Fifth Amendment is another obstacle to the prosecutor's desire to garner more evidence. So the trial subpoena from a prosecutor was not the strongest mechanism for saying that the courts should overturn a presidential claim of privilege.

The grand jury process that provoked the original subpoena and the dismissal by the president of Special Prosecutor Cox was the stronger setting because at the grand jury stage there is a semi-independent entity, the grand jury, that is composed not of professional prosecutors but of representatives of the citizenry, whose job is not simply to accuse someone of crime. Their task is rather to indict the guilty and exonerate the innocent. I thought we had been able to argue effectively in the original case that it was unthinkable that the grand jury should have withheld from it evidence in the custody of Richard Nixon that might show that the accusations being made by the president's former counsel, John Dean, were false, and that the persons who stood publicly accused of heinous felonies were in fact innocent and could have been shown to be innocent by the White House tapes. That was the stronger setting for saying that the courts, acting in a relatively independent and neutral fashion, should balance the serious competing interest of the grand jury in the truth-finding process, pursuing innocence as well as guilt against the president's claim of a right to withhold information.

In any event, by firing the special prosecutor, and then as a result of this "Saturday night massacre" and the fire storm that resulted and giving up the tapes, the constitutional issue was ripe for Supreme Court review only in this later context of a trial subpoena. The judgment that we made to go immediately to the Supreme Court without awaiting a decision by the court of appeals was based on a variety of tactical factors. In part, of course, we did not want to brook the additional delay of perhaps several months that would be occasioned while the criminal case languished. Nor did we want to be forced to proceed to trial with the Watergate cover-up case, thus conceding, in effect, that the sub-poenaed White House tapes were not necessary for the criminal trial.

But beyond that, there was a certain sense that the case would come to the Supreme Court in a better posture if we could take the initiative. We anticipated, I must say, a successful outcome in the court of appeals, which had already sustained the prosecutor's right to get White House evidence in the earlier grand jury subpoena case. Although we anticipated a favorable ruling in the court of appeals, we thought that if the president was petitioning for Supreme Court review, we would be fighting the battle on his turf. My recommendation was that it was useful in setting the stage for this drama for us to stake out its boundaries and to show, as we ultimately styled the case, that by being the petitioners, we had control of the title of the case. This was part of the strategy for litigating the separation of powers problem. This was not, as the president was saying, an intra-executive branch dispute between the president and the lowly officer of the Department of Justice who happened to have the title "Special Prosecutor." This was not a constitutional clash between the branches; rather, this was the United States in its sovereign capacity, pursuing a trial of persons who had been indicted by a lawfully composed grand jury, and trying to get evidence from a person who happened to have material evidence. The posturing of the case was to try to portray to the Court that that person, named Richard Nixon, happened to have this evidence, and it made no legal difference that he also was president of the United States. So the case was not *United States* versus *the President* or *United States* versus *President Richard Nixon*; it was styled *United States v. Richard M. Nixon*, for very deliberate reasons.

By going first we also had the opportunity to do some other things; for example, all briefs submitted on behalf of the United States utilize an extraordinary and unique color that only the solicitor general uses. The president wound up using a different color (because of our preemption) than a private party would be using. There were other physical elements that we tried to structure in a way to shape this controversy, not as a separation of powers dispute, but as a rather garden variety controversy between the United States and a person who had relevant and important evidence. The Court took the case and, somewhat to my surprise, the vote was unanimous from the very earliest discussions on the merits, as Professor Ball's essay has shown.

The question whether the Court would take the case was one that I was reasonably confident of. I thought that the Court would step up to recognizing the duty-to-the-country element that apparently Justice Brennan did articulate to his brethren and he did ultimately persuade at least six of the justices to take the case out of order at that extraordinary time in our political history. As I mentioned earlier, the president had been saying for nine months or so by that time that he might obey a definitive ruling of the Court, although he was leaving his options open even on that. That meant that the most reasonable prospect for getting compliance depended on getting unanimity and, for that purpose, we knew that any opinion that came out would have to include those justices, especially Chief Justice [Warren] Burger and probably Justice [Harry] Blackmun, who would be most unlikely to want to overturn the president's claim of privilege. As Professor Ball has pointed out, although the opinion was ultimately signed by Chief Justice Burger, it was the amalgam of recommendations on most issues by virtually all the justices; but what was significant was that the chief exercised his prerogative as the senior justice in the majority to assign the opinion to himself. That has turned out in history to be highly important because it committed him, I think, to the opinion, to voting in this way. It brought Justice Blackmun along and led to a unanimous opinion.

It would be fair to say that although the Court did not use the extraordinary mechanism that had been used in the *Cooper* v. *Aaron* case in 1958 (one of the desegregation cases where all of the justices personally signed the opinion), I think that is the only time in history that this has been done to show that this was not only a document approved by the justices but was actually their personal commitment to the result. Although that didn't happen in this case despite Justice Brennan's suggestion that it should happen, the fact that it was an opinion by the chief justice—President Nixon's hand-selected chief justice—was of enormous importance, not only in securing the unanimity that was politically dispositive, but also in showing to the president that the law on this matter was crystal clear. Although scholars have aptly noted since then that the issues are far more complex and far more debatable than the Court's opinion made them out to be, the Court did announce, as we had requested, a definitive and unanimous ruling.

One of the comments that Professor Ball quoted in his essay is that the president announced that he was gratified by the Court's opinion; that may sound ironic, but I think there is more than a grain of truth to it. Although Richard Nixon lost the case, the presidency, whose interests he had been at least nominally championing, won. When we read the opinion, there was the momentary euphoria that the Court had come out unanimously upholding the subpoena that was of the most immediate concern to us in the Special Prosecutor's Office.

As we stepped back and began to analyze its longer term jurisprudential foundations, however, it was a lot more troubling. President Nixon had a lot to be gratified about, because part of the price for Chief Justice Burger's writing of the opinion and holding on to the unanimous court was that his view prevailed on the most central issue in the case, which is the existence and source of executive privilege. Not only did he say that executive privilege exists (and many commentators had been urging the Court to deny the very existence of the privilege in any form) but the Court through his opinion unanimously established that the privilege is constitutionally based. It derives from the inherent fabric of the Constitution, from the separation of powers. That is a decision of enormous consequence, because it means that the president has constitutional legitimacy when he says he wants to withhold evidence from those who are seeking it—not just from grand juries, not just from prosecutors like an independent counsel today and the various investigations that are underway, but from Congress as well. Congress is equally subject to the countervailing strictures of the separation of powers doctrine when the president chooses to invoke them as a justification for refusing to cooperate with a congressional inquiry. So by announcing not only the existence of the doctrine—something that the Court could have side-stepped with an even-if analysis—the Court constitutionalized the doctrines, which it also could have sidestepped within an even-if analysis.

The Court handed the presidency a very strong victory that we will be living with for years or centuries to come. It was not simply of significance on the technical question of executive privilege, but also on the notion that the president has inherent constitutional prerogatives that derive from his status as head of one of the branches, a principle that has had further radiations of great consequence on other matters of privilege. For example, the Court since then has held the president absolutely immune from civil liability for acts engaged in in the course of his duties.

The president's inherent constitutional powers as ratified by the Supreme Court in the Nixon tapes case were also at the core of the debate in the Iran-Contra affair, where the president has said his role as the chief executive, with all of the various constitutional functions that this carries, gives him the prerogative to disregard or at least to sidestep all but the most precise legal restrictions that Congress may choose to impose on his conduct of various national policies. So the Nixon tapes case has provided a legitimate justification for many of the assertions of constitutional prerogative by the executive that we have seen in the last thirteen years, and will continue to do so, I suspect, under Democratic as well as Republican administrations that we will see in the future.

Just one final thought: The Court's decision to constitutionalize the executive privilege claim by relating it to the separation of powers doctrine is somewhat at odds, in my view, with the Court's—from my perspective happy, but, I think, from a scholar's or citizen's perspective, cavalier—decision to override the privilege. The analysis engaged in by the Court was that it was ultimately for the courts to decide when the privilege will be respected or overridden, and the rationale is that we certainly can't allow the president to be the final judge of the scope of his own claim of privilege. A person cannot be the judge in his own controversy. That is a slogan that we urged the Court to adopt and apply in this context, but if you think about it for even half a second, it does not get you very far, because the argument could have just as easily been turned back on the Court.

If this is a constitutional privilege that the president enjoys, why is it that the Court is the ultimate judge of its own power, that is, its own claim that its need for the evidence or its desire for the evidence for judicial functions must be given greater weight in some larger sense than the president's claim that the evidence should not be turned over because to turn it over would interfere with his functions? What the Court said is, "When we want it, we will be the ultimate judges of whether our need is sufficiently compelling." There is no more logic to that position, probably in law as well as in theory, than there is to the president's position, once the Court conceded that the separation of powers—that is, the establishment of coordinate branches with independent functions—was to be the basis for the president's claim of privilege itself. So although the Nixon tapes decision did lead, I think, ineluctably to the president's resignation, it is a mischievous decision in many respects, and it is a decision that lawyers, prosecutors, politicians, and people attending conferences will have to grapple with for years to come.

THE PROTEST MOVEMENT

Discussant: Tom Hayden

Let me say that though my purpose is to talk about the past, obviously the past cannot be separated from the present. A decade after Watergate, we see many of the same patterns in what has come to be known as Irangate or secret military operations, shadowy groups functioning outside the law even though they make the law, and in the White House, a philosophy which was once enunciated by Richard Nixon, that when the president does it, that means it is not illegal. The point is that Watergate did not originate and did not end with the person of Richard Nixon.

These patterns that we have seen revealed again this week [November 19–21, 1987] in the congressional report on Irangate seem to be rooted in a persistent struggle by some right-wing elements using official state power, and a climate, at least condoned by the president, to circumvent the democratic process for their own private agendas, as though they were elected officials. This is a deep institutional problem from decade to decade that we have still not resolved.

But having said that, let me now try to explore with you what we can learn from the Nixon period and the protest movements of those times.

The main thing that I think a historian would want to look at is that the rise and the fall of Richard Nixon was closely related to his preoccupation with left-wing or protest movements during his political career. His whole character was revealed in his response to those movements. His early political success, as you know, coincided with, and was based on, development of the Cold War. His later judgment, and I believe that this is true of most of us, was based on applying the principles of his early years to new conditions. He viewed Vietnam as if it were another case of aggression like China invading Korea, and he assumed, as with Korea, that the outcome in Vietnam would be a partition of the country into two Vietnams as there were two Koreas. He saw the New Left as a sinister conspiracy aiding and abetting foreign powers. He saw in Daniel Ellsberg a new Alger Hiss; he saw in George McGovern the echo of Henry Wallace; and compiling an "enemies list" was not different from going to a House Un-American Activities Committee meeting in the early 1950s.

Conspiracy indictments (there were some sixty-five on the federal level during the Nixon years) were nothing more than a continuation of the Smith Act prosecutions of the previous era.

In short, Richard Nixon was gripped by what I would consider to be a paranoid view of the world, a society that was divided into two camps, good and evil; and his opponents, therefore, were at best dupes, and at worst traitors or "bums."

What is remarkable about this, and I think we all tend to replay our earlier experiences over and over again—even the president—is that there were tremendous changes from the late 1940s and early 1950s to the late 1960s. Even Richard Nixon was cognizant of some of these changes. But not being able to make an adaptation, he instead applied his early successful experience which, under new conditions, led to his downfall.

The differences were that the New Left was entirely homegrown and was speaking to widespread domestic concerns, racial justice, university reform, environmental despoliation, women's rights, and so on. There was no organized political party or conspiratorial web behind these forces. Even the CIA tried to point this out to the administration in a report. The American public, unlike in the late 1940s, no longer automatically believed in the pronouncements of the government. Both juries reflecting middle America and appeals courts turned down the sixty-five indictments from Chicago to the Pentagon Papers case. *The New York Times* printed the Pentagon Papers and won the Pulitzer Prize. The Vietnam War, to make a final parallel, was fueled primarily by indigenous nationalism, not by outside dreams of communist expansion.

Ironically, as I said, President Nixon, in his own way, undermined the presidency by the recognition that there were some changes in the communist world, but it was an incomplete recognition. Think about it: When Nixon and Mao Tse-tung toasted each other in Peking, what was left of Nixon's rationale for the Vietnam War or his case against domestic traitors? He was not able to draw the right conclusions about a changing world and, somewhat like a tragic Shakespearean character repeating his early experiences, he went off-track, provoked a constitutional crisis, and precipitated his own collapse. Instead of sending his supposed enemies to prison, he created an environment in which many members of his own administration went there instead.

What of the protest movement? I know that is the subject of this panel, and it would take hours to go into it, but briefly, I think that the protest movements of the 1960s deserve more credit than we are likely to receive, at least in the foreseeable future, and that is because history is never written by activists or rebels, but usually by middle-of-the-road observers who are very far from the fray.

The country that we live in honors its rebels, if at all, only after they are dead, and then they generally seem to have streets named after them. Yet our generation, in my view, has been acquitted not only in the courtrooms. We acquitted ourselves well where it really mattered, when it was time to stand up for our beliefs in a society that was silently amoral.

We had a definite impact in ending Southern segregation, leading the most massive resistance to a war in American history, and opening up the political process to all those constituencies that had been excluded. We paid a price that Dave Dellinger has referred to as "the scars." One thing I noticed in thinking back on that time is that there is no record anywhere of the tangible price that was paid. You can't find out how many people died, how many people were injured, how many people went to jail. I worked with a graduate student this summer just on this subject, and my preliminary conclusions about the decade are that over twenty thousand Americans were killed in protests and a hundred thousand were arrested. Those are minimal figures, and I have none for the number of people who were kicked out of school or lost their jobs, not to mention the psychic toll.

We, however, were not perfect. We fell into the absolutism of the either-or, the good-or-evil, categories ourselves. One belief that my friend Abbie Hoffmann shares with Richard Nixon, I think, is that neither of them has any profound regrets about the past. There are two schools of absolute thought on that decade; that it was the greatest ever on the one hand, and that it should be repealed and erased from history on the other. I think that this derives from a human short-coming that we all have, and the shortcoming is the defensive inability to express regrets about one's past because of a feeling that it is a betrayal of one's beliefs.

I think one of the toughest problems we have as Americans and as plain human beings is trying to reach in our lifetime the maturity to acknowledge mistakes, to acknowledge and reject the tendency towards absolutism and self-righteousness. In searching for the truth, it seems to me, one is certainly bound to commit errors and obligated to change one's mind. There is nothing wrong with admitting wrong if we learn from it, but we have a human shortcoming, the tendency to defend in entirety our past.

Let me give you an example. I think all of us in the Chicago Conspiracy Trial, the defendants, were wrong in overpredicting that America would become so repressive that it would eventually become a police state in which we would certainly be found guilty and, as our lawyers advised us, spend a minimum of seven years in jail. In response to the belief that we were inevitably going to jail, we developed, in retrospect, a paranoid style of our own, assuming the worst every day, alienating many Middle Americans, and embracing whatever preparations we thought necessary for life behind bars during a period of certain civil strife in the outside world. We all thought we would go to jail for five to ten years, and some of us thought that the Nixon Administration was so powerful that we would not ever get out on appeal because all the appellate judges would be changed by Washington, the Constitution would be abridged, and none of our bases of appeal would be successfully heard.

Instead, what happened was that we were in jail for two weeks after the trial. Dave was in jail for a couple of months, Bobby Seale was in jail during virtually all of the trial. Bobby Seale was eventually cleared of his contempt charges and Connecticut murder charges because the government acknowledged that it was wiretapping his phone lines to his lawyer from jail. Dave, I believe, was ex-onerated from all contempt charges; I was exonerated; the other defendants were found guilty of one count and not guilty of the other. The Seventh Circuit Court of Appeals granted us bail when Judge [Julius] Hoffman denied it, and then overturned the verdict in the case. The appeals court, a year or two later, condemned the judge and prosecution for grievous errors of law.

In other words, we thought we were going to jail for life, and in fact, it was people like John Mitchell, the attorney general, who did. In other words, the democratic process worked more than we could have imagined and more than our ideology would permit us to imagine, and even later we struggled to explain it by saying, it really was the outside force of public opinion that made this happen, because we could not acknowledge that the system worked on our behalf and against the Nixon Administration. It took me almost a decade to acknowledge that forthrightly and say, "We were wrong, we vastly overstated the potential of a police state"; not that there were not the seeds of it there, not that there wasn't repression, not that there was not Watergate with all of its dread implications.

I guess the last thing I'd like to say is that the legacy of those years to me, the legacy of the Nixon years, is a stronger America. But not in a definition of strength Richard Nixon would employ. I think that we are stronger because the country rejected secret wars and domestic spying in favor of an open and pluralistic process of decision making. Last year when I was in the legislature, Charles Colson, who once was proud of having said of the Vietnamese people, "If you get their balls, their hearts and minds will follow," came to me to lobby for prison reform in Sacramento. I told him he was becoming "soft on crime." My conclusion is that the Founding Fathers, in addition to being brilliant political architects, must certainly have had an ironic sense of humor.

Discussant: David J. Garrow

Professor Silverman at the beginning was kind enough to note that I was only sixteen in 1969 and so, by generational identification, perhaps I fall a little bit closer to many of the students in the audience than I do to most of my fellow panel members.

I think it is worth mentioning at the outset that just this year we are beginning to get some first-rate studies of the protest movements of the late 1960s. In Jim Miller's recent book focusing on Tom Hayden and the evolution of SDS[1] and Todd Gitlin's recent book *The Sixties*[2] we now have some good, solid, reflective scholarship that people can benefit from. I think in light of this panel's title, "The Protest Movement," singular, it is appropriate for me as both an academic and as a representative of the younger generation here to highlight a point Sandy Gottlieb talked about, which is that *the* movement, singular, was not of a piece both with regard to the antiwar community of the late 1960s and with regard to the black freedom struggle of that era. Within the antiwar movement there was a very significant tension, one might even say division, between the moderate wing, the SANE wing (namely, those who simply opposed the war), and those whom SANE viewed as the excessively radical foes of the war, who openly favored the Vietcong. Similarly, there was also considerable division within the black movement by the late 1960s.

I know that both the organizers of this session and my fellow panelists regret the fact that we don't have any representatives here of either the black movement of the late 1960s or of the feminist movement that was starting to emerge during those years. Nonetheless, I think it is quite important for us to realize that there had been a tremendous evolution between where the communities of dissent, particularly within the black civil rights movement, had stood in 1965–66 and where they stood by 1969–70.

The most successful period of the protest movement had come in the 1963–65 era. Then, in the years after 1965, America saw very extensive urban disorders in the Northern cities and also witnessed the emergence of black power and black nationalism as stronger tones in the black freedom struggle. By the fall of 1966, the unity and the sense of shared purpose and shared goals that had characterized most of the progressive community in the mid-1960s began to break down.

One example which I think is a very important example concerns Bayard Rustin, who died only two or three months ago. Rustin was one of the most important and influential black intellectuals and political activists, not only of the 1960s but of the two previous decades as well. As of 1963 or 1964, Rustin's emphasis and argument was that the civil rights forces had to turn toward economic issues and had to start raising questions about an economic redistribution of wealth in America. These ideas were viewed as very radical and dangerous, and were arguments that many white Americans who might support desegregation of public facilities did not want to deal with. However, by 1966–67 Rustin had come to be viewed as a conservative, indeed by some as an "Uncle Tom," and what had happened, to put matters perhaps a bit simplistically, is that Rustin's emphasis upon an agenda focusing on economic issues, focusing on the problems of what we nowadays most often call the black underclass, had lost out among both blacks and whites. In many liberal white communities, that issue now had a very secondary status relative to opposition to the war, but it also had secondary status to the interest in nationalism, to the interest in the cultural concerns and black pride, that for many black activists the black power slogan represented.

What Rustin wanted to do, and indeed to some extent what Dr. King as well wanted to do as of the time of his assassination in 1968, was to build a multiracial coalition that would address fundamental economic redistribution in the United States. The strategy that Rustin wanted to follow at that time was a strategy of electoral action, a strategy of political organizing, and the slogan that both Rustin and his mentor, A. Philip Randolph, spoke of was "from protest to politics," namely, that the future was politics and the era of protest was now mostly in the past. With reference to some of the effects of protest that Mr. Gottlieb highlighted in his remarks, it needs to be appreciated that the disruptive, angry, and even bitter demonstrations that were often seen between 1968 and 1970 did not have simply a negative effect, did not have only the effect of turning off white middle America. Those demonstrations also had the effect of making moderate groups, both in the antiwar movement and in the black civil rights struggle, such as the National Urban League, look more attractive to the government, to foundations, and to the Nixon Administration. What one sees in the civil rights arena in those initial years of the Nixon Administration is an eagerness on the administration's part to assist and to advance those so-called "responsible" elements—for example, the Urban League and James Farmer, the one-time national director of CORE, the Congress of Racial Equality, who took a sub-cabinet post in the Department of Health, Education, and Welfare in the Nixon years. In other words, these individuals were accorded more respect, more input, and more influence because of the fact that other people were in the streets, that other people were viewed as dangerous. Hence, I think our interpretation of protest in those years needs to have that double-edged appreciation that the radicals *helped* the moderates just as much, and perhaps more so, than the radicals *hindered* support for mainstream civils rights efforts and/or mainstream opposition to the war. I think, however, that it is very crucial for us to appreciate that the economic agenda that the black freedom struggle and its white supporters had in 1968–69 at the outset of the Nixon era was an agenda that essentially was not pursued, an agenda that in all frankness we have not done a very good job of addressing or advancing in the almost twenty years since.

I would also like to highlight, particularly for the undergraduates who are present, the fact that our scholarship and our current-day historiography are relatively weak and oftentimes incomplete in appreciating the negative effects of government repression and government hostility toward the protest movement, particularly with regard to the actions of the FBI against both black groups and antiwar groups. We tend at times, I think, to look at the movement and to look at the protests of those years somewhat apart from other things, and do not appreciate very fully just how harmful all of the government COINTELPRO[3] types of activities actually were. Most significantly, I think, we oftentimes minimize just how deleterious were the effects that the thousands upon thousands of paid government informants within the movement had on those organizations and on the tone and the feel of relations among people. What existed in many instances at that time, and what is perhaps nowadays often best forgotten by some of the people involved, was a very great fear of that panoply of informants and an attendant distrust of one's movement colleagues. Thus, the worst effect of the government's disruption and harassment of the movement was perhaps not so much what the informants or even J. Edgar Hoover's dirty tricks themselves wrought, but was instead the worry and the fear, and at times even paranoia, about government penetration and government threats that was generated.[4] On occasion these worries did fundamentally harm the strength and the unity of the movement and movement organizations.

In conclusion, while our growing academic appreciation of the protest movement is very good at noting, and at times celebrating, the moral strength and courage that thousands of people manifested during those years, I think that we need to appreciate equally the more painful story about the harm and the scars and the casualties that people suffered during that time, often at the hands of the government itself.

NOTES

1. Jim Miller, *Democracy Is in the Streets* (New York: Simon and Schuster, 1987); see also Tom Hayden, *Reunion: A Memoir* (New York: Random House, 1988).

2. New York: Bantam, 1987.

3. For Counterintelligence Program. See generally David J. Garrow, *The FBI and Martin Luther King, Jr.: "Solo" to Memphis* (New York: Norton, 1981), pp. 173–203, 220–227.

4. See generally David J. Garrow, "FBI Political Harassment and FBI Historiography: Analyzing Informants and Measuring the Effects," *The Public Historian* 10 (Fall 1988): 1–14.

Discussant: Sanford Gottlieb

I come with a question and, I hope, an insight. My question really is to Mr. Krogh, and I hope you will answer it later. It is on a personal level. Since I was on Nixon's enemies list, I wonder if you could tell us who was it in the White House to whom we can address our thanks for that distinctive honor?

On the insight, I think we haven't quite yet edged up to the real lessons of the protest movement. Tom has been getting there but we haven't quite faced it, and to me it is not a terribly enjoyable task. But it is one I think we have to go through, not just because we have been invited here to speak but because there are some very important lessons in it.

The moderator posed the question, was this a simple protest? The obvious answer is "no." We had come on the scene at a time when a new generation had arrived in the United States, a generation part of which, and I stress the part, was largely affluent, largely white, and in revolt against authority. In retrospect, much of what passed for an opposition to and a protest against the Vietnam War was in reality a protest against all forms and symbols of authority: the schools, universities, government, business, the military, Mom and Dad. That vastly complicated the task of those people who thought that we were protesting essentially against the Vietnam War. It was a tremendously volatile, emotional, complex protest movement that we had there. For those of us who were in the moderate wing—we had two wings, broadly speaking, we had moderates and we had radicals—those were pretty difficult times because of the complexities of the protest.

Let me give you a specific. It came during the Nixon Administration in 1970. Senators George McGovern and Mark Hatfield had introduced an amendment to cut off the funds for the Vietnam War. SANE, the organization of which I was executive director at the time, published a full-page ad in *The New York Times* urging people to support the McGovern-Hatfield amendment. The ad was essentially a petition in which people were asked to send their names to us, and we would give them to the senators.

Well, to our office in Washington came a petition signed by twenty-odd policemen from New York City. There was a cover letter from John Donellan, and he said the following—this was printed in an August 1970 issue of *The New Yorker* magazine:

Dear Sirs:
All of the twenty-one signatures belong to New York City policemen, my co-workers. We feel very strongly that individuality must be expressed and that no group (police, construction workers, students, parents) should be labeled and saddled with iron-clad ideologies. The media has stressed the affinity between the superficial "flag-wavers" and violence prone "hard-hats" with the "police mentality." We policemen resent this and

express our whole-hearted support of the amendment to end the war now.

John Donellan and Fellow Officers

I wrote to him, and he came back with the following answer:

I don't know any typical cop. You really can be an individual and human being even while wearing the blue uniform. The "police mentality," the right-wing conservative John Birchite, George Wallacite bigot and bully image, is unfair and inaccurate. I suppose there are many who fit the description. I know a few personally, but needless to stress, there are many decent, confused, open-minded, fair men who get labeled "pigs." This small gesture we made, the petition, was the first time for many of us to have done anything politically orientated or involved. We are not a group, just individual guys.

Now, that reminded me, when I got the exchange of correspondence, of an incident that took place the day after the first large nonstudent march against the Vietnam War, which I helped organize in November of 1965. The next day Dave Dellinger had organized a meeting of what was then called the National Coordinating Committee, which in effect represented the radical wing of the movement, to which I could come and offer my explanations for what were considered high crime and misdemeanors at the time. I had made the mistake of telling *The New York Times* that I was talking to the police in Washington, D.C., about the problem, in advance of the demonstration, of how to keep out of our demonstration the people who did not belong there, namely those who were carrying Vietcong flags. That became the issue for the radicals for a short period of time—the fact that I could dare talk to the police about such a problem. The people who carried the Vietcong flags had nothing to do with the purpose of the demonstration, which was to promote a negotiated settlement.

Well, I showed up at this meeting and I was asked about it by a young lady. She asked about dealing with the police, and I made the answer, "The police are our friends until they hit us over the heads." She dissolved into tears. Now, that was a rather extraordinary event, but it was indicative of the kind of mind-set that I am talking about.

The cops, already in 1965—forget about 1970—the cops were the enemy, the cops were the "pigs"; the government was the enemy, the government was "pigs." We were already seeing the kind of ideological self-indulgence that has already been talked about, and this is precisely what made the task a whole lot harder.

Then it took a form which—and I get now into the insight which I think is important to this day—it took a form which had a political effect. Violence was not the issue; by and large, the demonstrations were not violent. However, there was always a very visible minority, such as the Vietcong flag-bearers in my demonstration, and later the people who burned draft cards. Ultimately, the most visible act was the burning of the American flag. All of this occurred on camera.

What we are talking about here is not violence, it is values. The people hold certain things dear to them—they cherish certain values, they believe in certain things—and traditional patriotism is one of those values. We are a middle-class country with middle-class values. The radical movement didn't want to know that they came from that class, or they came from the upper-middle class but they didn't want to accept it. They wanted in many cases to flaunt their revolt. I am not talking about the agents provocateurs who abounded in many of the demonstrations. I am talking about the people who through their own emotions, and I won't try to analyze those emotions here today, were using demonstrations to flaunt their own revolt against society. Meanwhile, across the country millions of people were watching this on television. It is the combination of television with a minority of the antiwar movement that I would suggest to you created something that is going to be discussed later this afternoon, the Silent Majority.

By 1968 there was in the public opinion polls a majority against the war in Vietnam. By 1968, over 50 percent opposed the war in Vietnam for a whole variety of reasons, not always ours. By 1968, other public opinion polls showed a majority even larger against the war protesters. I will repeat that by 1968 there was a majority against the war; by 1968 there was an even larger majority against the war protesters. Why? Because we live in a television age, ten people in a demonstration of a hundred thousand could get on camera—by the time they started burning American flags on camera, and it could have been one or two people in a demonstration—and five hundred thousand were guaranteed to see it on the evening news. It was guaranteed absolutely, there were no exceptions. That potent combination—TV; a revolt against authority; abusing the symbols that people held dear, especially the American flag—helped create the Silent Majority. These were people who already were mostly against the war but didn't know how to express it. They were politically impotent. They didn't know how to express it because that meant getting into bed with Abbie Hoffmann or flag-burners, or a whole crowd of what they considered really abnormal types. They saw those people on camera, and those people were unrepresentative even of the protest movement. But that's what got on television and that's what formed the American mentality of sitting out the war in Vietnam.

Why else did it go on for eight years? The war lasted eight years, from February 1965, which marks the start of the systematic bombing of North Vietnam and the major introduction of U.S. ground troops. You can count it further back into the Kennedy Administration, but let's count it from February of 1965 to 1973, with the final withdrawal of American troops. Eight years, that's longer than the combined American involvement in World War II and Korea combined. Why else did it go on for eight years? The Silent Majority was silent, and President Nixon was basically free to do what he wanted. Although many things were accomplished, I'm glad nobody so far has said that the antiwar movement shortened the war, because it is not provable.

I do not enjoy saying this, but I think the lesson we have to take away from this is that, while we taught a lot of people how to dissent at a time when they didn't know how to dissent—they didn't know how to criticize the government very easily in 1965, and one of our earliest problems was teaching them how to dissent—and while a lot of what went on was in fact affirmative, the flaunting of values that the majority holds dear can paralyze people politically and have unexpected and largely negative political consequences. I think that is the main lesson we have to take away from the protest movement of that time.

I am glad to say that people have learned that lesson today. We don't see any of that in any wing of any movement. Maybe that was a unique time. Maybe that was a generational question more than anything else; for reasons which I don't understand, it appeared and then disappeared. We don't have whole masses of people now in revolt against authority. Perhaps people are wiser than they were in the 1960s. Yet I think what we have to say, and it is certainly painful for me to say it, is that this movement in the 1960s, despite all its positive aspects, had negative political impacts which made it difficult to end the war when it could have been ended. Had we turned one-tenth to one-quarter of our energy and our brain power into focusing on Congress earlier on and trying to get money cut off for the war, as eventually happened in the 1970s, we could have ended it by the late 1960s.

SECRECY, THE GOVERNMENT, AND THE MEDIA

6

Secrecy and Democracy:
The Unresolved Legacy of the
Pentagon Papers

JOHN KINCAID

Publication of the Pentagon Papers by leading newspapers in June 1971 was a significant event in modern American history. The contents of the papers fueled the fires of antiwar movements at home and abroad; the release of the papers provoked an unprecedented criminal prosecution of two American citizens; and the reaction of the administration of President Richard M. Nixon to publication of the papers led ultimately to the Watergate scandal and the first resignation of a president in American history. Often overlooked, however, is the fact that the trial of Daniel Ellsberg and Anthony Russo for photocopying the Pentagon Papers revealed the imperial and lawless side of the Nixon Administration, and this brought into sharp relief the dilemmas of government secrecy in a democratic polity.[1]

Never before had citizens been charged with a crime for disclosing presumably "Top Secret" information to the general public through the American press. Heretofore, except for narrow fields of secrecy legislatively sanctioned by the Congress such as certain atomic energy information, the keeping of secrets had been understood to be an executive prerogative but not a statutorily vested authority. Once the cat was out of the bag, the press was free to make use of information. After all, the leaking of classified information had been, and still is, a very common practice.

The principal restraint on the press was the ability of the president to persuade the press not to publish information. Unlike Britain's prime minister and most other heads of state, who can protect secrets under an Official Secrets Act, the president possesses no statutory authority to block press publication of classified information. Prior to the trial of Ellsberg and Russo, moreover, it was not generally believed that the president could lawfully prosecute citizens for leaking classified information to the American press.

Indeed, the threat posed by such authority to informed debate in a democracy and to disclosures of governmental malfeasance made such executive authority virtually unthinkable. In passing the Espionage Act of 1917, for example, the Congress denied President Woodrow Wilson's requests for broad authority to control war information. Members of Congress deliberately limited the scope of the law so that it could not be used as an instrument for presidential censorship of the press. Over the years, the Congress has consistently refused to allow the executive branch to draw a statutory veil of secrecy around itself.

The Nixon Administration's prosecution of Ellsberg and Russo, therefore, was an audacious attempt by an "imperial" executive branch to secure from the judicial branch a broad measure of power and authority long denied it by the legislative branch.[2] Nonetheless, the Congress sat by while the administration creatively fashioned extraordinary criminal charges out of novel interpretations of existing statutes covering conspiracy, theft, and espionage. Although the administration failed in its effort to imprison Ellsberg and Russo, the reluctance of the court to quash the prosecution at the outset fundamentally altered the rules of executive secrecy in the United States by converting what had been a political game of hide-and-seek between presidents and the press into a potentially criminal game of cat-and-mouse. Hence, the long-term significance of the Pentagon Papers—and the fundamental clash between secrecy and democracy—lay not so much in the unauthorized publication of the documents, but in the abuse of the Rule of Law by the administration—an abuse that has had the effect of hanging a judicial sword of Damocles above the heads of citizens who would disclose classified information to the public.

THE PRINCIPAL EVENTS

On Sunday, June 13, 1971, *The New York Times* began to publish excerpts from a U.S. Defense Department study marked "Top Secret" and entitled *History of U.S. Decision-Making Processes on Vietnam Policy*, popularly known as the Pentagon Papers. The compilation of documents had been assembled during Lyndon B. Johnson's administration at the request of then-Secretary of Defense Robert S. McNamara. Initially, President Nixon was not especially disturbed by the publication of the papers. Their contents, after all, dealt with policy-making prior to his administration and were, therefore, likely to be embarrassing to the Democrats just before an election year. However, the president's national security adviser, Henry Kissinger, prevailed on the president to do something about this "massive hemorrhage of state secrets."[3]

On the evening of June 14, after two days of publication and after various White House consultations, Attorney General John Mitchell asked *The New York Times* to cease publishing excerpts from the Pentagon Papers. Mitchell asserted that publication of the documents violated the Espionage Act. *The Times* refused to comply, saying, "It is in the interest of the people of this country to be informed of the material contained in this series of articles." The U.S. Department of Justice obtained a temporary restraining order against *The Times*. The newspaper appealed to the U.S. Supreme Court on June 24.

While *The Times* was restrained from publishing excerpts from the Pentagon Papers, *The Washington Post* began to publish portions of the study. *The Post* distributed extracts to some 345 client publications through the *Washington Post–Los Angeles Times* News Service. The Department of Justice obtained a temporary restraining order against *The Post*, and then appealed to the U.S. Supreme Court when the U.S. Court of Appeals for the District of Columbia ruled that *The Post* had a constitutional right to publish the material. Extracts from the Pentagon Papers were also published by *The Boston Globe*, *The Los Angeles Times*, *The St. Louis Post-Dispatch*, *The Christian Science Monitor*, and a number of other newspapers during June 22–29. The Department of Justice obtained a restraining order against *The St. Louis Post-Dispatch* on June 26.[4]

On that day, the U.S. Supreme Court heard public oral arguments from Solicitor General Erwin Griswold for the United States, Alexander Bickel for *The Times*, and William Glendon for *The Post*. In a swift and extraordinary flourish of activity, the Court rendered a 6–3 decision on June 30, and issued a short per curiam opinion for the Court, with justices Warren Burger, John Harlan, and Harry Blackmun dissenting. The decision was accompanied by nine opinions. The per curiam opinion held that the United States had not overcome the heavy constitutional presumption against prior restraint on the press. Justices Hugo Black and William Douglas took a nearly absolute view of a First Amendment prohibition of prior restraint on newspapers. Justices William Brennan, Thurgood Marshall, Potter Stewart, and Byron White acknowledged that there could be conditions that would justify a prior restraint on press publication of national security information, but that such conditions were not present in this case. Chief Justice Burger objected to the "unseemly haste" with which the Court handled the cases. Justices Harlan and Blackmun also objected to the "frenzied train of events [that] took place in the name of the presumption against restraints created by the First Amendment." The dissenting justices believed that publication of the Pentagon Papers should have been delayed until an assessment could have been made of the papers' potential effect on national defense and security.[5]

The New York Times and *The Washington Post* hailed the ruling as a victory for freedom of the press, and resumed publication of excerpts of the Pentagon Papers on July 1. Although the Nixon Administration had succeeded in temporarily imposing the first U.S. government prior restraint on newspapers in American history, an event that outstripped even the Sedition Act of 1798, the attempt to control leaks by judicially restraining the press did not stick. In the view of the administration, something else had to be done to defend executive prerogatives over the dissemination of information.

SELECTIVE PROSECUTION?

The setback at the Supreme Court did not deter the Nixon Administration from pursuing criminal charges against Daniel Ellsberg. The White House had identified Ellsberg as the person responsible for the Pentagon Papers leak almost immediately after publication of the documents. According to H. R. Haldeman, Kissinger was especially outraged "because Ellsberg had been one of his 'boys.' (He had lectured at Kissinger's Defense Policy Seminars at Harvard in the 1960s.)" Kissinger apparently told President Nixon that Ellsberg "had weird sexual habits, used drugs, and enjoyed helicopter flights in which he would take potshots at the Vietnamese below."[6]

Ellsberg was first indicted on June 25, 1971. He surrendered to U.S. authorities in Boston on June 28. Not fully satisfied with the strength of its case, however, the administration continued to seek incriminating evidence, both legally and illegally, and to examine its prosecutorial options. During the Labor Day holiday, members of the White House Plumbers unit burglarized the office of Ellsberg's psychiatrist in an effort to obtain information that might be used to damage Ellsberg's credibility and cast doubt on his motives.

On June 19, the FBI questioned Anthony J. Russo about his role in the release of the Pentagon Papers. Russo refused to answer FBI questions. On June 23, he was subpoenaed to testify before a federal grand jury in Los Angeles. Despite a grant of immunity, Russo declined to testify unless his testimony could be made public. On August 16, he began serving a forty-seven-day jail term for contempt of court. On October 1, U.S. District Court Judge Warren J. Ferguson released Russo from prison and ordered the government to provide Russo with a transcript of any testimony he might be required to give to the grand jury. Assistant U.S. Attorney David R. Nissen held the order to be "unlawful" and refused to comply with it. Russo again declined to testify before the grand jury. On December 29, 1971, the grand jury issued a new, secret indictment in the Pentagon Papers case, one that added new charges against Ellsberg and also included criminal charges against Russo.

The defendants were charged with fifteen counts of criminal conduct, including conspiracy, espionage, and conversion of government property (theft) for photocopying in 1969 substantial portions of the Pentagon Papers. Contrary to a common belief, Ellsberg and Russo were not indicted for giving the Pentagon Papers to any newspapers or for making the documents public in any way. They were indicted for temporarily removing the Pentagon Papers from the premises of the RAND Corporation in Santa Monica, California, and for photocopying the documents at an advertising agency owned by Russo's friend, Lynda Sinay. Listed as unindicted coconspirators were Lynda Sinay and Vu Van Thai, a former South Vietnamese ambassador to the United States. Thai had evidently been present at one of the photocopying sessions. The charges against Ellsberg carried maximum penalties of 115 years' imprisonment and $120,000 in fines. Those against Russo carried maximum penalties of 35 years' imprisonment and $40,000 in fines. During the trial, however, U.S. District Court Judge William Matthew Byrne, Jr., directed an acquittal on one espionage count each against Ellsberg and Russo.

There are several reasons for believing that the trial of Ellsberg and Russo— popularly known as the Pentagon Papers Trial—was a case of selective prosecution undertaken for political reasons. For one, Ellsberg and Russo were the first citizens in American history to be criminally prosecuted for activities associated with a leak of classified information to the public. Second, the leaking of classified information by public officials from the president to low-level subordinates had been, as it continues to be, a common practice. Henry Kissinger has argued that publication of the Pentagon Papers "was selective, one-sided, and clearly intended as a weapon of political warfare."[7] Political warfare may not be the appropriate term in this case, but even so, political warfare is a common motivation for leaking secrets, whether it be by presidents, national security advisers, or persons outside an administration. Furthermore, a full compilation of available documents was soon published by Beacon Press with the assistance of Senator Mike Gravel.

Third, no members of the press, who actually published the documents, were indicted by the government. Indeed, the indictment of Ellsberg and Russo steered clear of any possible collision with the press by limiting the alleged criminal behavior to the period of March 1969 to September 1970, a time span that ended more than nine months before the publication of the Pentagon Papers. Fourth, no attempt was made to prosecute other private citizens formerly associated with the Lyndon Johnson Administration who possessed copies of the Pentagon Papers, or portions thereof, and who arguably drew on those documents, directly or indirectly, for books, articles, and speeches.

The available records of White House discussions of how to proceed against Ellsberg suggest that the decision to prosecute was a political strategy designed to make an example of him. The administration wished to stem what it regarded as a rising tide of sensitive leaks by indirectly intimidating others who might consider disclosing information to the press. The principal problem facing the administration was one of finding a statutory basis for prosecution. To do so, the U.S. Department of Justice had to bring to bear on the case considerable creativity. All charges involved novel interpretations of standing statutes.

CONSPIRACY—TO VIOLATE AN EXECUTIVE DECREE?

The first count in the indictment charged the defendants with "conspiracy to defraud the United States and an agency thereof by impairing, obstructing and defeating its lawful governmental function of controlling the dissemination of classified Government studies, reports, memoranda and communications." This count also charged the defendants with conspiracy to violate the espionage and theft of government property statutes.

The allegedly classified government documents specifically cited in the indictment were eighteen volumes of the Pentagon Papers; eight pages of a report on the situation in Vietnam by General Earle Wheeler dated February 27, 1968; and a memorandum entitled *Negotiations and Viet Nam: A Case Study of the 1954 Geneva Conference* written by Melvin Gurtov, a former RAND consultant. On this latter document, however, Judge Matthew Byrne ruled that the government could not present any evidence showing whether this memorandum could have injured the "national defense" if it had been released during the period of the defendants' alleged offenses. The judge's ruling was based on the prosecution's failure to turn over an exculpatory report by government experts. The report stated that the memorandum contained no information "related to the national defense which could have caused injury to the United States if disclosed."

Although the government often employs conspiracy charges to increase the odds of obtaining a conviction—because the rules of evidence are relaxed and the prosecution need prove only one "overt act"—in this case, the government went far beyond the customary uses of conspiracy charges by asserting the existence of a nonexistent information law—that is, the allegedly "lawful governmental function of controlling the dissemination of classified" information. The charge was unprecedented. The executive branch had never before asserted the existence of such a "lawful" function as a criminal matter. No one had ever been prosecuted for conspiracy to defraud the United States of such a function. This charge had never even been brought against citizens who had committed genuine espionage by giving classified information to foreign governments.

The key issue in this charge hinges on the meaning of "lawful." Although many persons have been charged and convicted of conspiracy to defraud the government of lawful governmental functions, Ellsberg and Russo's actions did not impinge on a governmental function that is "lawful" in a civil or criminal sense, because the Congress has never passed a law giving the president statutory authority to establish a classification system for keeping information secret (except for certain atomic energy information and military codes, none of which pertained to the Pentagon Papers or to the government's charges against Ellsberg and Russo).

The system of classification used by departments and agencies in the executive branch was established by executive order for internal housekeeping purposes. Government employees who compromise that system have always been subject to possible administrative reprimand but not criminal prosecution. Persons who are not government employees cannot be administratively reprimanded and, until the Pentagon Papers, could not presumably be prosecuted for leaking classified information to the general public.

Constitutionally, every lawful governmental function, a violation of which would entail criminal penalties, must be defined by an act of Congress, the people's legislative representatives. Criminal charges of conspiracy to defraud the government of "lawful" governmental functions must, presumably, have as their bases congressional statutes, or executive orders issued pursuant to express congressional statutes.

In the conspiracy charge against Ellsberg and Russo, there was, and continues to be, no statute or "classification law." Instead, the government made the extraordinary contention that executive orders "have the force of law whether promulgated under a direct statute or under the authority of the Executive, which is not by statute, which comes from his Constitutional power. There is *no* distinction between those two." In a manner similar to President Johnson's interpretation of the Gulf of Tonkin resolution as being the functional equivalent of a declaration of war, the government in this case interpreted an executive order, having no statutory foundation, as being the functional equivalent of a criminal statute.

This contention was extraordinary in terms of customary understandings of the constitutional powers of presidents, but quite consistent with the Nixon Administration's expansive understanding of its constitutional powers and broad view of such related matters as executive privilege. Had the court upheld the contention put forth in the Pentagon Papers Trial, it would have sanctioned, in effect, rule by executive decree whereby the president could cause criminal penalties to be brought against citizens for violating executive orders having no statutory grounding in criminal law, and especially in this case, an executive order being used to do what the Congress has consistently refused to do by means of legislation. To allow presidents to create crimes by decree would violate fundamental principles of democracy.

At another point in the trial, the government argued that there is a statutory basis for executive orders regarding the classification of information. That basis is the Freedom of Information Act (FOIA), which the prosecution contended is the functional equivalent of an Official Secrets Act even though the purpose of the act is to make more information available to the public. That is, by enacting the FOIA, the Congress implicitly provided a statutory foundation for the executive classification system, and thereby implicitly recognized the authority of the executive branch to defend that system by prosecuting persons who compromise it. The court was not receptive to this extraordinary argument, so the government abandoned it.

Aside from these constitutional issues, there was also the question of whether individuals can be prosecuted for leaking information that is improperly classified as "Secret" or "Top Secret." Executive orders governing classification provide rules for classification. The rules are ostensibly designed to prevent officials from classifying, and thereby secreting, information that properly belongs in the public domain. It is well known that officials often violate these rules and improperly classify as "secret" large volumes of information that should be placed in the public domain. In the Pentagon Papers trial, the government contended that Ellsberg and Russo should not be permitted to challenge the propriety of the classification markings on the documents; however, the judge elected to allow the defense to present testimony on this matter—testimony that raised serious doubts about whether the Pentagon Papers had been classified properly and whether certain of the documents should have already been declassified for public use.

An ironic dimension of this issue with regard to selective prosecution is that executive orders governing classification also provide rules and mandates for declassifying documents. No case could be found of an official being prosecuted or administratively reprimanded for failing to declassify documents when required to do so by the executive order.

ESPIONAGE—ARE THE AMERICAN PEOPLE THE ENEMY?

Ellsberg and Russo were not charged with giving or selling information of any kind to any foreign government or entity. Nor, as noted, were they charged with violating any congressional statute that makes it a crime to release classified information to the public. Given that the Pentagon Papers were released through the American press to the American public, and given that Ellsberg and Russo were not charged with giving information to any foreign enemy of the United States, the espionage charge was a most curious one. Does the release of classified information to the public constitute espionage? This charge, quipped Russo, implied that the Nixon Administration regarded the American people as "the enemy," foreigners in their own republic.

The espionage charge was all the more curious when one considers that Ellsberg and Russo were charged only for photocopying the documents, not for releasing them to the public. The government contended that mere possession constituted espionage, and argued that the defendants were obligated by law to "deliver" the documents to an official or employee of the United States "entitled to receive them." In principle, under this theory, a person who finds a "Top Secret" document on a public street and who throws it in a trash can or puts it in a closet at home is guilty of espionage.

Furthermore, according to the nearly eighty-year history of U.S. espionage law, the disclosure of properly secret national defense information is a crime only when that disclosure is made "with intent or reason to believe that the information to be obtained is to be used to the injury of the United States, or to the advantage of any foreign nation." However, in the Pentagon Papers trial, for the first time in the history of espionage prosecutions, the U.S. government sought to exclude "intent." The government acknowledged that the law had never been used in this manner, but argued that the subsections under which Ellsberg and Russo were being tried did not require proof of "intent." "Intent," however, is a crucial feature of the law, one insisted upon by the Congress. Without the obligation to prove an intent to injure the United States or aid a foreign nation, presidents would have wide latitude to use the Espionage Act to prosecute citizens whose only intent was to disclose governmental wrongdoing to the public.

This novel interpretation of espionage, coupled with the fact that Ellsberg and Russo were not charged with giving the Pentagon Papers to anyone else, led to a bizarre, surrealistic mode of testimony. Not wishing to rule on the substantive issues of espionage law before hearing testimony, Judge Byrne required the government to prove, and the defense to disprove, an entirely hypothetical situation, namely, whether the Pentagon Papers "would have aided a foreign nation or injured the United States" if they had been released to the newspapers or the public during the period of photocopying covered by the indictment.

Given the absence of a verdict in the trial, one cannot say which side won this debate. Subsequently, however, officials of the Nixon Administration, including Henry Kissinger, acknowledged that publication of the Pentagon Papers did no noticeable harm to the United States and gave no noticeable aid to the nation's enemies—namely, the North Vietnamese, with whom the United States was not officially at war. Furthermore, from the very first White House debate over how to respond to the publication of the Pentagon Papers, serious consideration was given to declassifying them on the spot, in part as a way of defusing the importance attributed to them by critics of the war. The White House also consulted Richard Allen, who supported declassification.

THEFT—WHO OWNS WHAT IN A DEMOCRACY?

Many commentators still refer to the Pentagon Papers as having been stolen. In *Breach of Faith*, Theodore H. White goes so far as to say that "there was no doubt that the Pentagon Papers had been stolen from government files. They had been stolen by one Daniel Ellsberg . . . in violation of both civil laws and laws of national security."[8] White is wrong on every point. Furthermore, regardless of the actual circumstances regarding Ellsberg's possession of the documents, in the absence of a conviction for theft, one cannot properly say that the documents were stolen.

The theft charge raised several knotty issues. The threshold issue, however, was: What was allegedly stolen? At first, the government contended that Ellsberg had stolen the physical documents. The defendants introduced evidence showing that the documents photocopied by Ellsberg and Russo were the private, personal copies of Paul C. Warnke, Leslie Gelb, and Morton H. Halperin. These individuals had housed the documents at the RAND Corporation in Santa Monica and had given Ellsberg permission to check the documents out of RAND's security library. Furthermore, other private citizens, including Lyndon B. Johnson and Robert S. McNamara, had taken copies of the Pentagon Papers into their own possession when they left public office. Hence, the prosecution found it difficult to contend that the physical documents belonged to the government in the first place, let alone that Ellsberg had "stolen" the documents from the government. The documents were not in the possession of, or under the control of, the U.S. government. If charges of theft of government property were to be lodged, they logically should have been directed against Gelb, Halperin, and

Warnke. Such an approach, however, would have exposed many former government officials, including Johnson and McNamara, to theft charges for leaving public service with classified documents in hand.

At this point, the prosecution modified its strategy by claiming that Ellsberg had stolen "the arrangement of the words on the pages and the ideas conveyed by that arrangement," and that Russo had unlawfully received those contraband words. This was an extraordinary and unprecedented charge because the U.S. government cannot "own" information and, therefore, cannot have information stolen from it. In a democratic republic—the word comes from *res publica*, meaning "a public thing"—public information or information generated by the government belongs to the public. The public cannot be construed as stealing its own information. Hence, the government cannot copyright public information, and the Congress has always denied the government property rights over information. As Melville Nimmer testified before the court: "The Copyright Act announces to the public that it may copy governmental documents without incurring criminal liability." The theft of government property statute, in any event, "does not purport to make a special rule as to classified or 'sensitive' or even unpublished documents."

The theft charge was further complicated by the fact that Ellsberg had given or shown copies of the Pentagon Papers to some members of the Congress. A conviction for theft, therefore, would have implied that the executive branch is the government and that the Congress is not, and that members of the Congress, like Anthony Russo, could be prosecuted for receiving classified information "stolen" from the executive branch.

Thus, the theft charge had implications of presidential imperialism similar to the other charges. The conspiracy charge implied a right of the president to rule by decree. The espionage charge implied that the president viewed the American people as an enemy. The theft charge implied that the presidency can possess public property not belonging to the people or the Congress, and own information that is immune from a democratic public's right to know.

GOVERNMENT MISCONDUCT

The Pentagon Papers Trial began in Los Angeles on July 10, 1972, with selection of the jury. On July 24, Judge Byrne revealed that the government had filed a wiretap transcript of a conversation by a member of the defense staff, but ruled that the contents need not be disclosed because they did not bear on the case. The defense appealed the ruling to the U.S. Supreme Court. The trial was stayed until November 13, when the Supreme Court upheld the judge's ruling. Immediately thereafter, the trial was again stayed when the defense appealed for and obtained dismissal of the jury. Selection of a new jury began on January 8, 1973.

On May 11, 1973, however, near the close of testimony, Judge Byrne dismissed all charges against Ellsberg and Russo, and declared a mistrial because

of "improper government conduct" which offended "a sense of justice." Among
other things, the White House Plumbers had burglarized the office of Ellsberg's
psychiatrist in 1971; FBI wiretap transcripts of telephone conversations by Ellsberg in 1969–1970 had disappeared; on several occasions the government had
failed to make a timely disclosure of exculpatory evidence; and presidential
assistant John Ehrlichman had flown to Los Angeles in April to offer Judge
Byrne the directorship of the FBI. A poll of the jurors after the mistrial indicated
that most would likely have voted for acquittal if they had had the opportunity
to decide the case.[9]

CONCLUSION

The Pentagon Papers trial was a political trial in the classic sense. It was also
a prosecutorial effort that conformed to the Nixon Administration's often extraordinary constitutional claims to power and its cavalier disregard for the Rule
of Law. The decision to prosecute was a high-level one made by the president,
and the charges brought against Ellsberg and Russo represented a creative political construction of statutes designed to make a noncrime into a crime.

The proof is in the pudding, so to speak. The concern of the Nixon Administration with leaks was so great that, in addition to the Pentagon Papers trial,
it sought to achieve the same ends in its proposals to the Congress to reform the
federal criminal code. All the legal issues raised in the Pentagon Papers trial
and the creative constructions of statutes used to prosecute Ellsberg and Russo
were contained in the administration's criminal code "reform" proposals. Those
proposals, if enacted, would have provided a firm foundation in criminal law
for prosecuting persons for disclosing classified information to the public, and
would have prohibited defendants from raising such questions as ownership of
information and the propriety of any government classification of documents.
Improper classification would have been no defense against criminal charges.[10]

The Congress rejected the president's proposals, Nixon resigned from office,
the imperial presidency came to an end, and the Vietnam War also came to an
inglorious end two years later, but the issues raised in the Pentagon Papers trial
have continued to haunt public life, affecting every administration since Nixon.
Because Judge Byrne elected to defer rulings on the substantive legal and constitutional issues until the end of the trial, the mistrial left all the issues judicially
unresolved.

Hence, the possibility of prosecution continues to stand as a potential threat
to citizens who disclose classified information to the general public, although
any decision to prosecute, and the basis for doing so in cases similar to the
Pentagon Papers case, continue to remain in the realm of politics rather than
statutory law. The state of the law, as it now stands, neither permits nor prohibits
a president from prosecuting persons who leak classified information to the
American press.

A key question for Americans, then, is whether the issues raised by the

Pentagon Papers trial can be resolved legislatively or judicially. Although it is generally recognized, as John Jay argued in *The Federalist* nearly 200 years ago, that executive secrecy is sometimes necessary for the conduct of effective foreign policies, it is difficult to reconcile in any precise way the practice of secrecy with the openness required for democratic policy-making. Legislative and judicial solutions would necessarily be imperfect, and perhaps dangerous to democracy, because one cannot say in advance and in detail what kinds of information should be kept secret. Even genuinely sensitive national security secrets might occasionally have to be exposed in order to root out malfeasance or otherwise protect the public good. Given that officials already err on the side of secrecy when they can get away with it, any further encouragement via legislation or judicial support may aggravate the problem. The ability of presidents and their agents to protect secrets that are genuinely vital to the security of a democratic nation can easily be expanded to protect secrets that are vital only to the power and interests of public officeholders.

Thus, unless there is to be no secrecy, reconciliation of the need for secrecy with the prerequisites of democracy requires, in the final analysis, public-spirited officials who are able and willing to exercise sound judgment based on honest assessments of the national interest as determined by democratic processes. Such was not the case in 1971.

NOTES

1. See also John Ricks, "Daniel Ellsberg," in *Dictionary of the Vietnam War*, ed. James S. Olson (Westport, Conn.: Greenwood Press, 1988), pp. 133–135; and John Ricks, "Anthony J. Russo, Jr.," in *Dictionary of the Vietnam War*, ed. James S. Olson (Westport, Conn.: Greenwood Press, 1988), pp. 400–401.

2. Arthur M. Schlesinger, Jr., *The Imperial Presidency* (Boston: Houghton Mifflin, 1973).

3. Henry Kissinger, *White House Years* (Boston: Little, Brown, 1979), p. 730.

4. Sanford Ungar, *The Papers and the Papers* (New York: Dutton, 1972).

5. *New York Times Co. v. United States*, 403 U.S. 713 (1971).

6. H. R. Haldeman, *The Ends of Power* (New York: Dell, 1978), p. 155.

7. Kissinger, *White House Years*, p. 730.

8. Theodore H. White, *Breach of Faith* (New York: Dell, 1975), p. 191.

9. See also John Kincaid, "Pentagon Papers Trial," in Olson, *Dictionary of the Vietnam War*, pp. 361–362.

10. See also John Kincaid, "Nixon Strategy for Secrecy," *American Report* 3 (May 7, 1972): 1.

7

President Nixon's Conception of Executive Privilege: Defining the Scope and Limits of Executive Branch Secrecy

MARK J. ROZELL

The Nixon Presidency is remembered most for its involvement in one of the great constitutional crises of our history. This paper focuses on a central issue of that crisis: the scope and limits of executive privilege in our separation of powers system. My plan is to identify and discuss President Nixon's conception of executive privilege. I compare President Nixon's contribution to our understanding of the doctrine of executive privilege to traditional conceptions of that doctrine found in American political thought, practice, and constitutional history. I argue that while the doctrine of executive privilege has legal and historical bases in our separation of powers system, President Nixon's conception of that doctrine was too broad and lacks legal or historical foundation. Furthermore, while adoption of the Nixon standard would undermine the delicate balance of power between the branches of government, one should not generalize from the Nixon case, as some leading critics have, that all claims of executive privilege are baseless.[1]

EXECUTIVE PRIVILEGE

Executive privilege can be defined as the right of the president and important executive branch officials to withhold information from Congress, the courts, and the public. The purposes for withholding information are varied (namely, protecting state secrets, protecting confidentiality of White House deliberations, or protecting privacy). There is little agreement among legal scholars as to (1) whether executive privilege is a legitimate power, and (2) if it is legitimate, what the limitations are on claims of privilege.

For conceptual purposes it is important to distinguish executive privilege from the executive power of prerogative. The latter term refers to the notion that executives may take any action deemed necessary, in times of emergency, even if such action is contrary to the law. Executive privilege is therefore one form of the prerogative power. In times of emergency, a chief of state may exercise his prerogative to withhold sensitive information.

Controversy over claims of executive privilege has a long history in the United States and is rooted in our separation of powers system. The Framers were not explicit about the role of executive privilege in our governmental system. The Constitution lacks any reference to the privilege power, leading some critics to conclude that executive privilege is a "constitutional myth"[2] and others to argue that the privilege is such an obvious executive power that the Founders believed it need not be explicitly granted.[3]

The Founders' lack of clarity on executive privilege has encouraged a good deal of presidential discretion in withholding of information. The Founders, it appears, intended there to be an area of discretionary power for presidents who may assert a right to withhold information. The Founders recognized their inability to identify in advance all the possible contingencies under which presidents may prudently withhold information. Their solution to potential abuse of that power was not to delineate explicitly its scope and limits. Instead, they relied on the institutional checks and balances provided by our system of separated powers.

Over two hundred years experience under the Constitution provides ample historical evidence and legal precedent to help us more precisely define the scope and limits of executive privilege. My view is that both historic precedent and legal sanction clearly legitimize executive privilege. Generally prudent presidential exercise of executive privilege and important court decisions also reveal that executive privilege is not an absolute power limited only by the president's self-imposed restraints. As I shall argue, executive privilege may legitimately be invoked under four general circumstances:

1. when the nation's security may be threatened by divulging information;
2. when the confidentiality of internal White House deliberations may be jeopardized;
3. when the personal privacy of executive branch officials may be compromised for no public gain; and
4. when the enforcement of criminal justice may be threatened.

Admittedly, these are broad categories and are open to interpretation. The imposition of more precisely defined boundaries would destroy the realm of presidential discretion that is needed to protect the public interest. These categories are compatible with the traditional conception of executive privilege found in American political thought, action, and constitutional development. Before establishing the intellectual, historical, and legal bases for executive privilege,

I shall identify and discuss President Nixon's conception of executive privilege. I conclude by discussing the proper scope and limits of executive privilege in our separation of powers system.

PRESIDENT NIXON'S CONCEPTION OF EXECUTIVE PRIVILEGE

The most benevolent interpretation sometimes given for President Nixon's eventual downfall was that, unlike his predecessors, President Nixon was caught by his enemies misusing presidential power. According to this interpretation, President Nixon's actions, including his claims of executive privilege, were not extraordinary. The real difference, allegedly, was that (1) President Nixon provided indisputable documentation of executive branch wrongdoing and (2) his enemies in Congress and the national media were exceptionally vigilant.

This argument is in opposition to my view that President Nixon's conception of executive privilege lacks historical and constitutional foundations. In comparison to his predecessors' claims of privilege, the scope of President Nixon's claims was more broadly based. President Nixon went beyond notions of protecting the nation's security, the public interest, and the privacy of his aides, to using claims of privilege for purposes of political expediency, withholding of embarrassing (not vital) information, and covering executive abuses of power. Establishing that President Nixon's claims of executive privilege lack a historical and constitutional foundation requires an examination of his own administration's words and actions in comparison to the way in which Nixon's predecessors viewed and exercised the privilege. Let us first identify and discuss the Nixonian conception of executive privilege.

Executive Privilege Is Used for Reasons of Political Expediency

There is a common folk saying that where you stand on an issue depends on where you sit. Applied to our separation of powers system, this could mean that for reasons of political expediency, the position one adopts as a member of the legislative branch differs from the view one adopts as a member of the executive branch. The problem with this perspective is that if carried too far, it means that there are no enduring principles governing the exercise of political power in our system—only incessant battles for power driven by self-interest.

Nixon's actions indicate that the view he adopted on executive privilege was influenced by his institutional perspective. Nixon opposed the principle of executive privilege as a member of Congress, and made the most broadly based claims of privilege in history as president. For example, in 1948 President Harry S. Truman refused to release the text of an FBI letter concerning a prominent scientist accused of disloyalty by the House Un-American Activities Committee. On April 22, 1948, a member of that committee, Representative Richard M. Nixon (R-Calif.), protested Truman's invoking of the privilege:

The point has been made that the President of the United States has issued an order that none of this information can be released to the Congress and that therefore the Congress has no right to question the judgment of the President in making that decision.

I say that the proposition cannot stand from a constitutional standpoint or on the basis of the merits for this very good reason: that would mean that the President could have arbitrarily issued an Executive order in the Meyers case, the Teapot Dome case, or any other case denying the Congress of the United States information it needed to conduct an investigation of the executive department and the Congress would have no right to question his decision.

Any such order of the President can be questioned by the Congress as to whether or not that order is justified on the merits.[4]

This statement is ironic given President Nixon's vigorous defense of executive privilege a quarter-century later. As president, Nixon adopted the view that Congress lacks the legitimacy to question or contest executive claims of privilege. In President Nixon's conception of the separation of powers, the president reigns supreme, and may unilaterally determine the scope and limits of his own powers. President Nixon claimed that whenever a dispute between the political branches over executive branch information occurred, the president's claim of privilege resolved the dispute. Nixon's presidential view of executive privilege, therefore, was one adopted for reasons of political expediency. In a sense, this view of the president in the separation of powers system elevates the role of the chief executive to that of participant *and* referee in a political struggle. President Nixon even questioned the legitimacy of the courts as referees in our governmental system. In a revealing quote, Nixon stated during the Watergate controversy that "the manner in which the president exercises his assigned executive powers is not subject to questioning by another branch of the government."[5]

During oral argument in *U.S. v. Nixon*, President Nixon's attorney, James St. Clair, candidly rejected the right of the judiciary to contest presidential claims of privilege. The following exchange between the Court's justices and St. Clair revealed the president's view that although the Court could declare the law, the president still had the final word:

Question: You are submitting the matter to this Court. . . .

St. Clair: To this Court under a special showing on behalf of the president. . . .

Question: And you are still leaving it up to this Court to decide it.

St. Clair: Yes, in a sense.

Question: In what sense?

St. Clair: In the sense that this Court has the obligation to determine the law. The President also has an obligation to carry out his constitutional duties.

Question: Well, do you agree that this is what is before this Court, and you are submitting it to this Court for decision?

St. Clair: This is being submitted to this Court for its guidance and judgment with respect to the law. The President, on the other hand, has his obligations under the Constitution.

Question: Are you submitting it to this Court for this Court's decision?

St. Clair: As to what the law is, yes.[6]

Executive privilege not only serves political expediency but also, for President Nixon, was an unquestionable presidential prerogative. This leads to the second basis of the Nixonian conception of executive privilege—that there are no legitimate limits on presidential exercise of this power.

Executive Privilege Has No Limits

If the judiciary lacks authority to question executive activities, then, logically, anything the chief executive does is legitimate. President Nixon most clearly identified this belief in his televised interviews with journalist David Frost. When questioned on May 19, 1977, by Frost about the limits on presidential power, Nixon replied: "When the President does it, that means it is not illegal."[7]

This statement implies that there are no limits on presidential authority, including the power to withhold information. All that is required is presidential approval of an action. In a clear refutation of the more common constitutional view that no person is above the law, Nixon argued that presidential actions had higher standing than the law itself. For example, Nixon justified the burglary of Daniel Ellsberg's psychiatrist's office as a legitimate presidential action. While asserting that he did not know of the burglary in advance, Nixon responded that, if told, "I would have said, 'Go right ahead.' " Nixon continued: "I didn't want to discredit the man as an individual. I couldn't care less about the punk. I wanted to discredit that kind of activity, which was despicable and damaging to the national interest."[8]

Nixon added that such normally illegal activities become lawful when sanctioned by the president. The causes for sanctioning such activities are varied, and may, Nixon asserted, include the "national interest" or "national security." The activities of members of the executive branch are also exempted from normal legal limitations if conducted on the president's behalf:

If the President, for example, approves something, approves an action because of the national security or . . . because of a threat to internal peace and order of significant magnitude, then the President's decision in that instance is one that enables those who carry it out to carry it out without violating a law.[9]

President Nixon, therefore, adopted the most broadly based definition of the privilege imaginable. In practice, the former president rejected even any general limitations on the use of this presidential power. His conception of the privilege was that of a presidential power subject only to limitations accepted at the chief executive's discretion. This absolute privilege claim was asserted by President

Nixon's defenders, who argued that "such a privilege, inherent in the Constitutional grant of executive power, is a matter of presidential judgment alone."[10]

Executive Privilege Belongs to All Executive Branch Officials

For President Nixon, executive privilege was not a right possessed only by the president and selected White House insiders. Rather, in Nixon's view, executive privilege could be invoked by the president on behalf of *all* executive branch officials. As noted above, Nixon claimed that the president's exercise of power could not be questioned by the other branches of government. The president's aides also could not be questioned: "If the President is not subject to such questioning, it is equally inappropriate that members of his staff be so questioned, for their roles are in effect an extension of the President."[11]

Nixon applied this reasoning not only to his White House staff but also to the entire executive bureaucracy. Nixon's attorney general, Richard Kleindienst, asserted on behalf of the president that Congress lacked authority to call any employee of the federal government to appear before it if the president decided to bar such testimony.[12]

Members of the executive branch, in Nixon's view, could also assert for themselves a claim of executive privilege. In fact, Congress held a number of hearings on the matter of whether "agency" or "departmental" privilege was a legitimate executive branch power. The invocation of executive privilege by numerous subordinate officials in the Nixon administration prompted legislation to curtail such claims of privilege. For example, H. R. 6228, introduced by Representative John N. Erlenburn (R-Ill.), proposed that all executive branch information be made available to Congress and the comptroller general of the United States "except in cases where the President himself invokes the claim of executive privilege."[13] The purpose of this proposal was to make the president alone accountable for all claims of executive privilege. However, the legislation was successfully opposed both by (1) advocates of a broad definition of the privilege, and (2) strict opponents of the privilege, who claimed the proposal would effectively legitimize executive privilege.

TRADITIONAL CONCEPTIONS OF EXECUTIVE PRIVILEGE

President Nixon adopted an extremely broad conception of the executive privilege power. One result of Nixon's theory of executive privilege, and of the events surrounding Watergate, is that they indirectly increased the stature and recognition of strict opponents of the privilege, most notably, historian Raoul Berger, who claims that executive privilege is a "Constitutional myth."[14] In Berger's view, all claims of executive privilege are indefensible.[15] Berger's carefully researched studies identify four general arguments supporting the assertion that the privilege lacks legitimacy in our constitutional system: (1) The Founders' fear of tyranny, which inspired these Constitution-makers to avoid creating a too-powerful chief executive, (2) the lack of an explicit constitutional foundation for the privilege (more specifically, the Constitution nowhere grants an executive power to withhold information), (3) as the "Grand Inquest" of the nation, it is Congress's right to receive all executive branch information, and (4) the well-documented historical misuses of the privilege by executive branch officials.[16]

Each of these four arguments is defensible. However, Berger's thesis that executive privilege is completely groundless is as problematic as Nixon's claim that there are no legitimate limits on executive privilege. Both these views attempt to find a completely unambiguous answer to the nature and limits of presidential power in our separation of powers system. The search for absolute answers is fundamentally misguided. The attempts of critics of the privilege to prove that it is a "myth," as well as the attempts of some advocates to defend an absolute privilege power, are based on incorrect understandings of our separation of powers system.

My purpose now is to show that, although President Nixon's claims of executive privilege were excessive, the abuse of this power is not an argument for its elimination. The Founders recognized that any power once granted could be abused, and that the only guarantee against such occasional abuses—eliminating power altogether—was an unacceptable solution. We can reject President Nixon's conception of executive privilege and still accept the legitimacy of that power. In what follows I argue that executive privilege—in more limited form than the Nixonian conception—has intellectual, constitutional, and historical roots in our separation of powers system.

Intellectual Roots

The intellectual origins of executive privilege can be traced to the two most influential thinkers of modern constitutionalism—John Locke and Charles Louis de Secondat, Baron de Montesquieu. These constitutional thinkers concerned themselves with how to limit executive power without undermining the executive's ability to protect the public security. Locke and Montesquieu therefore sought to devise political regimes characterized by both strength and liberty.

In his *Second Treatise of Government*, John Locke offered a three-fold distinction of government powers: legislative, executive, and federative.[17] While on the surface Locke's emphasis on legislative supremacy seems unequivocal, he invests considerable power in the executive branch. For example, the "federative power"—the power to make war, peace, treaties, and alliances—is placed solely in the executive realm.[18] Locke's chapter "Of Prerogative" is most revealing. In times of emergency, when the legislature is not in session, or where the laws are silent, the executive is given "the power of doing public good without a rule."[19] For Locke, the "supreme law" of the land is the preservation of society. Only the executive can be empowered to act with power and "despatch" in times of emergency. While the legislative branch has supreme law-making powers during normal times, Locke does not deny the executive the power to take extraordinary, even extralegal, actions in emergencies.

Baron de Montesquieu was also concerned with the problem of reconciling freedom and strength. Individual liberty, he wrote, can best be protected by preventing any one power from holding the authority to formulate and execute the laws. He devised a governmental triad—legislative, executive, and judicial powers—as a means of preventing any one arm of the government from becoming tyrannical.[20] Although Montesquieu set forth a separation of powers system to limit governmental power, he did not advocate weak government. Montesquieu's executive—the "monarch"—was empowered to act with discretion during emergencies, even if the legislature did not specifically recognize the actions taken. Montesquieu therefore advocated a strong executive, independent of direct pressures from the "popular will," and capable of acting with force and discretion.

The writings of Locke and Montesquieu influenced the development of the ideas of the American Framers, who sought to construct a vigorous executive within a framework of republican liberty. In the celebrated *Federalist* papers, "Publius" cited Montesquieu's insights on the separation of powers doctrine. A number of references in the *Federalist* exhibit Publius's understanding that the president must have a realm of discretionary authority, especially in foreign policy-making. Alexander Hamilton's *Federalist 70* provides a strong defense of the executive secrecy and prerogative concepts: "Decision, activity, secrecy and despatch will generally characterize the proceedings of one man in a much more eminent degree than the proceedings of any great number; and in proportion as the number is increased, these qualities will be diminished."

In *Federalist 64*, John Jay observed that "secrecy" and "despatch" were inherent in the executive, and that successful diplomatic negotiations cannot be undertaken by a numerous assembly. Jay noted that presidential secrecy may be necessary to the treaty-making process:

There are cases where the most useful intelligence may be obtained, if the persons possessing it can be relieved from the apprehensions of discovery. . . . Although the President must in forming them [treaties] act by the advice and consent of the Senate, yet he will be able to manage the business of intelligence in such a manner as prudence may suggest. So often and so essentially have we suffered from the want of secrecy and despatch, that the Constitution would have been inexcusably defective if no attention had been paid to those objects.

It is clear that the American Framers, following Locke and Montesquieu, advocated a dominant role for the executive in foreign affairs, and in so doing they recognized the prerogative of the president to withhold information from Congress, the courts, and the public. The Framers recognized that presidential discretion was limited, and that through the separation of governmental branches, the potential abuse of executive powers could best be checked. In the writings of Locke, Montesquieu, and the American Framers, we find that executive prerogative should be exercised under unusual circumstances, such as an impending threat to the national security. These thinkers did *not* recognize an unqualified, limitless executive prerogative power.

Historical Roots

Discerning the Framers' views on executive secrecy requires more than just reviewing their writings. We can learn much about the Framers' intentions by assessing their actions.

It is significant that the Constitutional Convention was conducted in secret.[21] The debates of the convention were not officially recorded. The official journal of the convention listed only formal motions and roll-call votes by state. The journal was made available only to the Convention delegates, who believed that secrecy was necessary to protect the proceedings of the convention from external pressures. James Madison recalled, "No Constitution would ever have been adopted by the Convention if the debates had been public."[22] Daniel Hoffman summed up the views of the convention delegates:

Few thoughtful observers . . . would have endorsed the radical claim that secrecy is an unqualified evil. Where national security was involved, in particular, most men were ready to grant that secrecy was often necessary. . . . [The] most ardent devotees of popular sovereignty accepted this fact reluctantly.[23]

The historical roots of executive privilege can also be traced to governmental decision making in the early republic. The frequent exercise of the privilege by our early presidents established the precedent for numerous historical claims of executive privilege up to the modern era. I shall not list the early uses of the privilege because that has been done elsewhere and would require a degree of attention beyond the size and scope of this chapter.[24] The events surrounding the St. Clair incident, the Jay Treaty, and the Burr conspiracy are very well documented. The importance of these incidents is that they reveal the acceptance of the legitimacy of executive withholding of information by our early presidents (George Washington, John Adams, and Thomas Jefferson). In House debates over executive refusal to disclose documents to Congress pertaining to the Jay Treaty, for example, our chief constitutional architect, Representative James Madison, proclaimed that "the Executive had a right, under a due responsibility, also, to withhold information, when of a nature that did not permit a disclosure of it at the time."[25]

Our early presidents asserted the right to withhold information very cautiously. Each expressed some reservation about such presidential authority, yet recognized the need for executive branch secrecy under certain vital circumstances (namely, to protect executive branch deliberations, to enhance treaty negotiations, and to protect national security). Most important, Congress exhibited a degree of deference to executive claims of such authority, indicating that the legislative branch also accepted the legitimacy of executive branch secrecy under certain conditions.[26] Throughout history Congress has deferred to claims of executive withholding of information under the following circumstances: (1) when national security and foreign affairs crises are involved and (2) when the president has demonstrated that public disclosure of information would damage the candid nature with which deliberations are carried on within the executive branch.[27] This is not to suggest that all presidents have exercised such authority judiciously. Rather, there are clearly established precedents that lend credence to the legitimacy of executive privilege.

Legal Bases

We have seen that the Founders recognized that the president is much more capable than Congress to act with unity, secrecy, "despatch," and resolve. The chief executive's preeminence in national security and foreign policy making has also been recognized by the judiciary on a number of occasions.[28]

Foreign policy has often been conducted according to less democratic principles than domestic policy making. Justice George Sutherland gave credibility to this distinction in *U.S. v. Curtiss-Wright Corporation*.[29] He noted that it is important to "consider the differences between the powers of the federal government in respect of foreign or external affairs and those in respect of domestic or internal affairs. That there are differences between them, and that these differences are fundamental, may not be doubted."[30] The Court clearly recognized the notion that the chief executive has a "discretion" in foreign affairs to act beyond what the realm of the law allows.[31]

Perhaps the Court's strongest defense of executive withholding of national security information is found in *U.S. v. Reynolds*: "It may be possible to satisfy the Court, from all the circumstances of the case, that there is a reasonable danger that compulsion of the evidence will expose military matters that, in the interest of national security, should not be divulged."[32] With regard to sensitive national security information, therefore, the Court believed that it was truly necessary that such information not be disseminated publicly.[33]

The most relevant case for this analysis here is, of course, *U.S. v. Nixon*. The unanimous decision of the Court in the *Nixon* case affirmed the legitimacy of executive privilege as it is implied in the Constitution. The Court decided as well that executive privilege is not an absolute presidential power. Rather, the specific circumstances surrounding any claim of executive privilege must be considered. The Court also affirmed the jurisdiction of the judiciary to resolve disputes between the political branches over executive privilege. Finally, the Court declared that in resolving such controversies it shall use a balancing test, weighing the public interest aspect of executive privilege and the public's "right to know."[34]

THE SCOPE AND LIMITS OF EXECUTIVE PRIVILEGE

President Nixon's legacy to the executive privilege controversy has been, in part, to contribute to the polarization of this debate into two extreme positions: (1) that of the modern-day Whigs, such as Raoul Berger, who, based on a narrow and legalistic view of the Constitution, claim executive privilege has no foundation in our governmental system, and (2) that of the presidential supremacists, such as former president Richard Nixon and his defenders, who claim the executive privilege is an absolute presidential prerogative.

In this paper I have argued that both these positions are problematic. There is considerable precedent in political thought, action, and constitutional history to legitimize executive privilege. Likewise, there is little basis for the belief that executive privilege is an unqualified, unlimited presidential power. The major debate, therefore, should not be over the legitimacy of executive privilege. Rather, scholars should concern themselves with the question of where to draw the line between acceptable and unacceptable claims of privilege. Reasonable people will, of course, disagree as to where the line should be drawn.

My view is that the Framers' conception of separation of powers provided a timeless remedy to the problem of executive branch secrecy. The resolution of the controversy over President Nixon's overly broad claims of executive privilege is instructive of this point. A solution true to the Framers' intent is to encourage Congress and the courts to make prudent use of their institutional powers to encourage executive disclosure of information. The separation of powers doctrine therefore provides the vital mechanism by which the other coequal branches can challenge claims of executive privilege.

For example, if members of Congress demand the disclosure of executive information and the president refuses, Congress may retaliate by withholding support for the administration's policies. Congress may also choose to withhold appropriations for administration-favored programs. This gives the president the option to weigh the importance of privileged material against the prospect of legislative stalemate. As Gary Schmitt observed, the "solution to executive excess is not elimination of the power from which that excess may come but rather the vigorous use by Congress of those tools it has at its disposal."[35]

In extreme cases, Congress may threaten to assert its impeachment power. The president then must weigh the importance of maintaining secrets against the possibility of impeachment proceedings. Most likely, presidents will make accommodations to congressional requests rather than withstand increased pressure from the legislature.

The separation of powers doctrine also encourages mutual accommodation and compromise to overcome any stalemate precipitated by executive branch secrecy. For example, the president may choose to divulge sensitive information to a few highly respected members of Congress. Ideally, the president will be candid with these individuals and, likewise, these legislators will not abuse their trust by divulging any of the information for policy or partisan reasons. For example, regarding treaty negotiations, Chief Justice William Rehnquist noted that "frequently the problem of overly broad public dissemination of such negotiations can be solved by testimony in executive session, which informs the members of the committee of Congress without making the same information prematurely available throughout the world."[36]

The role of the judiciary in resolving controversies over executive branch secrecy is important as well. The Supreme Court affirmed in *U.S. v. Nixon* that the separation of powers doctrine does not guarantee an "absolute, unqualified presidential privilege of immunity from judicial process under all circumstances."[37] In this contest of governmental powers, the Supreme Court asserted the legitimacy of the judiciary to pose as a viable check on abuses of executive branch powers.

As noted at the introduction, the temptation to impose strict boundaries on the realm of the president's privilege power should be resisted. However, to help this debate rise above the notion that the only resolution available is found in what the separate branches may permit under particular circumstances, I propose that executive privilege be granted legitimacy by the other branches under four general conditions: (1) those protecting national security, (2) those protecting the confidentiality of White House deliberations, (3) those protecting the personal privacy of executive branch officials, and (4) those protecting the enforcement of criminal justice.

These categories are intended only as a set of general guidelines to move away from the Nixonian conception of executive privilege as an unlimited presidential power used for purposes of political convenience. These guidelines also reject the view of those opponents of executive privilege, who believe that the only way to overcome the potential abuse of power is to strip away power altogether.[38]

NOTES

1. See, for example, Raoul Berger, "The Incarnation of Executive Privilege," *UCLA Law Review* 22 (October 1974): 4–29.

2. Raoul Berger, *Executive Privilege: A Constitutional Myth* (New York: Bantam Books, 1975).

3. Gary Schmitt, "Executive Privilege," in *The Presidency in the Constitutional Order*, ed. Joseph Bessette and Jeffrey Tulis (Baton Rouge: Louisiana State University Press, 1981), p. 160.

4. Norman Dorsen and John H. F. Shattuck, "Executive Privilege, the Congress and the Courts," reprinted in U.S. Congress, Senate, *Executive Privilege, Secrecy in Government, Freedom of Information, Hearings Before the Subcommittee on Intergovernmental Relations of the Committee on Government Operations and the Subcommittees on Separation of Powers and Administrative Practice and Procedure of the Committee on the Judiciary*, 93rd Congress, 1st Sess., April 10–12, May 8–10, 16, and June 7, 8, 11, and 16, 1973, Vol. 3, p. 155.

5. U.S. Congress, House of Representatives, *Availability of Information to Congress*,

Hearings Before a Subcommittee of the Committee on Government Operations, 93rd Congress, 1st Sess., April 3, 4, and 19, 1973, p. 308.

6. *U.S. v. Nixon*, 94 S.Ct. 3090 (1974) at 60–61. Quoted in U.S. Senate, *Executive Privilege—Secrecy in Government, Hearings Before the Subcommittee on Intergovernmental Relations of the Committee on Government Operations*, 94th Congress, 1st Sess., September 29 and October 23, 1975, p. 598.

7. "Nixon: A President May Violate the Law," *U.S. News and World Report*, May 30, 1977, p. 65.

8. Ibid.

9. Ibid.

10. Brief of Richard M. Nixon in Opposition to Plaintiffs' Motion for Summary Judgment, *Senate Select Committee on Presidential Campaign Activities v. Nixon*, 366 F. Supp. 51 (D.D.C. 1973), p. 16. During the conference panel discussing the Nixon legacy, John Ehrlichman characterized my description of Nixon's conception of an absolute privilege power as "historically inaccurate." According to Ehrlichman, I argued that Nixon did not believe that claims of executive privilege are ever subject to review. Ehrlichman explained that the Nixon White House had an internal review process for examining each instance in which executive privilege might be asserted. Ehrlichman misunderstood my argument. My point was that, according to Nixon, presidential claims of privilege are never subject to review *by another branch of government*. Nixon's own words and actions are sufficient to substantiate my argument.

11. U.S. Congress, House of Representatives, *Availability of Information to Congress, Hearings Before a Subcommittee of the Committee on Government Operations*, 93rd Congress, 1st Sess., April 3, 4, and 19, 1973, p. 308.

12. Dorsen and Shattuck, "Executive Privilege, the Congress, and the Courts," pp. 158–159.

13. U.S. Congress, House of Representatives, *Availability of Information to Congress, Hearings Before a Subcommittee of the Committee on Government Operations*, 93rd Congress, 1st Sess., April 3, 4, and 19, 1973, p. 1.

14. Raoul Berger, *Executive Privilege: A Constitutional Myth* (New York: Bantam Books, 1975), especially chapter 1.

15. Gary Schmitt, "Executive Privilege, the Congress, and the Courts" p. 157.

16. These views of Berger's are summarized from his work *Executive Privilege: A Constitutional Myth*; his statement before the Senate Subcommittee on Separation of Powers of the Committee on the Judiciary on July 28, 1971; and his article "The Incarnation of Executive Privilege," *UCLA Law Review* 22 (October 1974): 4–29.

17. John Locke, *Second Treatise of Government*, ch. 12, sections 143–148.

18. Ibid., sections 146–148.

19. Ibid., ch. 14, section 166.

20. Charles Louis Baron de Montesquieu, *Spirit of the Laws*, Book 2.

21. Raoul Berger argues that since Article I, Section 5(3), of the Constitution provides for legislative secrecy, and no such mention of secrecy is made in the executive articles, "the fact that the Convention deliberated in secret is therefore of no moment" (see Berger, "The Incarnation of Executive Privilege," pp. 15–16). The Supreme Court in *U.S. v. Nixon* drew on the fact that the convention was conducted in secret as evidence of the Framers' recognition of the need for secrecy in government.

22. Quoted in Daniel Hoffman, *Governmental Secrecy and the Founding Fathers* (Westport, Conn.: Greenwood Press, 1981), p. 21.

23. Ibid.

24. For a detailed discussion of the early use of the privilege, see U.S. Congress, Senate, *Hearings on S. 921 Before the Subcommittee on Constitutional Rights of the Committee on the Judiciary*, 85th Congress, 2nd Sess., 1958, pp. 33–146.

25. *Annals of Congress* (1796), p. 773.

26. Mark J. Rozell, "In Defense of Executive Privilege: Historic Developments and Modern Imperatives," *International Social Science Review* 59 (Spring 1984): 67–81.

27. Ibid.

28. *First National Bank v. Banco Nacional de Cuba*, 406 U.S. 759, at 765–767 (1972); *Haig v. Agee*, 453 U.S. 291 (1981); *Oetjen v. Central Leather Co.*, 246 U.S. 297 at 302 (1918); *U.S. v. Curtiss-Wright Corp.*, 299 U.S. 304 (1936); *U.S. v. Truong*, 629 F.2d 908 at 914 (1980).

29. 299 U.S. 304 (1936).

30. Ibid., at 305.

31. Ibid., at 307–308; see also *Zemel v. Rusk*, 381 U.S. 1 at 17 (1965).

32. 345 U.S. 1 at 10 (1952).

33. See also *Chicago & Southern Airlines v. Waterman Steamship Co.*, 33 U.S. 103 (1948).

34. *U.S. v. Nixon*, 418 U.S. 683 (1974).

35. Schmitt, "Executive Privilege," p. 179.

36. William Rehnquist, "Statement Before the Subcommittee on Separation of Powers of the Committee on the Judiciary," U.S. Congress, Senate, *Executive Privilege*, 92nd Congress, 1st Sess., August 4, 1971, pp. 431–432.

37. 94 S.Ct. at 3106–3107.

38. Ronald Ziegler's thoughtful comments during the panel discussion evidence the need for presidents and presidential advisers themselves to understand that they alone can foster an environment under which claims of executive privilege do not lead to conflict and stalemate between the political branches. To establish credibility, Ziegler asserted, a White House should never cloak embarrassing situations by asserting executive privilege; never knowingly mislead or lie; never "shoot from the hip"; never overreact to criticism since such a reaction will look negative and defensive; and most important, a president and his advisers must have a realistic view of how they are going to be perceived on the outside. I agree with Ziegler's comment that there need not be additional judicial or legislative action to define the scope and limits of executive privilege. This view is in opposition to the argument made by Tom Brokaw during our panel discussion that we need a statutory definition of executive privilege to resolve disputes quickly. The problem with implementing a statutory definition of executive privilege is that it is impossible to define precisely all the possible circumstances under which presidents may claim executive privilege. A statutory limitation may severely constrain a president's discretionary authority when it is needed most.

Moderator: Victor Navasky

I want to compliment the organizers of this conference on selecting as impartial moderator the editor of a left-wing radical rag. And to put on the panel as presumably impartial participants, among others, a network news anchorman and a former editor of one of our most distinguished newspapers. These guys always claim that they are impartial but in fact, at another time, on another panel, on another occasion, I would argue that they have what I would call the "ideology of the center." We are delighted also to have the spokesmen for the Nixon White House, but their problem, if I may say so as impartial moderator, is that at the time they misperceived and misrepresented the mainstream press as some sort of liberal conspiracy when in fact the media were "ideological centrists." So those of you who were at the last panel and heard the complaint that it was stacked because it had too many people from one side, consider this: You have here two alumni of the administration, you have two representatives of the ideology of the center, you have two academics who also present themselves as impartial, and then, because as moderator I am supposed to be impartial, I don't get a chance to tell you what's *really* going on—but forgive these immoderate remarks from your moderator.

Now I can think of no panel more relevant to the present circumstance than one on the subject of secrecy, the government, and the media. How much, if any, of secrecy, lies, and illegal actions revealed in the recently released Iran Contragate report are a legacy of our failure to address properly the pre-Reagan systematic breakdown associated with Watergate and Vietnam as an assault on constitutionalism? How much of what was stamped secret in the Nixon years— I could add, by the way, the Kennedy years and the Johnson years, but we happen to be talking about the Nixon years—could safely have been made public? Have we really accepted the idea that the less the public knows, the greater our national security? We hear much about the harm to our national security if certain information gets out. Forget that our supposed adversary, the U.S.S.R., like the National Security Agency, listens in on everything we say anyway. But what about the disasters that occur as the result of information kept from the public? What is the relationship between Richard Nixon's comment to David Frost, "If the president does it, it's not illegal," and Fawn Hall's reference to "higher law?" Is it, in retrospect, desirable or necessary for government officials to make statements which quickly become, if you'll forgive the expression, "no longer operative"? The papers this morning are sharply focused on the legacy of the Pentagon Papers and President Nixon's conception of executive privilege. These are important starting points for a serious probing of the larger issues posed for this panel.

I have cruelly requested our panelists that they try to restrict their summaries of the learned papers to ten minutes each. We then will move from the papers to the commentaries, and then we will see what happens. Our first paper* is going to be on secrecy and democracy, "Secrecy and Democracy: The Unresolved Legacy of the Pentagon Papers." And the author of this paper is John Kincaid, who is the director of research of the Advisory Commission on Intergovernmental Relations in Washington, D.C. Mr. Kincaid got his Ph.D. from Temple University, he has an M.A. in Urban Affairs from the University of Wisconsin, and he did additional study at the University of Michigan in Ann Arbor. And he has a list of publications that is more than I could carry to the platform, but it is very impressive. The second paper is called "President Nixon's Conception of Executive Privilege: Defining the Scope and Limits of Executive Branch Secrecy." Mark J. Rozell, who will deliver it, is a member of the Department of Political Science at Mary Washington College. He got his Ph.D. from the University of Virginia, and he got his M.A. from the University of Virginia in Public Administration. He too has won many academic awards, both at the University of Virginia and at Eisenhower College. He has had a distinguished academic career and list of publications.

Our commentators need little introduction from me; they are for the most part, I suspect, known to you. First we are going to hear from Tom Brokaw. Tom Brokaw, as you know, is the anchor of "NBC Nightly News," and he, during the period of 1973–76, was NBC News White House correspondent, and during that period he covered all important Watergate developments. He is only three years overdue with an article he has promised to *The Nation* magazine. Our second commentator will be Howard Simons, who was managing editor of *The Washington Post* for thirteen years; he was managing editor during the Watergate period. He became curator of the Nieman Foundation for Journalism at Harvard in 1984. And as was pointed out to me earlier, he is the only man in this room who knows the identity of Deep Throat. Gerald Warren is presently the editor of the *San Diego Union*. He graduated from the University of Nebraska in 1952 with a Bachelor of Arts degree and a major in journalism. From January of 1969 to August 1975 he was deputy press secretary to the president in the Nixon and Ford administrations. He became editor of the *San Diego Union* in September 1975. Ron Ziegler has been president of the National Association of Truck Stop Operators since November of 1980. He served as chief spokesman for President Nixon and the White House staff from 1969–74, and directed and administered a staff responsible for press core logistics and communications policy. He was a familiar figure on television during all of those years.

*Moderator Navasky's presentation preceded the Kincaid and Rozell papers at the conference.

Discussant: Tom Brokaw

I want to make a couple of clarifications at the outset. One of the reasons that Victor Navasky is so pleased to be here this afternoon, to have this as his audience, is because the attendance here today exceeds the circulation of *The Nation* by a factor of two. And the reason that I'm three years overdue on my promised piece to *The Nation* is because, in the words of our mutual friend Calvin Bud Trillin, "Mr. Navasky pays for a piece in his magazine, a fee somewhere in the upper two figures."

I have already learned a great deal here this afternoon, especially from our distinguished professors, but also from Jerry Warren. I, with some regularity when we would travel, would take Jerry out for dinner and ply him with martinis all evening long and always would go home terribly impressed at how he had not given up anything. It wasn't until today that I realize he didn't know anything that he could give up. The gentleman at the outset of this session, who raised the eighteen and a half minutes, brought back to my mind and to Ron's, I think, at least one memorable day in the White House press room. We had just been, I think, about four days before, on a tour of the South. President of the United States Richard Nixon had assembled Southern governors and told them there would be no more bombshells. About thirty-six hours later, Ron called me into his office with a few of my colleagues, and he said, "I am not quite sure I know how to explain this, but there are eighteen and a half minutes missing from the tape here." So we learned very early on that when they said there were no more bombshells, that meant that the heavy artillery was just getting ready to fall at the White House in those days.

I'd like to talk first about secrecy in government. I do think that it is worth remembering that two hundred years ago, when the Founding Fathers gathered in Philadelphia to formulate that remarkable document, the U.S. Constitution, they did so in great secrecy. They sealed the windows and pulled the shades. It must have been terribly uncomfortable in there, but they felt it imperative that, if they were to resolve all of the differences in this fledging nation on that occasion, they had to do so in secrecy. I have to come to wonder, Howard [Simons], what might have happened if the current press corps, in its current makeup, had been in Philadelphia that summer. Think about it. James Madison nearly suffocating in that hall, taking those notes in that tiny handwriting, finally deciding that he needs a breath of fresh air. So, late in the afternoon, he leaves Constitution Hall to go for a walk through the streets of Philadelphia and he runs smack into Helen Thomas and Sam Donaldson. They're badgering him all the way down the street. "Well, what's going on in there, Mr. Madison? Don't you have enough faith in the American people to tell them what you're doing in their behalf? We hear that you're creating a monarchy and that you're going to control most of the money in the country. . . . " I can just see that going on.

I'm frankly very grateful that the Framers did that in secrecy, and that Sam and Helen weren't around. We wouldn't have a First Amendment today. I'm absolutely persuaded.

Secrecy in government. It's like beauty and the beast. It's in the eyes of the beholder, very often. The Pentagon Papers and the other cases of secrecy in the Richard Nixon administration it seems to me are the direct result of Richard Nixon's attitude that nothing the president could do would be illegal. Moreover, this compulsion of secrecy in that administration, I am persuaded, was in large part the by-product of an attitude on the part of the president and Henry Kissinger that they knew best. The exercise of power and authority, after all, is worth remembering in seminars like this and in our review of the history of those years, and recall that President Nixon and Henry Kissinger kept secrets from the secretary of state within the administration. Classified documents and privileged information in any administration, this one, the Carter Administration, Lyndon Johnson, and John Kennedy before it, are the coin of the realm for people who are in power in Washington. They spend it selectively. They spend it in Congress to win appropriations. They spend it with the press to win public favor. They spend it in the corridors, really to win internal struggles.

Yes, there are occasions when secrecy is required on the part of the government, when there are documents that should be classified and limited to only a few authorized, select officials for review. We've had any number of examples of this need for secrecy recently in our lives. The day that the Libyan bombing attack took place is one. Any number of American news agencies were aware by deductive reasoning, based on the information that we had been able to develop that day, that if one of the U.S. planes had left its base in Great Britain, that if our carrier task force was steaming south in the Mediterranean, given the fore-warnings that we had received in the highest levels of the Pentagon and in the Middle East, the attack on Libya was imminent. Yet no one went on the air or published that beforehand. It is an interesting discussion within journalistic seminars about whether that was an appropriate thing to do. Did it occur during the Jimmy Carter Administration while the American hostages were being held in Iran? Richard Valeriani of NBC News learned in December that a group of Americans had escaped the embassy in the initial confusion and that they were being held at the Canadian embassy in Tehran, and yet Dick Valeriani did not disclose that information. We had a series of exchanges with the secretary of defense and the director of the Central Intelligence Agency when the first military payload went up in the space shuttle system. We delayed broadcast twenty-four hours at NBC News based on their arguments. It turns out that at least two technical publications had described in much greater detail than what we knew the week before what in fact was in the space shuttle.

We have dealt with secrecy; we will deal with it again. I think that it requires a vigorous discussion between the press and those people who are in executive power and in the Congress of the United States. I believe, as well, that it is useful to reflect on what Mr. Kincaid said in his paper that release of the Pentagon

Papers also diminished the ability of presidents to conduct foreign policy with secrecy and dispatch, relatively free from the usual political restraints on presidential behavior in domestic fields.

Now, in this country we are bound up in the Iran-Contra affair. It was a secret operation that went on for almost two years in a wide-ranging fashion in Central America and in the Middle East, without any congressional oversight. I believe, and I believe that the American public believes, that this administration paid a terrible price for that secrecy and deception. Jerry said he was troubled by the release of massive amounts of classified information; I'm just as troubled by the classification of massive amounts of government papers. It is also worth remembering, as Mr. Kincaid has written, that subsequently, officials of the Nixon Administration, including Dr. Kissinger, acknowledged that publication of the Pentagon Papers did no noticeable harm to the United States and gave no noticeable aid to the enemies (with whom the United States was not officially at war). Furthermore, from the very beginning in the White House debate over how to handle the publication of the Pentagon Papers, there was serious consideration given to declassifying them on the spot. There are carloads of classified papers throughout Washington, even as we sit here today, that need not be classified. They're there because they protect the position of the people who are making decisions which may or may not be in your best interest.

Let me talk briefly about executive privilege and my experience with it as a journalist covering the Nixon White House. I have a trivia question for you here this afternoon. Many of you no doubt will remember that celebrated Houston news conference; it was the last public news conference of President Nixon while he was in office. Dan Rather and the president had a memorable exchange, "Are you running for something Mr. Rather?" the president asked. "No sir, are you?" Who asked the succeeding questions? Well, I did. It's lost in the backwash of history. I'll tell you something interesting about that. I had been intrigued by the question of executive privilege as claimed by the president at that time and how it may apply to a chief executive who was the subject of impeachment proceedings. I'd worked very hard in the days leading up to Houston. I talked to the leading constitutional authorities on that very point. I asked them if they could help me with research, and this included conservative, liberal, and moderate constitutional scholars, about claiming executive privilege, including the case of Madison and Jackson. The research came back that all of them claimed executive privilege, but uniformly with the caveat: except in criminal proceedings or in impeachment. That night, after the exchange with Dan Rather, as I was the last questioner on the panel, I asked Mr. Nixon if he had been historically inaccurate or misleading. He acknowledged the soundness in my research but he stuck by his original position.

What really always amused me about the Nixon doctrine of executive privilege was that it was applied selectively. Dealing with the Judiciary Committee, it was absolute, except when the White House felt it would gain advantage by making a conspicuous display of cooperation by shipping a truckload of expurgated transcripts to the Hill. Were they "green binders"? Jerry, I remember you being outside the West Wing of the White House and summoning the reporters that day so that they could see into the trunk of the car. There were about forty of them. It made it look like it was a large shipment of transcripts going to Capitol Hill, when in fact there were about four pages in each binder. They filled up the entire trunk of the car; each binder was on a specific point, and believe me it was a very specific point. The White House was attempting, obviously, to make the best impression that they could on the evening news that night. Moreover, some of you may also recall that they decided that John Stennis might be the lone legislative exception to the right of executive privilege by giving him permission then to listen to some of the tapes and offer his interpretation and then his judgment as to whether they were right or wrong. Executive privilege, it seems to me, does have its applications.

I do believe there are times when the president of the United States ought to be able to protect matters of national security, especially involving military operations. I think there ought to be exchanges that he can have with his advisers that should be privileged, and that there are individuals who work in any given administration whose privacy should be protected as well. But as we learned in the Iran-Contra affair, the definition of national security and the need for security is not an airtight proposition. That was, by any reasonable interpretation, a perilous undertaking in which it seems to me the risks outweighed the reward by any conceivable standard of measurement. I believe that the reporting procedures must be tightened. I think that the current recommendations on the Joint Committee of the Iran-Contra affair make some salient points when they say there ought to be a single committee on the Hill made up of a smaller group of people. The fact of the matter is that there is a good deal of leakage there, but, in fairness to those people who serve in Congress, there is a great deal more leakage in almost every agency of the executive branch of government, and that includes the White House. It's done with more sophistication because they are the people who are in control of the information, and they do it selectively. I believe as well, however, that when it comes to executive privilege, there should be some kind of statutory definition of it; how and when it applies ought to be determined by law. Most importantly, there must be a mechanism for a speedy resolution of a conflict on the use of executive privilege.

Let me just leave you with this thought. I believe that during the days of Watergate, the White House press corps erred on the side of caution. We knew what was at stake, and we were talking not just about the historic fate of one man, but about the great office, the engine, of the federal system of government in this country, the presidency. The republic was at stake. When information came to us, it was very carefully checked, and sifted again, and again, and again. Tested not just for its accuracy, but for its relevance as well. It was too easy in those closing days of the Nixon years to be able to pick up information from people who were attempting in a cheap way to make their own mark in that great scandal. I think that the press ultimately acted responsibly, by and large. It is worth remembering that the American press is not in the business to foster anarchy. It is worth remembering that we are there on a daily basis, acting on behalf of the people to tell them what is being done in their name and about whom they have a right to know.

For two hundred years the system of the U.S. government has been the envy of the world really. The foundation of our system of government has been a free and vigorous exchange of information. We are strengthened by that free and vigorous exchange, not weakened by it. We are strengthened by knowing who is acting in our name and in what fashion. Finally, let me leave with something I stole from David Brinkley some years ago. I don't do a great Brinkley. But I think that it's important to have some of the candescence of Brinkley in this. He said, "It's worth remembering that there are many countries in the world where the politicians have seized the power, they've seized the power and muzzled the press. But so far there are no countries in the world where the press has seized the power and muzzled the politicians." Thank you all.

Discussant: Howard Simons

Thank you. I am the clean-up discussant. So I'm going to do just that and clean up. I don't know if Judge Wiggins is here, but I want him to know that Hauptmann is innocent; I am the Lindbergh baby. For those of you who were at the earlier meeting, I was the managing editor of *The Washington Post*, and Ben Bradlee was the executive editor. I met President Kennedy once in my life, and I've never met President Nixon. For Victor Navasky, everywhere I speak, particularly to groups of journalists or groups interested in journalism, I am asked three questions. Who is Deep Throat? What ever happened to Janet Cooke? (She is the young lady who made up the story about Jimmy the heroin addict, and we had to give back the Pulitzer Prize; we didn't deserve it for a made-up story.) The third pressing question in American journalism is, When are you going to invent an ink that doesn't come off on your hands? To Tom Brokaw, James Madison would have been the leaker. To my ex-colleague and friend, Jerry Warren, I think that respect for the White House will return when the White House shows some respect for people and law. As my friend and colleague Haynes Johnson put it recently, one administration had the arrogance of power and the present administration has the arrogance of popularity. To Ron Ziegler, on his six steps, I think we need only one, and that is to tell the truth.

Finally, I'd like to refer to something Judge Wiggins said that bothered me about "Where were you?" meaning the press. He also reminds me of a wonderful story told by a journalist, the late Peter Lisagor who was from Chicago. When Ron Nessen took over from Ron Ziegler, he made this wonderful speech saying that he wasn't going to do what Ron Ziegler did, how things have changed and how the White House would be different. Lisagor raised his hand and said, "Mr. Nessen, two Rons don't make a right."

In Mr. Kincaid's paper, he says about the Pentagon Papers, which I also was involved in at *The Post*, that first, President Nixon was not especially moved about the publication of the papers. Their contents, after all, dealt with policy-making prior to his own administration and were, therefore, likely to be embarrassing to the Democrats just before an election year. Henry Kissinger prevailed upon the president to do something about this massive hemorrhage of state secrets. The most delicious thought of all, and one that I've harbored from time to time, is that a temper tantrum by Henry Kissinger resulted in Watergate. That it, indeed, started a chain of events that led to the resignation of Mr. Nixon.

The Pentagon Papers were fascinating, but no one read them at the time. The side issue became the issue, and that was the papers—the newspapers, *The New York Times*, *The Washington Post*, the fight between them and the administration. To this day I don't know how many people have really read the Pentagon Papers. There weren't many secrets in them. The volumes that had something that might compromise security were left out by the newspapers.

I'd like to talk a bit about secrecy, because my experience in Washington over thirty years is that you can't work there or even live there without bumping into a secret. The overclassification system is so vast that everything is classified, and classified for many reasons. Very few secrets are classified because they are true secrets. Many more are classified to save embarrassment, high cost overrun, to protect someone's turf, to do lots of things. Indeed, another reason for classification is habit. It's easier just to stamp something secret than to argue whether it should or shouldn't be so stamped. My experience in Washington has been that most real, honest-to-God secrets walk out the door; they don't just show up in *The Washington Post* or *The New York Times*. It used to be, in the good old days, that the secrets were taken by people who had an ideology; they were pro-Russian, pro-Nazi, or pro–something else. Those days are gone; now it's just purely greed. People sell the secrets. Most of the important secrets that have been given away in the last ten years have all been for money only and have been the most important secrets, like the KH–11 spy satellites, or what the Walkers did to our submarine fleet.

I think I want to get to Watergate for just a moment, because there are three things about Watergate that are fascinating to me among the many unanswered questions. I would hope that young journalists would go back and revisit it. There are three things that still puzzle me, and I understand that Mr. Magruder may have answered one here yesterday. The three questions are first, Who is "Deep Throat?" It seems to me that unless Bob Woodward comes forward or "Deep Throat" comes forward, we may never know. Second, What was really on the eighteen and a half minutes? Unless somebody in the audience knows or Mr. Nixon, who knows, comes forward and tells us, we may never know. Finally, What were they doing in the Watergate? There's lots of speculation. I understand Mr. Magruder suggested it had to do with Kenny O'Donnell and Howard Hughes, and that's what the bug was planted for, and that's been an avenue of speculation for a long time. But nobody has really come forward and said this is it. So I think there are three primary questions, and as I've said, I would love to have Watergate revisited.

Finally, I have a crude measuring rod about the free press. It's that the freer the press, the freer the society. I go around the world with my little string for measuring, and find that arguably we have the freest press in the world. I think that is an essential part of democracy, and something that we ought to treasure. We may not be civil all the time, Jerry, and that's okay with me.

In the latter days of Watergate I had a pang of conscience that said to me that I know what the administration's up to. They've got a unique way to celebrate the Bicentennial: They are going to do away with the Bill of Rights. I think no paper is that good all the time or that bad all the time, but the press, good or bad, is the one ingredient that's an essential part of democracy, and we ought to all be grateful for the First Amendment.

Discussant: Gerald L. Warren

Thank you, Victor. For those of you who could remember Victor's introduction on me earlier in the day, you will note that I am perhaps the embodiment of the dichotomy the Founding Fathers had in mind when they set up this whole business of government and the press. I've been both a government official and a newspaper editor, which makes me doubly hard to believe. I've noticed that there's a certain discipline in sitting up here. I've been out in the audience for most of the panels throughout the week, and there's a discipline up here where you feel that you must listen to the academic papers being read, something that I hadn't felt before. But I appreciate very much having the chance to hear two such middle-of-the-road papers. I cannot speak to the learned dissertations of the fine legal points of secrecy. As a matter of fact, I'm the wrong person on the wrong panel, because if anyone thinks Jerry Warren knew any secrets to the Nixon Administration, then he hasn't talked to Tom Brokaw or any other White House correspondent of the era. If it was secret, it was generally kept secret from me as well. Ron Ziegler's dictum, and I'm sure he'll talk about this, was that what Warren doesn't know won't hurt me. And in most cases it worked, but not always.

The Pentagon Papers: I'm fascinated by that subject. I was not only nervous but aghast when the papers were published in *The New York Times*. Now, as an editor, to carry out the dichotomy, I'm delighted that they were published, because they established in law—and I do believe, Professor, that this is one concrete thing that came out of the Pentagon Papers—it established in the Supreme Court the case law that prior restraint was not allowed in our system. So in that regard, I'm delighted. I'm amused about the fact that the Nixon Administration, or the allegation that the Nixon Administration, wanted to create an official secrets act. There was no thought about that, that I know of, during the discussion about the Pentagon Papers; there were already laws on the books to keep things secret. That I believe is what the Nixon Administration was trying to invoke in the Pentagon Papers case. As a deputy press secretary, as I've indicated, I hated leaks; as an editor, I looked forward to them. They are obviously titillating, but one of the reasons I hated them was that nobody would admit who leaked what to whom, and you could get absolutely no guidance on this leak, which Tom would have had on his show or one of the others might have had.

I'm also amused as I watched a sequence of White Houses continue to make the same mistakes that the Nixon White House made. Why they cannot learn from our mistakes, I don't know. I'm reminded of a White House chief of staff seminar, a symposium we had at the University of California in San Diego, in January 1986, last year. It was a wonderful seminar; Bob Haldeman was there, and he talked about the system of the Nixon White House and how it worked, and how in the last analysis it failed in the most serious crisis of the Nixon Administration. He was asked, if he had to do it all over again would he have done it differently? And his answer was "No." "In terms of the structure we set up to begin with I think we established a superb self-management system and structure, much of which still survives today. The thing I wished we had done was to have kept the system intact with the greatest crisis that hit us. Had we followed our system, we would have resolved the matter satisfactorily overall." And here he referred to his belief that it would have caused some suffering to some of the people involved, but that would have been necessary. He went on to say, "The fault is not that we had a bad system at all, in my opinion, it's true that we didn't use the system when we needed it most."

I believe that applies to White Houses of today. I believe where the Pentagon Papers were concerned, I still believe as an editor, even though they make great stories, that the massive unauthorized release of government papers is very troubling. It troubled me then, and it troubles me now. When I think of the guarantees of our freedoms under the Bill of Rights, I believe that a democratic government has a very difficult time conducting its business in some sense of privacy. The Constitution may not specifically grant these executives the power to keep secrets, although there's certainly some argument on that and I would argue that. I believe that some secrecy is helpful in the formulation of public policy, and the most troubling leaks of all are those leaks that Henry Kissinger talked about the other evening, of position papers, which lead up to the formulation of policy. When I left newspapering for government, I did not renounce my principles and my sense of ethics. When I returned to journalism as an editor after leaving the White House, I did not renounce my dedication to orderly government and my yearning for that orderly government, nor did I renounce my citizenship, which I believe carries with it the full faith in our form of government and a concomitant hope that it will succeed. That probably differentiates me from some newsmen you've talked to, but I really believe that. And for that reason, I support executive privilege when it's used in a balanced way. I'm not going to argue with the paper we've just heard. Obviously, the executive privilege power is being narrowed by the courts and by the legislatures as being discussed. I agree somewhat with the four points that Professor Rozell presented, but I think they were a bit too sharp in most cases. When I was in government, it was my job to keep secrets, whatever secrets they allowed me to have, and now as an editor, it's my job to find those secrets out.

I can think of maybe two secrets that I knew about in the six and a half years that I was at the White House. The first one, and the most interesting one, was the time that Henry Kissinger came down with a stomach ache in Pakistan. And a notice came out of Washington indicating how he failed to complete his schedule that day. We were at San Clemente and Al Haig called me in since Ron Ziegler was on another mission. I asked him about this, and he said, "I can't tell you anymore than you know right there, than you've seen right there. But let me tell you this, you're walking on eggs out there"—which was to tell me that I shouldn't say anything, I guess. He said just to rely on the statement from Islamabad and I would be all right. Well, I did that. And it was another case of stonewalling, I suppose, but it worked. There was no suspicion that the reason that Henry Kissinger had gastritis, or whatever it was (if he did) was that he had gotten out of Pakistan and flown to Beijing to set up the president's visit. This was the summer of 1971 and he came back and announced to the press corps at San Clemente. It was a complete surprise to the U.S. press corps, including the White House press corps. But I remember a week earlier, less than a week earlier, we'd stopped in Kansas City, Missouri, on the way to San Clemente and the president spoke to a domestic briefing, and he turned his remarks into a famous Nixon tour de horizon on the geopolitical system in the world. In hindsight, from what he said in the opening remarks, we should have realized that he was aiming toward China. However, Jim Deacon, who was a very veteran White House correspondent, left that briefing, slammed his notebook down and said, "That's the worst speech I've ever heard a president give." Even though he'd been in the White House a very long time, he had missed it entirely. There was definitely a tip-off in there that he was going to China and what he had hoped to do. Those listening back in the State Department detected a change in formulation. When we got back to San Clemente, the switchboard lit up with all the Asian and commonwealth reporters who wanted to come to San Clemente, those who rarely did. So they detected something, but our White House didn't.

The other secret I can remember is the December 1972 bombing of Hanoi, when the president was in Camp David, and Bob Haldeman, John Ehrlichman, Henry Kissinger, and Ron Ziegler were all on special assignment to Palm Springs, and Al Haig was in Saigon trying to talk President Thieu into this. I was called into the National Security Council (NSC) office by Colonel Dick Kennedy, and he told me that I was to call in a special group on Saturday, and that I would announce the end of the bombing in Hanoi and the fact that Henry Kissinger was going back to Paris to resume the broken talks with Le Duc Tho. Well, I was atingle of course, and that afternoon we flew up to Camp David and talked to the president about it, going through some questions and answers. I thought, well, here we are, a colonel and a deputy press secretary running the government. I was just a little bit nervous about that, even today. But it worked. That night I went to dinner at a friend's birthday party dinner at the Madison and I sat next to an official from the Soviet embassy. I had called a briefing and it went out on the wire. Everybody gets the wire, and everybody at the White House staff was somewhat nervous about it. It was unusual, but they said if Warren's going to do it, it can't be too important.

So they went home and didn't think about it. The only speculation was that there would be a cessation of hostilities during Tet. That happened before, and it's pretty good speculation. At the dinner that evening in a private room at the Madison, this Soviet counselor turned to me and says, "I know what you're going to announce tomorrow." He probably did, I thought to myself. I was scared to death. I quickly left that dinner, and went home and was nervous about it. Obviously, he didn't know, or thankfully, he didn't know, and he did think it was going to be a cessation of hostilities for Tet. Well, that's a diversion. Those are the two secrets I can tell you about, the only ones that I remember.

Also, in the chiefs of staff symposium, Don Rumsfeld quoted Winston Churchill, talking about the Normandy invasion, and I think that is appropriate here. Don said, "Sometimes the truth is so precious that it must be accompanied by a bodyguard of lies." Well, we could argue that, and I think I would argue that. But I am sure that the nation was well served by having the time to conduct this diplomacy after these two decisions were taken—the decision to send Henry to Beijing and the decision to send Henry to Paris to talk to Le Duc Tho. It was orderly to have that secret so that the diplomacy could continue. So perhaps that's one of the belligerent secrets that were held during the Nixon Administration.

I'm going to close by giving you my hope that at least two things have come out of this splendid conference. One, I think this conference has proved that you can have a reevaluation of the Nixon Administration that is neither a whitewash nor so blindly acrimonious as to render it meaningless. Also, I believe and hope that the students who attended this conference, the next generation of scholars, will see the President's Men in a more objective light. They will see that these men did not enter a government with the sole aim of obstructing justice and committing other felonies, that they are intelligent, thoughtful, patriotic persons who have made mistakes. I also hope, but I have no optimism about this; I would like to think that perhaps some of the present generation of scholars might think the same thing. However, I'm not very optimistic about that. I would hope the main benefit to come out of this conference would be a sense of civility in the examination of the Nixon years. I would hope that the Nixon years could be examined, as I've heard some historians talk about it during the conference, in a less than passionate way. I would hope also that civility somehow, sometime, could come into the White House briefing room; and that there would be normal, civil relations between the president and the press, and between the people and our government, because I firmly believe that we will continue to sputter and lose our way unless we can find that respect for orderly government and for our leaders that they deserve. Thank you so much.

Discussant: Ronald L. Ziegler

I think it has been pointed out that the issue of secrecy in government has been an issue that has confronted this country from the outset of our republic, particularly since World War II, and it did not necessarily begin with the Pentagon Papers, nor has it ended with the Pentagon Papers. Let me talk briefly about the Pentagon Papers. It was the day after Trisha Nixon was married to Ed Cox in June 1971, when *The New York Times* ran on the front page the fact that it was going to publish from the archives extensive volumes of decades of progressive involvement of the United States in Vietnam. At that time we in the government, we in the White House, had absolutely no idea what was contained in this material. In fact, we did not know that the vast majority of this material was classified "Secret" or "Top Secret." We did not at first feel that action was required. In fact, President Nixon points out in his memoirs that he felt that politically we should move ahead without any action on the Pentagon Papers, because, in fact, they traced involvement in Vietnam on the part of the Kennedy and Johnson administrations and this could have been a political advantage to the Nixon Administration.

However, as President Nixon points out, from the standpoint of policy, the issue focused on protecting national security interests. Now it's sometimes overlooked that we did not know what was in the Pentagon Papers, but we had people within the government, Henry Kissinger being one of them, who cautioned President Nixon in the most extreme terms, most severe terms, that the publication of the Pentagon Papers, the publication of these secret documents, could, in fact, break codes, reveal clandestine sources, and have a severe and negative impact on the national security of the United States. So President Nixon's decision to move to prior restraint had the purpose of giving the government an opportunity to evaluate the impact of those papers. The purpose was not to restrain the press, the objectives were not antipress; the dilemma that President Nixon faced is what we're talking about, secrecy in government. Where do you draw the line between the protection of national interests and national security and the public's right to know in our democracy? It was felt for national security purposes that we had to move ahead. I believe that as distinguished as the presented papers have been, the point is stretched in both Mr. Rozell and Mr. Kincaid's papers as to the purpose of our actions, the purpose of the president's actions. Prior restraint was seriously considered and the impact of prior restraint was seriously considered before the decision was made.

I'd like to cover one additional point and make an additional comment regarding John Kincaid's paper. Mr. Ellsberg and Mr. Russo were indicted. The question was, even after the papers were published, what does one do, what does a government do, when documents are stolen and released illegally to the public. It's not a new issue, and it's not an issue that ended with the Pentagon

Papers. Teddy White pointed out that in his view clearly Mr. Ellsberg stole papers and acted against the national defense of the United States. I agree with Teddy White; Mr. Kincaid does not. I was surprised that it was not pointed out in the papers the fact that we as a country have a very important court case pending before the Fourth Circuit Court relating to the 1979 Espionage Act. That case is the case of Sam Morrison. Sam Morrison was, as many of you know, an employee of the Pentagon with "Top Secret" clearance. Sam Morrison was also a stringer reporter for *Jane's Naval Review*. In 1984 Sam Morrison picked off the desk of a colleague "Top Secret" photographs taken by our satellites of Soviet submarines under construction, and he sent them to *Jane's Naval Review*. In 1985 the federal government sought and received an indictment to prosecute Sam Morrison under the 1979 Espionage Act. Mr. Morrison was convicted by a jury trial. In this case, the government did not move to prove the intent, the intent that Mr. Morrison had to do harm to the United States government. It simply prosecuted and won its case without the proof of the intent. I would think that this would be a substantial concern. It is a substantial concern to me in terms of focusing on the issue. Is there, in fact, a difference between an individual like John Walker stealing material and supplying it to another government for eighteen years with clear intent to do harm to the United States and an individual working in government, who for political or for other motives (Morrison's motive is unclear) takes secret documents and leaks them to *Jane's Naval Review*, which the Associated Press picked up and which ultimately appeared in *The New York Times* and *The Washington Post*.

The issue does not stop with the Pentagon Papers. The Fourth Circuit decision, which is going to come down, I believe, after the first of the year, is a significant decision relevant to the question of prosecuting those who are in government and steal classified materials. We have gone through periods in this country of the extensive use of executive privilege. Historically, those of you who are studying history will recall John Moss, a Congressman from California, who in the early 1950s, when it was felt that there was extensive government secrecy on non–national security items, chaired the Subcommittee on Information Policy in the House of Representatives. At that time, the bureaucrats and the Truman and Eisenhower administrations were using executive privilege in refusing to submit materials asked for by the press and by the Congress. The John Moss committee also led to the 1967 passage of the Freedom of Information Act.

I believe that we have progressively, through the conflict of our democracy, tried in numerous ways to deal with this very complex issue of executive privilege and secrecy in government. Clearly, secrecy in government should be limited. President Nixon, as a matter of fact, felt that there was too much classification of government papers, and attempted to move with a study to limit the declassification. I believe that there should not be judiciary or legislative activity dealing with executive privilege. I think we have enough already. I believe in the *U.S. v. Nixon* case, which was referred to earlier, we brought executive privilege to the constitutional level under Article II. I do not favor any additional judicial or legislative activity regarding executive privilege. In my opinion, the issue of executive privilege is grounded in the attitude and credibility of the executive branch. I believe that the greater the credibility and the better the attitude on the part of government and federal officials in dealing with the release of public information, the more easily our public will be able to deal with the issue of executive privilege. I agree with the point of view that those who are elected and are pointed to positions of executive authority must recognize that government in a democracy cannot be wiser than the people. I believe that the attitude held by government in a democracy cannot be wiser than the people. I believe that the attitude held by government is extremely important in establishing credibility. The American people, in my opinion, must feel that they are receiving from their government in a credible fashion what they feel they should be receiving. And I believe that the establishment of credibility on the part of the government is relatively simple, relatively easy.

I believe that there are six basic, fundamental steps that a government can follow to establish credibility and therefore allow for greater ease and acceptance of executive privilege statements when they are applied for national security and legitimate purposes. First of all, government should not cloak embarrassing situations and conceal shortcomings by exerting executive privilege. It is rapidly found out and is rapidly understood by the public. I think that the spokesman and the United States should only and always, from the standpoint of establishing credibility, speak from a basis of fact. It should never shoot from the hip, and it should never assume the answers. I also feel that the president and the spokesman for the president should never knowingly mislead or lie. I think that history has already shown that democracy will not tolerate deception. I think we have seen that in the contemporary time since World War II. I also believe that the president and his spokesman should never overreact to criticism, and that they should never look at the press as their enemy because, if they do, then the press tends to react in a negative and defensive fashion. I also feel, finally, that a president and the administration must have a realistic view of how they are going to be perceived by the public and by the press. What is good for one individual is not good for the other. A firm and clear recognition of that perception is very important. So I think, in terms of executive privilege and secrecy in government, it goes beyond legalities, even though they're important; it goes beyond establishing in our democracy a set of rules. I believe it goes to attitude, I believe it goes to communications, and I believe that it goes fundamentally to the credibility of the presidency of the United States. A president has the responsibility to establish and maintain the credibility of his office.

Now, just to conclude, I have heard, and we have read, about the many faces and many personalities of President Nixon. I was one of the president's staff men who spent time with him when power passed, flying over Missouri on the way to San Clemente, in the self-imposed exile. I was with President Nixon for almost a year in San Clemente. Richard Nixon is an extremely complex individual. In the time that I dealt with him, in a period of over seven years, I

personally saw only one face of Richard Nixon—that of a very intent, complicated, complex individual who was constantly strategizing, constantly working
at his position as president and president-elect, and constantly reevaluating and
reassessing himself and his positions. One thing I saw in San Clemente, California, during the period shortly after the resignation and during the year that
he was there and I was there with him (he was there longer) was that President
Nixon fully and totally recognized the shortcomings of his administration. He
struggled in that evaluation, and he agonized about the dilemma he had placed
his men in. He saw the sacrifice that they had to make. I saw him go through
that struggle. I also saw a man with courage accept his shortcomings, accept his
failures, accept the disgrace that he received in resigning. He did not destroy
himself. I believe in his memoirs—and I believe those studying the presidency
should read Nixon's memoirs—he said that the period of his presidency, including the Vietnam War and Watergate, was a period of great division in the
country, a period of great controversy. There were excesses on the part of many
parties that will be judged by history, and, as he has pointed out, he is prepared
to live with that judgment. I believe he feels that way today.

Response: John Kincaid

There is time to respond only to several comments. For one, the U.S. Supreme Court did not declare prior restraint out of bounds in the American system. The Court ruled only that, in the Pentagon Papers case, the government had not demonstrated a compelling case for prior restraint. A number of justices held open the possibility of future prior restraint on the publication of national security information where the government might be able to make a compelling and lawfully based argument for such restraint.

A key question is: What laws apply in such situations as the publication of the Pentagon Papers? If the law were clear, then the Department of Justice might not have had so much difficulty prosecuting Ellsberg and Russo. It might even have been in a credible position to prosecute newspaper reporters and editors. The law is not at all clear on these matters. This is one reason why the Nixon Administration steered clear of any criminal charges against the press, and even of criminal charges against Ellsberg and Russo that would have implicated the press directly by covering Ellsberg's release of the papers to *The New York Times*.

The administration was willing to risk a courtroom clash with two unknown citizens over their late-night photocopying of the documents, but a courtroom clash with *The New York Times*, *The Washington Post*, and several hundred other newspapers over publications of the documents would have been political suicide for the administration. Even in regard to Ellsberg and Russo, the criminal case was so weak that the administration felt a need to burglarize the office of Ellsberg's psychiatrist to gather evidence for a smear campaign that would strengthen its hand by making Ellsberg look bad in the public eye and reduce him from the status of a middle-class hero of conscience to that of disturbed weirdo, if not a traitor.

What helped to propel the case along for the administration, the courts, the Congress, and even many members of the public was little more than the mystique of national security secrecy. Amazingly, some members of Congress refused to look at the Pentagon Papers when the documents were first made available to the Congress because they believed that they were not authorized to read them. Many people simply assumed that Ellsberg had broken the law. Even Ellsberg apparently assumed that he was violating a law when he gave the documents to *The New York Times*. What made the Pentagon Papers trial all the more bizarre, therefore, was the fact that Ellsberg and Russo were being tried, not for releasing the papers to the press or to the Congress, but merely for photocopying the documents.

Again, the point is that documents are classified "Secret," "Top Secret," and so on, by executive order, not statute. The question is, then, can a citizen be criminally prosecuted for violating the executive order? If the answer is yes, then we do not need the Congress to make law; the president can simply issue executive decrees—surely a more efficient process of law making.

The U.S. government has millions of rubber stamps with classification markings. Government employees routinely use these stamps to "classify" documents. The executive order specifies strict rules for classifying documents. The ostensible purpose of the rules is to limit classification to what is essential to national security. Yet government employees receive little or no training in how to apply the rules.

During the Pentagon Papers trial, Defense Department witnesses were asked what training they had received as to what they should classify and not classify. Most said that they had received no formal training. They simply had the rubber stamps on their desks and used them regularly because everyone else did so. One witness said that he had been shown a movie, the theme of which was, beware of good-looking women with blonde hair. Such was the extent of his training. The actual operating rule, therefore, is to classify unless a superior official says not to. It is better to risk an unlikely reprimand for classifying a document that requires no classification than to be reprimanded, demoted, or fired for not classifying a document.

Thus, in cases like the Pentagon Papers, a private citizen or a newspaper may be vulnerable to criminal prosecution for releasing information that has been improperly or even inadvertently marked "Top Secret" by some functionary. Meanwhile, the Nixon Administration was arguing that defendants should not be allowed by the courts to challenge the markings on the documents or require the government to prove that the documents were in fact classified properly in accordance with the executive order. By this logic, a citizen could, in principle, go to prison for fifty years for violating an executive order that has no statutory basis because he or she disclosed or discovered a document containing a "Top Secret" marking that was the result of a cleaning person accidentally dropping the rubber stamp on the document while dusting an official's desk.

This was the point I was making about the Nixon Administration's criminal code reforms. While the administration was pursuing its unorthodox prosecution of Ellsberg and Russo, it was trying to get the Congress to sanction such prosecutions by enacting the administration's criminal code proposals, which contained the same legal points as those raised in the Pentagon Papers trial. The administration would have gotten its cake and eaten it too, if it had won in both the courts and the Congress. Unfortunately, it got a pie in the face instead.

It is true that the administration did not propose an "official" Official Secrets Act. Together, however, its various criminal code reforms would have amounted to a de facto Official Secrets Act. For example, Nixon's proposals would have explicitly made government documents government property. Disclosure would be constituted the theft of government property. Improper classification would have been no defense against criminal charges. Furthermore, the Espionage Act's "intent to injure the U.S. or advantage a foreign nation" clause would have been changed to "prejudice the safety or interest of the United States."

Finally, Mr. Ziegler's point about the Samuel Loring Morrison case is well taken. That case is precisely the kind of legacy I was pointing to in my paper. I did not address the Morrison case because this is a conference about Richard M. Nixon, and my paper focused on the Pentagon Papers trial. I agree, though, that the Morrison trial raised most of the same knotty legal issues as those debated in the Pentagon Papers trial. However self-serving Morrison's behavior, his likely conviction will accomplish much of what President Nixon tried to accomplish in the Pentagon Papers trial.

Please note, moreover, that my seemingly absurd example of a person being convicted of theft or espionage simply for finding a "Top Secret" document and putting it in a closet at home has been made rather real by the Morrison case. Morrison was not only convicted for giving photographs to *Jane's Fighting Ships*; he was also convicted of theft and espionage for having two other navy documents in an envelope in his apartment.

The chickens hatched in the Pentagon Papers trial have come home to roost in the Morrison case. The press is now vulnerable to criminal prosecution, not only for publishing classified information without the express permission of the executive branch, but also for merely possessing it. Does this mean that a member of Congress might also be subject to prosecution for possessing classified information or leaking it to a reporter? What is also not clear is who in the executive branch can give permission to publish classified information.

Considering the totality of developments since 1971—including the absence of shield protections for reporters in federal cases, the use of lie detectors to ferret out leakers, judicial support for contracts of postemployment silence on the part of certain government officials, and court recognition of executive privilege—one sees a significant expansion of the authority of the president to keep secrets and to enforce secrecy with tools of criminal law. Thus, an administration that was overly preoccupied with secrecy in the pursuit of foreign policy goals that did not always enjoy full public support or understanding and a president who had long had a reputation for being less than trustworthy bequeathed to us a legacy of less, not more, openness in the conduct of democratic politics.

IMPEACHMENT PROCEEDINGS

8

The Nixon Impeachment and Abuse of Presidential Power

DAGMAR S. HAMILTON

The broadly political charges brought against Richard Nixon by the House Judiciary Committee under Article II of the 1974 impeachment proceedings are the most significant of all the impeachment charges against him (see chapter appendix).[1] This article received more votes from members of the House Judiciary Committee, both Democratic and Republican, than any other article.[2] Because it concentrates on the presidential duty to preserve the Constitution and to take care that the laws be faithfully executed, it is also the most important in terms of historic guidelines for future presidents.

In order to understand fully the importance of Article II, it is first necessary to distinguish the impeachment proceedings from the other events often associated with the process.

For many people, the terms Watergate, impeachment, and forced resignation are synonymous. Few recognize the differences between the Senate Select Committee under Sam Ervin, the Special Prosecutor's Staff under Archibald Cox, and the House Judiciary Committee under Peter Rodino. Although impeachment is the sole prerogative (constitutionally) of the House of Representatives,[3] and removal from office the sole prerogative of the Senate,[4] without the confluence of all these three—the Ervin Committee, the Cox/Leon Jaworski staff, and the House Judiciary Committee—it is less likely that Article II would ever have been drafted and unlikely that President Nixon would have resigned.

The Senate Select Committee, under Senator Sam Ervin, was set up primarily to investigate the suspicious circumstance related to the break-in of Democratic National Committee offices in the Watergate Building. Its mandate was perhaps political in the partisan sense, but its purpose was primarily to investigate President Nixon's actions related to Watergate, not those (as in Article II) more broadly related to the power of presidential office. The Ervin Committee is instead remembered principally for the testimony of John Dean concerning the presidential cover-up of the break-in; and for Alexander Butterfield's disclosure of the existence of Oval Office tapes.[5]

The Special Prosecutor's Office was created by the White House in order to quiet growing public criticism resulting from televised disclosures of the Ervin committee. It was originally headed by Archibald Cox and then by Leon Jaworski. The mandate of the Special Prosecutor's Office was to see if any federal crimes, as defined by federal criminal statutes and punishable only after trial in a federal court, had been committed. The primary concern was to determine whether the White House—or the president—had been involved in such violations of the law as breaking and entering, bribery (the hush money), and obstruction of justice. Significantly, the special prosecutor was looking only at possible crimes to prosecute, not the broader category of abuse of power.[6]

When President Nixon fired Archibald Cox, and Attorney General Elliot Richardson as well as Deputy Attorney General William Ruckelshaus resigned rather than carry out the firing, the public protest swelled to previously unimagined proportion. Members of Congress, particularly those in the House of Representatives, were deluged by mail following the firing of Cox, and calls for investigation and possible impeachment by the House began to be heard. Although few Representatives wanted to take on a popularly elected sitting president, constituent demand could not be overlooked. As a result, a special Impeachment Inquiry was voted by the full House, to be overseen by the House Judiciary Committee.[7] The role of the House Judiciary Committee was much broader than the other two investigative groups; impeachment is not as narrowly defined as a criminal investigation.

The House Judiciary Committee legal staff, hired especially for the Nixon investigation, looked at a very wide range of presidential actions. It produced, five months before the drafting of actual articles, a report published by the Judiciary Committee as *Constitutional Grounds for Presidential Impeachment*.[8] This report, referred to as familiarly as "the grounds memo," did not link allegations of specific impeachable offenses by President Nixon to the standards defined therein; it set out, instead, to clarify the phrase used in the Constitution (along with treason and bribery), "high crimes and misdemeanors." The most important thing about the staff report, in retrospect, was its conclusion, after a careful examination of American and earlier English impeachments as well as language relating to the drafting and adoption of the Constitution, that impeachable offense need not be criminal in nature.

This report, little noticed outside the committee and the president's lawyers, really set the stage for the eventual adoption of Article II. Analysis of the 1787 Constitutional Convention in Philadelphia, the state ratifying conventions, and the First Congress indicated that the Framers were much more concerned about impeachment as a constitutional check on abuse of presidential power than they were about criminality.[9] The purpose of impeachment, said the report, is not to send the president to jail nor to fine him (as in a criminal case), but rather to remove him from office. His misconduct must be substantial, may show a pattern of abuse rather than a single event, and derives from his constitutional obligations.

As applied to President Nixon, the standards for presidential conduct set forth in the staff report are most closely connected to the charges adopted by the House Judiciary Committee in Article II. That article goes to the heart of what is, or is not, presidential duty.

Article II, adopted by the Judiciary Committee 28–10, is summarized in the committee's final report:

Richard M. Nixon, in violation of his constitutional duty to take care that the laws be faithfully executed and his oath of office as President, seriously abused powers that only a President possesses. He engaged in conduct that violated the constitutional rights of citizens, that interfered with investigations by federal authorities and congressional committees, and that contravened the laws governing agencies of the executive branch of the federal government. This conduct, undertaken for his own personal political advantage and not in furtherance of any valid national policy objective, is seriously incompatible with our system of constitutional government.[10]

By concentrating on "abuse of power," Article II sets a definitive standard for *all* presidential impeachments. More important, in its attempt to distinguish between what is acceptable and nonacceptable presidential conduct, Article II helps to set constitutional guidelines for other presidents, including those who have followed Nixon. For example, the accountability of President Ronald Reagan in some of the episodes related to the Iran/Contras problem can be analyzed in light of President Nixon's accountability for the creation of the Plumbers unit and the break-in of Daniel Ellsberg's psychiatrist's office, as characterized in Article II.

It is important to remember that Article II focuses on abuse of power of the *office* of the presidency. Its passage indicates that there are certain duties, both constitutional and implied, that are inherent on assuming that high office; and that among these is the obligation to act always in a manner consistent with both the letter and spirit of the Constitution. Article II calls attention, for the first time, to the Presidential Oath of Office, which mandates two major presidential duties: "to faithfully execute the Office of the President of the United States," and "to preserve, protect and defend the Constitution" to the best of his or her ability. The oath becomes not merely antiquated language to be dusted off for each new Inaugural and then forgotten, but living language to guide presidential conduct. In President Nixon's case, the House Judiciary Committee found that his actions as set forth in Article II did not meet the standards imposed by the Oath of Office.

Article II also rests on a similar duty, explicit in the Constitution, to "take care that the Laws be faithfully executed." While the constitutional language is broad, in the congressional debate it became clear that such actions as misuse of the tax system to punish enemies, misuse of the Federal Bureau of Investigation (FBI) to wiretap critics of the White House, and threats to use the Federal Communications Commission to revoke the television license of *The Washington Post* added up to conduct not in keeping with faithful execution of the laws. Congress was sending a powerful message to President Nixon and future presidents that he could not pervert the power he had as chief executive in order to contravene the lawful purpose of these agencies.

Article II is also important because it is clearly a *noncriminal* charge. During the days of the Nixon impeachment, there was lively debate over the question of whether an impeachable offense must be criminal, in the sense of violating a specific criminal statute, or whether it could be broader and noncriminal. (This was particularly important since, only a few years earlier, Justice William Douglas had defended himself from impeachment charges on the grounds that his conduct had violated no criminal standards; and Nixon's defense in the Senate was expected to be similar.) Article II instead left the *statutory* crimes of Watergate—burglary, obstruction of justice, and so forth—to the vehicle of Article I; and treated these offenses only within the context of abuse of presidential power.

Article II commanded more votes on the Judiciary Committee than any of the other four articles introduced. It was different from Article I, which could have been drafted in criminal law terms only. It was broader than Article III (failure to comply with the congressional subpoena), which was more an assertion of the congressional power to investigate than an examination of the president's conduct of office. Although it did not meet the War Powers issue head-on, as did Article IV (Cambodian bombing, which failed to pass), it did touch on national security and secrecy issues in its allegations of use and misuse of the FBI and the Central Intelligence Agency (CIA). Last, in the substantiality of its allegations, it charged what most regarded as more serious abuses of office than those of Article V (understated tax returns and improvement of private property; which also failed to pass).

In retrospect, Article II of the Nixon impeachment is probably closest to the *original idea* of impeachment as a check on the feared proposal to concentrate power in a single chief magistrate. Historical studies show, and Article II affirms, that the impeachment clause is *political*: not in the partisan sense of the word, but in its broadest and best sense.[11]

Although other presidents before and after Richard Nixon may have been tempted to abuse their power in similar ways, the fact remains that a bipartisan majority of the House Judiciary Committee concluded that he had indeed acted "in a manner contrary to his trust as President and subversive of constitutional government." The totality of his conduct and the climate of that time make it likely that Article II would have passed in the Senate as well as in the full House.

While the great majority of Americans today probably link Nixon's resignation only to the Watergate break-in because their memories are short and the break-in is easiest for the average citizen to understand, it is my conviction that by far the most serious long-run charges in the Nixon impeachment are those encompassed by "abuse of power" in Article II.

Would the abuse of power charges alone have resulted in President Nixon's resignation? Probably not. It was the combination of investigations, both criminal in the courts and noncriminal in the Congress, that uncovered the evidence that ultimately led to President Nixon's resignation.

Popular memory tends to connect President Nixon's resignation to the release of the evidentially damaging last tape, referring to it as "the smoking gun." What tends to be forgotten is that the resignation was not that immediate; it also occurred only after the House Judiciary Committee had voted to support, by a bipartisan majority, three articles of impeachment. It seemed likely at the time that these three would pass the full House; had they done so, the abuse of power article might well have gained, as it did in committee, the greatest number of "yes" votes.

At the time of resignation, much careful planning had already gone on for a full Senate trial, anticipating that the House would impeach. Selected members of the House would have proceeded to act as prosecutors, titled managers, in the Senate; and each of these managers, having already voted to support Article II, would have pressed the abuse of power charges with dedication before the Senate. Had the Senate finally voted on Article II, it is also highly likely that a two-thirds majority would have passed it. The abuse of power charges would then have been affirmed as a significant part of the Senate conviction.

Anticipating that he would likely be impeached in the House and convicted of impeachment charges in the Senate, President Nixon resigned. By resigning, he avoided the constitutional impeachment penalties which would have required his removal from office, barred him from holding any federal office ever again, and deprived him of his retirement pay and related benefits.[12] To think that he did so only because of the Watergate break-in is, however, a mistake. The mood of the legislature at the time, the turn against him by the public, and the possibility that the trial might have publicized and imprinted on the public memory much more sharply some of the lesser known abuse of power violations were also significant factors. It is impossible to assess the exact weight of each factor; but each one had a weight.

How likely is it that abuse of power charges would in effect bring another president down? On the one hand, the fact that they were taken as seriously as they were, and received as many votes as they did, is an indication that the legislative checks and balances on the chief executive, intended by the Framers, do work. For political scientists and democratic optimists, it is a positive message.

On the other hand, were the abuse of power charges, per se, enough? Few people would claim so. It is easy to imagine that another president, committing similar abuses of power, could remain unchecked. If such an abuser were highly popular, if Congress were unwilling to take him or her on, and if previously discovered criminal charges had not paved the way for Congress to act on civil charges as well, cynics could imagine future presidents "getting away with" serious abuses of civil power. While no one anticipates another Watergate, in the literal sense of that word, it would probably take an accumulation of very serious charges to set the stage for an impeachment based on abuse of presidential power alone. It is not impossible, merely unlikely.

Lying to the public, or obstructing justice with respect to the trials of other accused persons, might be sufficient to shift the popular mood from one of support to one of severe disillusionment. Even then, a single legislative committee would be hard-pressed and would probably lack the resources to do a thorough investigation of presidential abuses on its own. It is more likely that abuse of presidential power, as a ground for presidential impeachment per se, will continue to serve only as a kind of red flag warning, cautioning future presidents from abuse of power–type actions, but powerless to halt them if they do occur.

As presidents come and go, one hopes only that a sense of honor (and perhaps understanding) will keep them faithful to the constitutional duties imposed by the office. President Nixon may well feel that he was held to a higher standard than other presidents, and that he got caught where others did not. Certainly the converging forces of the criminal charges against him (as well as the unindicted coconspirator charges in the courts) conspired with the abuse of power charges to present a situation difficult to defend. In the long run, however, the affirmation by Congress of abuse of power charges in the Nixon impeachment makes the constitutional framework a bit stronger, whether one takes an optimistic or pessimistic view of its future utility.

APPENDIX

ARTICLE II, PARAGRAPH (1)

(1) HE HAS, ACTING PERSONALLY AND THROUGH HIS SUBORDINATES AND AGENTS, ENDEAVORED TO OBTAIN FROM THE INTERNAL REVENUE SERVICE, IN VIOLATION OF THE CONSTITUTIONAL RIGHTS OF CITIZENS, CONFIDENTIAL INFORMATION CONTAINED IN INCOME TAX RETURNS FOR PURPOSES NOT AUTHORIZED BY LAW, AND TO CAUSE, IN VIOLATION OF THE CONSTITUTIONAL RIGHTS OF CITIZENS, INCOME TAX AUDITS OR OTHER INCOME TAX INVESTIGATIONS TO BE INITIATED OR CONDUCTED IN A DISCRIMINATORY MANNER

The Committee finds clear and convincing evidence that a course of conduct was carried out by Richard M. Nixon's close subordinates, with his knowledge, approval, and encouragement, to violate the constitutional rights of citizens—their right to privacy with respect to the use of confidential information acquired by the Internal Revenue Service; their right to have the tax laws of the United States applied with an even hand; and their right to engage in political activity in opposition to the President. This conduct involved an attempt to interfere with the lawful administration of the Internal Revenue Service and the proper conduct of tax inquiries by misusing confidential IRS information and the powers of investigation of the IRS for the political benefit of the President. In approving and encouraging this activity, he failed to take care that the laws be faithfully executed and violated his constitutional oath faithfully to execute the office of President and to preserve, protect, and defend the Constitution.

I
WALLACE INVESTIGATION

On various occasions, President Nixon's subordinates acting under his authority and in order to serve his political interests sought and obtained information from the Internal Revenue Service about tax investigations of citizens. The first instance of which the Committee has evidence involves Governor George Wallace. In the spring of 1970, Wallace was running against Albert Brewer in the Alabama primary for the Democratic party's gubernatorial nomination. A Wallace defeat was considered helpful to the President because it would lessen Wallace's prospects in the 1972 presidential election. Four hundred thousand dollars in campaign funds remaining from the President's 1968 campaign was secretly contributed to the Brewer primary campaign. (Kalmbach testimony, 3 HJC 565, 664–66)

IRS information about Wallace was also used to try to defeat Wallace in the Alabama gubernatorial primary. In early 1970 Haldeman learned, apparently from an IRS sensitive case report,[1] about an investigation of George Wallace and his brother Gerald. Haldeman directed Clark Mollenhoff, special counsel to the President, to obtain a report of the IRS Investigation. (Book VIII, 38) According to Mollenhoff:

I initially questioned Mr. Haldeman's instruction, but upon his assurance that the report was to be obtained at the request of the President, I requested the report of IRS Commissioner [Randolph] Thrower. (Book VIII, 38)

Mollenhoff obtained the IRS report on the Wallace investigation from Commissioner Thrower. (Book VIII, 38, 41) On March 21, 1970, Mollenhoff delivered it to Haldeman on his assurance that it was for the President. (Book VIII, 36, 38)

Material contained in the report was later transmitted to columnist Jack Anderson. Portions of it adverse to George Wallace were published nationally on April 13, 1970, several weeks before the primary election. (Book VIII, 37, 39, 41)

After the publication, Commissioner Thrower and the Chief Counsel of the IRS met with Ehrlichman and Haldeman and discussed the seriousness of the leak and the fact that an unauthorized disclosure constituted a criminal act.[2] Haldeman and Ehrlichman assured Thrower that they would take steps to prevent a recurrence. (Book VIII, 42)

II
INFORMATION AND AUDITS

In the fall of 1971, John Dean's assistant, John Caulfield, sought and obtained information from the IRS on the financial status and charitable contributions of Lawrence Goldberg in order to assess Goldberg's suitability for a position at the Committee to Re-Elect the President. (Book VIII, 138–42) Confidential IRS material was also obtained about a journalist investigating the affairs of a campaign fundraiser and about various prominent entertainers. (Book VIII, 156–60, 211)

At Haldeman's request, and under Dean's direction, attempts were made to have tax audits conducted on various other persons. There is no evidence that these audits were in fact undertaken. (Book VIII, 176–80)

III
O'BRIEN INVESTIGATION

During the spring or summer of 1972, John Ehrlichman learned from an IRS sensitive case report that an investigation of Howard Hughes's business interests was under way. The report reflected a connection between the Hughes matters being investigated and the personal finances of Democratic National Committee Chairman Lawrence O'Brien. (Book VIII, 223–24) Ehrlichman sought and obtained information about O'Brien's tax returns from Assistant to the Commissioner Roger Barth. (Roger Barth testimony, SSC Executive Session, June 6, 1974, 3–6) Ehrlichman also told Treasury Secretary Shultz that the Internal Revenue Service should interview O'Brien. The IRS policy then in effect was that audits and interviews, absent statute of limitations and other compelling considerations, would not be conducted during an election year with respect to candidates or others in politically sensitive positions. (Book VIII, 219–20) Since the 1972 election campaign was in progress, the IRS would not have interviewed O'Brien until after election day, November 7, but because of Ehrlichman's demands the IRS had a conference with O'Brien in mid-August. (Book VIII, 219–21) According to Vernon Walters:

> IRS interviewed Mr. O'Brien on or about August 17, 1972. Mr. O'Brien was cooperative although the interview was limited timewise, and Mr. O'Brien suggested that any further interview be postponed until after the election. My recollection is that IRS furnished a copy of the Conference Report to Secretary Shultz. A short time thereafter, Secretary Shultz informed me that Mr. Ehrlichman was not satisfied and that he needed further information about the matter. I advised the Secretary that IRS had checked the filing of returns and the examination status of those returns (closed) and that there was nothing else IRS could do.
>
> On or about August 29, 1972, at the request of Secretary Shultz, I went to his office with Roger Barth so that we could conclude review of the O'Brien matter and dispose of it. Secretary Shultz, Mr. Barth and I discussed the matter and agreed that IRS could do no more. We then jointly telephoned Mr. Ehrlichman. Secretary Shultz informed Mr. Ehrlichman of that; I stated that IRS had verified that Mr. O'Brien had filed returns, that those returns reflected large amounts of income, that IRS already had examined and closed the returns, and that we (Shultz, Walters and Barth) all agreed that there was nothing further for IRS to do. Mr. Ehrlichman indicated disappointment, and said to me "I'm goddamn tired of your foot dragging tactics." I was offended and very upset but decided to make no response to that statement. Following the telephone conversation, I told Secretary Shultz that he could have my job any time he wanted it. (Book VIII, 234–35)

In early September, Ehrlichman telephoned Kalmbach and told him that O'Brien had IRS problems. He gave Kalmbach figures on O'Brien's allegedly unreported income and asked Kalmbach to plant the information with Las Vegas newspaperman Hank Greenspun, a friend of Kalmbach. Kalmbach refused to do so, despite subsequent requests by Ehrlichman and Mitchell. (Kalmbach testimony, 3 HJC 615–17)[3]

NOTES

1. The full text of Article II, which appears in the appendix to this paper, may be found as adopted by the House Judiciary Committee on Monday, July 29, 1974, in U.S.

Congress, House Judiciary Committee, *Final Report*, 93rd Congress, 2nd Sess., H. Rept. 93–1305, August 20, 1974, pp. 1–3.

2. The breakdown of total votes cast by members of the House Judiciary Committee on each of the five articles voted on may be found in U.S. Congress, House Judiciary Committee, *Debate on Articles of Impeachment Hearings . . . Pursuant to H. Res. 803*, 93rd Congress, 1st Sess., Vol. 19, July 24, 25, 26, 27, 29, and 30, 1974, following the transcript of debates on each article.

3. United States Constitution, Article I, Section 2.

4. United States Constitution, Article I, Section 3.

5. U.S. Congress, Senate Select Committee on Presidential Campaign Activities. See also Theodore H. White, *Breach of Faith: The Fall of Richard Nixon* (New York: Atheneum Publishers, 1975), pp. 235–236; and Frank Mankiewicz, *U.S. vs. Richard M. Nixon: The Final Crisis* (New York: Ballantine Books, 1975), pp. 22–23.

6. See, generally, Leon Jaworski, *The Right and the Power: The Prosecution of Watergate* (Houston: Gulf Publishing, 1976).

7. U.S. Congress, House, H. Res. 703, *A Resolution Authorizing and Directing the Committee on the Judiciary to Investigate Whether Sufficient Grounds Exist for the House of Representatives to Exercise Its Constitutional Power to Impeach Richard M. Nixon, President of the United States of America*, 93rd Congress, 1st Sess., Vol. 119, November 15, 1973.

8. U.S. Congress, House Judiciary Committee, *Constitutional Grounds for Presidential Impeachment*, Report by the Staff of the Impeachment Inquiry, 93rd Cong., 2nd Sess., February 1974.

9. Ibid., see also John R. Labowitz, *Presidential Impeachment* (New Haven: Yale University Press, 1978).

10. U.S. Congress, *Final Report*, p. 139.

11. U.S. Congress, *Constitutional Grounds*, pp. 7–11.

12. United States Constitution, Article I, Section 3.

NOTES TO APPENDIX

1. Sensitive case reports are used by the IRS to inform the secretary of the treasury, the IRS commissioner and, at their discretion, other administration officials of the existence of proceedings or investigations involving prominent individuals.

2. 26 U.S.C. §7213 provides in part that it "shall be unlawful for any officer or employee of the United States to divulge . . . to any person the amount or source of income, profits, losses, expenditures, or any particular thereof, set forth or disclosed in any income return." This section makes such activity a misdemeanor and requires the discharge of the guilty officer or employee. The IRS considers data obtained in an IRS investigation to be income return information; IRS Reg. §301.6103(a)–1(1) (3) (i) (b).

3. According to an affidavit of Senate Select Committee (SSC) Minority Counsel Fred Thompson, he was informed by Special Counsel to the President J. Fred Buzhardt that John Dean reported to the president on the IRS investigation of O'Brien on September 15, 1972 (Book VIII, pp. 337–339). In a staff interview, Dean said he did not recall discussing O'Brien's taxes with the president. On June 12, 1974, Judge Sirica held that the conversation from 6:00 to 6:13 P.M. on September 15, 1972, is relevant to the Watergate special prosecutor's investigation of alleged abuse of the IRS.

9

Domestic Legislative Coalitions
and Impeachment

TERRY SULLIVAN

Two points are common to characterizations of the Nixon impeachment.[1] First, congressional support for impeachment slowly accumulated. Some have suggested that this steady accumulation resulted from the foresight of the congressional leadership who systematically prepared their institution. For example, writing about the impeachment Congress, Jimmy Breslin says:

He doesn't remember the date, he wasn't keeping notes on everything at the time, but Congressman Thomas P. O'Neill, Jr., does know that it was just after he had become Majority Leader in the House of Representatives in January of 1973 that he walked into Speaker Carl Albert's office and said, "All my years tell me what's happening. They did so many bad things during that campaign that there is no way to keep it from coming out. They did too many things. Too many people know about it. There is no way to keep it quiet. The time is going to come when impeachment is going to hit this Congress and we better be ready for it." (Breslin, 1975, p. 12).

The second characterization of the Nixon impeachment is that "the system worked" because those in Congress realized that institutional power was fundamental to governing. For example, Elizabeth Drew made the following notation in her *Washington Journal*:

—August 7, 1974—

A Democratic senator says on the telephone, . . . "The fear that was welling up within me over what I thought was the impotence of the institutions was such that I wondered whether they would last. Suddenly, I realized that your position on the issues wasn't very important—that you have to have a framework of institutions within which to fight for your position on the issues, and that without the system nothing else matters.'' (Drew, 1974, p. 400)

Comments of this sort harken back to the Founders' expectations that a politician's "identification with place" ultimately would defend the constitutional balance. For example, James Madison articulated such an argument in his *Federalists* number 51:

[T]he great security against a gradual concentration of the several powers in the same department consists in giving to those who administer each department the necessary constitutional means and personal motives to resist encroachments of the others. Ambition must be made to counteract ambition. The interest of the man must be connected with the constitutional rights of the place. It may be a reflection on human nature that such devices should be necessary to control the abuses of government. But what is government itself but the greatest of all reflections on human nature? If men were angels no government would be necessary. (Hamilton, Jay, & Madison, [1789] 1961)

In this view, the system of checks and balances *worked* during the impeachment crisis in something like the way that the Founders had imagined it would, balancing the ambition for controlling policy decisions in one branch against similar ambitions in another.

Evaluating such summations is difficult because so much of what takes place in coalition formation and governing necessarily takes place in private. Leaders strategize and persuade in private, typically presenting a facade to the public that aids their cause rather than reflecting their activities. Members of Congress seldom publicly acknowledge when they have given in to leaders or to presidential pressures, and instead prefer to portray themselves either as steady supporters or as being single-mindedly dedicated to the wishes of their own constituents. Thus, analysts typically place such topics as drafting strategies, agenda control, coalition building, and leadership inside an empirical "black box," while systematically analyzing only those data that are secured outside of the coalition process.

Using data from *inside* the coalition process, the research reported here evaluates these two characterizations of impeachment by proposing answers to two questions:

1. Did coalition building on impeachment differ from coalition formation on domestic policy issues, accumulating slowly over time?
2. Does restoring the power balance between the Congress and the president ("institutional identification") account for that difference?

There is sufficient theoretical reason to expect that impeachment is a special issue, involving as it does the power balance between the two central policy-making institutions. Answering the first question is intended to establish whether there is an *empirical* justification for such theoretical expectations. In assessing the evidence, the analysis assumes that domestic policy issues represent the typical policy question and, thus, are a fair benchmark by which to compare impeachment.[2]

AVAILABLE DATA

The data employed in this study originated in the Majority Whip's Office during the 93rd Congress (1973–1974), and includes "headcounts." A headcount is a confidential poll of members about their intentions on issues prior to voting. Members respond to questions designed both to illicit information from members and to convey the leadership's position. These responses are coded into several categories ranging from *Right* to *Wrong*. Typically, counting on an issue began with an "initial" count, usually concluded weeks ahead of voting, and ended with a "final" count, completed only hours before the leadership went onto the floor. The counts used here cover thirty-four subjects, including sixteen counts on domestic policy issues and seven counts on various aspects of the impending impeachment process in the House. Similar counting takes place in the administration (compare Collier and Sullivan, 1986; Rosenthal and Sullivan, 1988; Sullivan, 1983, 1987a, 1987b, 1988).

EMPIRICAL PATTERNS

In order to answer the two central questions, member responses on initial counts (the earliest in the typical sequence on an issue) were compared over time and between issue groups. In addition, some comparisons were made between members who supported the leadership early on but then later deserted their position and the leadership.

Initial Support

The first question to address is: Based on initial headcounts, does it appear that impeachment differs from domestic policy, and did it accumulate over time? Figure 9.1 illustrates the patterns of initial support on the sixteen domestic counts (the diamond data points) and the seven impeachment counts (the crosshatches). Trend lines for the two groups also are plotted. The figure clearly illustrates that impeachment attracted more initial support than did domestic legislation, but that neither garnered more than 50 percent of the members. Moreover, it suggests that support on impeachment-related issues was close to a majority only right after the "Saturday Night Massacre."

Figure 9.1 also indicates that initial support on impeachment issues deteriorated rather than accumulated at a much faster rate than did support on domestic policy questions: more than twice as fast. Thus, these patterns do not support the idea that the leadership slowly built up support for impeachment. Indeed, the data suggest just the opposite: Over time, the coalition on impeachment drifted away

Figure 9.1
Initial Support on Selected Counts: Domestic Policies and Impeachment

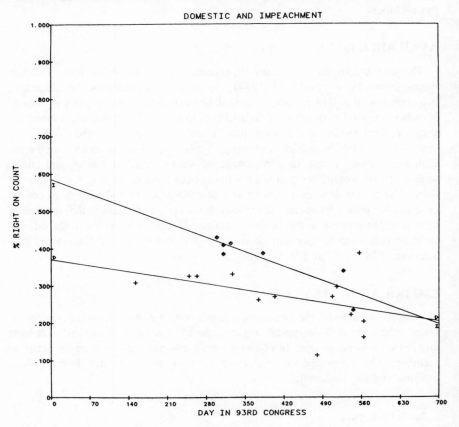

Note: Diamond symbol = domestic policies; crosshatch symbol = impeachment.

from the majority leadership and began to resemble closely the common coalition
for the Nixon domestic agenda.

Power Balance

Since the first characterization of impeachment as an increasingly stronger
movement is not supported by the data, it seems likely that the second characterization—having to do with the importance of the institutional balance—is
inaccurate, as well. This analysis utilizes evidence from a comparison between
members of Congress who were ''lost'' on impeachment, on the one hand, and
who were ''lost'' on domestic policy, on the other. On impeachment, some

Table 9.1

Lost Commitments by Institutional Identification, Region, and Ideology

Proportion of Targeted Group
Changing Their Earlier Commitment

Groups	---- Domestic ----		-- Impeachment --	
	Losses	% Change	Losses	% Change
Institutional				
Leader	40.7%		30.1%	
Follower	53.7%	31.9	41.4%	37.5
Regional				
North	45.2%		29.2%	
South	68.8%	52.2	50.0%	71.2
Ideological				
Liberal	39.1%		26.2%	
Moderate	52.4%		31.3%	
Conservative	72.7%	85.9	53.8%	105.3

Source: Compiled by author.
Note: The "stable" group is indicated with boldface.

sixty-three Democrats who had committed on the first impeachment count did not commit on the last count taken eight months later. On domestic policy, about fifty members who had committed earlier would not commit later.

Table 9.1 summarizes the lost commitments by comparing losses across issue types using three descriptors of those losses. The first variable is a composite leadership score which simply identifies all those members who held a position as a subcommittee or committee chair or as a majority party officer.[3] It is assumed that being a member of this loosely defined "leadership" constitutes an approximation of those likely to have the kind of strong institutional identification necessary to maintain the Madisonian balance between the president and Congress. The second variable utilizes a standard measure of regional identification, and the third variable identifies standard ideological preferences by dividing the membership into three groups: liberals, moderates, and conservatives.[4]

For each comparison, two bits of data are reported. The first column for each issue group reports the percentage of the target group of initially committed Democrats who lessened their commitment over the time period. For example, the figures in the first row indicate that of those leaders who committed on the early domestic count, nearly 41 percent did not commit on the final domestic count. The second column compares the rate of loss in the last subgroup with the rate of loss in the first subgroup. Thus, among conservatives on domestic policy, the rate of loss was almost 86 percent greater than the rate of loss among liberals.

Two comparisons will be made, between groups and across issues. In the between-group comparisons, the important comparison is made between what could be called the "stable" group and the "volatile" group. For example, if Madison's institutional identification were important, then we would expect that "leaders" would be less volatile than "followers," namely, that the rate of loss would be smaller for leaders than for followers. If ideology were key, then we would expect that in this data liberals would be less volatile than conservatives. In the comparisons made between groups, the important question is which volatile group is describing the biggest losses by comparison with its stable group, namely, which group is associated with the largest percentage change described in the second column?

Two patterns emerge in these data. The first is between groups. Clearly, the difference in losses in the volatile group is consistently larger than losses in the stable group. That pattern would suggest that each of these variables plays at least some role in describing the losses in initial support in both issue groups. The most dramatic percentage changes, however, are registered in the ideological comparison. On both issues, the difference between stable and unstable ideological groups is more than double the instability in the institutional group. Moreover, on impeachment, the instability among the ideological group is almost *three times* the instability in the institutional group. This is fairly strong, though indirect, evidence that ideological differences are at the base of the declining support on both kinds of issues.

The second pattern to emerge from Table 9.1 is across issues. In comparing issues, clearly impeachment has a higher rate of instability in each member group. This pattern reflects the fact that the trend in decline in impeachment support is steeper than the decline in support for the majority leadership on domestic policies. The important pattern to note, however, is which of the patterns of instability is the most dramatic; on which level is the decline in impeachment more rapidly overtaking the decline in domestic policy support? Comparing the changes across issues, it is clear that it is along regional and ideological lines that the leadership experienced the most instability. The rate of instability, for example, is nearly twice as great in the regional groups as in the institutional groups.

Thus, the evidence clearly suggests the importance of regional and ideological (namely, constituency) forces as central to the decline of initial support on normal domestic policies. Moreover, and more important, over time, the force of ideological and regional interests undercut initial support on the impeachment question as well.

PRESIDENTIAL LEADERSHIP AND COMPETITION

What can we conclude then? Congressional leadership is a competitive game. The Founders presumed that the power of the government naturally would flow disproportionately to the legislative branch—the embodiment of the sovereign "people." Thus, it was the intent of the separation of powers system not only to check generally the powers of the various branches but, more specifically, to undermine, and thus adjust for, the natural power of the Congress. Since the Founding, the development of an active presidency has further checked the power of Congress by creating several loci of leadership. Now, the president and the majority leadership compete for control over congressional policy-making.

The importance of that competition becomes apparent when a constitutional crisis develops. Moreover, in general, analysts correctly have interpreted constitutional conflict as a struggle for leadership and the maintenance of that Madisonian balance. Seen in that light, constitutional crises typically have been resolved in favor of the balance, and in that sense, it is correct to conclude that "the system works."

The empirical evidence presented here, however, suggests that more than institutional balance was involved in the constitutional crisis that culminated in the Nixon impeachment investigation. Moreover, by extension, the evidence suggests that these "political" (or policy) considerations may be important in the resolution of other conflicts, as well.

The results reported here suggest that it is possible that the congressional leadership actually experienced a great deal of difficulty maintaining its support, *even on impeachment*, because the administration successfully maintained a policy presence in the congressional process. While the struggle over the balance of constitutional power was very obvious, the struggle over the course of domestic policy carried on. In the latter arena, it may be that the Great Society leadership in the majority party was being outmaneuvered by a resurging conservative movement that would develop more fully later under Jimmy Carter and then Ronald Reagan.

In light of this possibility, one trend in the data is worth noting further. Figure 9.2 illustrates initial support on *all* counts. This falls into two clusters, one in 1973 and one in mid-1974, approximately split by Day 350. The first cluster is composed primarily of institutional questions, including the Budget and Impoundment Control Act, War Powers, Creating a Senate Confirmation for the Office of Management and Budget (OMB) director. These are indicated by closed circles. The second cluster is composed almost exclusively of domestic policies (the diamonds) and two counts on impeachment (crosshatches). It could be concluded that the first session of the 93rd Congress was dominated by institutional issues while the second session was dominated by domestic policy concerns.

The issue of impeachment bridged these two policy clusters by moving from one to the other. As such, support on the issue of impeachment was affected directly by the nature of the other policy conflicts present in the period through which it passed. In the first, impeachment was one issue among many focusing on the proper balance between the power interests of the presidency and the power stakes of the majority (congressional) leadership. In the minds of members, then, the impeachment issue could be cast in wholly institutional terms; terms that led members to conclude that "your position on the issues wasn't very

Figure 9.2
Initial Support on All Counts, by Type

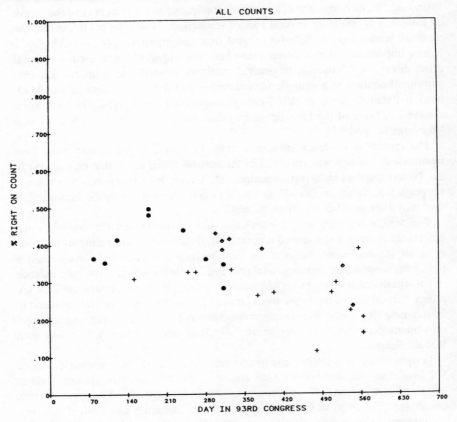

ALL COUNTS

Note: Diamond symbol = domestic policies; crosshatch symbol = impeachment.

important'' without the institutionally based authority and power to act on those positions, the kind of Madisonian response expected to motivate members to defend the constitutional balance by defending their institution.

With the issues of institutional balance resolved in 1973, however, only impeachment remained an open question. In the second period, the period dominated by domestic policy questions, impeachment probably raised for some the specter of a domestic agenda dominated by the moderately liberal Democratic congressional leadership. In that environment, how one stood on the institutional question of the day may have become entwined easily with one's position on the issues. To moderate and conservative Southerners, for example, the key issue in impeachment may have become who would be left to lead on domestic policies without President Nixon. When presented with the recurring and growing possibility of impeachment (now cast in an environment of policy confrontation rather than institutional confrontation), these members may have preferred to hold their commitment rather than freely associate themselves with the congressional leadership, even if they had done so in the previous period. To the leaders sitting inside this process trying to guide it, the situation must have appeared precarious. If members were becoming increasingly more accustomed to contemplating impeaching the president, they were also becoming increasingly less willing to demonstrate a commitment on the issue.

If this interpretation is true, then the notion that the system "worked" is accurate in the strongest possible sense. The Founders envisioned a system in which personal ambitions became linked with and dependent on institutional fortunes. They understood the central institutional design problem to be how to properly counterbalance an ambitious institution, whether it was a monarchical executive or a "republican monarchy" dominated by the legislature. They expected that inhabitants of an institution would identify with its position in the system and recognize that their influence over developments depended on the power of their institution. The Founders would expect that in a constitutional crisis, a senator or representative would realize the need for "framework of institutions within which to fight for [his or her] position on the issues, and that without the system nothing else matters": that their power stakes depended on the power of the Congress remaining intact vis-à-vis the presidency, and that eventually they would act on that realization.

The Founders did not anticipate that the policy preferences of institutional "inhabitants" might actually curb the power of institutionalized ambition. Surely such a development would place the system of checks and balances in great peril. The data support the conclusion that, in fact, the system of checks and balances was indeed in great peril because of the force of such policy preferences. Nonetheless, "the system did work." Many members of Congress clearly set aside their personal policy preferences in order to render a damning judgment on the very president who could and did deliver the policies they preferred. That is strong testimony to the strength of the Founders' constitutional design.

NOTES

1. First and foremost, I owe a great debt to Lawrence C. Dodd, who obtained many of the counts used in this study while working in the Majority Whip's Office in 1974, and who earlier worked with me on related projects (see, for example, Dodd and Sullivan, 1982). In addition, Stuart Zisman assisted me in some of the data analysis.

2. While there is a literature on the differences between foreign policy coalitions and domestic coalitions, there is very little debate over the fact that domestic policy represents normal relations between Congress and the executive, and only some debate over the extent to which foreign policy is different from normal (namely, domestic) coalition formation. This debate is summarized well in Edwards, 1980, and includes such research as in Peppers, 1975; LeLoup and Shull 1979; and Wildavsky, 1966.

3. The latter included only zone whips, whips, caucus officers, majority leader, and Speaker. It excluded members of Steering and Policy and the Committee on Committees.

4. The score used is provided by Americans for Democratic Action and is averaged for the 92nd and 94th Congresses. Any member not in both Congresses is given his or her score in the one Congress in which he or she was a member.

REFERENCES

Breslin, Jimmy. 1975. *How the Good Guys Finally Won: Notes from an Impeachment Summer*. New York: Viking Press.

Collier, Kenneth, and Terry Sullivan. 1986. *Presidential Influence and Support*. Austin: University of Texas Press.

Dodd, Lawrence C., and Terry Sullivan. 1982. "Majority Party Leadership and Partisan Vote-Gathering: The House Democratic Whip System." In *Understanding Congressional Leadership*, ed. Frank MacKaman. Washington, D.C.: Congressional Quarterly.

Drew, Elizabeth. 1974. *Washington Journal: The Events of 1973 and 1974*. New York: Random House.

Edwards, George, III. 1980. *Presidential Influence in Congress*. San Francisco: Freeman.

Hamilton, Alexander, John Jay, and James Madison. [1789] 1961. *The Federalists*, ed. Clinton Rossiter. New York: Mentor.

LeLoup, Lance T., and Steven A. Shull. 1979, March "Congress Versus the Executive: The 'Two Presidencies' Reconsidered." *Social Science Quarterly* 59 (March): 704–719.

Peppers, Donald A. 1975. " 'The Two Presidencies': Eight Years Later." In *Perspectives on the Presidency*, ed. Aaron Wildavsky, Boston: Little, Brown.

Rosenthal, Howard, and Terry Sullivan. 1988. *The Spatial Position of Members and Presidential Coalition Strategies*. Austin: University of Texas Press.

Sullivan, Terry. 1983. "Position-Taking and Conversion: The Correlates of Presidential Support During Lyndon Johnson's 90th Congress." *Working Papers on Institutional Design and Public Policy no. 21*.

———. 1987a. *Presidential Leadership in Congress: Bargaining and Strategic Responses*. Paper presented before the Society for the Study of Public Choice, Tucson, Arizona.

———. 1987b. "Presidential Leadership in Congress: Security Commitments." In *Congress: Structure and Policy*, ed. Mathew McCubbins and Terry Sullivan. New York: Cambridge University Press.

———. 1988. "Expectations, Headcounts, and Presidential Coalitions in Congress." *American Journal of Political Science* 32 (August): 567–589.

Wildavsky, Aaron. 1966. "The Two Presidencies." *Trans-Action* 4 (December): 7–14.

Discussant: John Doar

Not being a member of the House of Representatives, I assume and conclude that I am exempt from the last speaker's challenge. I will tell you that a week ago, a friend of mine told me that an English producer who was in the process of developing a television documentary about some event or events during the civil rights days was talking to my friend, who was a colleague of mine in the Justice Department in the 1960s. And after the producer had talked to him and quizzed him for quite some time, my friend said, "You shouldn't be talking to me, you should talk to John Doar," to which the English producer replied, "Well, I considered that but I've talked to a number of people and they say his memory is not very good."

With that I'd like to turn back to the impeachment proceedings. If one were to reread Alexander Hamilton's article on the impeachment process in the *Federalist Papers*, I think one would see that Alexander Hamilton's prediction as to how the impeachment process would move through the legislative branch did not come to pass. Hamilton certainly did not foresee that it would be the Committee on the Judiciary of the House of Representatives that would play such a central role in the inquiry. It has always been interesting to me to think back about the procedure and process of the House Judiciary Committee.

No inquiry into the conduct of a president had occurred for about a hundred years. When the legal staff of the Judiciary Committee first gathered together, we decided that if there was to be one standard to measure our performance, it was that if, and I say if, the members of the committee concluded, at the end of their deliberations, that they would vote "up" on one or more articles of impeachment, that the vote be by a two-thirds or better majority. Our task was to present the facts as clearly as we could, as impartially as we could, so that the effect would be that not only a narrow majority of the committee but a considerable majority of the committee would agree upon the committee's recommendation to the full House.

In order to do that, it seemed to us that there were two things that were necessary. One was that there should be a conviction that there was a foundation in law in each of the proposed articles of impeachment. As you've heard this morning, the staff of the committee did spend considerable time in developing a paper on the constitutional basis for impeachment, and we demonstrated, I think, that historically, impeachment involved conduct that seriously undermines the institutions of constitutional government. The second thing that we concluded was that there had to be some focus in the factual presentation. Time was important in the sense that we didn't have an endless amount of time to present material to the Judiciary Committee. Thus, there had to be some control over the substance of the material presented.

You have to recall, at that time, that there was a very, very serious intellectual debate as to whether or not impeachment reached beyond narrow criminal offenses. And coupled with that conceptual argument as to the grounds for impeachment, the Special Prosecutor's Office exerted strong pressure to confine the impeachment articles to as narrow a set of events as possible. In that way, it was argued, you would attain as close to 100 percent certainty with respect to the fact that criminal activity occurred. We, on the special counsel's staff, didn't feel that that was the best strategy in presenting the material to the committee. We thought that it was important to present facts concerning a course of conduct or a pattern of conduct stretching over a considerable period of time. And if the proof wasn't quite as strong, nonetheless it was a better and more principled way of presenting the facts and the evidence to the committee.

It is important to recall the way the process unfolded. The committee elected to prepare itself in closed sessions, absent reporters, absent cameras, absent television. Then, when they appeared before the American public, the committee members, after having worked very hard in mastering the facts, demonstrated that they were in control of them. As a result they, I think, were very persuasive in explaining why they voted as they did. The committee members, and I admire them very much for this, also demonstrated considerable humility before the television camera, almost an indifference to the television camera, and that was an admirable performance, in my view.

With respect to the differences between Article I and Article II, I don't believe that if there had not been an Article I, that Article II would have carried 28–10. If you read Article I, you see that there were a considerable number of allegations of abuses of power that formed the basis of that article. I believe that if you're going to ask that Congress pass on the ultimate constitutional question of removing the president of the United States from office, and if you need a two-thirds vote to do it, you want to try to focus the charge in a way that is understandable, clear, and certain.

Now finally, and this is a personal observation, one of the great things about the House Judiciary Committee was the vote that they cast on the first article. The inquiry occurred eight or nine years after the civil rights revolution had finally broken the caste system in this country. When the vote was taken, as we watched in the committee room and you watched before your television screens, we saw four conservative white members join with three black members to vote on the same side of the ultimate constitutional issue. And for me that was an exceptionally thrilling moment.

Discussant: Elizabeth Holtzman

Thank you very much. I'd like to begin by focusing on some of the little-discussed procedural factors that contributed in an important way to the outcome. At the outset of the impeachment process the question was: ''Who in the House of Representatives would be given the authority to commence an inquiry?'' The Speaker could have set up a new panel with hand-picked members. Instead, he chose to use a preexisting committee, in particular, te House Judiciary Committee. While the House Judiciary Committee traditionally sat on impeachment matters, there were some risks. The committee chair was new, and there were five new Democratic members on that committee, completely untested and unknown. Ultimately, it was to the Speaker's credit that he chose the Judiciary Committee (not just because I happened to be a member of it), because it eliminated the potential charge that the Speaker stacked the deck in setting up a new committee. There was no stacked deck in the Judiciary Committee. The membership of this committee had been formed before anyone in the country had seriously spoken the word ''impeachment.'' In fact, the committees were basically organized before the start of the 1973 term.

The second point is that the members of this committee for the most part took the issue of impeachment extremely seriously. There was much evidence to master and abstruse legal arguments to become acquainted with and to understand. I think most members of the committee dug deeply into the history of the constitutional phrase, ''high crimes and misdemeanors,'' and into the facts. This helped produce public credibility in the result.

The last important factor was that the public hearings were televised. It was not decided at the outset of the hearings that they would be televised. In fact, there was quite a bit of debate about whether or not they would be. This may be where the new members of Congress made a key contribution. Without their insistence, the hearings might not have been televised. Without television, I think the public's reaction to the hearings would have been very different. Instead, I think the country's ability to see the members of the committee publicly searching their conscience, publicly articulating in a solemn manner the serious reasons for voting for impeachment, helped gain widespread acceptance and credibility that the process never would have had otherwise.

I would like to add one comment to respond to the challenge thrown out by Professor Sullivan. I think there are things beyond concern about power, institutional power, that motivate members of Congress from time to time. Based on my experience and my conversations with other members of the committee, there was very deep concern about constitutional norms, about preserving a system of democracy, and about insuring that we would not have violations of the law and serious abuses of power carried out by the executive. I think the question of whether Congress is going to reign supreme or not did not enter into the committee members' minds. Instead, many of us saw our responsibility, our constitutional responsibility in preserving the Rule of Law in America.

I agree about the significance of Article II; I think the committee determination that it was not necessary to prove that the president actually engaged in a crime was a correct one. We were bolstered in our decision making on that by the fortuitous publication of a book by a professor at Harvard Law School, Raoul Berger, who discussed in depth the question of impeachment and whether the term "high crime or misdemeanor" requires, in fact, an actual violation of criminal statutes. He came to the same conclusion as the overwhelming majority of the committee.

I would like to focus here on something that I consider to be one of the failings of the impeachment process. And that is the failure to come to grips with one of the most serious abuses of executive power in the Nixon administration which, in my judgment, was the bombing of Cambodia, the use of American troops and the risking of their lives, the killing of people in a neutral country through the process of lying and deception of the Congress and of the American public. This article—proposed Article IV—was not approved. This failure raised very, very, serious questions about our constitutional system of government. Many people do not know very much about that article and the background behind it, but I think its relevance for today is especially clear.

The facts show that shortly after the Nixon Administration took power, the president authorized the bombing of Cambodia. It was a neutral country that was not at war with us at that time. In order to conceal this bombing from the United States Congress, the Joint Chiefs of Staff were ordered to, and in fact did keep, two sets of books. A false set of records was submitted to the United States Congress to deceive them. Oddly, the Cambodians knew they were being bombed, the North Vietnamese knew Cambodia was being bombed, the Vietcong knew about it, the Russians knew about it, the Chinese knew about it. But the United States Congress did not know, and neither did the American people.

Considering the significance of the war-making power itself—whether or not Congress would have acquiesced had it been told, whether or not the American public would have approved had it been told—the fact that this awesome power to commit American troops and authorize them to take the lives of other people in a country with which we were not at war was exercised by deceiving Congress and the American people about it, was in my opinion, a very gross abuse of power. It was a very serious undermining of our democratic system, which functions on a basis of public accountability.

The public cannot approve or disapprove of war carried on in secret. The significance for today is obvious, because in the end what happened, it seemed to me, was that failure to impeach for lying to Congress about the secret bombing of Cambodia may have sent a signal to other presidents that when it comes to foreign affairs, the president can deceive the Congress and can deceive the American public and can act with impunity. Indeed, it is very interesting to read—and I just looked at them recently—the views of those who voted against that article of impeachment. They recognized the serious undermining of the Constitution that was involved in the secret bombing; nonetheless, ten or more members—who would have constituted a majority for that impeachment resolution—said that Congress has never enacted the War Powers Resolution, and I'll quote the last line of their view: "Certainly any President who violated the provisions of that law"—meaning the War Powers Resolution—"would invite congressional action through the impeachment remedy to protect the constitutional separation of powers against abuse by the executive." Well I do not think that their prediction that violations of the War Powers Resolution would invite the remedy of impeachment has come to pass. Indeed, it may well be as we look back on the impeachment process that the refusal of the Judiciary Committee to deal with the abuses of power in the area of foreign affairs may come back to haunt us.

The other issue I want to raise has to do with fortuitous factors, having to do with the quality of evidence. This raises the question of how effective impeachment will be in the future. We had the benefit of not only the prior excellent work of the Senate Watergate Committee, but we also had the benefit of the materials that the special prosecutor, through a grand jury investigation, had accumulated. The grand jury voted to turn over materials it had accumulated to us. So we profited from the important evidence accumulated by substantial and important prior investigations. That is not in any way to minimize the very fine job that John Doar and his staff did. But how many times is the Congress going to be in a position before it undertakes an impeachment inquiry of having the benefit of prior intense congressional and grand jury investigations? So it may well be that the fortuitousness of these other investigations contributed in a way that may make repetition of impeachment unlikely or difficult even in circumstances in which it is desperately needed. Thank you very much.

Discussant: Judge Charles E. Wiggins

Thank you very much ladies and gentlemen. Greetings to my friends John Doar and Liz Holtzman. I haven't seen them for a number of years. I thank the school and our chairman for inviting me to talk about a subject of some interest to me. While I have been here I have heard that the holding of this conference about the Nixon presidency has generated some controversy. I am told that there are a number of professors who thought it to be inappropriate to hold such a conference, since it might be considered as an implicit endorsement, I think, of the Nixon Presidency. Others argued to the contrary, including our chairman. He maintained that there would be some balance struck in the presentations of views. And I note here today John Doar, who was an adversary in Congress, accompanied by Liz Holtzman, who was his cohort. We have also Professor Hamilton, who worked for John Doar. Finally, we have Terry Sullivan. I cannot figure out yet which side he is on. We have here today the kind of balance that I grew accustomed to in Congress.

In all events, I want you to know that I will not speak from a partisan point of view, although I am frankly and deeply offended by what occurred in 1974. As you know I've since become a member of the bench and I am apolitical. I don't have any political thoughts any more, but nevertheless, with that introduction, I want to proceed.

It's my purpose to speak briefly about the historical aspects of impeachment in our society. Then I want to relate that to the Nixon experience and particularly to Article II, since that is the focus of Professor Hamilton's remarks. And then I would like to conclude with a few personal views about Richard Nixon himself.

Impeachment was not invented in 1787. Impeachment existed on the continent of Europe for hundreds of years prior to our Constitution. Indeed, the expression "high crimes and misdemeanors" was borrowed from the European experience. There was this background of experience in Europe that the Founders of our Constitution called upon when they included the impeachment power in the Constitution. But what was this experience?

I found that it did not convey a single message. The earliest impeachments began around 1200 A.D. Thereafter there were a number of impeachments, and they tended to reflect the ebb and flow of parliamentary power vis-à-vis the monarchy. In England, there were times when the Parliament was in ascendency, and it would vigorously assert its power to superintend others in the government. And then there were times when the king himself asserted a strong control over the government. At such times the monarch did not and would not tolerate the exercise of an aggressive impeachment authority in Parliament. And so there was not a single lesson to learn. There was an example where the Parliament impeached one of the king's ministers for sleeping with the queen. The defense was characterized as a high crime or misdemeanor.

As we approach the eighteenth century and the formulation of the United States Constitution, the relevant European experience was one that confined its attention to criminal misconduct and not these excesses by various other king's ministers. Nevertheless, notwithstanding that experience, roughly at the time of 1787, the writings of Alexander Hamilton and of James Madison after the adoption of the Constitution in the *Federalist Papers* give a rather expansive definition of the power of impeachment. It's clear that Hamilton, at least, viewed the power as the opportunity to conduct a grand inquest over the affairs of public men. That's an ill-defined standard, but it represented Hamilton's view after the Constitution was formed. The American experience is probably the more relevant experience—it is clear that we got started earlier on by using it for blatant political purposes. The first impeachment effort was for Senator William Blount. He was guilty of something very close to treason, clearly a crime. As you know, the precedent in that case is that the impeachment power does not extend to a member of Congress. It was a decision you would expect Congress to reach, I suppose.

There were really only three major impeachments if we except the typical judicial impeachment. One was the attempted impeachment of Mr. Justice Chase. That was a conflict between Federalism and anti-Federalism. Justice Chase was an old Federalist, and there was a resurgence of the anti-Federalist, Democratic-Republican Jeffersonian wing coming into power. The impeachment of Justice Chase was purely political. It did not succeed.

The impeachment of President Andrew Johnson after the Civil War was clearly a political act by Congress challenging the authority of the president in the Reconstruction period. It was an exercise, a political exercise of contending political forces in our government.

And then, thirdly, the impeachment effort against Richard Nixon. In my view, a view not shared apparently by many in this room nor at the podium, the impeachment against Richard Nixon was purely a political exercise. And I'll speak more about that later on. Well, let me turn to this Richard Nixon case. I think I should discuss it in light of Article II especially. I admit that my memory is failing and that I don't have a perfect recollection of all the events that occurred.

First of all, the House Judiciary Committee debated the question of what should be the standard of review. Should we adhere to a criminality standard or does the power of impeachment reach to excesses of power? There was a rather structured debate and a party line vote on that question. The Democrats adhered to the standards that impeachment would reach excesses of power, whereas the Republicans voted, and I was among them, that in this case we should adhere to the standard of criminality.

Let me tell you that I believed then and believe now that the power to impeach does not require the commission of a criminal act. I felt then and I feel now, however, that it was necessary for the Congress to demonstrate that Richard Nixon had committed a criminal act. I say that because this issue evolved and developed from the breaking and entering of the Democratic National Committee Headquarters, a criminal act. That is why the impeachment committee was formed. It was charged with the duty of investigating into that act. And we concluded that Richard Nixon had nothing to do with that criminal act. He was innocent. But, could we have found that he would have been impeached for bombing Cambodia? I don't believe that the American people would have tolerated such a view by Congress. I think they would have viewed it as an egregious excess of power by Congress if it focused on what they would perceive to be collateral matters.

Well, we lost that debate. Congress concluded that it would subject the president to the power of impeachment for acts other than criminal acts, specifically for abusing his power, his authority. I'll take a personal aside here and say at the conclusion of that debate, after the House Judiciary Committee had voted to subject the president to impeachment for abusing his power, I questioned the chairman as to what this power meant. That is, what is abusive? I suggested that if it was going to be abusive, that it had to be something extraordinary. We had to have a standard to test whether or not President Nixon had done something out of the ordinary. And the way that you did that, accomplish that end, was to examine what his predecessors had done.

Now that was regarded as a cheap political shot. But was it? I mean how else are you to determine whether a president of the United States has abused his power on a objective basis unless you test it against the conduct of others? Well the majority in the House Judiciary Committee did not yield to my offer that they investigate Lyndon Johnson, for example, or Jack Kennedy, for example, in order to set a standard against which this abuse could be tested. And for good reason. Because they knew, and I knew, and *The Washington Post* knew, and everybody in town knew, that few presidents had more grossly abused power than had Lyndon Johnson. Be that as it may, I lost that battle too. And the Congress proceeded.

I want you to know some of its conclusions. One: Did Richard Nixon authorize the breaking and entry of the Democratic National Headquarters? I think the general perception is that he did. The evidence is to the contrary. There's no evidence that President Nixon personally authorized or knew about the breaking-in of the Democratic Headquarters in advance. The committee concluded that. The special prosecutor also found that the evidence supports that conclusion. Nevertheless, the committee concluded that he was guilty of a cover-up. What were the facts relevant to the cover-up? Well, it appeared that a lot of dollars were paid to Mr. [Gordon] Liddy and to others who were involved directly in the crime. If the money was paid to secure their silence, it was an act of obstruction of justice and a crime. If the money was not paid for that purpose but merely to pay the attorneys and to support their families, during a time when they were subject to accusations, it was not a crime. The key issue, then, was why was the money paid? Well, nearly everybody was certain of the answer, but they didn't have the evidence. They "knew the answer" because they didn't like Richard Nixon. They assumed that the Nixon Administration, which was really the defendant, here the respondent, had authorized the payment of money to secure silence. It was called "hush money." It was characterized as bribery. But the evidence that it was bribery or was hush money was not presented. At the time the vote was taken on Article I, the so-called criminal article, there was no evidence that Richard Nixon was personally involved. And he was the person subject to impeachment, not the administration, not the people who were in trouble in his administration, but President Nixon personally.

Well after the vote was taken, many felt they were vindicated by the so-called smoking gun evidence that came to public light after the vote was taken. I too felt that it was the final straw. Not because Richard Nixon deserved to be impeached, goodness no. It was evidence that linked Richard Nixon for a brief period of time with the obstruction of justice. What did the evidence show? It will only take me a moment to repeat it. A meeting was held in the Oval Office two days after the break-in, a meeting between the president and H. R. Haldeman. They talked for a couple of hours, but during the course of that two hours they got around to talking about Watergate. Haldeman took the lead and said that he was reporting a conversation that he had had with the Attorney General John Mitchell and John Dean. They had looked into this matter known as the Watergate, and decided that the FBI was getting close to information that they should not be involved in by tracing the money, following the money into Florida. They believed that the CIA should contact the FBI and tell them to lay off.

The president simply listened, he grunted a couple of times, and then he said approximately, "Well, I'm not going to second-guess John," meaning John Mitchell, his attorney general. "You, Haldeman, Ehrlichman, go talk to the FBI and the CIA." And they did so. Well, I think any law student writing on this subject could conclude that there was evidence that the president was attempting to interfere with a criminal investigation and that he obstructed justice. But that does not mean necessarily that you would impeach the president if that's all the evidence there was. Nevertheless, it was a crime. The evidence further disclosed, about two weeks later, that Pat Gray of the FBI called the president and said, "Mr. President, certain of your people are interfering with our investigation," and the President said, in approximate words, "Pat, you go ahead with your investigation, make a complete investigation, pay no attention to these people." The legal significance of the conversation was that perhaps the president withdrew from the conspiracy after joining it. However, there was a period of exposure of two weeks in which he was perhaps guilty of a criminal offense.

All of this evidence came to light after the committee had voted. It was persuasive enough for me to recognize that the presidency of Richard Nixon had been effectively destroyed. I felt that, whether he was subject to impeachment or not, we had to have a new president.

Article II was the abuse of power article. My concern then and now is what does it mean, and who determines whether power is abused in our society. The essence of the article that was approved by the committee was that a committee of Congress can determine when a president has abused his power. The conduct that it looks to is, essentially, political conduct.

I don't want to yield to a committee of Congress or to Congress itself the power to remove a president because it believes that the president has abused power. Congress pours whatever meaning it wants into that concept. The concept is an extraordinarily jump . . . an extraordinarily powerful jump in the transfer of power from the people to a legislative body. It resembles the parliamentary system in that the Parliament may have a vote of no confidence with respect to the prime minister at any time and replace him. What this says to me, and what perhaps we will say in the future, is that the Congress may be declaring that the president has abused power, vote him out of office. I think that's a dangerous precedent in our society. It usurps authority that ultimately belongs with the people. I vote against the article.

The third article—I don't think it's necessary to dwell on it. The House Judiciary Committee was offended because President Nixon would not respond to its subpoenas. He did not invoke the Fifth Amendment; of course, had he invoked the Fifth Amendment, the House would have backed down. Rather, he presented a principled argument about executive authority, executive power, and the House impeached him for doing so. They said the president had a duty to respond to our subpoenas, his argument of executive authority to the contrary notwithstanding. It is not very good form, I would think, to force the president to confront impeachment when he has an issue of executive power, and the extent of executive power that he wants to present to the Congress.

Well, I want to conclude by just a word or two about Richard Nixon. And I feel that after listening to a number of speakers today that somebody today should say something nice about Richard Nixon. I don't speak as a long-time friend of Richard Nixon. I know that people in the press portray me as some sort of in-pocket friend of the president. That is not the case. I was elected from what happened to be Richard Nixon's old district in California. I saw him speak on one occasion when he ran against Jerry Voorhis, a prominent New Deal Democrat. Mr. Voorhis retired to Claremont, California, and became one of the foremost Nixon critics for years thereafter.

After his election, Nixon was assigned to the House Committee on Un-American Activities at a time when anticommunism was on the rise in our society. And he got involved in the matter of Alger Hiss. He played a role in sending Alger Hiss to jail. Alger Hiss was not a light-weight in the Democratic party. He was a major political figure, and I think you can trace his demise to the activities of this young congressman, Richard Nixon. Nixon on the strength of that notoriety and publicity ran for the Senate. He took on Helen Gahagan Douglas, another prominent, well-placed Democratic leader. I was away in the service during that campaign and I just read about it. I read about how dirty it was. But I also noted that the dirt was flowing freely on both sides. It was a rather typical, closely contested senatorial race. Richard Nixon disposed of Helen Gahagan Douglas, and in doing so he made no friends among the Democratic party. Then, two years later he was elevated by Dwight Eisenhower to be vice president. I don't think Dwight Eisenhower knew him. He was just a young

Senator from California who would lend a balance to the ticket. But he was elected.

Well, it was in the context of all of this that Richard Nixon was eventually elected to the presidency. He had a host of political enemies with wounds that dated back for years. He was partisan. It was in that light that a partisan Congress considered whether to impeach him. They did not consider, ladies and gentlemen, whether or not the evidence would sustain an article of impeachment. The committee was formed to impeach Richard Nixon. The decision to impeach Richard Nixon was made not in the light of television, but in the Speaker's office. That is the way decisions are made in Congress.

In all events, I was deeply offended by this. I think Richard Nixon deserved far better. I believe that he served his country well. I believe that the conduct that is wrong, attributed to him and to his administration, was unexceptional in the history of American politics. I believe that people in power in Washington then and today knew that it was unexceptional; in fact, some were active players.

In my opinion, Richard Nixon is one of the strongest, and will be recorded ultimately as one of the strongest, presidents in this century. I am honored to have served with him, although independently of him. I regret his near-impeachment that led to his resignation.

___ Part II ___

Reexamining Nixon

Herbert S. Parmet remarked at the Conference that Richard Nixon was the "dominant political figure of the postwar period." Yet even those who spent their professional careers studying him—his biographers—were baffled by Nixon, the man, his motivations, goals, hopes, and fears. Roger Morris emphasized the roots from which he sprang, Southern California and the factionalism of the Republican party in the postwar years, all of which left important imprints on Nixon. Stephen E. Ambrose focuses on Nixon's relations with and contrast to Dwight Eisenhower, who was his mentor and idol, and for whom he did so much nasty political work. And Herbert S. Parmet saw Nixon as the embodiment of the postwar conservative reaction to the social welfare politics of the prior decades.

Part of the difficulty in understanding and writing about Nixon has been due to the lack of research materials from his presidency. James J. Hastings, the deputy director of the Nixon Presidential Materials Project of the National Archives, describes the legal status of the Nixon presidential materials and the special legal restrictions governing their access and release. Joan Hoff-Wilson explains how these legal restrictions on access and the ability of Nixon's representatives to challenge the release of broad categories of papers has made it very difficult to research important segments of his administration.

A final assessment of the Nixon legacy is examined in papers by Barry D. Riccio and Sherri Cavan, who focus on the difficulties of trying to place him in either the liberal or conservative mold. H. R. Haldeman and Robert H. Finch, who worked with him over a number of years, point out the many contradictions in the man. Finally, Arthur Schlesinger, Jr., evaluates Nixon in the "long trajectory of American history."

Reexamining Nixon

NIXON BIOGRAPHERS

Moderator: Louis W. Koenig

It is a great pleasure to participate in the Hofstra Conference once again, and especially on this panel on Nixon biographers. I suppose President Nixon is a perfect target for biographers with the complexities that we have learned about his personality in some of the sessions we have had so far. I speak of this mindful of a statement Adlai Stevenson once made that Mr. Nixon was once a man who wore many masks. He was, many would say, a divided man; a man whose life had many contradictions; a man of peace, but on the other hand one who made or ordered extensive bombings of North Vietnam; a supreme anticommunist, but also one who established friendly relations with the People's Republic of China.

I think of him as a model of deportment as vice president in the illnesses of President Eisenhower; a model of deportment in the 1960 contest with President Kennedy, as he conducted himself most commendably in that close election and during those results slowly coming in from Illinois and Texas. Then we get the picture of the Watergate disaster. Some have seen President Nixon in terms of personality, and I am very confident we will be getting into that in our discussion shortly. Others have stressed very much the nature and circumstances in which he was placed, so that some will say part of the Watergate explanation is that he had too many enemies in Congress with an opposition party controlling the legislature, as well as other factors possibly. I am mindful of a cartoon in which two men are standing at a bar and one of them is saying to the other, "Look, Nixon is no dope. If the people really wanted moral leadership he would give them moral leadership." In any case, we look hopefully to our biographers to explain the Nixon puzzle.

Discussant: Stephen E. Ambrose

I thought I would start with a continuation of what I did yesterday, that is, the comparing of Ike and Dick, and in this case, compare the sources for their lives that we biographers have to rely upon to try to put together the story of what this man did, how he did it, how he accomplished it, who his friends and associates were, and so on. With regard to Eisenhower, the situation is as close to ideal as a scholar could possibly want. The papers have been open for a long time. Only a tiny percentage of them, mainly covering nuclear warfare, are still sealed today by security classification. The staff and the director of the Eisenhower Library in Abilene are absolutely top people. The result is for the student of the 1950s and of the Eisenhower Administration almost an ideal situation.

Nixon's different. With Nixon it is very difficult to get into sources past 1963–64. His papers in Laguna Niguel, California—those vice presidential papers, so called—actually cover the period from his entry into politics in 1946 through the California gubernatorial campaign of 1962. Those papers at Laguna Niguel are very rich, and they do offer the kind of insight into the life Nixon led, the schemes that he plotted, the actions that he carried out, which a biographer could want. We come not to an absolute dead end, but pretty close to it after 1964–65, and certainly after 1968, although the National Archives has struggled valiantly to open up the papers of the Nixon Administration to researchers and scholars who want to explore the history of the late 1960s and early 1970s. The archives have been hampered in this effort, as I think everyone in this room knows, and a very great deal of the documentary record of the Nixon Administration remains under a seal, the subject of struggles in the court. There seems to be a determination on the part of Nixon himself, not so much, I gather, on the part of members of his administration, to continue the cover-up, to keep these basic working materials of the Nixon Administration hidden and unavailable to scholars. It is a dreadful situation. People such as Jim Hastings sitting here in front of me, among others, are working hard on this situation. We are going to have a panel on it tomorrow afternoon, and I am looking forward to that very much, but it is really a dreadful situation.

I want to comment on one part of it. The first thing any biographer, anybody thinking about Nixon, comes to realize is that the man is capable of enormous self-pity. The second thing, once you start a serious look, is that a lot of times he is right, and I end up feeling sorry for him too. On one particular case about the records of his administration, for example, he has quite a legitimate complaint that he is being treated differently from other presidents.

The Lyndon Johnson tape-recorded material down in Austin is under seal, and my understanding is it will remain under seal for some fifty years. Nixon has a very legitimate complaint there, that the archives have taken the Johnson papers and kept them under seal while they are trying to force the Nixon transcripts into the public realm.

In general, with regard to his papers, Nixon's complaint is that he is being treated differently from other presidents. Now the quick and glib answer to that is that he *is* different from other presidents since he is the only one who resigned, and so on. Actually, in the case of the archives, don't waste an awful lot of sympathy on Nixon. He is not being treated differently by the National Archives from other presidents (except on the matter of the tapes). To the best of my knowledge and understanding, the delay in the opening of the record of the Nixon Administration is a delay that is brought on by one man. It would disappear if he would leave aside his objections. That one man, of course, is Nixon, and here you have something so typical of Nixon, or so it seems to me. The man is shooting himself in the foot. Who is going to benefit most from the release of the records from the Nixon Administration?

I don't think it is possible for anyone to think any worse of Dick Nixon than very many of us in this room, certainly myself, did in 1974. I don't think there is anything in those papers that is going to make me regard Dick Nixon in a more negative way than I did then. I am very confident of that. The worst that can be said about Nixon I think has been said. For him to continue to insist that there are some 100,000 documents he objects to the release of certainly makes John Q. Public think, "My God, you mean there are 100,000 cover-ups in those Nixon papers?" Actually, a great deal that happened in the Nixon Administration was positive, innovative, forward-looking, and imaginative, but we historians can't tell that story until we can get at the record, and Nixon is the one who stands in the way.

Now going to the subject of sources for a life of Nixon: At the time when he was at the pinnacle of power and when he was in the presidency, we are denied the opportunity to look at the record of what he did, of what he was communicating, of what the memos said about meetings, and so on. But we do have a source that is a brand new thing which no historian, no biographer, has ever before had available to him, and that is the transcripts and the tapes themselves of the most intimate conversations between the president and his closest advisers at a time of great stress. They are wonderfully revealing. I'd never come across a better source, one that made me feel such a sense of how Nixon operated, how Haldeman operated, how they played off against each other. One of the things from long periods of time reading those tapes, for example, struck me very forcibly. I don't know if I would have come to it any other way. This is just judgmental on my part—it is that Richard Nixon was actually afraid of John Mitchell. This was not in the sense that a lot of politicians were afraid of J. Edgar Hoover, and not in the sense the Mitchell had something on him. It was in the sense that Mitchell was the only man that Nixon had ever met who had a more powerful personality than he did and who could dominate a room. Well, that is the sort of thing that you can't get out of documents but you can get out of these tapes.

However, for the Nixon Administration, despite the lack of evidence in the ordinary forms that we are accustomed to from other presidents, there is another place in which we have a special insight into Nixon and his people and how they operated. No administration in American history has produced so much in the way of memoirs, starting with the man at the top. Taking all of the presidential memoirs into account, none is so revealing as that of Richard Nixon. None print such intimate details as Nixon's does. None is as thorough in its coverage as Nixon's memoirs.

Then we go to some of the principal actors. There is no secretary of state in history that has come even close to Henry Kissinger with his twenty-five hundred pages of intimate details, self-serving arguments, reprinting of documents, insights and criticisms of the president, and some praise for him. However, you come away from it feeling you really do know more about Kissinger and the State Department than you really wanted to. For the researcher, that's exactly what you are looking for. Then, for so many others in that administration, because of the way that administration came to an end, and, one suspects, not least because so many members of the administration found themselves in difficulties that required big legal fees, it meant that they had to get those memoirs out in a hurry if they were ever going to pay those lawyers' bills. It resulted in a flood of memoirs that beats any previous administration, and especially from the speech writers, two of which are more of the memoir variety, those of Bill Safire and Ray Price. For a biographer it is wonderful to get these speech writers, who have the most intimate contact of all with the man, and especially with Nixon, who worked more closely with speech writers then anyone else. So there are plenty of sources on the Nixon Administration. I do regret, however, that he doesn't make more of the official papers of his administration available to scholars.

Discussant: Roger Morris

I thought I would address primarily what benefits and advantages I can give you as a biographer. And by you, I mean principally those in the audience who are historians of the Nixon Presidency or political scientists trying to fathom the inner workings of the U.S. Government. I think there are some valuable contributions to be made to that study from political biography, especially the early career of notable politicians such as Richard Nixon. Let me share with you briefly some of the highlights of the early period with which my wife and I have been most concerned over the last several years, tying in those points of relevance to what you may be working on in the presidential years.

My main concern in undertaking the political biography of Richard Nixon was to repatriate an alien. It is a truism in American political biography that we tend to give our presidents place and time. We make them native to the American soil in some way, whether it is Tidewater, Virginia, for Jefferson, or the dust of Abilene for Dwight Eisenhower, or Hyde Park for Franklin Roosevelt. We do that with some facility with perhaps one exception—Richard Nixon. Most of the early biographers of the man tended to see him as an aberration, as a man as Gary Wills said, who lacked the color of time and place. I disagreed with that almost wholly, and wanted to give Richard Nixon back his country, his time, and his place. That was the essential approach of the biography. I thought, too, that political biography ought to tell us something beyond the surface about American politics, about how it works. Even though one was writing about a politician from the '40s or '50s, '60s or '70s, one ought to hold to the standards of the 1980s, and therefore we ought to know about money and power as much as possible.

With that in mind, let me begin with some of the insights and some of the high points of Nixon's early career as they relate to understanding Nixon the president and Nixon the major figure of the second half of the twentieth century in American politics.

First, of course, we had to look at the history of American Quakerism. It turns out, I think, that religion was one of the more important factors in the background, in the making of this man whom many Americans see as symbolizing immorality and amoralism in American political life. There is a memorable scene which takes place on a sultry September night in 1927 in Los Angeles at a large, old church downtown. A father who is grieving at the loss of his youngest son takes his other three boys for a revival, and during that experience they charge down the aisles with the rest of the very emotional and heaving crowd of converts to declare themselves for Jesus Christ. The middle son is fourteen years old. He writes about this experience later and is deeply touched by it. The older son is about to be sent away to a very spartan religious school in the East, mainly because the high school principal at Whittier Union is rumored to be a secret smoker and the whole place is thought to be quite licentious. The older boy returns from that experience—where he takes 5 A.M. showers in icy temperatures in the unfinished basement of the dormitories—with a raging case of tuberculosis, and that precipitates a second family tragedy. Well, the older son, of course, is Harold, and the middle boy who at fourteen is also sent away to school somewhat closer to home in Fullerton is Richard Milhous Nixon. He belongs very much to those wonderful little musty, wooden Quaker churches that dotted the landscapes in the Los Angeles basin in the 1920s and 1930s. One has to understand the difference between Eastern and Western Quakerism and the great wave of evangelical reform that swept that religious movement in the nineteenth century to understand the peculiar, and I think very important, religious provenance of this particular president.

He also, of course, has a personal life. He is not, in fact, a mystery, nor is he an aberration. He belongs very much to his time and place in American culture. He is capable of a flinty anger and also of great human tenderness. He is at once, for his time and place and for his age, sophisticated yet very naive. He has a love affair which has, I think, on the whole a traumatic effect on his youth. He comes from a family on his mother's side of some social, political, and economic pretense, which has an effect on his own future pretensions. He has a very strong and capricious father, who instills in him political views and at the same time creates a kind of cowardliness toward political and personal confrontation, which ends up haunting Richard Nixon's presidency.

So he belongs to those little churches. But he also belongs to that store in East Whittier. He belongs to that tract where his father tried to raise lemons without success in Yorba Linda. And he belongs to the special time and place of Southern California of his era. He belongs to the packinghouse where his mother worked for a while with great humiliation, and he belongs to those tents where the revivals took place and where the families went to see Billy Sunday and Paul Raider and all the rest.

He belongs also to a period that is often very neglected by biographers and by historians in general, and that is the early adult years during which he returns from Duke Law School and tries to set up a law practice. Despite his hopes and dreams of practicing in New York or somewhere outside Los Angeles, he ends up with a very small and in some respects rather seedy local law firm, Wingert and Bewely, in Whittier, and it is that period of 1937–42 that in many ways was the political crucible for what followed. It is in that period that he makes his first abortive run, in this case for a State Assembly job that he is not ready to get and in which he doesn't yet have the anointing of the Republican elders. He also maneuvers for the presidency of Whittier College and even for a city attorney's job in little La Habra. In those maneuvers, in those politics of that early period, one finds a great deal that's familiar form the later Nixon years, including the presidency.

In many respects, of course, it is the later political career which is the most intriguing and the most beckoning. For those of you who are on the trail for dirty money in Watergate or who want to talk about backers and powers, about coalitions and groups and special interests in Richard Nixon's political career, please begin by all means with 1946. That campaign is the beginning of something that was less than honesty in campaign-spending reporting. It's also the beginning of his lifelong alliance with some of the most powerful groups in Southern California. It is true, Virginia, there was a Committee of One Hundred. They were in many respects small businessmen. But it's true as well that there were many, many other supporters and forces behind Richard Nixon's start in American politics, some of whom were not small businessmen and some of whom were not on the Committee of One Hundred. It's also true that in the records in Sacramento you will find recorded campaign contributions and spending of $17,000, and that is roughly one-tenth to one-fifteenth of what was actually spent and at one time recorded before the records were destroyed. You will recognize in 1946 some of the methods that become so enduring and so important in 1968 and again in 1972, and you will, of course, see a very important role played by that other character in the early Nixon years that we all know, Murray Chotiner.

From the following years in the Congress, I was struck again and again by how much the habits of the Nixon Presidency were cultivated early in his first experience in American politics in the Capitol. One will discover in the first two years of the Eightieth Congress a remarkable early liaison with a kind of subterranean secret government that runs just beneath the surface of American politics. He has a number of crucial and really fateful alliances with the Catholic Church, with the U.S. Chamber of Commerce, and most of all with the Federal Bureau of Investigation. It facilitates some of the most startling and dramatic episodes in his political rise. It's a record which has been very largely secret, but which, I think, you will find very illuminating in terms of the later events in his presidency. He comes to Watergate, he comes to the White House, he comes to the pinnacle of American political power, with expectations and habits of government and of politics that were shaped in those first two years in the Congress of the United States. He also comes from that early period very much as the darling of the press corps. The man who is commonly assumed to have been hated by the American media begins his political career having it very much his own way. He is not only pampered by *The Los Angeles Times* and uniformly adored by the local press in the 12th District in California—to the point that many of the local editors and reporters served as veritable campaign aides—but he also has marvelous press relations in Washington. He has an early alliance with *The New York Herald Tribune* in the person of Bert Andrews and others who facilitate his rise and who play behind-the-scene roles in his eventual nomination as vice president.

Going on, you will find that 1950 and the whole race against Helen Gahagan Douglas, which is normally assumed to be most renowned for its smears and its anticommunist themes, really introduce something equally important in Richard Nixon's life—a series of machinations and schemes involving the opposition party. He has a remarkable liaison in 1950 with a man who ran against Helen Gahagan Douglas in the Democratic primary, and that tells a wholly different and, I think, unique story of how he emerged as a United States Senator. You find also that in 1952 the real story of his nomination is not so much in the convention in Chicago but in the events before that—and that there is a history in the Republican party at least a year before the actual convention itself in which Richard Nixon's nomination is all but a foregone conclusion.

I was amused by Henry Kissinger last night, my old and esteemed boss, when he so insistently demanded modesty in terms of his own accomplishments, a modesty I think for the most part that he deserves. When Henry Kissinger was writing that thesis he was telling us about and worrying about the British Foreign Ministry in the nineteenth century as a student at Harvard, Richard Nixon was already a U.S. senator. And later of course as a vice president he was indeed negotiating some fairly serious foreign political entanglements, and was indeed playing a role behind the scenes in the Eisenhower Administration as a diplomat and, most of all, as a politician at court. So Henry is right that President Nixon came with a good deal of experience and skill in terms of diplomacy, at home and abroad.

Finally, let me say that 1960 was perhaps the most startling chapter of all for us in the early years of the Nixon life, because that election turned out to be an even greater watershed than anyone had assumed. It is not only the point at which Richard Nixon sheds his old political persona and becomes a statesman in defense of an administration, but also the point at which he suffered the first real loss in his political career. He loses in an election which almost certainly, by what is available now in terms of documentation, was stolen by the Democratic party—and not simply by local functionaries in Chicago or in Nevada or Hawaii or New Mexico or Texas but by liaison with the Kennedy campaign in Boston. He loses that race and in so doing suffers such a tremendous disillusionment, such a jading of his own view of American politics, that he also sheds almost his entire staff and much of the style and tone of his basic political approach. He takes on, as you know, a whole new cast of characters, who emerge slowly in the 1960s, first in 1962, and go on to become some of the famous people you see on this stage and who play major roles in his presidency, and in his final scandal and fall.

Let me say in conclusion that I think that it's terribly, terribly important—if we are going to understand Richard Nixon the man, and Richard Nixon the president—that we place him, as we would any other American president or politician, in the context of his history; that we understand Southern California; that we understand the Republican party in California from which he sprang; that we understand the factionalism; that we understand the interests, the money, the power than he came to represent. It is no less vital that we forgive the man, if you will, and, perhaps grant him the compassion and the sensitivity to remember what it was to be a politician at that moment. His presidency was not always easy, as Henry Kissinger reminded us last night. Neither was his rise.

And it left on the man the scars and the imprint that we see in the record of his tragic fall from power. I hope biography can give you a sense of those beginnings, can clear away some of the mysteries about who he was, why he was what he was—and give you without simplistic causation some understanding not only of the past, but of what is to come in the future.

Discussant: Herbert S. Parmet

I do feel that those of us here today will basically be the vanguard of the process of examining Richard Nixon, but also of what I am also much more concerned with, the vanguard of the process of examining the United States and the world during the period when he was so prominent. That is what I think is the major need. This process will be going on, then, for an unlimited amount of time, as history invariably does.

The peculiarities of the Nixon personality have been exhumed ad nauseum. He has come down to us in various reincarnations; he is either an American Cataline or a Clyde Griffiths, the unfortunate protagonist of *An American Tragedy*, who was the victim, as Theodore Dreiser described it, of not only his own needs but of the society as well.

The point here is to get down to an understanding of why Richard Nixon has been such a commanding figure not only in the United States but in the world. It should be of some interest—and it was to me, and I came upon this after I began my work—to find out that on the day Richard Nixon resigned, on August 9, 1974, Anthony Lewis of *The New York Times*, who, as you know, is hardly a fan of Richard Nixon, made the observation in his column that "the Age of Nixon has come to an end." It was the culmination of an era, and that's what I am concerned with, and that is what my work primarily is trying to unravel, in trying to provide us with a perspective of the man and his presidency because, after all, in my lifetime and a good many of the lifetimes of most of us in this room, Richard Nixon was the dominant American political figure. He has been the dominant political figure of the postwar period. He has been a character we have seen in dozens in Herblock cartoons. We are all familiar with that: the devil incarnate; the archetypical opponent of Harry Truman, the man he supposedly implied was a "traitor" to the United States.

When we go back and realize the role that Nixon played, we begin to see that certain things fall into place. Of course, we historians have to be very careful about not trying too hard, too many times, to make things too tidy. But we do have to have some kind of language so that we understand what we are trying to do and trying to say.

His era—and by his era I mean from his California beginnings and the Voorhis campaign of 1946—coincided basically with the postwar world. The end of his presidency coincided with the end of that postwar world both at home and abroad. It was more than just the end of a presidency. Nixon's presidency served a function between Roosevelt and what followed Nixon as an attempt to rationalize two ongoing developments, the progression of the New Deal welfare state and the continuing Cold War. Nixon has always seen himself as somewhat of a broker playing this role in this thirty-year period of conflict. Contrary to the Herblockian view, and contrary to the view of many of us who have followed the Republican party, at heart (and I think you will find this going back to the California campaigns of 1946 and against Helen Gahagan Douglas in 1950) he has always been less the political partisan than a centrist who continued to believe in what he called—and he called it that back in 1946—"practical liberalism." He meant by that encouragement for the spirit of entrepreneurialism. In his emphasis, that did not assume that the various levels of government could or should remain indifferent to the needs to safeguard those who were victimized by the system. At the time at which he was most identified as an orthodox Republican, his role was to try to steer the Republican party along a middle course, somewhere between the contending impulses of the Rockefellers, the Goldwaters, and the Reagans—during, in other words, this vital period between the Age of Roosevelt and what Kevin Phillips has noted became "postconservative America."

Nixon embodied, epitomized the children of the New Deal generation who found their way back to a confidence that American capitalism could work and could work for their children as well. They rediscovered the values that seemed to have gone askew. Nixon keenly reflected the middle-class priorities that were especially important to those whom we might call the working middle class. They saw in Nixon not a figure of glamour at all, but in certain ways something closer to the real gut: a guardian of their intent to secure a piece of the American turf, or their idea of the American dream. And to do so without losing out to those who were insistent on changing the rules in the middle of the game by grabbing advantages that were not available to earlier generations. This was not only the coming of most Americans, the great majority, who were middle-class, but we must also understand it as the process of the acculturation and assimilation of generations of immigrants, which had achieved an American identity while at the same time reconciling that with their ethnic heritages as they had come to a point where they bought the American dream, felt themselves part of it, and did constitute a conservative, stabilizing force in the context of American traditionalism.

For reasons not too hard to fathom, an unusually large number of writers have been obsessed with trying to psychoanalyze the man. I suppose that in the hands of valid specialists, that kind of inquiry does have its place. But it is too bad if it obstructs our view of certain essentials.

Within the context of postwar America, then, I believe (with due respect to all the various analyses and examinations of the man) that Richard Nixon is, in the long run, less significant for the peculiarities of his own psychological makeup (does it really matter whether or not he had a "zest" for mashing potatoes?) than really as one who, in his attitudes toward both foreign and domestic policies, provided leadership for a wide variety of second- and third-generation ethnic groups and older line Republican stalwarts in protecting their interests from the excesses and abuses of welfare state liberalism—and what they regarded as well-meaning but utopian impracticalities that were envisioned by many humanitarian social reformers whose objectives they very often did not denigrate.

At the same time, to further help polarize the situation, the Democratic party increasingly came to be seen as the captive of dissidents and outsiders who were looking to the federal government for special privileges. Those who had made it through the postwar period were now concerned with consolidating their arrival and protecting it.

Nixon saw himself, then, as attempting to maneuver through this, and he hoped to bring together a bipartisan coalition of entrepreneurialists of various racial, ethnic, and class stripes, all bound together in not only a strong adherence to traditionalism but also a very strong sense of American nationalism. This included, most importantly, a regional unification. He thought in regional terms, so he meant the South as well as the North and the West. And if we really understand the much-discussed, the much-publicized "Southern Strategy," which we associate with the 1963 and 1972 campaigns, we can understand that it actually constituted a national strategy. From my work on Kennedy, I remember how Kennedy had to put off his action on open housing until after the congressional elections of November 1962 because of the number of Democratic congressmen and congresswomen from the North who were concerned in a way that was not very dissimilar to concerns of the South. Nixon was speaking not only to Southerners, he was speaking to those Democrats as well.

For the period from the end of the war until the rise of the New Right and their capture of the White House, the character of American politics and diplomacy was shaped by the essentials that were common to the Age of Nixon. It was an age of contention. It was an age of uncertainty about what kind of a role America could and should play in a confusing and dangerous world. We were about as unresolved about that as we now are about what to do with Richard Nixon.

Discussant: Raymond K. Price, Jr.

Good afternoon. It is good to be here and to be with this panel, although I do feel somewhat that I am here under false pretenses because I am not a professional scholar. Even the one book that I did was not a biography of Nixon as such but rather an interpretive retrospective on the Nixon years and on him as a person and as president—what he was like, what he and we confronted, what we tried to do, and where and why we succeeded and failed.

What I do perhaps bring, as the introduction suggested, is a somewhat different perspective from those of most who have written formal biographies as such. It is a perspective of twenty years of personal and professional association with Richard Nixon before, during, and since his presidency, including the exile in San Clemente and the return to New York. Just as a reader approaching any work on a public figure needs a shaker of salt to put on what the author writes, you obviously need a shaker of salt with me because I come from this very different perspective. I take a subjective approach. But at least it is one with the biases up front and out there to be seen.

I wouldn't have been associated with Richard Nixon for twenty years if I didn't believe in him and what he was trying to do. I certainly would not have stuck with him during the darkest days, at a time when doing so had a very high cost, if I didn't think he was on the right side in Watergate as in most other things, whether or not it was on the winning side.

I have argued for a long time that people were going to be surprised by the rapidity with which the Nixon Presidency would be reassessed. It took thirty years for Hoover to be reassessed. It took twenty years for Harry Truman. People forget that Truman was the only president since Gallup began measuring presidential approval whose actual approval rating while in office was lower than the Nixon Administration's at its lowest point. We dropped to 24 percent in the Gallup; Truman dropped to 23 percent, and he is now regarded as one of our better presidents. There are two reasons why I have always felt that Nixon's reassessment will come faster. First, the pendulum swings faster now. We have a shorter attention span. Things change more rapidly. Second, the assessments of the Nixon Presidency that came out of its last days were the product of nothing short of mass hysteria, and hysteria doesn't last. As hysteria fades, people begin to put things in perspective. They begin to look at the good and bad together— which is the job of history. Obviously, a lot went wrong as well as right in our administration. I do think that when these are put together into perspective he's going to be seen, to the surprise of many, to be in the top rank of American presidents.

In these few minutes I am not going to refight the Watergate battle. There are plenty of other people on the program these three days to do that. Rather, I would like to touch briefly on a few other aspects of the presidency and of Nixon.

Just to illustrate, let me tell you about my own first encounter with him. It was twenty years ago, on Washington's birthday, 1967. *The Herald Tribune*, of which I was the last editorial page editor, had folded a few months earlier. I was in New York, trying to get a novel written. For many years the *"Trib"* had been considered the voice of the Eastern establishment in the Republican party. I got a call that morning from Richard Nixon, whom I did not know. He wondered whether I might be interested in joining him in beginning to prepare for what might be a campaign for the presidency in 1968. My initial reaction was that I doubted it. I wasn't at all sure he was going to be my candidate, much less whether I would want to get involved. But he invited me to lunch that day, and I went. We spent three hours talking about practically everything under the sun—politics, people, philosophy, the world, the nation—where it's been, where it's going. As he skipped around the world he would skip from event to event, and place to place, and issue to issue. And he would do this at first in a seemingly disparate way but then he would tie it all together neatly at the end so that all the apparently unrelated pieces suddenly fit. I began to see the workings of an absolutely remarkable mind. I had been a professional observer of politics. I had thought I understood him pretty well. But I found that I didn't. I found him to be a more impressive person than I had imagined. At the end of the three hours he asked me to give him an answer in a week. Well, I went back home, trying to decide whether I now wanted to join him. The first question was whether he was my candidate. I had quite a few books and clipping files and so forth that bore on him. I also brought to the choice a lot of prejudices. I came out of the New York newspaper establishment and, to put it mildly, he was not the most popular political figure among my newspaper colleagues. But I found that the more I dug into the facts, the more the prejudices fell away. I found to my surprise that he *was* my candidate after all. Having finally decided that I should do it, I called him back on the seventh day and said that if he still wanted me to work with him, I'd like to. He asked me to come down to his office that afternoon. I did. He had an empty office at the law firm waiting. I started work that night.

The reason I tell you this is that I later found out how common this was for people whose whole perceptions of Richard Nixon had been formed by what they read and heard about him through the media. When they met him one on one, in person, they found he was vastly better than they had imagined. Almost everyone who did so had such a reaction, and this must tell us something about the way our impressions are formed—about how they became layered one over another until the life is drained out and a caricature is created.

Another thing happened shortly afterward that I think also tells something important about Nixon. A month later I accompanied him on a ten-nation tour of Asia and the Far East. It was a study trip. He was surveying that part of the world, putting his ideas together for the campaign and perhaps eventually for the presidency. We were in India at a time of intense difficulty in Indian-American relations because of a then-recent change in U.S. arms supply policies. The

Indians thought the United States had done this in such a way as to favor their bitter enemy Pakistan, and they were made as hell at us. The U.S. ambassador then was Chester Bowles, a veteran Democratic politician, former governor of Connecticut and president Kennedy's under secretary of state. Bowles had us over for dinner the night we arrived. It was a very genial evening, a couple of politicians sharing old war stories. However, the ambassador did have one very special request, a plea to Nixon: Would Nixon please hold a press conference at the embassy the next day to try to explain to the Indians why the Johnson Administration had taken the actions it had?

On this trip Nixon had been assiduously avoiding the press; it was a deliberately low-key study trip. But Bowles asked and he agreed. So the next day we went to a large hall in the embassy that was crammed with reporters—mostly Indians but some from other countries. For an hour they shot largely hostile questions. He fielded them, always explaining, never complaining, always walking meticulously the fine lines between Indian and Pakistan sensitivities and between their sensitivities and those of the United States, and explaining why the United States had felt that it must take these actions. At the end of the hour Bowles pulled him aside, thanked him profusely, and said he thought it was the best thing that had been done for Indian-American relations in years. Think about this. Nixon expected to run for the presidency against Lyndon Johnson. Only the most skilled diplomatist could have done this without a note, without a briefing paper, in such a sensitive situation, with those results. Only someone who is a statesman first and a politician second would instinctively and intuitively have spoken for the United States and on behalf of the administration he was going to run against, without putting an inch of distance between himself and the administration in a situation like that. Yes, he is a politician; yes, he is also a statesman.

What did we inherit when we came into office? I was fascinated by the way Herb Parmet is trying to put things in the perspective of history, which is the only way you can assess a presidency. And it has always fascinated me that if you divide the century neatly into thirds, you find that the middle third begins with the start of the Roosevelt Administration and ends with the close of the Johnson Administration. That was a third of a century of rapidly accreting power in Washington. We came to the White House at the start of the final third, and Nixon took office determined to reverse that flow—to get power moving back out of Washington toward the states and communities, and, most important, toward the people. This was the source of a lot of later friction. It meant taking power away from people and institutions that had come to think of it rightly as their own. These included a lot in Congress, a lot in the intellectual establishment, and a lot in the media establishment who felt it was their right to rule.

We also inherited the legacy of the 1960s, which I have called the second most disastrous decade in the nation's history—the only worse one being the 1860s, when we had an actual civil war. There were riots, burnings, and assassinations, with the civil discourse turning shrill as the nation tore itself apart with civility completely drained away. We inherited a bitterly unpopular war with half a million troops half a world away, with Americans not understanding why and with the previous administration having no plan either to win it or to get out.

Coming into office, Nixon's first inaugural plea was to lower our voices. For a while that happened. But pretty soon the honeymoon was over, the shrillness returned, and the curse of the 1960s was visited on the early 1970s, coloring all that happened in the coming years.

To me, Watergate was the last hurrah of the 1960s. From start to finish Nixon's was probably the second most embattled presidency in America's history, Lincoln's being the only one more so. In the end we looked out from the White House in those final days and saw many of the same adversaries. But in most things that happened, it was at a time of very high performance and very high purpose. I missed yesterday's sessions and last night's address by Henry Kissinger, but I think Henry probably covered a good deal of that high performance.

There are two things you have to bear in mind about Richard Nixon. One, he's a tough, resourceful politician. Two, he's a very shrewd and a very serious statesman. As a politician, he was in the tradition of Roosevelt, Kennedy, and Johnson; the difference being that when they did the same things as Nixon, they didn't get caught.

I often think of a remark that Jimmy Roosevelt made at the height of Watergate. We were out in California and I was sitting with Rose Mary Woods when she took a call from him. He complained bitterly to Rose about what his colleagues in Congress (he was a six-term Democratic Congressman from California, a liberal Democrat) were doing to Richard Nixon. He said "everything they ever accuse him of, Father did twice as much of."

Later in the same period I was chatting with "Tommy the Cork"—Thomas G. Corcoran, who was the great Roosevelt brain truster. With that Irish gleam in his eyes, he told me, "The trouble with your fellows is that they're always writing memos. When we did those things we never put it on paper." As a statesman I think Nixon really is in the tradition of the great European statesman of the past— the geopolitician who understands the use of force, understands the need to use it, and also understands that the threats to freedom in our world are real. He is not a saint, not by any means. But I would suggest to you that a saint would make a disastrous president, and any good president would never get past the first qualifying rounds for sainthood. The job descriptions are very different. Nixon is also voraciously studious. He is always reading and writing and thinking, and especially plotting alternative courses of action out through their multiple-order consequences in the future. Because of this, one trap that people trying to read his motives often fall into is to assume that a particular action is taken for the immediately apparent motive. In fact, he probably is thinking of what he hopes to achieve by it six or seven moves further along the way.

Since the presidency I have traveled with Mr. Nixon a number of times to

Europe and Asia. I have been struck every time by the respect in which he is still held over there, and by their puzzlement at the strange ways of these odd Americans who take a statesman like this and toss him away like a paper napkin. I agree with them. He certainly has left a major legacy diplomatically, even though his work was aborted before it was finished. Had he not been weakened by Watergate and forced from office, I still believe that Southeast Asia would be free today. In the Middle East, he saved Israel during its darkest hours while still restoring the historic friendship between the United States and Israel's Arab neighbors. He carved out a new pattern of relationships with the Soviet Union, in large part because, in the course of three summits, he and Brezhnev sat down together, argued together, talked together, reasoned together, and practically arm wrestled together at times. Each knew that the other was tough, each knew he couldn't roll the other. Each knew that the other was going to vigorously defend his own country's interests. Therefore, they were able to deal in the common interest of both. And of course he also did bring China back into the community of nations *on the right terms*, not the wrong ones, not shooting its way back in, but as a potentially great and progressing nation that was willing to live at peace with its neighbors.

Two days before he resigned on Tuesday of that final week, having been up and down on the question of whether to resign or not, he decided that he would. The next morning, August 7th, I put a first draft of his resignation speech on his desk. Let me just read you the memo that I attached:

August 7, 1974

MEMORANDUM FOR: THE PRESIDENT

FROM: RAY PRICE

SUBJECT: RESIGNATION SPEECH

A first draft is attached. I'll be working on additional thoughts for it.

As I believe you know, I think this had become a sad but necessary decision in the circumstances. But I hope you'll leave office as proud of your accomplishments here as ' I am proud to have been associated with you, and to have been and remain a friend. God bless you; and He will.

In the same circumstances I'd write the same note today. Thank you.

RESEARCHING THE NIXON PRESIDENCY: DOCUMENTS AND EVIDENCE

10

The Status of the Nixon Presidential Materials

JAMES J. HASTINGS

Many of the participants in this conference were once members of the Richard Nixon Administration, and they have provided us during these last three days with some reflections on their experiences. Other participants are scholars of the Nixon Administration, and they have provided us with their analyses of that important period in history. My role in this conference is somewhat odd in that, as the custodian of the official historical record of the Nixon Administration, I am the middleman between the document originator and the present-day user of the materials. My job is to ensure that the Nixon presidential materials are preserved and made available in an equitable and timely fashion. I am here today to report on the status of this task.

The Nixon Presidential Materials Project is part of the National Archives of the United States. Our goal is to provide access to the historical records of the Nixon Administration so that everyone—whether former staff member, scholar, or member of the general public—can have a better understanding of what everyone agrees was a presidency of great importance. A complete understanding of the Nixon Presidency is impossible without access to the original source materials.

I am proud to say that major portions of the Nixon materials are now available for inspection in the Nixon Project's research room in Alexandria, Virginia. Beginning in December 1986 and continuing through July of this year, we opened significant groups of files covering topics ranging from Arts to Utilities, and including the office files of President Nixon and many of the highest level staff members of his administration. In fact, the files of many of the participants in this conference are open, including H. R. Haldeman, John Ehrlichman, and Egil

Krogh. In addition, most of the audiovisual materials from the administration
are open—the one famous exception being the White House tapes.

How did we finally reach this point and how does our work with the Nixon
materials compare to the handling of the archival materials of other modern
Presidents? These are the questions I will answer today.

In 1973 the question of access to the records of the still-incumbent Nixon
Administration was one of the most profound issues confronting the American
government. "Smoking Gun," "Saturday Night Massacre," and "Modified
Limited Hangout" are but a few of the expressions that have entered the modern
American lexicon as a result of attempts to gain access to the Nixon materials
during the administration. Executive privilege was argued constantly at both ends
of Pennsylvania Avenue. Never before in American history had the issue of
access to the records of a president been so pivotal in the resolution of a great
national crisis. As we all know, it was access to one particular historical record—
a very reluctantly released tape recording—that brought about the accelerated
end of the Nixon Presidency.

However, the controversy over access to the Nixon materials did not end with
President Nixon's resignation. In September 1974, former president Nixon signed
an agreement with Arthur Sampson, the head of the General Services Administration, which was then the parent organization of the National Archives. This
so-called Nixon-Sampson agreement mandated the destruction of the tapes and
allowed considerable opportunity for destruction of some of the papers, too. It
left any true donation of the Nixon materials tentative, and assigned to the former
president very strong powers of control over access. This agreement was signed
without the knowledge of the National Archives. Needless to say, there were
those who were upset by the Nixon-Sampson agreement, and the ensuing furor
resulted in legislation, signed by President Gerald Ford in December 1974, that
seized all the Nixon materials and placed them in the custody of the government.
Nixon challenged this law, known as the Presidential Recordings and Materials
Preservation Act, and demanded in court that the prior agreement be followed.
In 1977, the Supreme Court ruled that the 1974 Act was constitutional.

Since the constitutionality of the act was upheld, we have been processing
the materials to ensure their preservation and to prepare them for opening to the
public. In working toward the goal of providing access to the Nixon materials,
we have followed four interrelated guidelines:

1. The requirement of the 1974 act that the National Archives make available to the
   public at the earliest reasonable date materials essential to the understanding of
   Watergate.

2. The agreement negotiated between Nixon and the National Archives in 1979 concerning the processing of the former president's materials.

3. The provisions of the Nixon materials public access regulations, promulgated by the
   National Archives and accepted by Congress.

4. The practices developed by the Presidential Libraries for use in processing materials similar to the Nixon materials.

Each of these points has influenced how we have performed our job and, ultimately, what we have made available for research use. How each of these affected our actions, together with Nixon's reactions, constitutes the history of the Nixon Project up to the present moment. Each warrants elaboration.

ACCESS TO WATERGATE INFORMATION AT THE EARLIEST DATE

Needless to say, at the end of the administration there was very little interest in any topic related to Richard Nixon other than Watergate. When Congress enacted the legislation that placed the Nixon materials in the government's custody, there was great concern that the recently pardoned former president would destroy the historical record of abuses of power in his administration, thereby frustrating the public's right to know the full truth about Watergate. One of the primary reasons for the passage of the 1974 act was to ensure that information about the abuse of power would be made available to the public.

Fulfilling this congressional mandate was not a simple matter for the National Archives. The first proposal put forward was that we examine each document in the forty million pages of files to look for and identify abuse of power–related items. In other words, the archivists were to become "Junior G-Men," ferreting out evidence of misdeeds. Such an assignment would have violated two of the most sacred tenets of archivists: we never engage in interpreting the documents, and we never release documents out of context. In addition to the archival problems inherent in this plan, Nixon's lawyers added the legal objection that such investigative processing would violate his Fourth Amendment rights. We decided to put away our badges and "heaters," and to conduct our processing in a more traditional, noninvestigative way.

However, we had to find some way to satisfy the law's mandate. We determined that the only reasonable way to accomplish the task of opening abuse of power–related documents was to process entire groups of files that would most likely include Watergate information. In this way we could fulfill the congressional mandate yet avoid violating either traditional archival principles or Nixon's rights. The files most likely to contain Watergate information were determined to be, first, the Special Files, consisting of the papers of the president himself and his chief advisers; and second, the White House tapes. The legal requirement to first open abuse of power–related documents left no alternative to beginning our processing with the materials considered to be the most sensitive. This procedure—which is not the normal practice in the presidential libraries—troubled both the National Archives and Richard Nixon, for different reasons, and even concerned parts of the research community, who faced the prospect of waiting far longer for less sensitive materials while we worked on the more difficult files.

THE NEGOTIATED AGREEMENT BETWEEN THE GOVERNMENT AND FORMER PRESIDENT NIXON

Former president Nixon did not cease protesting the treatment of the archival materials of his administration when the Supreme Court ruled on the constitutionality of the Presidential Recordings and Materials Preservation Act. He also contended in Court that the regulations implementing the act violated his constitutional rights in a number of ways. These challenges delayed all processing of the materials for more than four years after the end of his presidency. Because archival processing routinely begins in presidential libraries soon after the end of an administration, the parties in the litigation sought to settle the issues that were prohibiting the timely processing of the Nixon materials. This agreement was reached in February 1979, and processing began shortly thereafter.

This "negotiated agreement" between Nixon and the government certified that the first two file groups to be processed would be the Special Files and the White House tapes. The parties further agreed that no documents or portions of tapes would be released out of the context of an "integral file segment"—to use the term the lawyers invented. Perhaps the most controversial and historically far-reaching part of the agreement, which the archivists fought hard against, was the determination that any political document in the files that did not have a direct connection to the president's constitutional powers or statutory duties would be permanently removed from the files and returned to the former president. Returning such political documents, which are woven throughout every president's files, would necessarily result in permanently damaging the integrity of the file. The National Archives reluctantly agreed to this drastic departure from the practices of the presidential libraries because former President Nixon indicated that he would donate the withdrawn materials in the future to the National Archives. This agreement, although far from perfect, cleared the way for us to begin our work to make the Nixon materials available to the public.

THE PUBLIC ACCESS REGULATIONS

The 1974 act placed the Nixon materials in the government's custody and required the National Archives to promulgate regulations implementing the public access provisions of the law. The present set of regulations is the sixth set to have been proposed.

The most significant portions of the regulations specify what restrictions will be applied to the materials and what rights remain to the persons who created the documents or are mentioned in them. These restrictions were consciously drawn from the restriction categories that govern access to the materials of other former presidents, although the language used was based on that of the Freedom of Information Act. Essentially, the archivists look for and temporarily remove from the files that are to be opened to the public information that, if disclosed, would violate a federal statute, compromise national security, reveal confidential commercial or financial information, constitute an unwarranted invasion of privacy, or reveal investigatory information. These broad categories were designed for the same purpose as the restrictions categories applied to other presidential materials. They are a guide to a commonsense exercise whose purpose is to assure that documents are opened only if the disclosure will not break a law, inhibit the proper functioning of the Government of the United States, or infringe upon the rights of any American.

The regulations also provide extraordinary appeal opportunities to persons who believe that disclosure of the materials may violate their rights. In fact, the greatest departure in the Nixon regulations from the practices in the presidential libraries is the requirement to notify former Nixon administration officials before the National Archives opens materials that they either created or, in some instances, that name them. Former staff members are not routinely notified of the opening of materials in the presidential libraries.

ACCESS PRACTICES IN THE PRESIDENTIAL LIBRARIES

At the end of his administration, Nixon was not allowed to take possession of his archival materials and donate them to a presidential library as his predecessors had done. Instead, as mentioned earlier, the Nixon presidential materials were seized to ensure that the record remained complete. This brought about a unique relationship between the government and the Nixon presidential materials and, in fact, created a unique adversarial relationship between the government and the former president.

Traditionally, at the end of his administration a president would donate his presidential materials to a presidential library. Custom and practice since the days of George Washington had permitted former presidents to take their presidential materials with them and to establish the rules for eventual access to them. The opportunities for caprice in such personal custodianship are obvious. It is entirely possible that, at some time in the distant past, presidential papers were used to curl hair or drain fried chicken. It is certain that many presidential papers were destroyed or dispersed in the period from George Washington's term to that of Calvin Coolidge. Many of those that somehow did manage to survive often had extremely lengthy restriction periods placed on them.

However, then came President Franklin Roosevelt and his idea for a presidential library to house the documents and memorabilia from his administration. President Roosevelt stated that his intention was to create an institution that would enable the American people to study and enjoy the documents and other items that were created or received during his presidency. This new institution would be operated permanently by the federal government. This concept of a government-owned and operated presidential library represented a compromise that continued the private property principle yet established a claim that there was a public interest in presidential materials.

Public interest assumes public access. The way in which the Roosevelt Library processed and opened papers became the model for the work of succeeding libraries. The Roosevelt model was based on two principles developed by the archivist of the United States working together with a committee that President Roosevelt established to provide guidance in the review of his papers. The first principle was that every page of any series of documents proposed to be opened in the library would be reviewed by archivists prior to its opening. The second principle was that the president would provide general categories of restriction against which the papers would be reviewed. These principles have served as the basis for the National Archives access policy to presidential materials from Roosevelt to Jimmy Carter.

On March 17, 1950, only five years after Roosevelt's death, approximately 85 percent of his papers were opened for research. Major portions of the papers of every succeeding president except Nixon have been reviewed by archivists and opened for research within six or seven years of the end of the president's term of office. There has never been a serious breach of national security, personal privacy, or any other individual or corporate right because of premature or improper release of documents by the presidential libraries. This model and this performance have greatly influenced how the National Archives has treated the Nixon materials.

These, then, are the four influences bearing most heavily on the processing of the Nixon materials. Taken together they constitute a unique package; but in practical application, they have combined to provide access to the Nixon materials that is comparable to the materials of other presidents. As I have illustrated, the government's relationship with Richard Nixon's presidential papers and tapes has presented a great challenge to the National Archives because Nixon did not follow in the tradition of his predecessors. However, despite the complexities and the uniqueness of the Nixon case, we have managed to treat the Nixon materials according to the principles for processing and providing access to the archival materials of modern presidents that have been developed and learned over a forty-year period. When we opened the first segments of the Central Files last year and all the Special Files this year, more than thirteen years had elapsed since the end of the Nixon Administration. Access to similar groups of papers in the presidential libraries has occurred after considerably briefer periods of time from the ends of their respective presidencies. The delay was an unavoidable consequence of the lengthy period of disagreement and litigation that followed Nixon's presidency.

A mob of reporters came to our research room to look at the Nixon files on the days we opened them. Never before have presidential papers received such intense journalistic interest. The reporters, of course, were hoping for headline material in these documents that they had heard so much about. Judging from the stories that appeared in the newspapers and on radio and television, they were disappointed. Rather than sensational tidbits, they found an enormous volume of original documents that would require years, not hours, to comb through. The collective view of the disappointed journalists was that this stuff was history, not headlines. They quickly yielded their desks to the historians.

We are far from having everything from the Nixon Administration open to the public. We have available only 3 million of the 40 million pages. Furthermore, of the 3 million pages now open, we have removed approximately 150,000 pages according to the restrictions specified in our regulations. We were forced to remove another 150,000 pages from the Special Files because Nixon objected to their disclosure. It will take many months for the regulatory process necessary to resolve the issues raised by his unprecedented objections. The other recent former presidents have chosen to trust the judgment of the archivists in access matters. Since former president Nixon has chosen not to accept our judgment, we must conduct another review of the thousands of pages to which he has objected and then await his decision as to whether he wishes to contest our decisions in court. The litigation could go on for years. I am hopeful there will be no litigation on this issue. I am hopeful too that our processing and opening of the White House Central Files can go forward without significant objection from Nixon or anyone else. Everyone has agreed that the Central Files are not in the so-called "sensitive" category; they are real meat-and-potatoes documents, concerned with the issues and programs that constitute the substance of the Nixon Administration. We plan to open more of these Central Files early next year, and we are busy preparing for additional openings.

Unfortunately, it is still too early for those researchers with an interest in foreign policy to expect to see a full documentary record of the Nixon Administration's efforts in that field. The national security content in the Nixon foreign policy documents is still too recent to permit any kind of systematic declassification. I am not sure, either, that the National Security Council, which has declassification jurisdiction over most of our foreign policy documents, is yet ready to turn its attention, in a grand way, to the records of the Nixon Presidency.

I have said a great deal about the papers, but what about the tapes? The tapes are a problem for everyone. Richard Nixon is probably still wondering why he did not destroy them; he almost certainly is not happy at the prospect of any of you listening to them. There is a real possibility of continued disagreement over the tapes. We have almost finished processing them, and we are now considering what to do next. Let me give you a little background on the National Archives' experience with presidential tapes so that you can understand our position.

The National Archives had almost no experience with presidential tapes before it received those of Richard Nixon. There is a tiny collection of tapes at the Roosevelt Library, but neither archivists nor researchers understood that these scratchy recordings held anything more than a few press conferences until a particularly diligent researcher took them to a sound-enhancing laboratory. The Lyndon Johnson tapes—thirty-six cubic feet in volume, primarily dictabelt recordings of telephone conversations—came to the National Archives, after Johnson's death, under a deed of gift which locked them up for fifty years. Consequently, the National Archives' only experience with the Johnson tapes is as security guard. The Kennedy tapes present a more complicated story. Their existence was not made known until after the July 1973 revelation of the existence of the Nixon tapes; processing was not begun on them until 1981, two years after the beginning of the processing of the Nixon tapes. After a start in a different direction from that used with the Nixon tapes, the processing method being used by the Kennedy Library was made to conform with the Nixon tapes method. The portions of the Kennedy tapes that are both substantive and not national security–classified are now available to the public.

The National Archives had had a great deal of experience with presidential papers before the Nixon troubles, but we had had no experience with tapes. The most important initial decision that we made was to process the Nixon tapes, as much as possible, in the same way that the Nixon papers were being processed— and, in essence, in the way that the papers of any recent president were processed. Now that the work of review is almost complete, the National Archives is planning a phased schedule for opening the tapes. In 1989 we plan to open the tapes that the special prosecutor requested from the White House during the Watergate investigation. We believe the mandate of the 1974 act to open abuse of power materials as soon as we can requires that these Watergate-related tapes be processed and opened first. After the opening of the Watergate special prosecutor tapes, which consist of approximately eighty hours of recorded conversation, we will determine when we will open the first portion of the main body of tapes. The announcement of our intention to open additional segments of the tapes will come well before the actual opening. This will enable all affected parties to comment on the opening or make a claim against it.

I have said that the tapes are a problem for everyone. I have not yet spoken about the researcher. Whoever among you who comes to listen to the tapes, when we have the entire file group open, will have to confront, as a first step, a twenty-seven-thousand-page finding aid. This is our Tape Survey Log, which is essentially a chronological list of names and subjects mentioned in the tapes. Once past this hurdle, the researcher will face four thousand hours of recorded conversations. Two years of eight-hour days will be required to listen to all the tapes, with no time for lunch allowed and no time permitted for turning the machine back to listen to a particularly tricky bit of conversation over again— and almost all of it is tricky. Using these unique materials should be as great a challenge for the researchers as processing them was for the archivists.

I should add that it looks like our researchers will be coming to the Washington, D.C., area for the foreseeable future. The Richard Nixon Presidential Archives Foundation plans to build a Nixon Library in California. However, we have been informed that former president Nixon does not wish at this time to follow in the tradition begun by Franklin Roosevelt and, instead, has chosen to operate, at least initially, a library that is not part of the federal government's system. Since the presidential materials by law must remain in the government's custody, they will remain indefinitely in the Washington area. We continue to discuss the proposed library with the Nixon Foundation, and the door is open for an eventual agreement to bring it into the system.

When Congress passed the Presidential Recordings and Materials Preservation Act in 1974, its primary concern was preservation of and access to the Nixon materials. Secondarily, however, Congress was concerned with the historical materials of future presidents. In Title II of the 1974 legislation, Congress established a commission to study the proper disposition of the historical materials of presidents who would come after Richard Nixon. The commission studied the history of how presidential materials had been handled, and recommended legislation that would make all official presidential records the property of the United States. In 1978, Congress enacted the Presidential Recordings Act which stated that, as of 1981, all documentary materials relating to the president's official duties would be owned by the United States, and access to them would be governed by restrictions based on the Freedom of Information Act. Thus, the experience with the Nixon materials contributed to the end of the tradition of private ownership of presidential materials. Beginning with President Ronald Reagan, the materials of a president that record the affairs of the public will be owned by the public.

As I look around this room and think of the people I have met and heard speak during this conference, I am impressed by the responsibility of the National Archives to keep the desires and interests of every one of you in mind as we process the Nixon materials. Many of you want to be able to use the Nixon materials as soon as possible. The National Archives feels the responsibility to grant your wish to the degree that the law and fairness allow. Those of you might be more concerned about how public access to the Nixon materials might affect you or your associates. We too share this concern. The 1974 law requires us to protect the rights of persons named in the materials, but this concern is deeply rooted in our history as well. Just as we have traditionally sought to serve our researcher community, so we have recognized the necessity of protecting the rights of persons mentioned in the documents in our custody. In the course of our work, we have been accused by some individuals of treating former president Nixon unfairly by making too much information available too soon. Others have accused us of continuing the Watergate cover-up by not making information available soon enough. Through it all we have remained neutral; no decision on access has ever been made on the basis of anything other than the law, the regulations, the negotiated agreement, and the traditions of the presidential libraries.

We are proud of the work we have done, and delighted that we now have researchers in our reading room. I am certain that all participants in this conference look forward to the better understanding of the Nixon administration that access to the Nixon presidential materials surely will bring. We have seen in this conference that Richard Nixon's career is of endless fascination. Those of us who have been entrusted with the almost equally endless historical record

of his administration feel honored to have a role in clarifying the presidency of
Richard Nixon.

Discussant: Joan Hoff-Wilson

I am beginning to think I am doomed to doing research on presidents whose papers don't open or don't open very readily. I first worked on the presidency of Herbert Hoover, and although he went out of office, as you know, in 1933, the papers did not open until the early 1960s. It is unfortunate, I think, not only for Nixon but for other presidencies, when any kind of a delay of this nature takes place. Historians know that when presidential papers are opened, the reputations of the presidents involved usually improves. While the participants in any given administration, particularly the president himself, are very often leery of having their papers opened, history will prove their fears are unfounded. It can only enhance the reputation of the given president.

I want to say some specific things about my use of the presidential papers with respect to the Nixon Administration, and then some very, very general things about the Nixon Presidency itself. Some of the difficulties in researching go beyond the access to the papers. Historians tend to differ from political scientists and journalists when it comes to writing contemporary history because we are so hung up about adequate documentation for what we are doing. Yet, obviously, writers of contemporary history are in extremely influential positions to influence, not only public opinion, but also the minds of public officials. Still I have trouble convincing my own colleagues that contemporary history really should be written more often by historians. It is too important—much too important—to be left to journalists alone. At the same time, I think that contemporary history has to be based as much as possible on nonprivileged information, and that is where I think the real problem lies with so much of the published words about the Nixon Administration. His papers are not available to the degree that historians like them to be in order to document their work. I would say categorically that the books and other published materials available on Nixon right now constitute the worst single body of literature on any president that I have ever read. This is largely because so much of it is based on anonymous sources and written by journalists.

Now having said that, let me indicate that historians often go to the other extreme of requiring excessive documentation. Reporters, and I think I would add lawyers to this category, have to be, given the nature of their work, satisfied not with the *best*, but with *any* evidence. Historians are looking for the best evidence and, more particularly, they are looking for aggregate evidence. In other words, historians are not concerned about the one document that is going to make the headline or win the case. We want an entire body of coherent evidence, and that is why we favor aggregate declassification of documents. The reason historians approach research in this way is that we are interested by and large in proving the generalization, not the exception, to the rule. Thus, atomized information is not as useful to historians as it is to journalists and to lawyers.

In other words, if you take that much-touted piece of federal legislation, the Freedom of Information Act, that act by its very nature, given the fragmented information obtained through it, tends to atomize material, tends to lend itself to producing the single document that will make or break a case or create a headline. Although I have used the Freedom of Information Act extensively, I do not believe that it is as useful to historians as it is to those in other fields. Consequently, too much has probably been made of the use of that act as far as historical documentation is concerned.

I think that Jim Hastings (director of the Nixon Papers and Materials Project) was quite right when he described the first day of the opening of the Nixon Special Files as a mob scene at the National Archives. The reporters were disappointed because they were looking for the kind of bombshell that comes up occasionally but not very often in such papers. I look back on that opening in December 1987 and then on the other openings later in the summer of 1988: the new material was enormously valuable for my purposes. I had been waiting since 1979 for the noncontroversial material on domestic policy to open up. A lot of it is there. It is very, very good material, and it is extremely well processed. Consequently, I was pleased with these openings because I was not looking for the quote by Pat Buchanan or some other specific information on Watergate. I personally believe that even when the National Archives' staff are finished opening up all these Special Files we are not going to find many significant details about Watergate that will change the overall picture of what we know now. At most, I think that some of these documents will widen the web of Watergate to include more who knew about the cover-up. And if some of these people are still vying or hoping for some kind of public office or public service, that will be an important revelation. I do not think we are really going to find out more about the actual details of Watergate as a historical event from these Special Files. Consequently, I am still waiting and will continue to wait when the bulk of the noncontroversial material will be opened, because it will provide the kind of documentation historians need.

I was, however, disappointed in one sense with the opening of these latest papers. As I went through what I thought were some relatively noncontroversial files on revenue sharing and the Equal Rights Amendment (ERA), I found out that what the Nixon representatives had done was not to remove, as the reporters suspected they had, abuse of power documents, because those had already been made available during the court trials resulting from Watergate. Instead, approximately 150,000 documents were removed just before the opening that were staff policy recommendations and that are important to historians because we try to document how decisions are reached. Therefore, I was disappointed because on some of these subjects it was clear that some of President Nixon's representatives were not trying to protect him, but were trying, very diligently I think, to protect some of his former aides. I do not think there is any way, for example, that you can protect Pat Buchanan from his own mouth. I do not even think that the attempt should be made. On the other hand, the removal of documents in the revenue sharing file by Ehrlichman or in the ERA file by Dean seemed to me to be overly protective on the part of the Nixon Administration's representative. Aside from these unnecessary removals, the papers were extremely useful to me, and will be for other historians who are not concentrating on Watergate.

As I look back, though, on the Nixon Presidency, I perceive two problems: One is that *we know so much*, and the other is that as yet *we know so little*. Part of that is because his papers have not been opened, but part of it is also because of the way he went out of office and the publicity that has been given to him as a result of Watergate. Additionally, behind that I think there's a problem that is seldom talked about—it is the whole division of the ex-presidency and its semiofficial status in this country. We simply do not know what to do with living ex-presidents, whether we like them or not. Consequently, it is not only difficult to research them, it is also difficult to make up our own minds about them because most of us doing the research have lived through the presidency that we are investigating. William Howard Taft once remarked that the best way to treat a former president was to "chloroform and ceremonially cremate him" when he left office in order to "fix his place in history and to enable the public to pass on to new men and new measures." Not even Nixon's most ardent enemies have publicly suggested this treatment. My point is that we would be having trouble dealing with his presidency and now his ex-presidency even if there hadn't been Watergate. Nixon is here, he is still around, and he is not going quietly away. And, contrary to the wishes of the fall 1987 issue of the *Columbia Journalism Review*, he is going to continue to be consulted as a specialist and consultant on foreign policy. I think the difficulty of using the Nixon papers is that one has to deal with him not only as an ex-president, but also as an enormously controversial figure in our recent past.

Having indicated how difficult this task is, I nonetheless believe that once all the problems with the tapes and with the remaining papers are resolved through litigation, Richard Nixon's presidency will be the best-documented one of this century. Consequently, given its significance as well as the documentation that will be available, there is no doubt that students, historians, and presidential researchers of all kinds will be working on this particular collection of papers well into the next century. The tapes in particular provide unusual documentation, not available in such quantity for other presidencies. As I noted at the beginning of my remarks, we already have a large body of literature based on interviews and/or leaked sources that constitute what might be a kind of informal oral history of the Nixon presidency.

I have done quite a bit of interviewing for this particular project on Nixon, but before I even thought about working on his presidency, I had already interviewed a very different group of people—70- to 80-year-old aging women who were former suffragists or early supporters of the Equal Rights Amendment. I conducted some of the last interviews, for example, with Alice Paul and others of her generation. Although I am not going to suggest that one can compare

Alice Paul with John Ehrlichman or John Dean, I believe that all such interviews reflect similar problems. These older female suffragists dissembled, exaggerated, forgot, embellished, or often indicated that they were involved in ways and events that they couldn't have been involved in, or exaggerated their positions in other ways. I found that it was not that much different when talking to considerably younger people from the Nixon Administration. I assume this is true of most administrations. In other words, I view most oral interviews as really political conversations. They are not really histories unless they are conducted by an agency like the National Archives or within the presidential library where there's follow up, where there is time to reflect, and where conditions are other than a quick telephone call or a brief hour or less sandwiched into somebody's busy schedule prevail.

As I conducted these interviews with former Nixon aides, I set two limits for myself. One was that there were to be no conditions or strings attached to the interview. The second was that I asked for papers to back up some of the statements being made. Now, I think you can imagine that I did not usually receive such papers, but occasionally I did, much to my surprise. The point I am making here is that we should neither overestimate or underestimate the value of these oral interviews with respect to Nixon or any other president. I do think we should be suspicious of the manner and way in which they are conducted. If they are not done in a systematic, professional way, and particularly if the source is not cited, I am increasingly of the opinion that they are less and less useful from a historical point of view. Although I refused to accept any privileged access on these interviews, I really cannot say that I have encountered less honesty or candidness or forthrightness on the part of an interviewee by not promising secrecy. I think that is a mystique about interviews. Most of the people who are going to grant you an interview, especially those in an administration that has obtained as much notoriety as Nixon's, are either planning to publish or have published, or they are revealing things that you could find in other sources. I really do not adhere to the concept that privileged access or secrecy has to be promised to obtain such interviews or that we should continue to give anonymous literature much relevance.

Finally, let me say something about shortsightedness and Nixon's papers. If there is anything that has impressed me, it is the way in which these documents have been processed by the staff of the National Archives under very difficult circumstances. However, other things have not impressed me. I think Congress was shortsighted in 1974 when it did not adequately fund the National Archives for processing the Special Files, let alone to begin processing the noncontroversial material. The next example of shortsightedness was repeated again and again as university after university turned down the Nixon papers and the possibility of having a Nixon Library on their respected campus. I have said this will be the best-documented presidency of this century. It is one of the most significant since the World Wars, if not the most significant, and any university with these papers would have become a major resource center for the study of the presidency. Yet at least a half a dozen major and not so major universities, because of faculty and other oppositions, turned those papers down in what I consider to have been mindless shortsightedness.

There is still another kind of shortsightedness that exists in the historical profession in general with respect to Richard Nixon. If you were at the opening session on Thursday, you heard that Nixon was rated in the latest poll of scholars as a failure; third from bottom in a list of all presidents. I find this rating incredibly shortsighted even though I am the executive officer of the Organization of American Historians which published the article. Generally speaking, these polls are based on presidential achievement. In 1983, when this one was conducted, few historians could think of any achievements on the part of the Nixon Administration, and so they classified it as a failure.

The shortsightedness I want to mention is that of Nixon and his representatives. They are still too concerned about what will be revealed if they finally reach a settlement of negotiation for opening up the remaining papers, and especially the tapes; and I think it is unbelievably shortsighted to consider opening a private presidential library, as they are, without the bulk of Nixon's presidential papers or even without the bulk of his vice presidential papers. This kind of library simply will not have academic creditability. So there has been shortsightedness on all sides with respect to Nixon and his papers.

One last thing I want to say about presidential papers is only peripherally connected to the recent decision to move what papers there will be in the Nixon Library to Yorba Linda. I have worked in most of the presidential libraries, and I really think we need a new federal law, one that will state categorically that no president can place his or her papers in a city of less than 250,000 people. Perhaps I say this because I once spent eight months in West Branch, Iowa, working on a biography of Herbert Hoover. Presidential papers should be easily accessible in metropolitan areas; they should be located where there are dry cleaners and movie theaters and the basic amenities of urban life. This is a consideration, I think, which all future presidents should hold in their minds. Regardless of where they were born, they should not be allowed to deposit their papers in that place unless it is a major city. This personal preference aside, I am very grateful to the organizers of this conference. I think that the headlines about it will clearly show there is a reevaluation of Nixon going on that is absolutely necessary. It has been too belated, partly because of the release of his papers, but also because of our own very dimmed memories of him with one exception—Watergate.

Discussant: Harry P. Jeffrey

In the rather short time allotted to me, I would like to speak from my particular vantage point. I am a historian, and an oral historian; I have been a member of the Nixon Administration, serving as a staff member of the Cost of Living Council; and I am one of that rare breed, a Southern Californian.

As a historian, I am concerned about the paucity of available materials concerning the Nixon Administration. Here it is 1987, almost 1988, over thirteen years since the end of the Nixon Administration, and only 3 million of the 40 million pages of the records of the Nixon Administration are open to scholars for research. That is just 7 percent. Of these 3 million pages, 150,000 pages have been removed from viewing by the National Archives staff, and another 150,000 pages have been excluded from researchers by the objections of President Nixon. These objections and the possible litigation could delay for some time the opening of these 300,000 pages, which obviously are some of the most important documents.

One can appreciate the unique situation that has caused this exceedingly slow release of Nixon Administration documents, but the result has been extremely frustrating for scholars. For many of us, the pace of release of manuscripts and other materials by the federal government is altogether too slow for "regular" government documents, much less the Nixon records. This is especially so in the case of documents which have a national security classification. Governmental restrictions to access need to be liberalized, not tightened. The Freedom of Information Act should be broadly, not narrowly, applied. Let us hope that the National Archives and Records Administration, now finally independent of the restrictive arm of the General Services Administration, will use its newly won freedom to aggressively promote the speeded-up release of documents. Also, let us seek an aggressive drive for more adequate funding of the National Archives after years of a subsistence diet, or rather, starvation rations.

The special situation of the Nixon Administration records disturbs scholars. The requirements of the 1974 Presidential Recordings and Materials Preservation Act that Watergate-related documents be made available to the public at the earliest reasonable date should not mean that the release of all the other Nixon Administration manuscripts should be delayed. This conference has, I believe, only reemphasized what many of us, scholars and former Nixon Administration officials, already knew: that the Nixon presidency definitely is one of the most important, if not the most historically meaningful, administration in the last forty-plus years. Like Professor Herbert Parmet, I believe that most of the post–World War II era can be called the "Age of Nixon." In fact, for well over ten years I have taught a course with just this title and this focus.

There are other things in the unique agreements regarding the Nixon Administration that worry many scholars. The 1979 "negotiated agreement" between

Mr. Nixon and the United States Government allows so-called "political documents" to be removed permanently from the National Archives and returned
to the former president. Indeed, as Jim Hastings has stated, this is a "most
disturbing and historically far-reaching" precedent. It certainly does, to quote
Mr. Hastings of NARA [National Archives and Records Administration], "result
in permanently damaging the integrity of the file." This "drastic departure from
the practices of the presidential libraries because former President Nixon *indicated* that he would donate these political documents *in the future* to the National
Archives" is indeed a slim reed on which to hang. (The emphasis is mine; the
question is from Mr. Hastings.)

Another question of scholars is the public access regulations of the Nixon
National Archives material. This sixth set of proposed regulations allow, as the
Hastings paper maintains, "extraordinary appeal opportunities to persons who
believe that disclosure of the material may violate their rights." Yes, as Jim
Hastings has written, it is a fact that "the greatest departure in the Nixon
regulations from the practices in the presidential libraries is the establishment
of the requirement that former Nixon administration officials be notified before
the National Archives opens materials which they either created or, in some
instances, which name them."

Of special concern to me, as an oral historian, is the status of the tapes of the
Nixon Administration. Please bear in mind that these tapes are not just the
Watergate tape recordings; they are an incredibly important record of this historical administration. A twenty-seven-thousand-page finding aid, the Tape Survey Log, the chronological list of names and subjects mentioned in the tapes,
is mind-boggling to a scholar. To adequately research four thousand hours of
recorded conversations is a monumental hurdle.

As one who has directed three oral history projects, I am keenly aware of the
long hours needed to listen to tapes. Therefore, I strongly urge the National
Archives to seek adequate funding and staffing to transcribe and edit the tapes.
To attempt to listen to the tapes would take much more than the two years of
eight-hour days estimated by Mr. Hastings. You cannot begin to realize how
many times you would have to stop the tape recorder and put it in reverse to
listen to the conversation again and again and again.

One of the things that will come from this conference is a better appreciation
of the great historical importance of the Nixon Administration. It is more, much
more, than just the Watergate scandal. We should all carry this message back
to our respective constituencies and our respective regions. Former Nixon Administration officials should promote, not retard, the release of materials to document
the crucial importance of Richard Nixon and the Nixon Administration in the
history of post–World War II America. These officials should impress on their
former colleagues, and on Mr. Nixon, the necessity to let scholars adequately
document the Age of Nixon. Scholars and journalists should press for the earliest
possible release of all the manuscripts and transcribed tapes. Archivists should
aggressively promote a sizeable increase in the funding of Nixon Administration

documents. The general public should carry this message of the need to have Congress fund and the executive branch process and open the record of the history of such a key individual and a historical administration.

Now I would like to make some comments about records of the Nixon Administration and of Richard Nixon which are available or, in some cases, that should be made available, to scholars, journalists, and the public. My institution, California State University, Fullerton, has a collection of 191 oral history interviews focused on Richard and Patricia Nixon, most of which were conducted between 1969 and 1972. This Richard Nixon Oral History Project, which I directed, interviewed relatives, friends, and others who knew the Nixon family and the Ryan family of Patricia Nixon in their "prepolitical years," that is, up to 1946. Topics highlighted include: the Nixon and Ryan families, relatives, and friends; the communities of Nixon's early years—Yorba Linda, Whittier, and Fullerton, and those of Pat Ryan's childhood in the Artesia-Cerritos area; California Quakerism; Nixon's school and college days; the Nixons' courtship and wedding; Nixon the young lawyer, businessman, and aspiring politician; and Pat Ryan the teacher. The interviews have been carefully transcribed, edited, indexed, and bound; they are completely open to the public. Also, the original tape recordings may be listened to. Authors who have used the Fullerton collection include William Leuchtenburg, Roger Morris, Herbert Parmet, Stephen Ambrose, Fawn Brodie, and Julie Nixon Eisenhower.

California State University, Fullerton, has provided a number of ways in which to research its Nixon Oral History Project. All the bound volumes are available for purchase. We are completing an agreement with a publishing company which will offer the interviews in bound volumes or microform. The university's Oral History Program also has a complete annotated catalogue of the Nixon interviews and of histories of additional Southern California communities. A book, *The Young Nixon: An Oral Inquiry*, contains the complete edited transcripts of a representative sample of eleven interviews. In addition, the Oral History Program will be publishing additional volumes of the interviews centering on such topics as Nixon's particular brand of Quakerism, his family, and his early environment, and a volume devoted to Patricia Ryan.

Moreover, California State University, Fullerton, has other Nixon-related material. The Oral History Program has boxes of Nixon memorabilia including yearbooks, speeches, and photographs. A Special Collections Division of the university library contains a collection of Southern California political material, including pamphlets and books highlighting the political climate of the area.

Whittier College, Nixon's alma mater, also houses an excellent collection of Nixon books and other material. Furthermore, the so-called Los Angeles branch of the National Archives and Records Administration has a Nixon collection. Located deep in Orange County, in Laguna Niguel, this material presents both opportunity and frustration for Nixon researchers.

Some of the NARA collection, the deeded part, is generally open to researchers. In the Pre-Presidential General Correspondence Series are 845 boxes (three

hundred linear feet, or twenty-four-thousand folder titles) of Nixon's correspondence from the late 1940s to 1963. It is primarily an alphabetical file, with some
subject classifications. There is a Vice Presidential Trip File, 1953–1959 (thirty-
seven linear feet), which includes Mr. Nixon's statements, briefing materials,
and handwritten notes. Campaign Files has records (four linear feet) of the 1960,
1962, and 1964 campaigns, and holds memos, speech drafts, tapes, and transcripts. Two boxes of drafts and research notes of Nixon's *Six Crises* book
mainly relate to chapter six, the 1960 campaign. Khrushchev's 1959 visit to the
United States is documented, but largely only via press clippings. Also available
are a newly opened, sixty-linear-foot section of Invitations, Replies, and Other
Records Relating to Appearances, 1953–1964; seven linear feet of Correspondence with Children, 1954–1962 (not Nixon's own children); miscellaneous me-
mentos and tapes (4 boxes); and photographs. However, a small amount of this
material is restricted in compliance with the deed by Mr. Nixon, but permission
may be requested to use it.

Unfortunately for researchers, there is a large portion of the Nixon prepresidential records at the Laguna Niguel archives which is not open to all researchers.
Special permission has been granted by Mr. Nixon to some, but not all, people
to use this material. This undeeded collection is merely stored at the National
Archives in a massive vault, and does not belong to the federal government. In
this 800-linear-foot collection is material from Mr. Nixon's political campaigns
from 1946 to 1968; his House of Representatives and Senate years, 1946–1953;
and his "public figure" years of 1961–1968, which include Nixon's law firms
and financial records. Within this collection are photographs, movies, memorabilia, and miscellaneous records, including a scattering of items dating as far
back as 1923: grammar school essays and assignments, high school annuals with
inscriptions from fellow students, college note books, letters received from Duke
University Law School classmates, and separation papers from the Navy. In
addition, there are approximately 500 cubic feet of other material, not all well
classified.

Moreover, the undeeded collection houses some material of the Nixon presidency. This includes photographs, memorabilia, miscellaneous records, and
even the dresses of the three Nixon women.

Of particular interest to oral historians at Laguna Niguel is a closed "official"
and "sanctioned" Nixon Oral History Project conducted by Whittier College in
the 1971–1973 period. This collection contains 395 interviews of some 355
people. It is a very complete record of Mr. Nixon up to 1946. Nixon, his family,
and his former secretary provided access to many people that the California State
University, Fullerton, Oral History Project, with a much more limited budget,
did not reach. This collection also includes photographs and other Nixon memorabilia. Unfortunately, this Whittier project, which has been completely transcribed, edited, and legally released by the interviewees, is totally closed, and
it appears that it will remain closed for years. Like other records of Richard
Nixon, the Whittier Oral History Project is caught up in a complex web of

competing jurisdictions, in this case among the federal government, the original and now defunct Richard Nixon Foundation, Whittier College, and the former president.

Most of you know that a Richard Nixon Presidential Library is to be built in Yorba Linda, California. The twenty-five-million-dollar library and museum is to be located on a site of nine acres at the birthplace of Richard Nixon. This home, in which Nixon was born, is standing and will be restored. Plans are to open the house to the public with many of the furnishings and furniture that were in it when Nixon was a boy. A Richard Nixon Presidential Archives Foundation is raising the money for the library, which will be the first private presidential library in the modern era, thus breaking a precedent begun by Herbert Hoover. The library will hold the prepresidential and postpresidential collections of Richard Nixon, and the undeeded presidential materials. Included will be Nixon's White House diaries, plus the documents and drafts he used in writing his six books.

Thus, the Nixon Library and Museum in Yorba Linda will be separate from and not a part of the National Archives Nixon Collection, which is now housed in Alexandria, Virginia. As I mentioned before, the Alexandria archives has forty million pages of Nixon's presidential records. It also contains two oral history collections. One is some 150 exit tapes of officials leaving the Nixon administration. The other is an oral history project just begun, the interviewing of former Nixon Presidency officials. I urge all those who participated in the administration, in and outside this room, to cooperate with this worthwhile effort. If you have not yet been contacted by NARA, please volunteer to be interviewed, and urge your ex-colleagues to consent to be interviewed. In addition, I suggest that Nixon archival staff seek augmented funding for the oral history projects. This should include monies for transcribing and editing both sets of tape recordings.

The National Archives Motion Picture and Sound Recording Section in Washington, D.C., has some eighty-five transcribed tapes of the Nixon Administration Cost of Living Council. This collection details the activities of the Economic Stabilization Program, which from 1971 to 1974 supplied the only peacetime wage and price controls in American history. Interviews were conducted with officials of the Cost of Living Council, Pay Board, and Price Commission; labor union and business leaders; journalists; and congressional and executive branch officials. They are of high quality, but perhaps I am biased, as I was the codirector of this project. Most of the transcripts are open. Included in the archival records of the Cost of Living project are audiovisual materials, speeches, press conference reports, and other miscellaneous items.

University Publications of America is beginning to put out in microform, under the title *Papers of the Nixon White House*, the National Archives collection of Nixon papers. Professor Joan Hoff-Wilson is the editor of this valuable series.

A few other sources of Nixon materials, or things related to the former president, deserve mention. At the University of Utah in Salt Lake City the author of *Richard Nixon: The Shaping of His Character*, the late Fawn Brodie, has left her tapes and notes. Some Nixon memorabilia has been collected by the San Clemente Historical Society; unfortunately, at the present time it is stored in a garage near the former Western White House. The American Political Items Collectors has a Nixon chapter, the Nixon Political Items Collectors. Headquartered in Orange County in San Juan Capistrano, it publishes a newsletter called *Checkers*. There are two oral history projects which relate to Nixon. One, the California State Government Gubernatorial Oral History Series, is a collection of interviews about California governors beginning with Earl Warren, who was first elected in 1942. A second project, the California State Government Oral History Series, tapes interviews of major post–World War II figures who played meaningful roles in California history and politics. However, Richard Nixon himself has not been interviewed by either project.

In conclusion, Richard Nixon probably will be the second most written-about president in the twentieth century, behind only Franklin Roosevelt. I believe that it is imperative that all of us, archivists, scholars, former Nixon Administration officials, and the general public, work for the quickest possible release of all Age of Nixon material, and that we strive for adequate funding to accomplish this task. We must preserve the rights of the individuals concerned; but we also should be very much aware of the necessity to present the complete historical record of this truly important man and his presidency. Thank you.

Discussant: Mark R. Weiss

On July 16, 1973, during a public hearing of the Senate Select Committee on Presidential Campaign Activities, Alexander Butterfield, then head of the Federal Aviation Agency, revealed that conversations that took place in offices of the president of the United States, Richard M. Nixon, had been recorded routinely, automatically, and secretly. The recordings included all room or telephone conversations held in the Oval Office, the president's Executive Office Building office, and the Cabinet Room, as well as conversations in the Lincoln Sitting Room of the White House and the telephone at the president's desk in the Aspen cabin at Camp David. A reported purpose of the recordings was to provide future historians with firsthand evidence of the day-to-day processes of decision making in the White House. If the existence of the recordings had remained secret and if greater care had been taken in the design of the recording system then these tapes might well have proven to be a historian's gold mine and, aside from other aspects of the Nixon Administration, would have established a unique place for the administration in the history of the presidency. Ironically, the "premature" admission of their existence accomplished just that. Few disclosures of presidential practice have had so great an impact on the subsequent conduct of an administration.

On November 21, 1973, Chief Judge John J. Sirica of the U.S. District Court for the District of Columbia appointed an advisory panel of six persons to examine the White House tape recordings which had been subpoenaed by the grand jury that was investigating the Watergate break-in. I was a member of that panel. Our task was to evaluate the authenticity and integrity of the recordings. On the same day that our appointment was announced, the judge was informed by the counsel for the White House that a gap of approximately eighteen-minutes duration existed in one of the recordings. This tape rapidly became the prime object of our examination, and provided us with an almost perfect opportunity to develop and test a variety of techniques for authenticating tape recordings. The results of our analyses indicated that the recordings we examined were all originals and not copies. In the case of the tape with the eighteen-and-a-half-minute gap, the analyses permitted two conclusions to be drawn. First, the strong buzzing sound that is audible in this interval resulted from the recording of at least five and possibly as many as nine segments over the material that was originally recorded in this region of the tape. And second, these over-recordings were made by use of manually operated controls on a tape recorder other than the one on which the original recordings were made. Our tests of this tape and of the other ones subpoenaed by the court also afforded us an opportunity to examine the recording system and to evaluate the quality of the recordings and the accessibility of the information they contained.

The system that was used to make the recordings was installed in the spring of 1971. Microphones were hidden in each of the rooms in which recordings were made. For example, microphones were implanted in the president's desk in the President's Office in the Executive Office building. In the Oval Office, microphones reportedly were placed in sconces on the walls. All of the microphones in a room were connected through long cables to an electronic device that delivered their combined outputs to the input of a reel-to-reel tape recorder. The tape recorders were outside the "bugged" offices, hidden in closets or enclosures to which only a handful of White House Secret Service men had access. These men maintained the recording system, and logged and stored the reels of recorded tape. To maximize the amount of conversation that could be recorded on a single reel, the recorders were sound-activated, and the recordings were made at a tape speed of 1.7 inches per second on 1,800-foot-long reels of tape.

While the general design of the recording systems was reasonable, the manner in which they were installed caused the quality of the recordings to be poorer than need have been the case. All analog tape recordings exhibit some form of degradation in the quality of the recorded sounds. In the case of the White House tapes, the degradation consists of significant levels of hum, tape hiss, and sound echoes. These forms of noise are almost always present in recordings made in large offices and with microphones in less-than-optimum locations. However, in many of the recordings of conversations in the Oval Office and in the President's Office in the Executive Office building, the noise levels are particularly high in comparison with the sound level of the recorded speech. As a result, parts of the conversations are difficult and sometimes impossible to understand.

The recorded hum appears to have been due to pickup of 60-cycle power-line radiation by the long cables that connected the microphones directly to the recorders. If the microphone outputs had been amplified first before being connected to the microphone cables, the relative hum level would have been much lower. The tape hiss was, of course, inherent in the tapes, which were of good quality. As a rule, tape hiss affects speech intelligibility only for speech sounds that are recorded at a level that is comparable to that of the hiss. Thus, at times when a talker was close to a microphone or was speaking loudly, the recorded speech sounds were much louder than the tape hiss and, consequently, are easily understood. However, at times when the person talking was far from any of the microphones or was speaking softly, the speech intensity at the microphones was frequently too low to be intelligible in the presence of the tape hiss. This condition was made even worse when the hum was comparable to or greater than the speech intensity. The tape recorders that were used to make the White House tape recordings were designed to automatically lower the sensitivity of the recording amplifier when the input signal level was strong and raise the sensitivity when the input level was weak. Normally, this is a desirable mode of operation since it increases the chances that weak signals will be recorded at a level well above that of the inherent noise of the tape. However, when the hum was louder than the received speech, the amplifier sensitivity was prevented from increasing adequately to record the speech above the level of the background tape noise.

The third source of interference in these recordings is due to reverberation. The speech sounds that were produced were reflected repeatedly from the walls, ceiling, and floor of the rooms where they were made, gradually diminishing in intensity with each reflection. For rooms the size of the Oval Office and the President's Office in the Executive Office Building, the amount and duration of reverberant sound energy can be substantial. Even the presence of drapes and rugs did not diminish it greatly. At the microphones, the reverberated sounds combined with the directly received sounds, resulting in confusions that impair speech intelligibility. Bad as this effect was, it was made worse by the way the recording system was set up. Usually, a multi-microphone system is employed to limit the maximum talker-to-microphone distance to some acceptable value. Then, if the system is set up to record only the output of the microphone receiving the loudest sounds, both the loss of speech intensity and the proportion of reverberant energy in the recorded signal will be minimized. However, if, as was done in the White House recording system, the microphone outputs are combined before recording, the result can be and usually is an increase in the proportion of reverberant energy, and consequently a decrease in speech intelligibility.

The tapes can be processed in ways that improve the apparent quality of the recordings. Using currently available signal processing techniques, the hum can be removed entirely, and some of the reproduced tape hiss and sound echoes can be suppressed. However, those components of tape noise or of reverberated sounds that overlay speech components and interfere with speech intelligibility cannot be attenuated without at the same time degrading the underlying speech. At best, processing these recordings would make it easier to listen to the recordings over extended periods of time. This in itself may be of value to future transcribers, in view of the many hours of conversation that have been recorded. It is conceivable that more effective methods of enhancing recorded speech will have been developed by the time, if ever, that the bulk of the recordings are made available for scholarly research. If so, then the tapes may yet prove to be a source of unusual insights into a critical period in our history.

THE EVOLUTION OF THE
NIXON LEGACY

Moderator: Fred I. Greenstein

This has been a rich, rewarding, and informative conference. Please join me in expressing appreciation to Hofstra University for making this forum possible for all of us.

The topic of this concluding gathering, the Evolution of the Nixon Legacy, has two elements to it which are represented by the two paper givers, whom I shall now call the paper condensers. I hope they can come as close as possible to ten minutes in their exposition so we can have an exchange with the panelists. The two elements are the Evolution of the Nixon Presidency's reputation, which begins when that presidency ended in mid-1974, and the evolution of the reputation of Richard Nixon, which depends on political events that are still to come in the public corner of a living ex-president—a man whose political demise was seen as far back as 1952 but keeps failing to occur.

The paper givers are Barry Riccio, a historian at the University of Illinois, who has written on intellectual history and figures of the twentieth century. His paper, "Richard Nixon Reconsidered: The Conservative as Liberal?" is a look at Nixon in his presidency and Nixon's political views. The second person who has contributed an essay paper, Professor Sherri Cavan of the Department of Sociology of San Francisco State, is the author of a book called *Twentieth Century Gothic: America's Nixon*. In her paper, Professor Cavan applies sociological theories of rehabilitation to the contemporary Richard Nixon who is with us now and whose reputation has reemerged.

In alphabetical order, I have a sequence of people acting as discussants, all of whom but one have been introduced at least once, and probably even before that you knew something about their curricula vitae. First, after the two paper condensers, I will be calling on John Ehrlichman, a political author, who in his Nixon period was counselor and special assistant to President Nixon; then H. R. Haldeman, who at the moment is president of Murdoch Hotel Corporations, and who was chief of staff of the Nixon Presidency. I will then call upon Robert Finch, who was secretary of Health, Education and Welfare, and then counselor to the president, and who today is a distinguished member of the bar in the firm of Fleming, Anderson, McClung and Finch in Pasadena. The person who has been introduced many times, including by me, but not here, Arthur Schlesinger, Jr., is Albert Schweitzer Professor at the Graduate Center, City University of New York. I could list your books, Arthur, but I would forget some, and then there would be no time for the panel, but in 1973 the appearance of *The Imperial Presidency*, which managed to take note of the early stages of Watergate, clearly marks one of many reasons why we belong here. Finally, it's a great pleasure to introduce C. L. Sulzberger, distinguished columnist and author of no less than twenty-one books. His recent *The World and Richard Nixon* is one further reason for his presence.

11

Richard Nixon Reconsidered: The Conservative as Liberal?

BARRY D. RICCIO

Richard Nixon has long been a curious figure on the American political landscape. An ardent anticommunist when a young member of Congress from California during the late 1940s, he was also the architect of Détente when a middle-aged president. Though he advocated lowering our voices in the noisy 1960s, he also contributed to the nation that connoisseur of rhetorical overkill, Spiro T. Agnew. More to the point for our present purposes, Richard Nixon qua president had a decidedly ambiguous relationship with American liberalism.

Clearly there is no one definition of liberalism that is wholly satisfactory. If one wishes to define liberalism in its historical context, however, as did political scientist and Harvard scholar Louis Hartz over thirty years ago in his masterly *The Liberal Tradition in America*, one cannot ignore the close connection between a democratic polity and a market-oriented economy.[1] According to Hartz (who was himself strongly influenced by Alexis de Tocqueville), the very individualism that most Americans extol is rooted in this liberal tradition. This is a liberalism, Hartz insisted, that owes more to John Locke than to John Dewey. On a less rarefied level, it found expression in the nineteenth-century novels of Horatio Alger. To Hartz, this brand of liberalism was unabashedly nationalistic and not particularly cosmopolitan. In fact, its practical implications were largely conservative, and especially so in the Age of Eisenhower, when Hartz put pen to paper. The Harvard scholar also held that America was the liberal nation par excellence, a country that was in effect liberal from birth largely because it had been blessedly free from the feudal experience. However, the seemingly monolithic—and provincial—nature of the liberal ideology unsettled Hartz, and he argued that it was high time for Americans to detach themselves from their culture in order to obtain a more mature understanding of it.[2]

It seems safe to say that the vice president of the United States was not much on Hartz's mind. A decade and a half later, though, an energetic and talented young social critic who had read his Hartz carefully put out a hefty book on Richard Nixon as the paradigmatic American liberal. Garry Wills's *Nixon Agonistes* was a splendid work, replete with vivid portraiture and acute social analysis.[3] At bottom, Wills's concern was with the political and cultural significance of Richard Nixon. For Wills, Nixon epitomized what the author called "the crisis of the self-made man."[4] Moreover, it was precisely this ethos of self-sufficiency that lay at the heart of liberal America. Other Nixon watchers had commented on Nixon's palpable ambition, of course, but Wills was perhaps the first person to link Nixon's striving so unequivocally to the ideology of liberalism. In a liberal society, Wills asserted, making it becomes something of a moral imperative. At the very least, it is evidence of one's character. In such a society, according to Wills, the marketplace serves as a testing ground for both one's morality—and his manliness. Success, then, becomes a kind of secular religion. Interestingly, Wills likened Nixon to Steadfast Dodge in James Fenimore Cooper's classic *Homeward Bound*. (Historian Alonzo Hamby later would go further and compare Nixon to Clyde Griffiths in Theodore Dreiser's unforgettable parable about the downslope of the American dream, *An American Tragedy*.)[5]

The individualism that Richard Nixon so perfectly reflected, Wills continued, is rooted deeply in our culture. At its most cerebral—and appealing—it expressed itself in, say, the writings of Ralph Waldo Emerson, who Wills flippantly tagged "the Horatio Alger of the educated."[6] However, whether articulated as the self-culture of an Emerson or the more rugged individualism of a Richard Nixon, Wills argued, liberalism always exaggerated the extent of man's sovereignty over himself. (After reading Wills, one almost expects Nixon to leap from the pages of our *McGuffey's Readers*.)

Even Nixon's "rootlessness," in Wills's eyes, could be traced to the liberal value system. Perhaps with R.W.B. Lewis's *American Adam* at the back of his mind, Wills portrayed Nixon as the ultimate solipsist, a man who prided himself on standing alone (his autobiographical *Six Crises* was telling testimony to that feature of his personality) and who was seemingly beyond ties to tradition or to any genuine community.[7] In Wills's mind, then, the impulse to get ahead and a liberal social order were inextricably intertwined.

This is not to say that this ruled out idealism, far from it, in fact. One of Wills's more tantalizing claims was that in many respects Richard Nixon was actually a latter-day Woodrow Wilson. For one thing, Nixon greatly admired the progressive (read liberal) president, and drew inspiration from his example. So taken was the California Republican with this Southern Democrat, in fact, that he even ordered Wilson's desk brought into the Oval Office. However, the connection does not end there, Wills contended. Both men were inscrutable loners who spoke in largely Protestant accents. Nixon's "forgotten American" was not unlike Wilson's "man on the make," a lower-middle-class individual who strove to better his condition in no small part because of the terror inspired within him over the prospect of becoming—or remaining—an employee. Finally, as Wills would have it, President Nixon's foreign policy was Wilsonian with a vengeance, "preaching democracy with well-meant napalm," pushing the destruction of a tiny country "in a seizure of demented charity."[8]

Now there are many problems with this Willsian analysis. To take the matter of Nixon qua "St. Woodrow" (as H. L. Mencken used to call him), first, Richard Nixon undoubtedly revered Woodrow Wilson and was given to quoting from him liberally. However, occasional "Wilsonizing" does not a Wilsonian make. More important, would a devout Wilsonian—that is to say, one for whom any semblance of realpolitik smacked of the Devil's handiwork—have tolerated Henry Kissinger for so long? Most historians would probably agree that President Nixon's Vietnam policy had more to do with saving the face of this nation than with ensuring self-determination for another. Whether Nixon's brand of "realism" was actually realistic is not so much the point as whether he and his advisers were acting out Wilsonian impulses. Wills had made a bold and provocative argument to that end, but ultimately it was a less than convincing one.

What of the more general argument that pervades Wills's book, namely the thesis that Nixon typifies American liberalism and may well be its final product? Regarding the latter claim, it now seems that the obituary Wills wrote was a bit premature. The liberal social order that had so disturbed Wills is no longer in jeopardy, as it had appeared to many an observer in the heat of the battles of the 1960s. However, can it still be said that Richard Nixon represents American liberalism? Given how Wills defines his terms, yes indeed. Nonetheless, I think it also can be said of Wills (and of Hartz, for that matter) that he homogenized liberalism. In his nimble hands, liberalism was Horatio Algerism and little else. To be sure, Wills placed historian Arthur Schlesinger, Jr., squarely within the liberal tradition. At last report, though, Schlesinger was not making neo-Algerian noises. (Wills does have some shrewd things to say, incidentally, about Schlesinger's conception of ideology.) The differences between Daniel Moynihan and Milton Friedman, or even between Hubert Humphrey and Barry Goldwater, Wills conveniently minimized. Admittedly, all four men are (or were) supportive of a pluralistic society with constitutionally guaranteed liberties. They are all closer to one another than to, say, a Fidel Castro. However, having said that, with what are we left? We are left with individuals who strongly agree with one another on some matters and who strongly disagree on others. Surely not all of them have bought into the myth of the self-made man. At times one can detect a certain impishness in Wills, a desire to infuriate liberal Harvard professors by insisting that even Richard Nixon—the man that columnist Murray Kempton once stated was "the President of every place in this country which does not have a bookstore"—is, after all, one of them.[9]

Perhaps it would have been useful for Wills to distinguish more clearly between the liberalism of Manchester and the liberalism of Mondale. Nineteenth-century liberals were given to treating the market as if it were a demigod, and the same can be said for such self-styled conservatives such as Ronald Reagan, who has repeatedly expressed his debt to the classical liberals Ludwig von Mises and Friedrich von Hayek. Liberals of the twentieth century, however, have been wont to advocate a larger and more vigorous public sector in order to broaden opportunities for the many and check the privilege of the few. One thinks of, in this regard, the progressive presidencies of Republican Theodore Roosevelt and Democrat Woodrow Wilson, the New Deal–Fair Deal administrations of Democrats Franklin Roosevelt and Harry Truman, and finally, Democrat John F. Kennedy's New Frontier and fellow Democrat Lyndon B. Johnson's Great Society. This latter-day liberalism has sought to use government—and especially the federal government—both to smooth out the rough edges in our economy and to assist the disadvantaged. It is what most Americans think of—explicitly or implicitly—when they hear the term "liberal."

At this point I am afraid we must take leave of Mr. Wills and address another question. How did President Richard Nixon's domestic policies (foreign policy will necessarily lie outside the scope of the present inquiry) measure up against twentieth-century liberal standards? That is to say, did the Nixon Administration reject or embrace the contemporary liberal tradition of affirmative government? Some observers, no doubt, would see the question itself as being too pat, for most presidents have embraced a strong federal government in some spheres and have rejected the selfsame approach as inappropriate in others. Franklin Roosevelt, for example, had no hesitation about utilizing the power and authority of the central government to combat the depression and lay the foundation for a welfare state. At the same time, however, he shied away from using government as an agency of moral uplift. More than a few old-line progressives, as historians Richard Hofstadter and Otis Graham have shown, thought FDR moved too much in the direction of positive government when it came to the economy and welfare and too little in that direction regarding matters of morals and character.[10] Since the Roosevelt era, however, most liberals have insisted on a distinction between private morality and public welfare. The former realm they are content to leave to the private sector, generally speaking, while the latter arena is in their eyes a most proper province for government action at all levels.

The nub of the matter, then, concerns the welfare state. While the Democratic party initiated and continually enlarged this creature, the Republicans have long indicated a profound discomfiture with it. To be sure, under Dwight Eisenhower the party reluctantly came to accept the welfare state as part of the established order, but the party continued to be known more for the reluctance than the acceptance. Representing the minority wing of the minority party in 1964, Republican presidential candidate Barry Goldwater mounted a frontal assault on the New Deal and its legacy. Needless to say, he was resoundingly defeated, and in the wake of his defeat came the "Second New Deal," or the Great Society.[11] The welfare state expanded considerably.

As is well known, Richard Nixon campaigned aggressively for Barry Goldwater in 1964. Nixon had never been an economic fundamentalist, however much he had paid lip service to his party's lingering hostility to the New Deal tradition. In 1968, however, the leading domestic issue was not so much the New Deal as it was the Great Society, and on the latter point candidate Nixon had made himself perfectly clear. Lyndon Johnson's Great Society was, quite simply, a failure. If Nixon expressed no intention to bury the welfare state, he was not about to praise it, either, and he certainly appeared in no mood to expand upon it.

"The New Deal is dead," quipped Nixon loyalist John Roy Price in 1968.[12] Speechwriter Patrick Buchanan—younger but no less confrontational then than now—spoke of the need for a "counterreformation."[13] Moreover, erstwhile president Lyndon Johnson, musing about Nixon's domestic policies to biographer Doris Kearns in 1971, delivered this grim postmortem. "It's a terrible thing for me to sit by and watch someone else starve my Great Society to death."[14]

The image of Nixon presented here is that of a right-wing restorationist, not unlike the Ronald Reagan of the 1960s and 1970s. However, as numerous columnists, economists, and historians have pointed out, there was more continuity than discontinuity between the Great Society and the Nixon years. When there was discontinuity, it was often in the direction of enlarging rather than contracting the welfare state.

First, take the matter of the budget: Defense costs had commanded nearly half the total budget under Jack Kennedy; when Richard Nixon left office in 1974, defense expenditures amounted to less than a third of his entire budget. In fact, under the Nixon administration, defense spending declined as a percentage of gross national product and also in real terms. Admittedly winding down—and ultimately concluding—the war in Vietnam had more than a little to do with this, but other factors were at work, too. By 1975, more money was being expended on transfer payments—or what we now call entitlements—than on defense.[15] Only a year before, significantly enough, President Nixon's fiscal 1974 budget proposed spending nearly 60 percent more on social programs than Lyndon Johnson had in 1968. Now one must look beyond Richard Nixon for an explanation of all this. Nixon was the first president in nearly a century to face a Congress controlled by the opposition party from the very beginning of his tenure. Irrespective of his personal sentiments, he operated under rather severe constraints. Moreover, the increase in and aging of the population served to increase entitlement spending automatically.

Detractors of the Great Society have long indicted it for seemingly extending the heavy hand of government—particularly the federal government—into the economy. Nixon's attitude toward government regulation was well known to his adversaries and allies alike. In a word, regulation was anathema to him. However, it is hard to quarrel with the conclusion reached by a prominent economist who served in Nixon's employ. "Probably more new regulation was imposed on the economy during the Nixon administration," Herbert Stein has said, "than in any other presidency since the New Deal, even if one excludes the temporary Nixon foray into price and wage controls.''[16] The ''even if'' clause is not without significance, for Nixon was the first president to institute wage-price controls during peacetime, something Lyndon Johnson never remotely considered. It goes without saying that the controls were no penny-ante operation. Nixon has told us that without his controls, the Democrats might have pushed for something more stringent, and that in any event he had to do something to both restrain inflation and reduce unemployment. Wage-price controls seemed to be a convenient, if temporary, way out of that dilemma. Nonetheless, Nixon's action shocked one young Republican. ''It was perverse. Everything the free market scholars said would happen—shortages, bottlenecks, investment distortions, waste, irrationality, and more inflation—did happen right before my eyes. . . . The experience . . . left me a born again capitalist.''[17] In less than a decade David Stockman would get an opportunity to translate his ''born-again'' faith into action.

President Nixon displayed an eagerness to embrace regulation in other areas, too. Less than a year earlier, he had signed the historic Occupational Safety and Health Act (OSHA) in the wake of mounting pressure not only from Congress but also from labor chieftain George Meany and consumer advocate Ralph Nader (an uncharacteristic alliance of the old politics and the new).[18] OSHA, of course, would later become one of the primary bugbears of the American right, but some of the men around Nixon apparently thought regulation of that sort would woo disaffected blue-collar Americans away from the Democratic party. Richard Nixon was, after all, consciously seeking to realign the party system to produce, in Kevin Phillips's words, an ''emerging Republican majority.''[19] Laissez-faire fundamentalism could hardly be expected to meet the needs of socially conservative working-class Democrats.

Other factors were conspiring to push President Nixon in the direction of more federal regulation. The emerging energy crisis late in Nixon's tenure convinced both Republicans and Democrats of the need for fuel efficiency standards, and as early (or as late) as 1970, the environment had become a ''hot'' political issue. In establishing the Environmental Protection Agency in 1970, Richard Nixon clearly went beyond any previous president in the matter of environmental protection. However, as James Sundquist and others have informed us, the Johnson Administration had already chalked up some notable accomplishments in that sphere.[20] By 1970, in fact, Congress wanted to go even further than the president on this issue, and perceived him to be a restraining force. Still, Nixon displayed the zeal of a convert when he preached environmentalism, and, more to the point, he came around to the view that some degree of central planning was essential if the ecosystem were to be preserved. To that end he committed himself to a national growth policy, long an objective of city planners and the American Institute of Architects. Even as late as 1973, when Nixon returned to speaking in the accents of antistatism and actually began cutting back on select Great Society programs, he was still advocating a national land-use policy.

Historian Otis Graham has suggested that planning appealed to Nixon's penchant for order and tidiness. Moreover, Graham went so far as to liken the Nixon Administration's National Goals Research Staff to Franklin Roosevelt's controversial (to the right, at least) National Resources Planning Board of the 1930s.[21] No laissez-faire sentiments were especially evident here.

In general, President Nixon's economic policies hardly suggested a slavish devotion to the "old-time religion." In company with virtually all Republicans, Richard Nixon had been horrified by deficit spending most of his life. Nonetheless, not long after he came to office, Secretary of Labor George Shultz and others (who were still devotees of freer markets) convinced Nixon that unbalanced budgets were desirable so long as the economy was not operating at full employment. It was this willingness to embrace planned deficits during recessions that led the president to declare himself to be a Keynesian. In his newfound enthusiasm for Keynes, Nixon might have been second only to Kennedy. To its critics on the left and right, "Nixonomics" was so flexible that it seemed opportunistic, for President Nixon apparently was not pursuing any consistent economic course during his reign. As Graham shrewdly observed, however, "When this happened with FDR, it was usually regarded by liberals as laudable pragmatism."[22]

Nixon prided himself on being a political pragmatist, of course, but he also saw himself as something of a reformer. Early on during his presidency, Nixon had said that the watchword of his administration would be "reform." If some feared that this meant an attempt to return to the status quo ante, Paul McCracken, Nixon's head of the Council of Economic Advisors, disabused them of that notion. "We are a liberal administration," McCracken tersely stated.[23]

Did that imply that tax reform was in the offing? Perhaps it did. Unlike, say, Robert Kennedy, Richard Nixon displayed no interest in that subject while on the campaign trail. However, LBJ's departing secretary of the treasury Joseph Barr astonished and angered the nation when he reported how many millionaires paid no taxes at all. Suddenly, tax reform was an "issue." Before long, President Nixon was considering eliminating the investment tax credit, a gift John Kennedy had bestowed on a skeptical business establishment in 1963. Nixon even proposed a minimum tax for wealthy individuals, a proposal that was flatly rejected in 1969 but that became an integral part of President Reagan's highly touted omnibus tax reform bill of 1986. Not unlike former President Kennedy, however, Nixon had better luck with tax reduction than with tax reform. Interest groups that stood to lose from real reform were unequivocally opposed to closing loopholes; moreover, Nixon was never really enthusiastic about tax reform.[24] It should be emphasized, however, that Nixon's tax policies were no less progressive than those of the New Frontier or Great Society. This is not to say that the Kennedy-Johnson administrations pushed for especially progressive tax policies. In fact, quite the contrary appeared to be true. Then again, as historian Mark Leff has demonstrated in his cogently argued *Limits of Symbolic Reform*, the tax policies put forth by the Roosevelt Administration during the early days of the New Deal were not very progressive either.[25] Progressive spending policies, then, do not necessarily entail progressive tax bites.

Now revenue sharing was one reform about which Richard Nixon was enthusiastic. Henry Clay had been the first to broach the idea; it had been part of his much vaunted "American system" of the early nineteenth century.[26] During the Kennedy Administration, liberal economist Walter Heller (of JFK's Council of Economic Advisors) suggested revenue sharing as a way out of embarrassing federal surpluses. Nixon was even more charmed by the potentialities of revenue sharing than had been Heller. In fact, when he proposed it to Congress in the summer of 1969, President Nixon let out a blast of hyperbole reminiscent of Lyndon Johnson. It was nothing less, Nixon intoned, than "a new American Revolution."[27] It was no such thing, of course. However, inasmuch as general revenue sharing was a supplement to existing programs of categorical aid rather than a substitution for them, it did not represent such a drastic departure from the Great Society after all. Moreover, inasmuch as localities as well as states received federal assistance under the new program, liberal mayors had little reason to complain. Admittedly, Nixon saw revenue sharing as one way of revitalizing federalism and granting more autonomy to the states. Those on the receiving end, not surprisingly, perceived the matter less abstractly. As it turned out, federal aid to cities was greater under Richard Nixon than it would be under Jimmy Carter.[28]

However, there was one reform that grabbed the attention of activists and editorialists alike, and that was welfare reform. Mark Twain once cracked, "Everybody complains about the weather, but no one does anything about it." Welfare was pretty much in the same state by 1968. Virtually everyone complained about it, but there were precious few concrete proposals put forward to reform it. The Democratic platform of that year did mention something about moving toward national standards, and Democratic Congressman William Ryan of New York was the first politician to propose a guaranteed annual income. Lyndon Johnson's Commission on Income Maintenance (the so-called Heineman Commission) advocated precisely that to Johnson, but LBJ indicated that he thought the "services strategy" of the Great Society (e.g., Medicare, Medicaid, food stamps, legal services, and compensatory education) was a more profitable route to take than the "income strategy" now put before him. Wilbur Cohen, Johnson's secretary of Health, Education, and Welfare, believed the American public would balk at yet another program for poor people.

Richard Nixon did not neglect the subject of welfare reform when campaigning across the country. In fact, he stated that he was dead set against a guaranteed annual income. Nonetheless, Nixon became the first president of the United States to advocate a federally guaranteed annual income for nearly all indigent Americans.

There was, in effect, a guaranteed income for millions of poor Americans already, but in about half the states, families could qualify only if they were fatherless. In the remaining states, intact families would receive government assistance only if the primary breadwinner were unemployed. Thus, the welfare system extant at the time placed a premium on both unemployment and family dissolution. What was more, terms of eligibility and payment levels varied greatly from state to state. New York State, for example, was five times more munificent than the state of Mississippi.[29]

Into this "mess" stepped President Richard Nixon. What he proposed was a striking departure from the status quo. The federal government would now assist poor families that were intact as well as those that had split apart. It would assist the working poor as well as the nonworking poor, and it would go a long way toward establishing national welfare standards. The ramifications of all this were several—and significant. Children would be guaranteed an income irrespective of whether their parents worked. The income of poor people living in the South would be tripled, and the welfare rolls themselves would double in size. According to not a few economists, 60 percent of all indigent people would be brought above the poverty line immediately were this proposal to be enacted into law. Lyndon Johnson never dared go so far.

Both architects of the programs—dubbed the Family Assistance Plan (FAP)—and correspondents, not to mention historians, have recognized the boldness of Nixon's proposal. Former policy planner Daniel Patrick Moynihan, who perhaps played the single most important role in converting the president to the idea, called the FAP "one of the half dozen or dozen most important pieces of social legislation in American history."[30] (To a certain extent, Moynihan was patting himself on the back.) Respected columnists such as James Reston hailed it as nothing less than revolutionary, and historian Alonzo Hamby has said that Nixon's guaranteed income for poor families was "the most significant failed initiative in the history of American social welfare politics since Truman's universal medical insurance proposal."[31]

Why had Nixon professed something so far-reaching, and so likely to eventuate in criticism of him by his party's right wing? He did so in part, no doubt, because so many mayors and governors—including Republican ones—were placing pressure on him to do something to relieve them of their fiscal burdens, burdens brought on largely by generous welfare policies in their own states and localities. He did so in part also because there were some economists around Nixon—Pierre Rinfret comes to mind immediately—who saw an income maintenance proposal of this sort as a way of stimulating the economy. Others in the Nixon circle saw the FAP as a compelling answer to black critics and an imaginative response to many of the nation's urban woes. Nixon himself was not about to throw up his hands in despair. As he put it in his memoirs, "I wanted to be an activist President on domestic policy."[32] No one, of course, could accuse the FAP of being quietistic. However, it satisfied more than the president's activistic itchings. It was also a most ingenious way of using liberal policy against liberal politicians.

In his superb *In the Shadow of FDR*, historian William Leuchtenburg made quite clear President Richard Nixon's intention to move away from the tradition of the New Deal.[33] That intention, in no small part because it was advertised so widely, led many opponents of the welfare state to sign up with Nixon. However, Nixon himself, as we have already established, did not display any special affection for an economy run on automatic pilot or, for that matter, a society without welfare. What he now proposed, in the form of the FAP, was a policy aimed at assisting the working poor, a group with which the president himself empathized because of his once lowly roots and a group that could hardly be called radical chic. It was Harvard professor Pat Moynihan, however, who made the most compelling case for out-liberalizing the liberals. Moynihan convinced Nixon that the current services strategy of LBJ's Great Society meant little more than "taxing factory workers to pay school teachers."[34] Regarding social workers, a group for which Nixon had little sympathy, the Harvard professor assured the president that a policy of putting money directly and immediately into the hands of the poor would have the desired effect—"It would wipe them out."[35] In his memoirs, Nixon stated that this was one of the greatest appeals of the Family Assistance Plan. It was this aspect of FAP that led Garry Wills to say, "It is welfare used against welfare."[36]

Moynihan had other cards to play as well. He correctly informed Nixon that the FAP was not unlike a negative income tax, the brainchild of Milton Friedman back when he was working for the U.S. government during the 1940s. (Sargent Shriver of the Office of Economic Opportunity had actually advocated a negative income tax to Lyndon Johnson, but LBJ would have none of the idea.) That is to say, the FAP was an idea of conservative provenance after all. Beyond that, Moynihan appealed to Nixon's sense of history. With a proposal such as this, he forcefully asserted, the president could go down as another Benjamin Disraeli, a Tory reformer whose own enlightened policies for the poor and near-poor would accomplish far more than the nostrums of professional liberals. Finally, Moynihan held that a guaranteed annual income would enhance what he had called in an earlier address before the Americans for Democratic Action (ADA), "the politics of stability."

Reaction to the proposal was mixed. It was also suggestive to the topsy-turvy nature of American politics. Not surprisingly, virtually all economists who had anything to say about the FAP liked it, much preferring it to the less efficacious minimum wage. This was even true of economists who were not known for their love of market mechanisms, such as John Kenneth Galbraith. The Ripon Society, an oasis of liberal reform within the Republican party, also warmly endorsed it. Newspaper editorial writers and civic groups such as Common Cause and the League of Women Voters generally gave the FAP high marks. The American business elite revealed cracks in its ostensibly monolithic structure, however. The Committee for Economic Development and the National Association of Manufacturers supported the bill, but the Chamber of Commerce firmly opposed the FAP on the grounds that it was an extension of welfare. Organized labor, or at least the American Federation of Labor and Congress of Industrial Organizations (AFL-CIO), initially saw the FAP as a government subsidy of stingy employers—and as a possible threat to the vitality of labor unions—but eventually came around to supporting the Nixon plan after being assured that there would be a jobs program as well.

Conservatives were divided on the issue. One right-wing supporter, Congressman James B. Utt of California, served as Nixon's trophy from the John Birch Society. Others on the right were not so easily won over, however. *National Review* and *Human Events*, flagships of contemporary American conservatism, made known their unhappiness with the proposal, and Governor Ronald Reagan of California assailed the FAP as yet another way of rewarding idleness. Conservative critics of welfare reform-cum-redistribution within Congress would examine the details of the bill in more depth than Governor Reagan, and in the end would help to bury the bill.[37]

However, an attack from the right was expected by both Nixon and Moynihan. What threw them off guard was the gradually mounting hostility of certifiably liberal organizations such as the American Friends Service Committee and the ADA. These groups, along with social democratic warhorse Michael Harrington, scored the bill for its inadequacy as a means of eliminating poverty. Though Catholic and Jewish organizations gave the FAP their critical support, the Protestant National Council of Churches (whose leadership was far more liberal than its rank and file) blasted it as "racist."[38] The National Welfare Rights Organization was less felicitous in its use of language; in its eyes, FAP meant "Fuck America's Poor."[39] Public sector unions and organized social workers, both of which had long ties with liberal politics, set their faces against the Nixon bill, even though Nixon had decided to mollify the opposition by not hacking away at the welfare bureaucracy. (It was in large part because the FAP would have been added onto our existing welfare structure rather than have served as a replacement for it that Milton Friedman himself turned against it.)

Some liberal observers were livid with the reaction of their ideological brethren. In response to those who held that the floor for the poor created by the FAP was insufficient, journalists Vincent Burke and Vee Burke queried, "Was it better to have no floor?"[40] Regarding the common charge of many liberals in and out of Congress that Nixon could not possibly be sincere, the Burkes had this to say in the aftermath of the all-but-inevitable defeat of FAP in the Senate. "Would only 'sincerely' motivated federal dollars buy shoes and toys for needy children?"[41]

However, we should resist the temptation to look for a rogues' gallery. Indeed, collective self-interest played a part in the killing of the FAP among both conservatives in the South and liberals in the North, but it was not the only factor. President Nixon's Cambodian "incursion" undoubtedly lost him the support of some liberal members of Congress who were prepared to go with him on the issue of welfare reform. In addition, some claims to the contrary notwithstanding, Nixon never put as much energy into the FAP as he did into, say, playing the chessboard of international geopolitics. Finally, Nixon's dressing up of the FAP in the costume of Horatio Alger (he spoke sternly of a "work requirement" that rested far more on the carrot of incentives than on the stick of coercion) made it appear more harsh than it actually was. Nixon acted as if "workfare" were an alternative to welfare when it was actually a compound of work and welfare, and he consistently refused to acknowledge that his plan was in reality a *guaranteed* income for a good many poor people, namely children. That he behaved this way is understandable enough. Nearly two-thirds of the American public had expressed its disapproval of a guaranteed income in 1968. (That same year, Democratic presidential candidate Robert Kennedy distinguished himself from opponent Eugene McCarthy by claiming that he was for jobs as an alternative to more welfare.[42] What both Kennedy and the American people failed to realize was that "full employment," if the nation should be so lucky as to experience it once again, will not eliminate poverty, and that the country already had a guaranteed annual income anyway—for those who were unemployed.) After Nixon's advocacy of the FAP, a majority of the public responded favorably to a negative income tax. If they suspected it was precisely what the president said it was not, they would have been irrevocably opposed from the outset.

The push for and debate over the FAP were significant in many respects. For one thing, the genesis of the plan was emblematic of what Moynihan had termed "the professionalization of reform."[43] President Nixon may have been the first president to propose comprehensive welfare reform (Jimmy Carter was the last, with his ill-fated Program for Better Jobs and Income, or PBJI), but the idea itself was supplied by economists and political scientists.[44] There was no mass movement of the poor or near-poor demanding anything like the FAP. Even after it was proposed, members of Congress who were supportive of it received virtually no favorable correspondence from its intended beneficiaries. For another thing, the fact that the FAP did make it through the House of Representatives suggested that nonincremental change was still possible in this country. During the 1950s it was fashionable in many academic circles to hold that in the American context, given our pluralistic economy and federal political structure, only incremental reform was possible. Political theorists such as Charles Lindblom admitted that there were exceptions to this rule—exceptions occasioned by, say, war or depression—but in general, ours was the politics of "muddling through."[45] The difference between the incremental and nonincremental often depends on who is doing the defining, of course, but it does not seem unreasonable to grant the FAP nonincremental status.

Finally, the raging controversy over the Nixon proposal demonstrated that ideology is not always the most reliable guide to the formulation of public policy. When Richard Nixon was elected president, *The Progressive* predicted that a conservative such as Nixon would display no appetite for something as bold as a guaranteed income for most poor Americans. Nixon, of course, displayed a healthy appetite for such a dish. That appetite moved John Osborne of the liberal *New Republic* to state in 1969 that the FAP "reflect[ed] and constitute[d] the best in domestic planning and policy that we have had from the Nixon Administration."[46] Not all liberals, as we have seen, concurred with this assessment. The crazy-quilt nature of the coalitions for and against the FAP led sociologist Nathan Glazer to conclude that on the matter of welfare reform, one "would be hard put to distinguish liberals from conservatives."[47]

At times, of course, it was difficult to distinguish the liberal from the conservative in President Nixon, at least during his first term. That culturally Nixon believed himself to be a traditionalist (or "square") is well known. However, he also viewed his actions in domestic policy to be those of a reformer, and not the kind of reformer who promises to resurrect a golden age of the past. His reformist conservatism (so distinct from the sort of standpat conservatism epitomized by the legendary King Canute) placed him near that band of intellectuals who subscribed to a gospel of "neoconservatism." Like most neoconservatives, Richard Nixon thought the Great Society was too messy and too intrusive. He had come to accept without reservation the inevitability and even the desirability of the welfare state, though, again like the neoconservatives, he wished to see things done a bit differently and by different people. Along with most—though not all—neoconservatives, Nixon harbored a strong resentment of the so-called New Class, that body of liberal-minded white-collar and largely public-sector professionals who were often perceived as the primary beneficiaries of the Great Society. It was his antipathy to these people that in part spurred on his commitment to welfare reform. Moreover, the man who had sold Nixon on the idea of an income strategy, Daniel Patrick Moynihan, was fast becoming one of the intellectual darlings of the burgeoning neoconservative movement. It is perhaps not surprising, then, that Nixon took to reading the respected neoconservative journal, *The Public Interest*, and to dining with its indefatigable editor, Irving Kristol. Not a few neoconservatives, in fact, took out ads for Richard Nixon when he ran against George McGovern in 1972.[48] Alonzo Hamby does not exaggerate when he suggests that Nixon may have been our first neoconservative president.[49] However, political analyst Kevin Phillips is no less on the mark when he asserts that the neoconservatives wish "to preserve the intellectual and institutional structure liberalism built."[50] This explains the attraction of many neoconservatives to Richard Nixon, and thus the attraction of Richard Nixon to a certain kind of reform.

Herbert Stein entitled a chapter of his recent book on presidential economic policies, "Nixon: Conservative Men with Liberal Policies."[51] Stein was on to something. Edmund Burke long ago demonstrated to the satisfaction (and, in some cases, dissatisfaction) of liberals and conservatives alike that reform and conservatism were by no means antithetical. To Burke, reform was often more a means of preservation than a prelude to revolution, notwithstanding the reflexive responses of some overwrought rightists. It was Otto von Bismarck, after all, who laid the foundations for the welfare state, as Tory (no "neo" about him) columnist George Will so often reminds us.[52] Moreover, much of Theodore Roosevelt and Woodrow Wilson's brand of progressivism, as historian Richard Hofstadter and others have shown, was motivated by a desire to stave off more

292   Barry D. Riccio

radical reform.[53] Nixonian conservatism, in different ways and for somewhat different reasons, was no less of a fusion. At the very least, Nixon's actions demonstrated (to borrow a leaf from Ralph Waldo Emerson) that the "party of conservatism" could also be a "party of Innovation." Even the doyen of liberal historiography, Arthur Schlesinger, Jr., in his recently published *Cycles of American History*, subsumed the Nixon presidential record under the rubric of the reform cycle. As a reformer with strong ties to the Democrats, Schlesinger had every partisan reason not to make such an observation.[54]

Richard Nixon was a paradoxical figure who despised liberals while endorsing liberal objectives. He was certainly not the "last liberal" in the sense in which Garry Wills used the term, but it is difficult to deny that his presidency witnessed more social reform than have the administrations of his successors.[55] It is unfortunate that in attempting to steal a piece of liberalism from the liberals, he also sought to snatch the Constitution away from the country. Both the FAP and Watergate were, each in its own way, attempts to outflank the liberal opposition. This was not a winning combination—in any sense of the term.

NOTES

1. Louis Hartz, *The Liberal Tradition in America* (New York: Harcourt, Brace and World, 1955).
2. Ibid., passim.
3. Garry Wills, *Nixon Agonistes* (New York: New American Library, 1971).
4. This was the subtitle of the book.
5. Alonzo Hamby, *Liberalism and Its Challengers* (New York: Oxford University Press, 1985), p. 282.
6. Wills, *Agonistes*, p. 157.
7. R.W.B. Lewis, *The American Adam* (Chicago: University of Chicago Press, 1955).
8. Wills, *Agonistes*, pp. 396–397.
9. Cited in Joe McGinnis, *The Selling of the President, 1968* (New York: Pocket Books, 1969), p. 170.
10. See Richard Hofstadter, *The Age of Reform* (New York: Vintage Books, 1955), pp. 302–328; and Otis Graham, *An Encore for Reform* (New York: Oxford University Press, 1967), pp. 24–100.
11. William E. Leuchtenburg, *In the Shadow of FDR* (Ithaca, N.Y.: Cornell University Press, 1985), p. 138.
12. Cited in Otis L. Graham, Jr., *Toward a Planned Society* (New York: Oxford University Press, 1976), p. 248.
13. See A. James Reichley, *Conservatives in an Age of Change* (Washington, D.C.: Brookings Institution, 1981), p. 27.
14. The LBJ statement appears in Doris Kearns, *Lyndon Johnson and the American Dream* (New York: Harper and Row, 1976), p. 286.
15. Most of the evidence for these assertions can be found in the appendices to Herbert Stein's *Presidential Economics* (New York: Simon & Schuster, 1985), pp. 397–405.
16. Ibid., p. 190.

17. David A. Stockman, *The Triumph of Politics* (New York: Avon Books, 1987), p. 34.

18. Steven Kelman, "Occupational Safety and Health Administration," in *The Politics of Regulation*, ed. James Q. Wilson (New York: Basic Books, 1980), pp. 241–242.

19. See Kevin P. Phillips, *Post-Conservative America* (New York: Vintage Books, 1983), pp. 53–62.

20. James L. Sundquist, *Politics and Policy* (Washington, D.C.: Brookings Institution, 1968), pp. 361–381.

21. Graham, *Planned Society*, pp. 200–201.

22. Ibid., p. 217.

23. Cited in Daniel P. Moynihan, *The Politics of a Guaranteed Income* (New York: Vintage Books, 1973), p. 172.

24. On the vagaries of tax reform during the Nixon administration see Rowland Evans, Jr., and Robert D. Novak, *Nixon in the White House* (New York: Vintage Books, 1972), pp. 214–223.

25. Mark Leff, *The Limits of Symbolic Reform* (Cambridge: Cambridge University Press, 1984), passim.

26. Reichley, *Conservatives*, p. 154.

27. Evans and Novak, *Nixon*, pp. 241–244.

28. See Kenneth Fox, *Metropolitan America* (Jackson, Miss.: University of Mississippi, 1986), p. 219.

29. An excellent discussion of the many problems with our welfare policy during the 1960s can be found in Vincent J. Burke and Vee Burke, *Nixon's Good Deed* (New York: Columbia University Press, 1974), pp. 7–39.

30. Moynihan, *Guaranteed Income*, p. 4.

31. Hamby, *Liberalism*, p. 318.

32. Richard M. Nixon, *RN: The Memoirs of Richard Nixon* (New York: Grosset and Dunlap, 1978), p. 353.

33. Leuchtenburg, *Shadow*, pp. 161–173.

34. Moynihan, *Guaranteed Income*, p. 53.

35. Ibid., p. 37.

36. Wills, *Agonistes*, p. 486.

37. Moynihan provides thorough coverage of how various interest and ideological groups responded to the FAP. See *Guaranteed Income*, pp. 236–347.

38. Burke and Burke, *Good Deed*, p. 130.

39. Ibid., p. 138.

40. Ibid., p. 135.

41. Ibid.

42. See Arthur Schlesinger, Jr., *Robert Kennedy and His Times* (New York: Ballantine Books, 1978), p. 843.

43. See Daniel P. Moynihan, "The Professionalization of Reform," in *The Liberal Tradition in Crisis*, ed. Jerome M. Mileur (Lexington, Mass.: Heath, 1974), pp. 69–80.

44. Leonard M. Greene, *Free Enterprise Without Poverty* (New York: Norton, 1983), pp. 87–88.

45. This was the thesis, for instance, of Lindblom's *The Intelligence of Democracy* (New York: The Free Press, 1965).

46. John Osborne, *The Nixon Watch* (New York: Liveright, 1970), p. 143.

47. Nathan Glazer, "The Limits of Social Policy," in Mileur, ed., *Tradition in Crisis*, p. 83.

48. On neoconservative support for Nixon see Peter Steinfels, *The Neo-Conservatives* (New York: Simon and Schuster, 1979), pp. 87–90, 219–254.

49. Hamby, *Liberalism*, pp. 316–331.

50. Phillips, *Post-Conservative America*, p. 44.

51. Stein, *Presidential Economics*, p. 133.

52. See especially George F. Will, *Statecraft as Soulcraft* (New York: Simon and Schuster, 1983), p. 126.

53. Richard Hofstadter, *The American Political Tradition* (New York: Vintage Books, 1948), pp. 216–282. The subtitles of his chapters on Roosevelt and Wilson are, respectively, "The Conservative as Progressive" and "The Conservative as Liberal." From a very different political perspective and with a different fish to fry, Gabriel Kolko has made a similar argument in his *The Triumph of Conservatism* (New York: The Free Press, 1963), passim.

54. For both Emerson and Schlesinger, see Arthur Schlesinger, Jr., *The Cycles of American History* (Boston: Houghton Mifflin, 1986), pp. 23–50.

55. This is the subtitle of the last chapter of Wills's book.

12

Richard Nixon and the Idea of Rehabilitation

SHERRI CAVAN

In 1974 everyone was saying that Richard Nixon's public career was over. By 1984, the word was "rehabilitation."[1]

Talk of rehabilitation began with his first public appearance four years after the scandal of Watergate forced his resignation from the presidency. In the ensuing years, some have seen his rehabilitation as an article of faith, something people believe in; others see it as a job, the work the former president has been doing since he left office. Some describe it as a struggle; others describe it as a flawless performance. Some see his rehabilitation as complete; some see it as partial; and still others search for a way to measure how far he has come from disgrace and dishonor (Thomas, 1978; Kaiser, 1984; Friedrich, 1984; Herbers, 1984; Glynn, 1984; Anson, 1984; Lewis, 1984; Alter, 1984; Fineman, 1985; Boyd, 1985; Kristof, 1986; Martz, 1986; Simes, 1987).

Rehabilitation is a social process. It involves a person who has a reputation that is flawed or defective in some way, and work that is undertaken to restore that reputation to a socially acceptable condition.

Some axioms of rehabilitation theory are relevant. First, the idea assumes that the person in question is worth the effort that rehabilitation takes. It assumes that the person is a good person gone bad, and not an irredeemably bad person. Conservative critics of rehabilitation in the prisons argue that some offenders are not worth the cost involved or have no redeeming social values to begin with, and indeed, the goal of rehabilitation has long since been discarded as an objective of imprisonment. Those of a more liberal persuasion argue that all human beings have socially redeeming qualities, and therefore that rehabilitation is a possibility for everyone, although it may not always happen (Wright, 1973; Newman, 1978; Johnson, 1987).

A second important principle of rehabilitation addresses the way the candidate approaches the process. Successful rehabilitation requires that those who are to be restored to honor and respect openly and freely admit the error of their ways, show remorse, be humble, and be embarrassed and distressed by those actions that resulted in their dishonor (Garfinkle, 1956). As Richard Nixon has said on various occasions, contrition is not his style. Thus, any application of the idea of rehabilitation to his case must treat his acknowledgement that "mistakes were made" as the equivalent of the self-criticism ordinarily required from those who seek social redemption.

Rehabilitation is a status transformation. The rehabilitation process takes a person whose moral character has been disgraced and degraded and transforms him or her into a new person who now deserves honor and respect. This transformation is not just something that happens, the unaided evolution of character. Rather, it involves active work on the part of agents of social control, persons acting in the name of moral responsibility (Garfinkle, 1956). Insofar as Gerald Ford's pardon effectively eliminated the involvement of any agency of social control, and insofar as Nixon has sought neither private practitioner nor self-help agency to aid him, his rehabilitation must be viewed as an instance of self-rehabilitation, a transformation of character done without any organized institutional assistance.

Finally, the measure of rehabilitation is change. The idea of rehabilitation implies that there is a new Nixon, and that this new Nixon is a function of recognizable changes in his character.

This paper addresses the question of Richard Nixon's rehabilitation first by addressing what kind of evidence exists that there is a new Nixon, and then by looking at the work that has been undertaken to create the image of rehabilitation, despite considerable evidence that the new Nixon is really an old Nixon.

THE NEW NIXON AND THE OLD NIXON

The new Nixon is an old Nixon in various ways. Most obvious is the repetitive drama of Richard Nixon coming back from the brink of oblivion, reemerging in the public arena like a phoenix rising from the ashes of political defeat (McGinnis, 1968; Witcover, 1970; Lurie, 1972; Cavan, 1979; Brodie, 1981).

The first example of his recurrent resurrection was in 1952 when charges were made that he was being supported by a secret fund contributed to by wealthy oil and real estate interests. Those charges evoked editorials in newspapers that supported the Republican ticket demanding his resignation from the vice presidential nomination. No support was forthcoming from party influentials. It looked like his career in politics was over. Nevertheless, Nixon mounted a television defense of his honor, and so effective was his appeal to the sentiments and emotions of the audience that, in a viewing audience of sixty million, five in every thousand were motivated to respond with a letter, a postcard, or a telegram. The Republican National Headquarters was overwhelmed by the mail, which ran 74–1 against his resignation, and Nixon was retained on the ticket (Stratton, 1964; O'Brien and Jones, 1976). When Dwight D. Eisenhower won the election, Richard Nixon moved from being a senator with suspicious connections to being vice president of the United States of America.

In 1960 and 1962, Nixon suffered two major political defeats. Groomed to run for president in 1960, he lost the popular election to John F. Kennedy; then he lost the contest for governor of California to Edmund G. Brown. Worse yet, in the wake of this second defeat he exploded in anger, declaring that the press would no longer have Richard Nixon to kick around, that this was to be his last press conference and, by implication, that he was through with politics. He took on the image of a loser, and a poor one at that. It appeared that his political career was over.

Moving from California to New York, Nixon began a long and active process of rebuilding his public image; selling himself first to the loyal supporters of the Republican party, and then to those with power and influence (McGinnis, 1968). In 1962, it looked as though Nixon's meteoric career in politics had come to an end; in 1968, he was elected President of the United States by a slim margin. Four years later, he was reelected by an overwhelming majority (Cavan, 1979; Brodie, 1981).

Two years after his reelection, the House Judiciary Committee voted three articles of impeachment: obstruction of justice, abuse of power, and unconstitutionally defying its subpoenas. Rather than face the open hearing of impeachment proceedings, Richard Nixon resigned from the presidency he had fought so hard to achieve.

Despite the immediate pardon granted by his successor, virtually everyone who voiced an opinion initially believed that Nixon's days of public influence were over. He was a man discredited and disgraced, stigmatized by charges of executive malfeasance that could not be denied and seemed too extraordinary to be forgotten (*The Washington Post* Staff, 1974; *The New York Times* Staff, 1974; White, 1975; Jaworski, 1976; Dunham and Mauss, 1976; Sirica, 1979).

However, his return to California did not signal retirement. On numerous occasions Nixon said that a man is not defeated until he quits, and he was not the kind of man who quit, playing golf, walking along the seashore, and withdrawing from the public arena (Frost, 1978; Anson, 1984). Consequently, after a short period of seclusion during which he recovered from an attack of phlebitis, he began a gradual return to public life by first testing the waters at a party at Walter Annenberg's; then, golf at LaCosta; and finally traveling around at home and abroad; voicing opinions in televised interviews, private phone calls and memos, and public books and speeches; meeting with foreign dignitaries, former associates, and former enemies; and being asked for opinions and assistance.

He was reemerging as a public figure, playing the role of elder statesman at home and diplomatic courier abroad (Sidey, 1981; Sanders, 1983; Alter, 1984; Bruning, 1984; Morrow, 1985).

Like Rocky Balboa, that ephemeral movie hero of the 1970s, Nixon has continually returned to the top, overcoming the most overwhelming obstacles. The drama of Nixon's return to power and influence is familiar. This new Nixon is an old one.

The old Nixon was a peripatetic campaigner who was almost always on the road, traveling from one place to another, holding meetings, making speeches, and shaking hands (McGinnis, 1969; Lurie, 1972; Cavan, 1979; Brodie, 1981). The new Nixon appears even more indefatigable than the old one. He can be found regularly traveling from one part of the country to another, from the United States to Europe, the Soviet Union, the Middle East, the Far East, Africa, and the Caribbean; meeting in private, speaking in public, and being interviewed on television. Moreover, when he is not engaged in his indefatigable travels, he can be found at home writing or organizing stag dinners for a handful of guests or lunching in New York City with someone notable and newsworthy. In addition, he spends considerable time on the telephone, networking with various people of power and influence. He has a copious correspondence, especially small notes of congratulations or condolences. He walks every morning, and spends time with his grandchildren whenever he can, and to get away from it all, he takes periodic vacations with his long-time friend, Bebe Rebozo (Sidey, 1981; Anson, 1984; Alter, 1984; King and Weaver, 1986; Martz, 1986; Schmemann, 1986). In short, he has spent his time out of office in much the same way that he spent his time when he was in office or was campaigning for office: on the go.

A new category of events has become part of Richard Nixon's itinerary in these postresignation years. As his patrons, his contemporaries, and his adversaries have died, the various funeral and memorial services have created social occasions of a special sort. Death brings people together. Conflicts that existed in the past may be set aside without negotiating the terms of the new agreement. In the case of Anwar Sadat's funeral, Richard Nixon traveled aboard a government plane, in the company of former presidents Gerald Ford and Jimmy Carter. This was his first officially sponsored appearance, and so it was a significant event in Nixon's return to the public spotlight (Anson, 1984). The trip also allowed the three former presidents to normalize their relationships with one another. In the same sense, the Washington memorial service for Hubert Humphrey brought Jerry Ford, Jimmy Carter, Walter Mondale, Henry Kissinger, Nelson Rockefeller, and Lady Bird Johnson together in an intimate (but not unreported) meeting in the office of Howard Baker (Sidey, 1978). While this occasion was not officially sponsored, it again provided an occasion for Nixon to begin to normalize his relationships with others of power and influence. Such relationships have always been crucial to Nixon's career (Cavan, 1979).

In addition to the deaths of Anwar Sadat and Hubert Humphrey, the deaths of the shah of Iran, Yuri Andropov, Elmer Bobst, and even Woody Hayes all became occasions for Nixon to make a public appearance and frequently to give a eulogy at the service or an interview afterwards (Clark, 1978; Anson, 1984; Alter, 1984; Martz, 1986).

Nixon has always thrived on hard work. He sees himself as being at his best when he is on the brink of fatigue. He chides anyone who suggests he slow down and relax (Nixon, 1962, 1978; Chesen, 1973; Abrahamsen, 1976; Brodie, 1981). Consequently, this new Nixon who is constantly on the go is no different from the old Nixon who was constantly on the go.

The new Nixon is an old Nixon in still other ways. The rhetoric of conflict and confrontation that has always been part of his aggressive political style continues in the imagery of the elder statesman. The Cold War is now the "Cold Peace" ("No enemies," 1984). Even where his published opinions suggest Détente and negotiation (thought not conciliation and cooperation), his public speeches continue to evoke the gothic imagery of his youth: the vision of en- trenched forces of evil, dedicated to the destruction of the moral order for diabolical reasons like power and greed. In a speech at Chapman College, he said, "The Soviet leaders are dedicated Communists; they want to rule the world" (Holley, 1984, p. 1). In this classic evangelical style, Nixon has continued to evoke strong sentiments from the public, using the language and metaphors of warfare to sell peace (Fuller, Kondracke, and Lindsay, 1986).

As before, Nixon continues to idealize strategy and tactics as the meaning of politics, if not the meaning of life. He continues to focus on the means and not the goals. He continues to subscribe to pragmatic advantage as the ultimate justification for action (Sidey, 1983). In his treatise on leadership, he writes of the need for deceit and duplicity on the part of those who make important decisions. However, he does not see how the exigencies of war are exceptional circumstances and not the definitive character of leadership, which also involves vision and compassion. He does not address the relationship between the leaders and the followers in a democratic society, nor does he see how routine duplicity and deceit borders on totalitarianism (Nixon, 1982). Though he is older and more experienced, his vision is still quite narrow.

Nixon's youthful commitment to winning and losing has softened some to admit the option of compromise, yet such compromise is not seen as a move toward consensus or conciliation. Rather, it is seen as the best of competing evils, or sometimes a bargain or an admission that the other side might not be all bad. He has even described himself as a "closet dove" (Thomas, 1978; Thimmesch, 1979; Sidey, 1981, 1983; Sanders, 1983; Holley, 1984). However, for the most part, this elder statesman talks tough (Cavan, 1979).

Like the Cold War warrior of his youth, the elder statesman has no vision that goes beyond winning, no vision of unified interests engaged in mutually supportive action. Peace is not a natural attitude but rather an unstable interval between outbreaks of war and hostility, a delicate flower and not a robust shrub (Holley, 1984).

Outside arenas of conflict, whether they be politics or sports, business or gambling, there is nothing of which to speak. He does not address himself to questions of morals and ethics, virtue or truth. Neither does he speak of natural resources, individual rights, human relationships, the arts, science, religion, or humanity. He continues to be political without ever becoming philosophical.

This new Nixon is an old Nixon in a literal sense. He is now seventy-four years old. For forty years he has been in the public arena, half of that time in public office. He was one of the original architects of nuclear politics, a political attitude based on physical control over monumental forces of destruction and the willingness to bargain with this destructive potential for strategic advantage vis-à-vis others similarly armed. Despite Nixon's current presentation of himself as a man vitally concerned with the issue of world peace, he remains the same person who by his own admission was willing to bring the planet to the brink of nuclear war on four separate occasions ("Four times," 1985).

In the years after World War II, when the destructive potential of nuclear weaponry could have been curtailed and inhibited and a path toward peaceful coexistence taken with the Soviet Union, Richard Nixon was at the forefront of a political position that argued for the development, testing, and stockpiling of nuclear weaponry as necessary to the defense of national interests in the conflict with insidious, imperialistic, nihilistic forces of communism. With political leaders propagating such imagery, nuclear weaponry proliferated at an alarming rate on both sides. Even if today's nations so armed were to forge an agreement to halt the continued proliferation of such weapons by the end of the century, the legacy left to the future are the stockpiles of lethal armaments and the toxic waste and by-products those armaments have produced. Though he speaks of a desire for world peace, Richard Nixon has never repudiated this youthful folly. It has merely faded from prominence.

Like the aggressive young congressman of the 1950s, this new Nixon still thrives on risk, threat, confrontation, and duplicity. He is still committed to the idea that winning is everything, even if winning now means getting a better bargain rather than overpowering the enemy (Thomas, 1978; Sanders, 1983; Sidey, 1983; Holley, 1984). As an elder statesman, Nixon's stature is more a function of his endurance and ambition than of some deep philosophical insight into the human conditions, some understanding that was not accessible to him in his youth.

Despite these similarities between the new Nixon and the old Nixon, this old Nixon, the septuagenarian, also shows evidence of a new Nixon, a Nixon unlike those versions of the past.

Observers of the postresignation period note that he is more secure, more relaxed, less anxious, and less ill at ease (Herbers, 1984; Fineman, 1985; Martz, 1986; Fuller et al., 1986). He is obviously a man who is much more experienced than the youthful version of his self, more in control, and less apprehensive and uncertain. He has seen a lot in his lifetime, usually from the highest places. He has also fallen from high places; he has experienced the abyss and lived to tell the tale on network television. Very little fazes him. He continues to struggle to write and rewrite the accounts of his life and times in order to validate his claims to honor and respect. However, now he does so with more assurance, more grace, and even occasional flashes of humor.

He is also much wealthier than he was in his youth. Through a variety of judicious real estate transactions, well-placed investments, royalties accumulated from his books, and payments received for his interviews, in addition to the pensions and perquisites of the presidency that his resignation and pardon insured, he has managed to amass a sizeable fortune (Anson, 1984; Alter, 1984; Herbers, 1984; Glynn, 1984; Martz, 1986). The modest circumstances that his wife's cloth coat symbolized in his youth have given way to a more imperial style. He lives in a spacious house in an exclusive neighborhood; when he travels, which is frequently, he travels first-class, accompanied by an extensive entourage of aides and assistants to facilitate his movements and a bevy of armed bodyguards to surround and protect him. All the logistics of his daily existence are managed by others, from planning his agenda to managing his wardrobe. Freed from the irksome problems of mundane existence, there is less to frustrate him and more time for contemplation (Dolan, 1984; Herbers, 1984; Glynn, 1984; Shapiro, 1985; Martz, 1986).

Nixon the septuagenarian has also had more time for his family. In his youth, constant campaigning for office made inordinate demands on his wife and left him little time to share with his growing daughters. The embattled years of Watergate drew the family together, and when the girls married, their husbands were brought into the fold. With the birth of three grandchildren, the Nixon family has begun to take the shape of a dynasty: Nixon the patriarch, portrayed next to an ailing wife, flanked by beautiful daughters and handsome sons-in-law, fondling his infant grandchildren, and taking the older grandchildren to baseball games. His family is one of his greatest assets, and the new Nixon spends considerable time and energy cultivating that resource (Thimmesch, 1979; Mehle, 1982; Friedrich, 1984; Fuller et al., 1986; Eisenhower, 1986).

In sum, there are indeed ways in which the new Nixon is a man changed from the past, but at least to this analyst, there seems far more evidence to suggest that the new Nixon is an old Nixon, not so much changed as renewed, starting over with fresh energy and restored ambition. Indeed, in one of his rare flashes of humor, he joked, "[there is not] a new Nixon or a reincarnation, but there sure is an old Nixon" (Shapiro, 1984, p. 32).

IMPRESSION MANAGEMENT

A man with a loyal and devoted family, projecting an image of vitality and ambition; visiting scores of nations, some repeatedly; meeting with almost every major political leader abroad and many important people at home; voicing opinions in books, speeches, phone calls, memos, and letters; being asked his opinion by others—in the thirteen years since his resignation, Richard Nixon has reemerged as a figure of considerable influence in the public arena and a growing influence in the backstage machinations of political life.

How does he do it? we may ask. How does Nixon manage to overcome the stigma of discrediting revelations about his career and his character and in so doing maintain a position of respect with the public at large as well as with power brokers in both political parties (Herbers, 1984; Shapiro, 1984; Brown, 1987; McGovern, 1987)?

If he has not changed, certainly there is an impression that he is different— more worthy and more honorable than when he left office in disgrace. It is this impression that I wish to address by asking, How does Nixon evoke this impression? What does he do that makes those who judge him do so in a favorable light?

Impression management is a part of dramaturgical theory (Goffman, 1958; Burke, 1962; Messinger, Sampson, and Towne, 1962). It addresses the practices that individuals employ in order to elicit a desired response on the part of targeted audiences. Scripts, props, settings, and supporting cast are all organized to sustain a particular image of moral character. This is as much the case for those who are judged respectable as it is for those who are judged deviant (Goffman, 1963).

Audiences make their judgments on the basis of what they know or come to see, or on what is implied by what they know and see. Thus, the ability to control information is fundamental to controlling others' impressions. In addition, how information is presented and who is available to help with these presentations are relevant aspects of impression management.

Nixon's overwhelming task in these postresignation years has been creating and selling an image of himself as trustworthy, reliable, sincere, and enlightened, despite abundant evidence of deceit and duplicity, opportunism and betrayal. This is not a new task. He showed considerable appreciation of the role of impressions in adolescence (Cavan, 1979) and, from the Checkers speech on, his political career has demonstrated an astute appreciation and cultivation of various techniques associated with creating an image. Thus, as one small example, he has recently changed his official portrait at the White House to one that projects an image more in line with how he would like others to see him (Vasari, 1982; Hosefros, 1984).

DIVISIONS

Impression management has its roots in theater. As an analytic metaphor, it directs our attention to the stage, and to the important distinction between "front stage," where the calculated performances of public character are enacted, and "backstage," where the dirty work of manipulation and collusion takes place (Goffman, 1958).

One important example of this division between front stage presentations and backstage machinations is Nixon's conscious control of his language. It was not until the publication of the White House tapes that most Americans had any idea that the man who presented himself as the embodiment of respectable standards routinely used profanity in his private conversations in the Oval Office. Because these transcripts were to be made public, the actual words were edited out and replaced by (expletive deleted), a technique that only further exemplified Nixon's appreciation of maintaining the illusions of respectability front stage despite the backstage realities. In accounts written subsequent to his resignation, the public could learn how he carefully controlled his language in front of "ladies" while he engaged in locker room vulgarities with "the boys" (Woodward and Bernstein, 1976; Cavan, 1979; Brodie, 1981; Anson, 1984).

The controlled public image Nixon projects hides the disreputable aspects of his character from view. Occasionally, accounts of this side leak from aides and associates and find their way into public record. However, the pious public Nixon is a very different person from the vulgar, private Nixon, and in large measure, his success with the American public is a function of his ability to control those aspects of himself that are considered dishonorable and disrespectful, and to present instead an acceptable image.

Creating a division between front stage performances, where the illusion of respectability is fostered, and backstage behavior, where a different image is available is one division integral to managing the image of rehabilitation. There are other divisions that serve the same purpose: projecting the illusion of respectability. Thus, Nixon proposes that the past is different from the present; that errors in domestic policy have no relevance for judgment in foreign policy; that behavior governed by the head is different from behavior governed by the heart; that the means employed to get from one place to another are different from the goals being sought by that action (Frost, 1978). He suggests that what is unlawful becomes lawful when the president authorizes it (Pear, 1980b). He said, in the televised interview with David Frost, "My motive was pure political containment, and political containment is not a corrupt motive. . . . [M]y motive was not criminal" (Frost, 1978, pp. 16, 13).

By splitting hairs, Nixon speaks to only part of the issue, while he appears to address the whole topic. The audiences' attention is diverted. The impression is of a man who has nothing to apologize for, and no basis for embarrassment or chagrin. There has been a misunderstanding, but it is insignificant compared to the larger, global issues (Cavan, 1979).

Now it is clear to the attentive audience that when the former president says, as he does frequently, "I never look back" (see, for example, Frost, 1978; Bruning, 1984; Shapiro, 1984; Anson, 1984; Friedrich, 1984), his reference is specifically to the events of Watergate and his resignation. Otherwise, one of his most characteristic behavior patterns *is* looking back. Reruns and reunions are frequent motifs in these years since Watergate. He attends the fiftieth reunion of his graduating class at Whittier College; he returns to China on the tenth anniversary of his first trip; when he travels to Burma, he rings the ceremonial bell he rang on his first trip thirty-three years ago; the twenty-fifth anniversary of the Khrushchev Kitchen debate is memorialized at the Smithsonian; the tenth anniversary of Nixon's reelection to the presidency is celebrated in Washington, D.C. All these reruns and reunions suggest a man who is very much focused on the past, with perhaps this one notable exception (McGrath, 1982; Friedrich, 1984; "Nixon makes rare sojourn," 1984; "Golden anniversary," 1984; King and Weaver, 1986).

INFORMATION CONTROL

Creating divisions by splitting hairs is one technique of impression management. Another technique is the control of information. From the available "pool of facts," members of the audience get their impressions of character as well as their understanding of history. By controlling the contents and availability of this pool, Nixon can control others' impressions of him as a person and of his role in history.

A review of the public record of Richard Nixon's activities since his resignation reveals the inordinate energy and attention he has directed toward restricting access to information that might discredit his claim to respectability. He has also been active in creating new information that contributes to the impression of his respectability and his role in the historical process.

Nixon's continued litigation over the "private and personal" definition of the papers and tapes of his presidential years in the face of counterclaims that the public has a right to know the "documented facts" of his administration has been an important arena of information control. From the time the existence of the taping system became known in the testimony of Alex Butterfield, a low-ranking White House functionary, Nixon has faced constant pressure to yield those documents, but he has yielded very little. When he was finally forced to give up the June 23 tape, it revealed the president conspiring with his chief of staff to obstruct the investigation of the Justice Department and deceive the American public about the lawful character of his administration. This was the evidence the House Judiciary Committee needed to complete its case for impeachment. Consequently, the loss of that piece of information was a major factor in Nixon's resignation.

In the years since his resignation, he has lost control of very little information from those copious archives. The major portion of his tapes and papers remain bound in litigation, offstage and impotent as sources of American history or Nixonian biography (Anson, 1984; "Still waiting," 1986; "Nixon loses," 1987). As sources of information, they may well change our understanding of the course of American history, ca. 1969–1974, and also our judgments of the moral character of the man who was our president during those years. Therefore, controlling this information is crucial to the former president's objectives of defining his place in history.

Nixon has been uniquely successful in limiting the public and private testimony he has given in the various suits and dispositions generated in the wake of the Watergate revelations. As he was pardoned of all crimes of commission and omission, there was no public trial to demand that he testify under oath, and whatever the outcome, to officially define his place in the history of the American presidency. Instead, his resignation was surrounded with ambiguity. Nixon used prime-time television to explain his action to the public. He claimed his resignation was motivated by altruism, by the desire to see that the nation had a full-time president and not one embattled in a prolonged judicial debate that had been instigated by his detractors in the first place (Woodward and Bernstein, 1976; Cavan, 1979). There was no way to counter his public explanation, and no way to object. Nixon had the last word.

In an ironic way, his hospitalization for phlebitis was a lucky break. It effectively protected him from having to testify under oath in the trials of his closest aides and associates. Then, over the years, his extensive (and expensive) retinue of lawyers have protected him from a multitude of lawsuits that might demand that the former president state under oath the nature of his actions in various crucial situations relevant to charges such as obstruction of justice, infringement of civil rights, backdating his tax papers, and various other violations of the criminal code and abuses of executive power. Indeed, until the spring of 1987, his only courtroom testimony has been in the defense of two Federal Bureau of Investigation (FBI) agents charged with illegal entry (Pear, 1980b). Despite Nixon's appearance, the two agents were found guilty. They were subsequently pardoned by Ronald Reagan (Anson, 1984).

One way to control information is by preventing discrediting information from becoming public. Another way to control information is by manufacturing it yourself, by being an active participant in what is being written and said. In numerous books, speeches, and letters to the editor that he has authored, singly or in association with others (including self-publishing his book *Real Peace*), Nixon has been active in creating a documentary record that attests to his continued involvement in world affairs as an informed critic. No occasion is too lowly or too insignificant. Thus, speaking before the Whittier Republican Women's Club, he mentioned that his wife was feeling better and that they went to Disneyland for their anniversary; then, he launched into a formal presentation about geopolitics. The next day he gave the same speech at his fiftieth college reunion ("Nixon makes rare sojourn," 1984).

In addition to public speeches, interviews on television and in magazines and newspapers all involve the former president's active participation in the creation of a documentary record. What is asked and what is said in response to those queries reflect on the image that Nixon hopes to sustain: sage and statesman, a brilliant geopolitical thinker and astute strategist, a man whose observations and advice advance world peace. Incidentally, he also portrays himself as a regular guy, as when it was reported that he drops in at Burger King for lunch, bodyguards and all (Frost, 1978; "Nixon to assess," 1980; Mehle, 1982; McGrath, 1982; Bruning, 1984; Friedrich, 1984).

These staged events are opportunities for Nixon to set the record straight, often in the face of an interviewer determined to wrench some expression of remorse or humility from the former president (Frost, 1978; Anson, 1984). Notable in this context is Nixon's extraordinary ability to stonewall, to refuse to give any account of his involvement in Watergate other than acknowledging that mistakes were made and conceding that for a man of ambition, resignation from the presidency was a great punishment (Thimmesch, 1979). Beyond that, there is no accounting. There is no acknowledgment of precisely what "mistakes" were made, much less any consideration of whether, for example, obstruction of justice is more than simply a "mistake of judgment." There are no expressions of remorse or embarrassment, much less humiliation. There is no admission of what he might have learned as a result of those "mistakes" other than an occasional bitter references about destroying the tapes (Morganthau, 1982; Anson, 1984).

Another way an individual can make information become part of the record is by keeping a high profile. Since the 1950s, Richard Nixon's name has made news, first in the local community, then nationally, and finally internationally. Over the years, the curious turns his career has taken have only made him more newsworthy. Thus, his various foreign travels, his meetings and phone calls, his lunches and dinners at home and abroad, his real estate transactions, his visits to the baseball game with his grandson, and even his opinions of Disneyland are all the objects of journalists' attention. From there, they make their way to the daily pool of electronic and print information available to the public and the historians, both loyalists and detractors. Even when Nixon stays home, continuous reviews and analyses of him and his administration mean that his name and his reputation are rarely out of view.

Not all Nixon's reviews are favorable. A major part of his mystery is his ability to evoke intense loyalty from some and intense hatred from others, so not all those who read the available documentary record do so with the same benign accounting that he wishes to foster (Lewis, 1984; Kaiser, 1984; Morrow, 1985; Hiss, 1986). Their interpretations have not been stifled, but neither have they inflamed the public to demand an open accounting of the past in order to better comprehend the meaning of the present.

In addition to critics' interpretation of the available records, there has been some information leakage, revelations of facts and observations that contradict the claims the former president has made about his conduct in office and his character as a human being. Books and articles by various investigative journalists as well as books and interviews with some of his former associates have yielded substantial documentation of another side to Richard Nixon (Woodward and Bernstein, 1976; Haldeman, 1978; "Nixon encore," 1981; Ehrlichman, 1982b; Hersh, 1982a, 1982b, 1983).

COLLUSION

Nixon has not sustained the illusion of his rehabilitation alone. Like any social judgment, it requires the collusion of others. In the first place, the network of contacts that he had as president remained relatively intact after he left office. This network provides him with an inside line to power and influence, and he spends considerable time and energy cultivating it. Accounts of his day at his New York office stress the intense round of telephone calls he makes each morning. Like a salesman generating leads and prospects, Nixon continuously makes contact and touches base with old associates as well as with old opponents, power brokers, and people of influence. Occasionally he makes contact with ordinary folk, like calling a police officer who has been injured. Personal notes and memos supplement his phone calls, actively maintaining connections that might be useful in the future (Thimmesch, 1979; Anson, 1984; Friedrich, 1984; Boyd, 1985; Martz, 1986).

In an interview for *Newsweek*, Nixon said quite candidly:

As far as President Reagan is concerned, I talk to him quite regularly. Usually he calls me from Camp David, usually after he has had one of those, you know, tough decisions. For example, he called me after the Libyan business [the bombing of Qaddafi's compound], and we chatted a bit about it. It's a very natural relationship. (Fuller et al., 1986, p. 33)

Access to a network of interpersonal influence has been crucial to Nixon's career. It began with the Committee of One Hundred, which selected him to run for Congress in the 1940s, and in the ensuing forty years, this network has continued to grow, encompassing influentials at home and abroad, in government, politics, business, and the military; and gradually even encompassing those who were once at odds with Nixon's objectives: Hubert Humphrey, George McGovern, Mark Hatfield, Mario Cuomo, Katherine Graham, and even the working press ("Why Carter invited Nixon," 1979; Thimmesch, 1979; Shapiro, 1984; Lewis, 1984; Friedrich, 1984; "No enemies," 1984; Martz, 1986; Brown, 1987).

These social connections are important resources. They provide aid and assistance in accomplishing Richard Nixon's objectives. Nixon's relationship with Alexander Haig illustrates the best feature of such interpersonal connections: their ability to provide mutual aid (Kropotkin, 1902). As Nixon's chief of staff in the months before his resignation, Haig managed the orderly transition of the presidency from a man who had been reelected to that office by an enormous popular vote to a man who had never been elected to any office higher than the House of Representatives. Haig was subsequently instrumental in managing Ford's pardon of Nixon. In the ensuing years, Haig was instrumental in arranging Nixon's various public trips abroad as well as being a regular source of inside information for the former president (Hersh, 1982a; Anson, 1984; Herbers, 1984).

At the same time Alexander Haig was being useful to Richard Nixon, his own career was advancing. Originally brought into the White House by Henry Kissinger, both Haig and Kissinger avoided the stigma of Watergate. When Nixon's

other aides and associates were going to trial and then to jail, Haig went to
Europe as commander of the North Atlantic Treaty Organization. After the
Democratic interlude of the Carter Administration Haig was brought back to
serve for two years as secretary of state for the Reagan administration, and
he was one of the candidates for the 1988 Republican presidential nomination
(King, 1987).

In addition to the active collusion of people with power and influence, Nixon's
claims to honor and respect are advanced by more general forms of assistance.
Nixon's public appearances have always evoked a cadre of staunch loyalists for
whom he can do no wrong. They can be found in the press, in politics, in
business, among the outstanding members of various local communities, and
among countless ordinary people. They can be found in the United States and
in many other parts of the world, although not all. To these people, Richard
Nixon is a hero. Some of them have been Nixon supporters from the beginning
of his political career; others were prepubescent at the time of Watergate, but
count themselves as loyalists nonetheless (Nelson, 1978; Axthelm, 1978; Dolan,
1984; Kaiser, 1984).

Whoever they are and whenever they were recruited to his cause, the devotion
of Nixon's supporters is intense and rarely deflected. No matter what is revealed
about the other side of Richard Nixon, this cadre of loyalists is able to provide
a benign interpretation. They are able to show that whatever he might have done,
he did it with the best intentions, that it was not as bad as his detractors claim,
or that other presidents did worse. Their dedicated support is crucial to Nixon's
objectives.

Aligned in opposition are the detractors and demonstrators, for whom everything Nixon does is wrong. As in the past, he has encountered fewer public
signs of disrespect when he is out of office than when he holds an official position,
and he has encountered less disrespect on the East Coast than he did on the West
Coast. Nonetheless, every so often, a vocal crowd convenes in the vicinity of
his public appearances to express their disapproval (Pear, 1980a; Anson, 1984).
Besides vocal crowds, there have been other outward signs of disrespect. The
opposition Nixon encountered in leasing a New York apartment is a minor
example. More significant were the objections raised by Duke University faculty
when they were faced with the possibility that the Nixon Library would be
established on their campus (Scott, 1981; Wilson, 1981). However, at the same
time the Duke faculty protested the library, there were many other communities
vying for the opportunity to house the documents of his administration. Over
the years, protests have become increasingly fewer, and in their absence, they
help foster the impression that Richard Nixon, the thirty-seventh president of
the United States, is a man worthy of honor and respect (Herbers, 1984).

CONCLUSIONS

Ill repute is not just the negativity of nihilists and haters, small-minded people
who hold a grudge and do not forgive. Sociologically, it has very important

consequences for people's understanding of moral conduct (Garfinkel, 1956; Schwartz and Skolnick, 1964; Erikson, 1969). Indeed, it is by the allocation of ill repute that the members of a society effectively establish moral boundaries. Ill repute illuminates the behavior that is not acceptable in terms of the prevailing value schemes. Those whose biographies are blemished by the stigma associated with such unacceptable behavior become walking reminders of what happens when people go too far.

Ill repute is also a warning to those who might associate with the stigmatized that their reputations are likely to suffer as well. Thus ostracism from respectable society serves as punishment for those who have gone astray and as a method of containment for those who might be seduced by association with such behavior.

Ill repute is a forceful social judgment; it illuminates social boundaries and gives expression to social values. It is one of the forces that create community.

Rehabilitation is the process by which individuals who have gone beyond the boundaries of the moral order can be reintegrated back into the community. By acknowledging the errors of their ways, by cooperating with the authorities, and by showing demonstrable changes in conduct and character, members of the community acknowledge in these individuals a transformation of status: the bad guy becomes a good guy again; the stigma of ill repute is gone.

Where there is no stigma associated with behavior and no ill repute accorded the actor, we read the behavior as normal and the person as respectable. We understand that this is a behavior and expression of character that can be expected in similar situations; we read it as acceptable human conduct. Therefore, the absence of ill repute also expresses social values (Goffman, 1963; Gusfield, 1963).

If, in the absence of rehabilitation, ill repute fades over time, we must read a change as indicative of changing ideas about what is acceptable conduct and what is not. Thus, community standards may change over time; what was once thought to be the exception comes to be the rule, and reputations follow suit.

In the foregoing pages I have argued that there is little evidence that Richard Nixon has been rehabilitated in any way congruent with the axioms of sociological theories of rehabilitation. Nevertheless, the widespread impression exists that this is in fact what is happening—that in the years since his resignation from the presidency, whatever brought him into disgrace and dishonor has been eliminated, and that he is now due all the honor and respect appropriate to a former president of the United States. This impression of rehabilitation is a function of continuous hard work on the part of the former president: splitting hairs, concealing information, fostering illusion, and colluding with others.

In social life the impression is often as good as the event. We are constantly called on to rely on representations of statements (for example, printed accounts that purport to represent actual conversations), images (such as televised events that are proclaimed to be live), inferences (things that go unspoken but are known nonetheless), and innuendos (where ambiguity is maintained and deniability possible). Given this gossamer fabric of social life, Richard Nixon's ability to manipulate the impression of his rehabilitation has been an effective method of managing the stigma associated with his resignation.

His ability to maintain this impression in the face of everything that has been revealed about the inside workings of the White House during his administration and in the face of the indictments, guilt, and punishment of many of those who collaborated with him as part of that administration is impressive. A lesser man might have given up in despair, surrendering to those old-fashioned ideas of truth, justice, and honor. But Mr. Nixon stood fast and stood firm. Gradually, people came to forget why he was infamous, and he became famous again.

In addition, of course, there have been numerous political scandals since Watergate. Abscam moved public attention from the White House to the Congress; the Iran-Contra scandal then returned the focus to the White House. So perhaps we see in the "rehabilitation of Richard Nixon" not the change in moral character of a single man but the transformation of community standards attesting to acceptable moral conduct (Ermann and Lundman, 1978; Eisenstadt, Hoogenboom, and Trefousse, 1979; Vidal, 1983).

NOTE

1. Methodological note: Since I am concerned with the nature of public character, I have taken my "observations" from the public record. In the various accounts documenting Richard Nixon's activities since his resignation, I asked, "Where does he go; what does he do; with whom does he associate; what do others say about him; where does that information get recorded?" As I began to collect these observations, "rehabilitation" emerged as a repetitive theme. To assess the meaning of "rehabilitation," I first assessed the record of Nixon's behavior against an ideal-type sociological model of "rehabilitation." There seemed little congruence between Nixon's behavior and behavior predicted by theories of rehabilitation. To explain this discrepancy between the actual and the expected, I turned to the idea of impression management as the method by which the illusion of rehabilitation is realized. I wish to thank Cary Gilliam for his faithful assistance in the library and in the bibliography.

REFERENCES

"A Decade After His Downfall, a Resurgent Richard Nixon Still Stirs Mixed Emotions and Memories." 1984. *People*, Aug. 13, 53–54, 57–58.

Abrahamsen, David. 1976. *Nixon vs. Nixon: An Emotional Tragedy*. New York: New American Library.

Alter, Jonathan. 1984. "Nixon: The Long Climb Back." *Newsweek*, Feb. 20, 53–54.

Anderson, Jack, and Joseph Spear. 1986. "Watergate Fallout Continues." *The Washington Post*, June 17, B13.

Anderson, Susan H., and David W. Dunlap. 1984. "In the Nixonian Hand." *The New York Times*, Dec. 4, II3.

Anson, Robert S. 1984. *Exile: The Unique Oblivion of Richard M. Nixon*. New York: Simon and Schuster.

Axthelm, Pete. 1978. "A Different Sort of Notoriety." *Newsweek*, July 17, 32–33.

Balkan, Sheila, Ronald J. Berger, and Janet Schmidt. 1980. *Crime and Deviance in America*. Belmont, Calif.: Wadsworth.

Beck, Melinda. 1982. "Where Are They Now?" *Newsweek*, June 14, 42–45.

Boyd, Gerald M. 1985. "On Nixon's Rehabilitation of Nixon." *The New York Times*, June 13, A32.

Bremen, Howard F., ed. 1975. *Richard M. Nixon 1913—Chronology—Documents— Bibliographical Aids*. Dobbs Ferry, N.Y.: Oceana.

Brodie, Fawn M. 1981. *Richard Nixon: The Shaping of His Character*. New York: Norton.

Brown, Peter A. 1987. "Cuomo Tells Reagan: Let Nixon Work on Arms Pact." *San Francisco Examiner*, Feb. 25.

Bruning, Fred. 1984. "Nixon is Ready; America Is Not." *Macleans*, June 4, 9.

Burke, Kenneth. 1962. *A Grammar of Motives and a Rhetoric of Motives*. New York: World Publishing.

"Carter Checks Are Sold for $1,098 at Auction." 1980. *The New York Times*, Oct. 29, A17.

Cavan, Sherri. 1979. *Twentieth Century Gothic: America's Nixon*. San Francisco: Wigan Pier Press.

Chaze, William L. 1984. "Ten Years Later, The Impact of Watergate," Aug. 13, 56–58.

Chesen, Eli S. 1973. *President Nixon's Psychiatric Profile*. New York: Leyden.

Clark, Alfred E. 1978. "Elmer Bobst, At 93, Gave Library to N.Y.U." *The New York Times*, Aug. 3, B2.

Clark, Champ. 1979. "Goodbye to Watergate—All the President's Men All Free At Last." *San Francisco Examiner and Chronicle*, Feb. 4, 40.

"Collect Call." 1981. *Time*, July 6, 21.

Crouse, Timothy. 1974. "The Long Ear of the Law: The White House Tapes." *Rolling Stone*, Dec. 5, 36–38.

Cummings, Judith, and Albin Krebs. 1980. "Nixon Interview." *The New York Times*, Apr. 29, II14.

Dibble, Vernon K. 1963. "Four Types of Influence from Documents to Events." *History and Theory* 3: 203–226.

Dobrovir, William A., Joseph O. Gebhardt, Samuel J. Buffone, and Andra N. Oakes. 1974. *The Offenses of Richard M. Nixon: A Guide for the People of the United States of America*. New York: Quadrangle/The New York Times Book Co.

Dolan, Maura. 1984. "The Return of Richard Nixon." *Los Angeles Times*, May 16, II1, 6.

Douglas, Jack D. 1970. *Deviance and Respectability: The Social Construction of Moral Meanings*. New York: Basic Books.

Dunham, Roger, and Armond Mauss. 1976. "Waves from Watergate: Evidence Concerning the Impact of the Watergate Scandal upon Political Legitimacy and Social Control." *Pacific Sociological Review* 19: 469–490.

Ehrlichman, John. 1982a. "Art in the Nixon White House." *Art News* 81 (May): 74–81.

———. 1982b. *Witness to Power*. New York: Simon and Schuster.

Eisenhower, Julie Nixon. 1986. "My Mother, Pat Nixon." *Good Housekeeping*, 131, 141–147.

Eisenstadt, Abraham, Ari Hoogenboom, and Hans Trefousse. 1979. *Before Watergate: Problems of Corruption in American Society*. New York: Brooklyn College Press.

Ellul, Jacques. 1973. *Propaganda: The Formation of Men's Attitudes*. New York: Random House.

Erikson, Kai T. 1969. *Wayward Puritan: A Study in the Sociology of Deviance*. New York: Wiley.

Ermann, M. David, and Richard Lundman. 1978. *Corporate and Governmental Deviance: Problems of Organizational Behavior in Contemporary Society*. New York: Oxford University Press.

Farrell, William E. 1975. "Literary Appraiser Guilty in Backdating Nixon Files." *The New York Times*, Nov. 13, 1, 23.

Fineman, Howard. 1985. "Nixon: The Comeback Kid." *Newsweek*, Oct. 28, 45.

Foley, Charles. 1975. "Richard Nixon's Comeback Plan." *The Observer*, Oct. 16–18.

"Four Times That Nixon Nearly Went Nuclear." 1985. *San Francisco Chronicle*, July 22, 49.

Friedrich, Otto. 1984. "Nixon: 'Never Look Back.' " *Time*, Aug. 13, 16–17.

Frost, David. 1978. *I Gave Them a Sword: Behind the Scenes of the Nixon Interviews*. New York: Ballantine Books.

Fuller, Tony, Morton M. Kondracke, and John J. Lindsay. 1986. "The Sage of Saddle River." *Newsweek*, May 19, 32–34.

Gailey, Phil. 1982. "Charitably Speaking." *The New York Times*, Jan. 22, 16.

Garfinkle, Harold. 1956. "Conditions of Successful Degradation Ceremonies." *American Journal of Sociology*, 61: 420–424.

Garth, Hans, and C. Wright Mills. 1958. *From Max Weber: Essays in Sociology*. New York: Oxford University Press.

———. 1964. *Character and Social Structure*. New York: Harcourt Brace and World.

"G. Gordon Liddy Tries Out on Broadway." 1983. *San Francisco Chronicle*, Aug. 4, 60.

Glynn, Lenny. 1984. "Nixon's New Influence." *Maclean's*, Apr. 23, 10–16.

Goffman, Erving. 1958. *The Presentation of Self in Everyday Life*. Edinburgh, Scotland: University of Edinburgh.

———. 1963. *Stigma: Notes on the Management of Spoiled Identity*. Englewood Cliffs, N.J.: Prentice-Hall.

———. 1969. *Strategic Interactions*. Philadelphia: University of Pennsylvania Press.

"Golden Anniversary Celebrated." 1984. *The Rock*, Summer, 18–19.

Goldman, Peter. 1985. "Rocky and Rambo." *Newsweek*, Dec. 23, 58–62.

Greenfield, Meg. 1986. "When 'Finished' Isn't Final." *The Washington Post*, May 27, A21.

Greer, William R. 1985. "Nixon Curbs Activities After Skin Cancer Surgery." *The New York Times*, Aug. 9, A15.

Grove, Lloyd. 1984a. "Watergate Earloom." *The Washington Post*, Apr. 9, D1, D8.

———. 1984b. "The Nixon Watchers." *The Washington Post*, Aug. 6, F1, F13.

Gusfield, Joseph. 1963. *Symbolic Crusade*. Chicago: University of Illinois Press.

Haldeman, H. R., with Joseph Di Mona. 1978. *The Ends of Power*. New York: The New York Times Book Co.

Herbers, John. 1984. "After a Decade, Nixon Is Gaining Favor." *The New York Times*, Aug. 5, A24.

Hersh, Seymour M. 1982a. "Kissinger and Nixon in the White House." *The Atlantic Monthly*, May, 35–68.

———. 1982b. "The Price of Power." *The Atlantic Monthly*, Dec., 31–58.

————. 1983. "The Pardon." *The Atlantic Monthly*, Aug. 55–78.

Hiss, Alger. 1986. "The Lessons of the Richard Nixon Case." *The New York Times*, Jan. 21, A30.

Hoff-Wilson, Joan. 1984. "Watergate Is Already a Dim and Distant Curiosity." *U.S. News and World Report*, Aug., 13, 59.

Holley, David. 1984. "Ex-president Ties Soviet Relations to U.S. Election." *Los Angeles Times*, May 16, II1, 6.

Hosefros, Paul. 1984. "Nixon Replaced by Nixon." *The New York Times*, Dec. 9, A30.

Jaworski, Leon. 1976. *The Right and the Power. The Prosecution of Watergate*. New York: Reader's Digest Press.

Johnson, Robert. 1987. *Hard Time: Understanding and Reforming the Prison*. Monterey, Calif.: Brooks/Cole Publishing.

Kaiser, Robert G. 1984. "What Power Does He Hold over Us?" *The Washington Post*, Apr. 5, C1.

King, Wayne. 1987. "Haig to Seek Republican Nomination for Presidency." *The New York Times*, Mar. 24, 10.

King, Wayne, and Warren Weaver. 1986. "Nixon Events." *The New York Times*, Feb. 28, B4.

Kristof, Nicholas D. 1986. "The Success of the President's Men." *The New York Times*, July 13, 1, 8.

Kropotkin, Petr. 1902. *Mutual Aid*. Boston: Extending Horizon Books.

Lewis, Anthony. 1984. "Still Nixon." *The New York Times*, Aug. 2, A23.

Liebert, Larry. 1986. "Wide-Ranging Speech in S.F. by Ex-President." *San Francisco Chronicle*, Apr. 22, 1, 16.

"Lunch Visit by Nixon Thrills a Burger King." 1986. *The New York Times*, Apr. 4, D20.

Lurie, Leonard. 1972. *The Running of Richard Nixon*. New York: Coward McCann and Geogehegan.

McClory, Robert. 1983. "Was the Fix Between Ford and Nixon?" *National Review*, Oct. 14, 1264–1266, 1272.

McGinnis, Joe P. 1968. *The Selling of the President*. New York: Pocket Books.

McGovern, George. 1987. "On Nixon and Watergate, Reagan and Iran." *The New York Times*, Jan. 6, A21.

McGrath, Peter. 1982. "Nixon at Home and Abroad." *Newsweek*, Oct. 11, 50–52.

Magnuson, Ed. 1982. "Aftermath of a Burglary." *Time*, June 14, 30, 32–33.

Mannheim, Karl. 1936. *Ideology and Utopia*. New York: Harcourt, Brace.

Martz, Larry. 1986. "The Road Back." *Newsweek*, May 19, 26–30, 32.

Mazar, Allan J. 1980. "Master of the Power Game." *Newsweek*, Dec. 29, 13–15.

Mehle, Aileen (Suzy). 1982. "Richard Nixon: 'My Wife Pat.' " *Good Housekeeping*, Aug., 101–107, 156–158.

Messinger, Sheldon, Harold Sampson, and Robert Towne. 1962. "Life as Theater: Some Notes on the Dramaturgic Approach to Social Reality." *Sociometry*, 25: 98–110.

Meyer, Donald. 1966. *The Positive Thinkers*. Garden City, N.Y.: Doubleday Anchor Books.

Miller, Judith. 1982. "Nixon Reunion Recalls a Victory and Some Ashes." *The New York Times*, Nov. 8, 12.

Morganthau, Tom. 1982. "The Legacy of Watergate." *Newsweek*, June 14, 36–37, 39–40.

Morrow, Lance. 1985. "Poof! The Phenomenon of Public Vanishing." *Time*, May 13, 86.

Nelson, Jack. 1978. "Nixon Indicates He Might Fight an Arms Agreement." *Los Angeles Times*, Nov. 12, 1, 24.

Newman, Graeme. 1978. *The Punishment Response*. New York: Lippincott.

The New York Times. 1978a. *The New York Times*, Aug. 29, 88.

The New York Times. 1978b. *The New York Times*, Sept. 14, 37.

The New York Times Staff, eds. 1974. *The End of a Presidency*. New York: Bantam Books.

"Nixon and Magruder." 1987. *San Francisco Chronicle*, Mar. 18, 15.

"Nixon Encore." 1981. *Time*, Oct. 5, 25.

"Nixon Ends Memos to Reagan on Campaign Tactics and Issues." 1980. *The New York Times*, Oct. 8, B6.

"Nixon Loses a Round in His Bid to Keep Papers from Public." 1987. *San Francisco Examiner*, Mar. 7, 1.

"Nixon Makes Rare Sojourn to Whittier." 1984. *Whittier Daily News*, May 13, 1.

"Nixon Talks About Lying." 1982. *San Francisco Chronicle*, Oct. 28, 12.

"Nixon to Assess Campaign on NBC's 'Today' Show." 1980. *The New York Times*, Sept. 3, III14.

"Nixon Welcomed to Kentucky by a Cheering Crowd." 1978. *The New York Times*, July 2, A16.

Nixon, Richard. 1962. *Six Crises*. New York: Pocket Books.

———. 1978. *R.N.: The Memoirs of Richard Nixon*. New York: Grosset and Dunlap.

———. 1982. *Leaders*. New York: Warner Books.

———. 1984. *Real Peace*. New York: Little, Brown.

———. 1986a. "Lessons of the Alger Hiss Case." *The New York Times*, Jan. 8, A23.

———. 1986b. "The Pillars of Peace." *Vital Speeches* 52 (July 15): 585–589.

"No Enemies." 1984. *Time*, May 21, 53.

O'Brien, Robert, and Elizabeth Jones. 1976. *The Night Nixon Spoke: A Study of Political Effectiveness*. Los Alamitos, Calif.: Hwong Publishing.

Pear, Robert. 1980a. "3 Ex-Attorneys General Testify on FBI Searches." *The New York Times*, Oct. 29, A17.

———. 1980b. "Testimony by Nixon Heard in FBI Trial." *The New York Times*, Oct. 30, A17.

"Poll Says Most Americans Now Back Nixon's Pardon." 1986. *San Francisco Chronicle*, May 12, 16.

Radcliffe, Donnie. 1986. "Nixon and the Cancer Cure." *The Washington Post*, Apr. 7, B3.

Raines, Howell. 1980. "Lyn Nofziger: Barometer in Reagan Strategy Shift." *The New York Times*, Sept. 28, 36.

Raven, Bertram H. 1974. "The Nixon Group." *Journal of Social Issues* 30(4): 297–320.

Reese, Michael. 1982. "Nixon: 'Never Look Back.' " *Newsweek*, June 14, 38.

Reeves, Richard. 1976. "What Ehrlichman Really Thought of Nixon." *The New York Magazine*, May 10, 40–56.

"Richard Nixon Calling." 1980. *Newsweek*, Dec. 29, 15.

"Richard Nixon Is Stirring, and Politicians Wonder What's Up Beside His Once Low Profile." 1981–1982. *People*, Dec. 28–Jan. 4, 139.

Rischen, Moses. 1965. *The American Gospel of Success: Individualism and Beyond.* Chicago: Quadrangle Books.

Robison, Robert K. 1981. "The Measure of an American President." *The New York Times,* Sept. 29, A26.

Sanders, Sol W. 1983. "Are Two Gray Eminences Shaping Reagan's Foreign Policy?" *Business Week,* Oct. 31, 60.

Schmemann, Serge. 1986. "Nixon to Pay a Private Visit to Soviet, Kremlin Aide Says." *The New York Times,* July 12, A2.

Schwartz, Richard, and Jerome Skolnick. 1964. "Two Studies of Legal Stigma." *Social Problems* 10: 133–38.

Scott, Anne F. 1981. "Profs Nix Prez Files." *The New York Times,* Aug. 30, IV17.

Shales, Larry. 1984. "Nixon's Long Look Back." *The Washington Post,* Apr. 6, D1, D2.

Shapiro, Walter. 1984. "Making It Perfectly Clear." *Newsweek,* May 21, 32.

———. 1985. "Campaign 1984: Nixon's Role." *Newsweek,* June 10, 51.

Sidey, Hugh. 1978. "An Illustrious Kaffeeklatsch." *Time,* Jan. 30, 26.

———. 1981. "The Private Travels of Nixon." *Time,* Nov. 2, 30.

———. 1983. "Advice from an Old Warrior." *Time,* Sept. 19, 27.

Simes, Dimitri K. 1987. "The Stakes in Arms Control." *The New York Times,* Feb. 24, 27.

Sirica, John J. 1979. *To Set the Record Straight.* New York: Norton.

Stein, Howard. 1973. "The Silent Complicity at Watergate." *American Scholar* 43 (Winter): 31–37.

Steinhorn, Leonard. 1981. "The Nixon Within Us." *The New York Times,* Sept. 13, 20.

"Still Waiting for the Nixon Papers." 1986. *The Washington Post,* May 1, A22.

Stratton, William. 1964. *A Content Analysis of the Responses to the Nixon Speech.* Unpublished M.A. thesis, Department of Sociology, Whittier College, Whittier, California.

Talbott, Strobe, and Stephen Smith. 1985. "We in the U.S. Are Suckers for Style." *Time,* Apr. 22, 14–15.

Thimmesch, Nick. 1979. "Richard Nixon Speaks His Mind." *The Saturday Evening Post,* March, 65–66, 106–108.

Thomas, Jo. 1978. "Nixon, Hailed in Kentucky Town, Stresses the Need for U.S. Strength." *The New York Times,* July 3, 1, 7.

"Those Nixon Papers." 1987. *The New York Times,* Apr. 23, 10.

"$2,500 Paid for '64 Note Nixon Signed." 1985. *The Washington Post,* Feb. 16, A8.

Vasari. 1982. "A Little off the Jowls." *Art News,* Mar., 13.

Vidal, Gore. 1983. "Nixon Without Knives." *Esquire,* Dec., 66, 68, 70–71.

The Washington Post Staff. 1974. *The Fall of a President.* New York: Dell.

Weschler, Lawrence. 1986. "The Latest New Nixon." *The Nation,* Jan. 25, 65.

White, Theodore H. 1975. *Breach of Faith: The Fall of Richard Nixon.* New York: Atheneum.

"Why Carter Invited Nixon to the White House." 1979. *U.S. News and World Report,* Jan. 29, 8.

Wilson, Robert L. 1981. "Duke and the Nixon Library." *The Christian Century,* Oct. 21, 1045–1046.

Witcover, Jules. 1970. *The Resurrection of Richard Nixon.* New York: Putnam.

Woodward, Bob. 1984. "Nixon's Private Tapes: A Key to His Character." *The Washington Post*, Apr. 5, C1.

Woodward, Bob, and Carl Bernstein. 1976. *The Final Days*. New York: Simon and Schuster.

"World Leaders Through Nixon's Eyes." 1982. *U.S. News and World Report*, Oct. 11, 13.

Wright, Erik O. 1973. *The Politics of Punishment*. New York: Harper/Colophon Books.

Discussant: H. R. Haldeman

I want to express appreciation to Hofstra for this opportunity and for the progress that has been made in moving toward some understanding of the Nixon legacy, which is the subject of the forum at this point this afternoon. We have gone through three solid, packed days of review and analysis. We have learned a lot and we have evaluated a lot; all of us have, I think. I've come away with a strong conviction that there is much more to be learned and much more to be evaluated rather than any thought that we have wrapped it up in this three-day period.

I was very willing and ready to go out on a limb in talking about things here, and I am willing now to say that the conclusion of this conference has to be factually incomplete, emotionally premature, and historically presumptuous. I think probably all of the historians would agree with me at least on this point, if nothing else. I think we have taken a giant step forward in these few days, and I think that is a wonderfully constructive thing to do, and something that Hofstra and the people who put this together should be very pleased to have done.

Since my role in the administration and my chosen role in life is that of a manager of progress and process rather than a developer of policy and a creator of initiatives, I am going to take that same role in the closing hours of this conference. And in approaching the legacy, I am going to offer my words to you humbly with the hope that some of them will be heeded, and with the recognition that much of them may not be and maybe perhaps should not be. I would like to offer some guidelines that you all can use in the ongoing process of defining the Nixon legacy, which I think has barely been started in these few days, and I think it would be presumptuous to try to draw the conclusions today. I hope the ultimate statement or view of the Nixon legacy will be as accurate, as balanced, as fair, as insightful, as critical, as laudatory, as unbiased, and as comprehensive as is possible in any effort that is essentially as risky and as difficult as developing and defining the Nixon legacy. We are evaluating an infinitely complex man operating in extraordinarily challenging circumstances, and we have to keep this in mind as we move toward trying to find that Nixon legacy.

I would like to take as my text for these remarks a thought expressed earlier today by as eminent an authority as the executive secretary of the Organization of American Historians [Joan Hoff-Wilson], who in her eminent wisdom stated that the body of the Nixon literature to date is the worst of any presidency. I had the rudeness to applaud that statement in her panel discussion this morning because I very much agree with that. So you historians, you scholars, and you journalists who are gathered here have a major challenge before you to correct that shortcoming. My opinion and my remarks are not just directed to the historians and the journalists; they also apply to everyone else here, to the customers of the historians and the journalists, the students and the general public, the voters, all the rest of us who care about our government, whether or not we are qualified to report on it or to evaluate it in cosmic terms. All of you have apparently strong views about Nixon. Some of your views are firm and inflexible and others of your views are changing and expanding, and I submit that in assessing Nixon and the Nixon legacy, we all need to open our minds, and I include myself. Everyone of us, from whatever position we start, we need to open our minds and to challenge our own viewpoints before locking them in forever as our view of the Nixon legacy.

In order to do that, I would like to offer a few guidelines: First, please don't use the presently existing literature as established fact. It is the biggest trap you can possibly fall into. It is an absolutely vital step, and this conference hopefully will launch the taking of that step, that we move forward, challenging all of the presently conventional wisdom regarding Richard Nixon, his actions, his character, his personality, and his results, rather than just codifying and rearranging or expanding what is already available. There is an enormous amount of gross inaccuracy in most of the present views regarding the totality and specific segments of the Nixon Presidency.

I mentioned in an earlier panel session a process that I went through during the years that I had the unenviable luxury of substantial time on my hands (which is not a normal state for me to be in), a process of going through a lot of the presently available literature on the Nixon Presidency in substantial detail, with three highlighter pens in my hand—one red, one green, and one yellow. I proceeded, as I read, to underline or highlight in red every statement of fact made in the literature that I knew of my own personal and absolutely certain knowledge was false. I concurrently highlighted in blue everything that I saw of any significance that I knew of my own personal and certain knowledge to be true; and then I continued with a yellow highlight for those things I recognized as significant, but did not of my own knowledge know whether they were true or not. In other words, they were important, but I couldn't either verify or deny them.

It was a fascinating exercise, and it led me to the conclusion that the way to solve my financial problems was to publish a book myself, entitled *Errata*, and it would be bought widely because people would think it was erotic and that would be something coming from Haldeman. The context of the book would be a summation of those red highlights in the many books that I have taken hours to go through, together with a statement of my own personal, direct, certain knowledge of what the fact was. It would have been a fascinating exercise, but fortunately that period in my life ended before I got around to doing it, so it has never been done.

Within this context of not using the present literature, I think that must also apply to all the material that is derived from sources in the White House: the books by those of us who have served there, including mine. They should be, and I am sure they are, viewed with substantial questions by all of you as you go through them. This very definitely must be the case, for in my view, each of those books inevitably reflects the writer's bias and it should, because to get a true history you need the biased viewpoints of those who participated in making that history. They also were written from the writer's necessarily limited viewpoint. Don't assume that everyone who held any post in the Nixon Administration knew everything about what Richard Nixon was thinking and doing every hour of the day and night. There are a few of us that come close. There is nobody who had total knowledge. You can't, therefore, rely on any single source, and you cannot accept as totally correct any one source, because the limited viewpoints have an effect on the result. Each of them, in others words, is part of the whole. Some of them were a bigger part, some of them a lesser part, and that incidentally applies to even President Nixon's memoirs and his other writings, which express his viewpoint, his biases. His viewpoint was limited, as was the rest of ours, because a lot of things went on in the Nixon Administration that President Nixon had absolutely no knowledge of whatsoever at the time and doesn't today.

Second, you have to view the materials written by contemporaneous outside sources—the journalists—very carefully also, because these also reflect the writer's bias, even though it is presumed that journalists have no bias. I suspect that a journalist will admit that a touch of bias creeps in here and there; plus those works are limited, of necessity, by their third-party nature. They are dependent upon someone else's original knowledge, rather than being original sources themselves. And the transmission of original knowledge has a tendency to become confused and distorted by the transitor and transmittor.

Third, the works by historians and scholars suffer from both of the above problems, the individual's bias and the fact that they are limited by their third-party nature; plus, they acquire the additional burden of interpretation of causality, intent, and significance. I submit that at this time at least, and maybe forever, they are at best incomplete and premature. And then to the so-called psychohistorians—I have modified my views that their works are 90 percent baloney; I would prefer to say 100 percent.

There are great sources beyond the present and future literature in the form of the things we have been talking about here: the archival notes, the White House Tapes, the Nixon memos and staff memos, which people gleefully chortle about our having produced and which sank a few of us without a trace in the process. Ironically, what sank the Nixon Administration could very well have inestimable value in its reevaluation because there is a lot of original material there that is irrefutable. It's precisely what was said by those people at that time.

But there is a real danger there. To use snippets here and there out of this memo, out of that note sheet and this tape, to pull those out as absolute statements, would be a mistake, out of context as to solving or confirming some view you decided to prove, as one of the papers presented here at the conference did with one line from my notes. I wrote the line, apparently. I don't question the accuracy of the reportage; I simply say I have no knowledge of what that was about or whether it indeed proves or disproves the point that was under discussion. I think it is vital to understand the various purposes that these documents were created for and of the resources that created them, and not to assume what they meant without trying to place them in the context of those purposes. It is great because there are lots of them, but it is scary because they can be very misleading, especially taken alone or in part.

Third, as I urged in one of the opening panels, don't ever, no matter what facet of the Nixon Presidency you consider, don't ever lose sight of Vietnam as the overriding factor in the first Nixon term. It overshadowed everything else all the time, in every discussion, in every decision, in every opportunity and every problem, and you have to take that into account as you deal in those subareas and other unrelated areas.

Fourth, a clue: Look for linkages in a relationship, probe some things and look for where one thing is a part of an overall something-else, and look for consistency of an objective. Some of you who don't believe there is such a thing will be astonished.

Fifth, don't let yourself accept easy conclusions. It is too easy to make quick conclusions about Richard Nixon. Challenge your conclusions, test and keep adding pieces to them, and let the thing grow in your own mind into something that may approach closeness to the reality.

Sixth, when you work with the White House tapes, which many of you undoubtedly will be doing in the years ahead, realize first of all that there is a real question in what you are listening to as to whom you are hearing talk and what that person is saying. The unassailable proof to me is the experience John and I went through at our trial, when we sat in the courtroom supposedly listening to ourselves on a tape. Both of us listened on one tape, and we looked up, and the transcripts said Ehrlichman: "this this this," and Haldeman: "this this this"; and John said, "You didn't say that, I did," and I said, "Yeah, you didn't say the next thing, I did." Even with hours and hours and hours of studying the tape to produce accurate transcripts, they got the wrong person. The irony of it is John and I both have listened to tapes where we couldn't tell whether it was John or me that was saying something or someone else.

The worst danger in the tape area is a suggestion made this morning that I think would be absolutely terrible, and that is that the tapes be edited and transcribed by the National Archivists, and the funding would be provided for them to do this, so they would be much easier for you folks to use as your source materials. I guarantee it would be much easier, but it would be the worst possible thing to do. If you want to use the tapes, you have got to listen to them, you have got to draw your conclusions from what is said rather than letting someone else tell you. As soon as they are transcribed, you tend to read the transcript and assume it's true, and I guarantee the best transcripts that could be produced for the trial were grossly inaccurate and misleading.

Let me conclude by saying that I urge you to recognize and accept the validity of what seems to me to be the constantly emerging theme of the conference, and it is one word: complexity. You are dealing with a complex man personally, politically, strategically; you are dealing with a complex time, Vietnam, an opposition Congress, a shift of eras, watersheds in many areas of domestic and international policy. You are dealing with complex resources; you have all the usual historic resources, plus incredible volumes of files and the White House tapes. You are dealing with complex analysis, because I will guarantee that the obvious is probably wrong. Using the theory of contradictory opinion, all of this adds up to a complex legacy, and it needs a lot of thought and a lot of work.

I am delighted to have been a part of the conference, and hope that it has, and I believe it has, taken a big step toward the effort to deal with all of these complexities.

Discussant: Robert H. Finch

Because I have a cold and my voice is about to go out, I will be mercifully brief and simply expand a bit on John's quick recital of the Nixon legacy, on the reorganization of the executive branch, the work of the Ash Commission, and some personal observations of Richard Nixon.

I believe that the day will come when the nation will get a president with election by a very large majority of the popular vote and with majorities of the same party in both houses. When that happens, we will hopefully see a smaller cabinet organized by "function" and not by "constituency." Under this rubric, my old department of HEW, for example, would become part of a "Human Resources Department," which then would include Labor and Education. Agriculture, Energy and Interior would go to a "Department of Natural Resources," etc. This would reduce the present cabinet to about nine or ten officers.

This smaller cabinet would, I think, be useful in many ways, but most of all because members then could really be "counselors" to the president. They would be fulfilling the historical and collegial role which has profitably marked many of our presidents' cabinets. Unfortunately, I must necessarily characterize most postwar cabinets, including Mr. Nixon's and Mr. Reagan's, as not noted for discourse, but really as "show-and-tell sessions." Some member is asked to bring in the report for the day, and the cabinet mulls that over, and then the president decides that that becomes the news story for the day. I think a limitation of cabinet officers would tend to fix budget responsibility a good deal more, and leave less authority in fiscal matters to the senior White House staff or OMB. The secretary would clearly be required to make and stand by the trade-offs among the various constituencies in his department.

The two most recently added cabinet officers are the Department of Education and the about-to-be-consummated proposal from Reagan for a cabinet seat for a Department of Veterans' Affairs. Both of these are the result of a blatant recognition of political dynamics, for in any rational scheme of looking at government by function and the percentage of the respective budgets affected, they are a redundancy. This is not to say that education and the rights of veterans are not important; it is to say that, given the limited role of education in terms of dollars under our federal system and the similar relative importance of veterans' entitlements as opposed to other constituent groups, they do not deserve cabinet status.

It was the keynote of the Nixon Administration that we were trying to put forward a package of proposals under the title of the "New Federalism" which would attempt to restore the relative balance of federal, state, and local governments and the historic role traditionally given to each of our three levels of government. Historically, local and state governments (being the closest to the voter) dealt with most of the housekeeping and humanitarian concerns, such as police and fire, health, transportation, etc., with state government filling the role in education, transportation, parks, etc., and with the federal government being the supporter of last resort, but beginning with the fundamental responsibility at the outset of defense, postal, and other clearly national needs. Obviously, the New Deal role of the ever-burgeoning federal government had distorted this balance, and this was one of our goals in trying to rectify and strengthen all aspects of our federal system. Given the overwhelming number of Democrats in both houses, we could not go directly at curtailing the federal establishment, as did Reagan, so we conceived of "revenue sharing," which would pass through money from the federal government to state and local governments in a way that would allow them to make use of their own judgment in the allocation of those precious tax dollars. We think history will vindicate this proposal even though it disappeared in the Reagan years.

Nixon's preoccupation with foreign policy, particularly in his second term, and the recognition and opening up of China overshadowed many of the domestic initiatives we started in the first term. One of these was a very concentrated effort on the part of Mr. Nixon and the Department of HEW with respect to a breakthrough on cancer research. This was propelled by an early meeting (even before we took office) that Nixon asked me to have with President Lyndon Johnson, and he [Johnson] made it very clear that one of the greatest disappointments of his term in office was that despite the multiplicity of programs proposed in Johnson's Great Society, his greatest disappointment was that they thought they were close to a cure for cancer and had been unable to achieve it. He devoutly believed that it was close at hand, and that if we focused a great deal of time and effort and dollars, we could bring it under control. Johnson in his typical persuasive way persuaded both the president and myself (and I was particularly supportive since both of my parents had died at an early age of the disease) that this cause deserved high priority.

Of course, we very quickly learned there was no single cure for cancer, and that there were no easy breakthroughs, since we have a great variety of cancers. But we did devote a great deal of effort, and the byproducts of this research paid off even into some of the early breakthroughs in our problems with AIDS when later this disease came to the forefront.

Another of our initiatives in health care was the recognition of the health maintenance organizations, which would enable prepayment through an alternative way to fee-for-service and yet maintain quality.

Yesterday at this conference, before a group of Long Island high school students, I was asked about some of Nixon's personal characteristics. The most outstanding of the Nixon qualities is an extraordinary ability to focus his energy and intellect on a given problem or to detach himself and conceptualize from the general to the specific or vice versa.

From the time I first became close to Richard Nixon, I was struck by his incredible work schedule. As a new member of Congress, where I observed him while I was working for another congressman, I was astonished at his long hours and his extraordinary focus on the assignment at hand.

He acquired an early taste for foreign policy which I think grew out of his exposure to the problem of European economic recovery and the proposal by the Truman Administration of the Marshall Plan. When he was first asked to go on the select committee to consider the Marshall Plan, the then Republican leader, Joe Martin, and other old hands told him the plan was going to be a political "boondoggle" and give-away, and that it might be his political suicide.

Nixon denied those suggestions. He then went on the fact-finding tour with Chairman Chris Herter and came back from the tour and gave the Marshall Plan strong and articulate support. That, I believe, triggered his broader interest in foreign policy, and when he later became vice president (and particularly with the amount of controversy that had ensued over the so-called slush fund and "Checkers speech"), one of his first decisions was to focus on foreign policy and immerse himself in an area which he had not had an opportunity to get involved in before. When he was later sent by Eisenhower on foreign assignments, he would go through incredible periods of study and concentration, and would absorb data on his trips like a sponge and then share this information with the secretary of state, John Foster Dulles, with whom he developed a very close relationship.

Nixon has an incredible recollection and can remember facts and people (and their names) to a greater extent than anyone I think I've ever known in public life. This has been used to good advantage throughout his political career.

Discussant: Arthur M. Schlesinger, Jr.

If the quality of the discussions on the panel today is representative of what's been taking place in this conference, then you have been very fortunate. The cautions that Mr. Haldeman and Mr. Ehrlichman address to historians are thoughtful and important. I trust all scholars will take them into due account.

I would like to relieve some of their apprehensions, however, and note that the verdict of history is never final. Richard Nixon is one of those characters about whom debate will continue to the end of time. The great Dutch historian Pieter Geyl once described history as an "argument without end." The present argument began in Nixon's lifetime, and it will go on for years to come. The word "definitive" can never be properly applied to any historical work. As Oscar Wilde once said, "The one duty we owe to history is to rewrite it."

The question this panel is discussing is, I guess, what difference did the Nixon Administration make in the long trajectory of American history? I can only give one historian's assessment of this legacy. I should begin by declaring an interest. Mr. Nixon did me the high honor, for which I am eternally grateful, of placing me on his Enemies List. All suitable discount should therefore be made for anything I may say.

I would like to discuss briefly just three elements, three dimensions, of the Nixon legacy. The first is foreign policy, which I take to be the part, judging from his sacred writings, that he most treasures about his own record. It is an area for which historians are bound to give him credit. Here Nixon carried forward tendencies that had begun in the Kennedy and Johnson administrations to bring about what can perhaps be described as the secularization of the Cold War. In the 1950s, with John Foster Dulles defining the contest, the struggle with the Soviet Union took on the aspect of a holy war. Kennedy did not regard it as a religious conflict. He regarded it as a power conflict, as did Johnson. But the Republicans clung to the idea of a jihad. Then Nixon and Kissinger took further steps toward the secularization of the Cold War—a process marked by the replacement of ideology by geopolitics as a way of thinking about the Cold War.

In the early years of the Reagan Administration this process of the secularization of the Cold War was somewhat reversed. We reverted for a season to the Dulles brand of rhetoric. But even President Reagan seems in the last months to be yielding to the pressures of reality. The Nixon-Kissinger team played a valuable role in encouraging sensible thinking about the conflict as seen in terms of the balance of power and of a movement from an era of confrontation, as Nixon said, to an era of negotiation.

I don't think, however, that we should overdo the virtues of the Nixon record in foreign policy. His response to the Chinese desire to break out of diplomatic isolation was quick and valuable, but the Sino-Soviet split had already forced the Chinese to seek an opening to the West. Nixon and Kissinger understood this, saw the opportunity, and responded intelligently. Moreover, as conservatives, they were able to get away with a rapprochement that, if proposed by President Hubert Humphrey, Nixon himself would very likely have attacked.

Mr. Haldeman reminds us that the Vietnam War overshadowed Nixon's first term. Here the Nixon policies seem indefensible. He could have secured the withdrawal of the American forces in 1969 on substantially the same terms that he finally accepted on the eve of the American presidential election in 1972. The sticking point had always been Nixon's insistence that the withdrawal of U.S. troops be accompanied by simultaneous and concurrent withdrawal of North Vietnamese troops from South Vietnam. With the presidential election looming ahead, he dropped that insistence. Had we done in 1969 what we belatedly did in 1972, thousands of Americans and many more thousands of Vietnamese and Cambodians who were killed between 1969 and 1972 would now be alive.

In other parts of the world Nixon made serious mistakes in foreign policy. He supported the dictatorship of the colonels in Greece. He trembled—Kissinger too—over the specter of Eurocommunism, that now-forgotten menace, and shared Kissinger's expectation that Portugal—Portugal?—was about to go communist. His Latin American policy, especially the overthrow of Allende in Chile and the support of the Pinochet dictatorship, was hardly edifying. His policy of unconditional support for the shah of Iran played a vital part in bringing on the curse of Khomeini.

As Nixon's foreign policy has been overrated, so I think his domestic policy has been underrated. As a defender of the notion of a cyclical rhythm in American politics, I cannot resist pointing out that Nixon came to office in the 1960s—a decade that, like the 1930s and the first decade of this century, was a time of innovation and reform. In the same fashion, at thirty-year intervals, we endure conservative phases in the cycle: the Reagan 1980s, the Eisenhower 1950s, the Harding-Coolidge-Hoover 1920s. Nixon was elected president (with only 43 percent of the popular vote) when the liberal tide was still running strong. Not a man of profound convictions, he rolled with the punches and went along with a reform-minded Congress.

The Environmental Protection Act, the Occupational Safety and Health Act, the Comprehensive Employment and Training Act (CETA) and its federal employment program, were all enacted during the Nixon Administration. After Pat Moynihan told him about Disraeli and Tory Democracy, Nixon even proposed a guaranteed minimum income in his Family Assistance Plan. He indexed social security benefits, increased federal support for the arts and the humanities, imposed price and wage controls, and presided over the fastest increase in social payments since the New Deal. When the liberal phase of the cycle began to run its course in the early 1970s, so did any liberal inclination in the Nixon Administration.

The third dimension of the Nixon legacy is, in my view, most damaging: his impact on the Constitution. Now all presidents are irritated from time to time by the separation of powers. Theodore Roosevelt, when president, once clenched his fist and said to his young kinsman Franklin D. Roosevelt, "Sometimes I wish I could be President and Congress too." FDR added thirty years later, by which time he was in the White House himself, "I suppose if the truth were told, he is not the only President that has had that idea."

It was an idea that, one feels, consumed Richard Nixon. I don't know that we have ever had a president who felt more indignant, more righteously frustrated, over the separation of powers than Nixon; none more determined to revise the American system in order to minimize the capacity of the separation of powers to prevent presidents from doing whatever they wanted to do. In particular, he sought to seize for the presidency three vital powers the Constitution had assigned to Congress: the war-making power; the power of the purse; and the oversight power, the power to find out what is going on.

Now the war-making power had already passed to the executive by the time Nixon became president. From the day in 1950 when Harry Truman rejected Senator Taft's proposal of a joint resolution to authorize a commitment of American forces to combat in South Korea, presidents had assumed a de facto control of the war-making power, even though the Framers of the Constitution had confided that power exclusively to Congress. President Nixon carried this even further than his predecessors, particularly with the incursion into Cambodia.

The second power was the power of the purse—perhaps the most important of Congressional powers. This power President Nixon did his best to counter by the device of impoundment, that is, by not spending sums that the Congress had directed him to spend. Impoundment had been used in a limited way by presidents under special circumstances but never before had it been used to nullify laws passed by Congress, and never before had it been claimed as a constitutional right.

The third power of Congress which Nixon resented—a power that Woodrow Wilson had thought even more important than the legislative function—was what Wilson called the informing function, that is, the power of investigation and oversight. Nixon sought to counter this by making claims of executive privilege as an inherent and unreviewable right—claims which far exceeded the most extravagant claims previously made by the Eisenhower Administration.

So in these ways Nixon sought to change the balance in our political order between presidential power and congressional power. Beyond this, Nixon had an intense dislike, perhaps a fear, of political opposition. In this respect he was quite unlike Eisenhower or Reagan. Reagan, for example, obviously regards opposition as part of political life. He does not assume that people opposed to him are enemies of the republic. But, as John Ehrlichman once said, there was another side to Nixon, like the flat, dark side of the moon. Nixon saw life as a battlefield swarming with personal enemies bent on his destruction. He saw political disagreement as a threat to national security, and did not hesitate to violate the laws and the Constitution in order to put it down.

I suppose Nixon's was the most corrupt administration in American history. More than forty members of the administration underwent criminal prosecution, led by those particular champions of law and order, Vice President Spiro T. Agnew and Attorney General John Mitchell. The vice president, two cabinet members, a dozen members of the White House staff, and fifteen others scattered through the executive branch pleaded guilty or were convicted. The Nixon people were on the whole less interested in stealing money than they were in stealing power, and it was this that finally resulted in the Watergate, the cover-up and so on, and finally the impeachment.

The young, bemused by the rehabilitation of Richard Nixon, hardly know what Watergate was all about. Let us recall the articles of impeachment: "In his conduct of the office of President of the United States, Richard M. Nixon, in violation of his constitutional oath faithfully to execute the office of President . . . and in violation of his constitutional duty to take care that the laws be faithfully executed, has prevented, obstructed, and impeded the administration of justice[,] . . . has repeatedly engaged in conduct violating the constitutional rights of citizens [and] . . . has acted in a manner contrary to his trust as President and subversive of constitutional government. . . . Wherefore, Richard M. Nixon, by such conduct, warrants impeachment and removal from office."

This was not an action lightly taken by Congress. It was an action supported by Republicans as well as by Democrats, and it led to Nixon's resignation—an act unprecedented in our history. The basic issue involved in Watergate is with us still. It was stated unrepentantly by Nixon himself in his interview with David Frost in May 1977: "When the President does it, that means that it is not illegal." The notion that the sovereign can do no wrong has been the premise of legal systems in earlier times. It is not, however, the idea of the American Constitution.

The Constitution, despite Richard Nixon, does not enshrine the divine rights of presidents. Yet Nixon's belief that when the president does it, it can't be illegal, has obviously permeated at least one later White House. When I wrote *The Imperial Presidency*, I observed that corruption in the White House seemed to come at fifty-year intervals: Grant in 1873; Harding in 1923; Nixon in 1973. I said that half a century seemed to be the length of time it took for a president and his staff to forget the disgrace visited on predecessors who had abused their power. I assumed that the Watergate scandal would inoculate the White House against such flagrant abuse until about the year 2023. Obviously, I was quite wrong. Probably I should have taken into account the short attention span instilled by our popular addiction to television. At any rate, Colonel North, Admiral Poindexter, and the furtive and devious atmosphere created in the Reagan White House seem an unexpectedly early tribute to the Nixon theory of the divine right of presidents.

The separation of powers is no doubt a great exasperation for presidents. But it has its virtues; for in a democracy, policy can succeed only if it is based on consent. Consent is obtainable only through debate and persuasion and education. The separation of powers is a means of assuring and guaranteeing the disciplines of consent. More than that, the separation of powers is a means of guaranteeing the liberties of the American people. As Senator Sam Ervin said during the Watergate investigation, ''One of the great advantages of the three separate branches of government is that it's difficult to corrupt all three at the same time.'' Most happily for the republic, Richard Nixon failed in his effort to establish a new theory of presidential supremacy.

HOFSTRA CULTURAL CENTER

RICHARD NIXON

SIXTH ANNUAL
PRESIDENTIAL
CONFERENCE

A Retrospective on His Presidency

NOVEMBER 19-21, 1987

HOFSTRA UNIVERSITY

HEMPSTEAD, NEW YORK 11550

HOFSTRA CULTURAL CENTER

CONFERENCES AND SYMPOSIA PROGRAM

Director for Liaison and Creative Development
NATALIE DATLOF

Director for Documentation, Finance and Planning
ALEXEJ UGRINSKY

Conference Coordinator and Special Assistant to the Directors
ATHELENE A. COLLINS

Assistant Conference Coordinator
LAURA J. TRINGONE

Secretaries
MARILYN SEIDMAN
JESSICA RICHTER

Development Coordinator
DONNA TESTA

ART PROGRAM

HOFSTRA MUSEUM
Director
GAIL GELBURD
Curator of Collections
ELEANOR RAIT

Galleries
DAVID FILDERMAN GALLERY
Curator
MARGUERITE M. REGAN
Coordinator of Special Programs
MARY F. KLERK
Special Assistant to the Cultural Center
BARBARA LEKATSAS
Gallery Staff
NANCY E. HERB
ANNE RUBINO

EMILY LOWE GALLERY
Director
GAIL GELBURD
Executive Secretary
MARY WAKEFORD

LONG ISLAND STUDIES INSTITUTE
Director
NATALIE A. NAYLOR
Curator
BARBARA M. KELLY

MUSIC PROGRAM
Director
SEYMOUR L. BENSTOCK

AMERICAN CHAMBER ENSEMBLE
Directors
BLANCHE ABRAM
NAOMI DRUCKER

THE HOFSTRA QUARTET
Artistic Director
SEYMOUR BENSTOCK

PUBLICATIONS
GEORGE SAND STUDIES
Editor
NATALIE DATLOF

TWENTIETH-CENTURY LITERATURE
Editor
WILLIAM A. McBRIEN

HOFSTRA UNIVERSITY CULTURAL
AND
INTERCULTURAL STUDIES
Editor
ALEXEJ UGRINSKY

THEATER PROGRAM
Director
ALBERT PASSUELLO
Creative Director
EDWARD DENNEHEY

HOFSTRA UNIVERSITY

J. RICHARD BLOCK
Vice President for Planning and Liaison

JAMES M. SHUART
President, Hofstra University

FRANK G. ZARB
Chair, Hofstra University Board of Trustees

332

SIXTH ANNUAL PRESIDENTIAL CONFERENCE

RICHARD NIXON:
A Retrospective on His Presidency

NOVEMBER 19-21, 1987

JAMES M. SHUART	*President*
LEON FRIEDMAN	*Conference Co-Director* *Hofstra University School of Law*
WILLIAM F. LEVANTROSSER	*Conference Co-Director* *Department of Political Science*
NATALIE DATLOF	*Conference Coordinator*
ALEXEJ UGRINSKY	*Conference Coordinator*

Hofstra University Richard Nixon Conference Committee: Faculty and Administration Members

MAYER BARASH
Sociology/Anthropology
SEYMOUR BENSTOCK
Music
DAVID J. CHIU
Asian Studies
MICHAEL DE LUISE
Public Relations
MICHAEL D'INNOCENZO
History
ROBERT L. DOUGLAS
Law
BERNARD J. FIRESTONE
Political Science
ANDREW J. GRANT
Grant Development
JAMES E. HICKEY, JR.
Law
RONALD JANSSEN
English

IRA KAPLAN
Psychology
HAROLD A. KLEIN
Research in Development
JAMES J. KOLB
University College for
Continuing Education
ROBERT J. KUHNE
School of Business
HAROLD LAZARUS
School of Business
HARVEY LEVIN
Economics
LINDA LONGMIRE
Political Science
JOSEPH R. MACALUSO
Student Activities
THOMAS PARSONS
Computer Science

SONDRA RUBENSTEIN
Communication Arts
ROBERT E. SALFI
Computer Science
SHASHI K. SHAH
School of Business
RONALD H. SILVERMAN
Law
MARION E. PONSFORD
English
KETTY SETTON
Political Science
ROBERT SOBEL
History
LYNN TURGEON
Economics
JOHN E. ULLMANN
School of Business

Hofstra Cultural Center Richard Nixon Conference Assistants

PATRICIA BARTO
Conference Assistant
KAREN CASTRO
Conference Assistant

CONRAD DAVIES
Graduate Assistant
ABDUL MACAN MARKAR
Graduate Assistant
DIANE PATERSON
Conference Assistant

MICHAEL QUATTRUCCI
Conference Assistant
TARA STAHMAN
Conference Assistant

Hofstra University Richard Nixon Conference Committee: Student Members

TAMMY ALBERT
CAROL ANGRISANI
PAMELA ANTHONY
ANGELA SUE BELLUCCI
LANE BORON
DARREN BOSIK
FELICIA BROWN

SAMIR P. BULSARA
MARIA CASTRO
CAROLYN CHIARELLA
LAWRENCE D'AMICO
SANDRA DONNELLY
LISA DUCKETT
SANDRA DUBE

ANITA ELLIS
ELIZABETH ENCK
STACY FELLMAN
ALAN FISHKIN
DAVID FOX
JONATHON FURR
JENNIFER FUSCO

(continued)

Hofstra University Richard Nixon Conference Committee: Student Members

BONNIE FYLSTRA
CLEM GARCIA
KATHY GERBER
CHRISTOPHER GHERADI
DENISE GIBSON
ELIZABETH GLASSER
CATHY GLICKSTEIN
CHERYL GREEN
MICHELE HADDAD
RALPH HEALEY
MICHAEL HICKEY
JOANN HIRSCHEL
KIMBERLY IMPERIALE
JOHN JENSEN
KAREN KULIG
MICHELLE LEVY
MOHAMED LUNAT

ELLIOT MARKOWITZ
CHRISTOPHER MENDORA
JOHN MOLINARI
JOSEPH E. MONTOYA, JR.
ANDREW MYERS
SCOTT NICHOLSON
JACQUIE A. NORTH
MICHELLE OLSON
CECILIA PAGKALINAWAN
PETER PERCIAVALLE
JANINE POPICK
DANIEL QUINN
MICHELE C. RAMIREZ
SCOTT REDHEAD
ANDREW RIPPS
LINDA RODI
LINDA RUSSO
DINA SANTORELLI

DAVID SARNOFF
BARI SCHLESSENGER
ANDREW SCHMERTZ
NICHOLAS SERRANO
CHRIS SHAKESPEARE
DOUGLAS STROTHER
THOMAS TARTARO
KARL THUGE
HOWARD TOLLIN
SHELLEY TREACY
MELISSA TUOHEY
TODD UTERSTAEDT
FRAN WASSERMAN
SUSAN WEINER
JENNIFER WESTON
STEPHEN D. YORK
JIAN ZHANG

Hofstra University Student Organizations

ECONOMICS CLUB
POLITICAL AFFAIRS CLUB
STUDENT GOVERNMENT ASSOCIATION
TKE
COLLEGE REPUBLICANS

DIRECTORS' MESSAGE

Perhaps no other political figure has occupied such a prominent position on the American political scene for so long a period as Richard Nixon has in the post-World War II era. Perhaps no other person in politics has demonstrated such perseverance and durability as the former president. More significantly, no other political figure has generated such strong public reactions, both positive and negative, as President Nixon. There has rarely been a period in American history in which the people have felt so intimately involved as participants in the political events of the time and identified themselves as closely either in favor of or against a President. Americans still have retained those identifications and allegiances. The events of the Nixon administration are not distant historical episodes to most Americans but personal occurrences.

The major events of the Nixon Presidency continue to generate controversy. To this day, intense debates and disputes are sparked by discussions of Watergate, the impeachment proceedings, the nominations of Haynesworth and Carswell, the impoundment of appropriated funds, the War Powers Act, the invasion of Cambodia and the ending of the Vietnam War, and the Middle East crisis and the oil embargo. Less controversial subjects but of equal or greater historical importance to the Nixon Presidency would include the opening to China, the establishment of revenue sharing, the beginnings of detente, the passage of the basic environmental protection laws, welfare reform proposals, and such important initiatives as going off the gold standard and instituting wage and price controls.

Hofstra's Sixth Annual Presidential Conference follows in the tradition of our prior conferences in assembling a group of former government officials involved in the subjects under consideration as well as leading scholars and journalists. Panels have been organized to focus on the key accomplishments of the Nixon years as well as those matters which generated the greatest controversy. Participants in these events will review their experiences from the perspective of the thirteen years since the Nixon administration ended. We have attempted to provide a variety of viewpoints so that whatever preliminary judgments are made will reflect a balanced array of evidence.

We urge you to visit the Richard Nixon Presidential Conference Exhibition in the David Filderman Gallery on the 9th floor of the Joan and Donald E. Axinn Library. The Exhibition includes memorabilia on loan from the National Archives and a large selection of books on President Nixon. Many are from the private collection of Paulette and Robert J. Greene of Rockville Centre, New York. They have graciously donated their collection to Hofstra University. Mr. and Mrs. F. Jarvis Page of Garden City, New York have lent campaign material to the Exhibition and have donated Nixon campaign posters to the University as well. The Exhibition has been arranged by the staff of the David Filderman Gallery of the library.

A program of this magnitude does not materialize without substantial assistance, and many thanks are due to those who have helped make this conference possible. A special thanks goes to the scholars who submitted papers and to the notables who agreed to participate in the various conference forums. Thanks also to the Hofstra Faculty Committee who read and helped to choose papers for the conference.

We are especially grateful to Frank G. Zarb, the Chairman of the Hofstra University Board of Trustees, who was an active participant in the planning and organization of the proceedings and whose good sense played a key role in the development of the program. We are also thankful to James Hastings and his staff at the National Archives who was very helpful in supplying information and material.

Finally, our sincere thanks are extended to members of the Hofstra community with whom we have worked so closely over the last several months: Mike DeLuise, Jim Merritt, Wendy Vahey, Marge Regan, Anne Rubino, M.F. Klerk, Donna Testa, Harold A. Klein and the Hofstra Cultural Center student assistants, a group of extraordinarily talented, resourceful and hard-working young men and women, all students here at Hofstra University. They include: Patricia Barto, Karen Castro, Conrad Davies, Abdul Macan Makar, Diane Paterson, Michael Quattrucci and Tara Stahman. A special word of thanks is extended to the Cultural Center's staff, Athelene A. Collins, Marilyn Seidman, Jessica Richter and Laura Tringone, whose dedication to the daily tasks contributed to the overall success of the conference.

The Hofstra Cultural Center's co-directors, Natalie Datlof and Alexej Ugrinsky, have worked tirelessly to build on the legacy of the late Professor Joseph G. Astman, who founded the Center eleven years ago, and this conference is a tribute to their efforts, as well as to those of the staff that serves them and the University so well.

We welcome our guests and we hope our three days together will be enjoyable, intellectually rewarding and historically significant.

Leon Friedman

Leon Friedman
Conference Co-Director
Hofstra University School of Law

William Levantrosser

William F. Levantrosser
Conference Co-Director
Department of Political Science

Thursday, November 19, 1987

8:00 a.m. - 8:00 p.m.	Registration Multi-Purpose Room, North Campus

9:30 a.m. **John Cranford Adams** **Playhouse, South Campus**	Opening Ceremonies

Greetings	*James M. Shuart,* President Hofstra University
	Frank G. Zarb, Chair Hofstra University Board of Trustees
Introductions	*William F. Levantrosser* Conference Co-Director Department of Political Science
	Leon Friedman Conference Co-Director Hofstra University School of Law
Addresses	PERSPECTIVES ON RICHARD NIXON
	Elliot L. Richardson Milbank, Tweed, Hadley & McCloy Washington, DC
	Hugh Sidey Contributing Editor Time Magazine Washington, DC
	Stephen E. Ambrose Alumni Distinguished Professor of History University of New Orleans

For Conference Exhibit Schedules see page 25
For Dining Facilities see page 27

11:00 a.m.	CONCURRENT PANELS
Panel Ia **Student Center Theater** **North Campus**	REORGANIZATION OF THE EXECUTIVE BRANCH

Moderator: ***James P. Pfiffner***
      Department of Public Affairs
      George Mason University

"The Implementation of Cabinet Government During the
Nixon Administration"
Shirley Anne Warshaw
Department of Political Science
Gettysburg College

"The Nixon Administration and the Federal Bureaucracy in Retrospect"
Bert A. Rockman
Department of Political Science
Research Professor, University Center for International Studies
University of Pittsburgh
and
Joel D. Aberbach
Department of Political Science
Director, Program for the Study of American Institutions, Politics, and Policy
Institute for Social Science Research
University of California—Los Angeles

Discussants: ***Roy L. Ash***
           Los Angeles, CA

           H. R. Haldeman
           Santa Barbara, CA

           Arnold A. Saltzman
           Chairman
           Vista Resources, Inc.
           New York, NY

Panel Ib **John Cranford Adams** **Playhouse, South Campus**	SOCIAL WELFARE POLICIES

Moderator: ***James E. Hickey, Jr.***
      Hofstra University School of Law

"Outflanking the Liberals on Welfare"
Joan Hoff-Wilson
Department of History
Indiana University
Executive Secretary
Organization of American Historians

"Legislative Success and Failure: Social Welfare Policy of the
Nixon Administration"
Carl Lieberman
Department of Political Science
University of Akron

(continued)

Thursday, November 19, 1987

Panel Ib
John Cranford Adams
Playhouse, South Campus

SOCIAL WELFARE POLICIES   (continued)

Discussants: **John Ehrlichman**
Santa Fe, NM

Robert H. Finch
Fleming, Anderson, McClung & Finch
Pasadena, CA

Elliot L. Richardson
Milbank, Tweed, Hadley & McCloy
Washington, DC

Panel Ic
Dining Rooms ABC
North Campus

ENVIRONMENTAL POLICY

Moderator: **William R. Ginsberg**
Rivkin, Radler, Dunne & Bayh
Distinguished Professor of Environmental Law
Hofstra University School of Law

"The Nixon Environmental Record: A Mixed Picture"
Charles Warren
Berle, Kass & Case
New York, NY

Discussants: **Barry Commoner**
Center for Biology of Natural Systems
Queens College–CUNY
Scientific Advisor to the New York State Legislative Commission
on Science and Technology

David Sive
Sive, Paget & Riesel
New York, NY
Board Member, National Resources
Defense Council (NRDC)

John C. Whitaker
Vice President of Public Affairs
Union Camp Corporation
Washington, DC

12:45 p.m.   Lunch–See page 27 for Dining Facilities

2:00 p.m.

Plenary Session
John Cranford Adams
Playhouse, South Campus

THE OPENING TO CHINA

Introduction: ***Frank G. Zarb,*** Chair
          Hofstra Universty Board of Trustees

Address: ***The Honorable Han Xu***
          Ambassador of the People's Republic of China in the United States

Moderator: ***Robert C. Vogt,*** Dean
          Hofstra College of Liberal Arts and Sciences

"The Asian Balance and Sino-American Rapprochement
During the Nixon Administration"
Robert G. Sutter
Senior Specialist
Congressional Research Service
Library of Congress
Washington, DC

Discussants: ***Jerome A. Cohen***
          Paul, Weiss, Rifkind, Wharton & Garrison
          New York, NY

          Kenneth Lieberthal
          Director
          Center for Chinese Studies
          University of Michigan—Ann Arbor

          C.L. Sulzberger
          Author and Former Journalist
          Paris, France
          Author of
          The World and Richard Nixon, (1987)

4:00 p.m.

CONCURRENT PANELS

Panel IIa
Student Center Theater
North Campus

THE FOREIGN POLICY PROCESS

Moderator: ***Bernard J. Firestone***
          Department of Political Science
          Hofstra University

"The Nixon Doctrine as History and Portent"
Earl C. Ravenal
Distinguished Research Professor of International Affairs
School of Foreign Service
Georgetown University

"Richard Nixon as Diplomat-in-Chief"
Elmer Plischke
Professor Emeritus, University of Maryland
Adjunct Scholar, American Enterprise Institute for Public Policy Research

(continued)

Panel IIa

THE FOREIGN POLICY PROCESS (continued)

Student Center Theater
North Campus

"Continuities and Contradictions in the Nixon Foreign Policy"
Kenneth W. Thompson
Director, White Burkett Miller Center of Public Affairs
University of Virginia

Discussants: ***Lloyd S. Etheredge***
Director, Graduate Studies
International Relations Program
Yale University

Roger Morris
Sant Fe, NM

C. L. Sulzberger
Author and Former Journalist
Paris, France
Author of
The World and Richard Nixon, (1987)

Panel IIb
John Cranford Adams
Playhouse, South Campus

POLITICS AND THE GOVERNMENTAL PROCESS

Moderator: ***Monroe H. Freedman***
Hofstra University School of Law

"Information, Dissent and Political Power:
The Paradoxes of the Nixon Administration"
Alan F. Westin
Department of Political Science
Columbia University

"Richard Nixon and the Politicization of Justice"
Michael A. Genovese
Department of Political Science
Loyola Marymount University
Los Angeles, CA

Discussants: ***Charles W. Colson***
Chairman of the Board
Prison Fellowship Ministries
Washington, DC

Egil Krogh
Culp, Dwyer, Guterson & Grader
Seattle, WA

John Shattuck
Vice President, Government, Community and
Public Affairs, Harvard University
Lecturer, Harvard Law School

6:00 - 7:30 p.m.

Dinner—See page 27 for Dining Facilities

8:00 p.m.
Plenary Session

Presiding   ***James M. Shuart,*** President
                                  Hofstra University

Moderator: ***Sanford Hammer***
                                  Provost & Dean of Faculties
                                  Hofstra University

Introduction   ***The Honorable Han Xu***
                                  Ambassador of the People's Republic of China to the United States

Address   ***Henry A. Kissinger***

Henry Alfred Kissinger was sworn in on September 22, 1973, as the 56th Secretary of State, a position he held until January 20, 1977. He also served as Assistant to the President for National Security Affairs from January 20, 1969, until November 3, 1975.

At present Dr. Kissinger is Chairman of Kissinger Associates, Inc., an international consulting firm. Dr. Kissinger is also a member of the President's Foreign Intelligence Advisory Board, a Counselor to the Chase Manhattan Bank and a member of its International Advisory Committee, a member of the Commission on Integrated Long-Term Strategy of the National Security Council and Defense Department, and an Honorary Governor of the Foreign Policy Association.

Among the awards Dr. Kissinger has received have been the Nobel Peace Prize in 1973; the Presidential Medal of Freedom, this nation's highest civilian award, in 1977; and the Medal of Liberty in 1986.

Henry A. Kissinger received the B.A. degree summa cum laude at Harvard College in 1950, and the M.A. and Ph.D. degrees at Harvard University in 1952 and 1954.

8:00 a.m. - 5:00 p.m.	Registration Multi-Purpose Room, North Campus

9:00 a.m.	CONCURRENT PANELS

Panel IIIa
Student Center Theater
North Campus

DEFENSE POLICY AND MILITARY MANPOWER

Moderator: ***Morris Honick***
        Chief, Historical Section
        Command Historian
        Supreme Headquarters Allied
        Powers Europe, (SHAPE)
        Brussels, Belgium

"Defense Policy During the Nixon Administration"
Lawrence J. Korb
Dean, Graduate School of Public and International Affairs
University of Pittsburgh
Adjunct Scholar, American Enterprise Institute for Public Policy Research

"The Making of the All-Volunteer Armed Force"
Martin Anderson
Senior Fellow
The Hoover Institution
Stanford University

Discussants: ***Martin Binkin***
        Senior Fellow
        Foreign Policy Studies
        The Brookings Institution

        Adam Yarmolinsky
        Provost and Vice Chancellor for Academic Affairs
        University of Maryland, Baltimore County

Panel IIIb
Dining Rooms ABC
North Campus

ECONOMIC AND MONETARY POLICY

Moderator: ***Lynn Turgeon***
        Department of Economics
        Hofstra University

"Market Integration Policies During the Nixon Presidency"
M. Mark Amen
International Studies
University of South Florida/Tampa

(continued)

Panel IIIb
Dining Rooms ABC
North Campus

ECONOMIC AND MONETARY POLICY (continued)

"President Nixon's Political Business Cycle"
Ann Mari May
Department of Economics
University of Nebraska–Lincoln
and
Robert R. Keller
Chair, Department of Economics
Colorado State University

"Nixon's Economic Policy Toward Minorities"
Maurice H. Stans
Pasadena, CA

Discussants: *Robert Lekachman*
Distinguished Professor of Economics
Lehman College and
The Graduate Center/CUNY

Herbert Stein
Senior Fellow
American Enterprise Institute for
Public Policy Research

Forum IIIc
John Cranford Adams
Playhouse, South Campus

THE PROTEST MOVEMENT

Moderator: *Ronald H. Silverman*
Peter S. Kalikow Distinguished Professor of Real Estate Law
Hofstra University School of Law

Discussants: *Sam W. Brown, Jr.*
Centennial Partners, Ltd.
Denver, CO

David Dellinger
Peacham, VT

David J. Garrow
Department of Political Science
The City College/CUNY

Sanford Gottlieb
Senior Analyst
Center for Defense Information

Tom Hayden
California State Assemblyman
Santa Monica, CA

Egil Krogh
Culp, Dwyer, Guterson & Grader
Seattle, WA

High School Colloquium
9:00-10:30 a.m.
See page 24

10:45 a.m. - 12:15 p.m.	CONCURRENT PANELS

Panel IVa
John Cranford Adams
Playhouse, South Campus

WATERGATE RE-EXAMINED

Moderator: **John DeWitt Gregory**
Vice Dean and Sidney and Walter Siben
Distinguished Professor of Family Law
Hofstra University School of Law

"Watergate and the Nixon Presidency: A Comparative Ideological Analysis"
David R. Simon
Department of Criminal Justice Administration and Sociology
San Diego State University—Calexico

"Nixon's Dismissal of Special Prosecutor Cox:
The Constitutionality and Legality of an Exercise of
Presidential Removal Power"
Nancy Kassop
Department of Political Science
State University of New York/College at New Paltz

Discussants: **Stanley I. Kutler**
E. Gordon Fox Professor of American Institutions
University of Wisconsin—Madison

J. Anthony Lukas
New York, NY

Rev. Jeb Stuart Magruder
Executive Minister
First Community Church
Columbus, OH

Earl J. Silbert
Schwalb, Donnenfeld, Bray & Silbert
Washington, DC

Panel IVb
Student Center Theater
North Campus

THE MIDDLE EAST AND ENERGY POLICY

Moderator: **Sondra Rubenstein**
Department of Communication Arts
Hofstra University

"Oil and/or the Olive Branch: The Nixon Administration's
Choices in Its Middle East Policies"
Gideon Doron
Visiting Professor of Political Science
New York University and
Tel Aviv University
Ramat Aviv, Israel

Discussants: **Alfred L. Atherton**
Harkness Fellowships
of the Commonwealth Fund
Washington, DC

(continued)

Panel IVb
Student Center Theater
North Campus

THE MIDDLE EAST AND ENERGY POLICY (continued)

Hermann Frederick Eilts
Director, Center for International Relations
Boston University

Jo-Ann Hart
Department of Political Science
Brown University

Dale R. Tahtinen
Director, International Program
Cray Research
Washington, DC

12:30 - 1:15 p.m.

Lunch: See page 27 for Dining Facilities

1:15 - 2:30 p.m.

Plenary Session
John Cranford Adams
Playhouse, South Campus

NIXON BIOGRAPHERS

Moderator: Louis W. Koenig
Professor Emeritus
New York University and
Visiting Distinguished Professor
Long Island University/C.W. Post Center

Discussants: *Stephen E. Ambrose*
Alumni Distinguished Professor of History
University of New Orleans
Author of
Nixon: The Education of a Politician, (1987)

Roger Morris
Sante Fe, NM
Author of
*Richard Milhous Nixon: To the
Threshold of Power, 1913-1960*, (Summer 1988)

Herbert S. Parmet
Distinguished Professor of History
Queensborough Community College and
The Graduate Center/CUNY
Author of
The Age of Nixon, (1988/1989)

Raymond K. Price, Jr.
President
The Economic Club of New York
New York, NY
Author of
With Nixon, (1977)

2:45 p.m.   CONCURRENT PANELS

Panel Va   THE WAR POWERS RESOLUTION
John Cranford Adams
Playhouse, South Campus   Moderator: *Linda Longmire*
                                                     Teaching Fellow, New College
                                                     Hofstra University

                                             "Nixon versus the Congress: The War Powers Act, 1973"
                                             Philip J. Briggs
                                             Department of Political Science
                                             East Stroudsburg University

                                             "The War Powers Resolution: An Intersection of Law and Politics"
                                             Nathan N. Firestone
                                             Department of Political Science
                                             Point Park College

                                             Discussants: *Harold H. Koh*
                                                          Yale Law Schol

                                                          Burt Neuborne
                                                          New York University School of Law

                                                          General Brent Scowcroft, USA (Ret.)
                                                          Kissinger Associates
                                                          Washington, DC

                                                          Stephen J. Solarz
                                                          Member, U.S. House of Representatives
                                                          New York

Panel Vb   THE NEW FEDERALISM AND REVENUE SHARING
Dining Rooms ABC
North Campus   Moderator: *Andrew J. Grant*
                                                     Director, Grants Development
                                                     Hofstra University

                                             "Nixon's General Revenue-Sharing and American Federalism"
                                             David Caputo, Dean
                                             School of Humanities, Social Sciences and Education
                                             Purdue University

(continued)

Panel Vb
Dining Rooms ABC
North Campus

THE NEW FEDERALISM AND REVENUE SHARING (continued)

Discussants: ***John Ehrlichman***
Santa Fe, NM

Richard P. Nathan
Professor of Public and International Affairs
Woodrow Wilson School of Public and International Affairs
Princeton University

Paul H. O'Neill
Director
Chairman of the Board and
Chief Executive Officer
ALCOA
Pittsburgh, PA

Forum Vc
Student Center Theater
North Campus

THE SILENT MAJORITY: SUPPORT FOR THE PRESIDENT

Moderator: ***Eric J. Schmertz***
Dean and Edward F. Carlough
Distinguished Professor of Labor Law
Hofstra University School of Law

Discussants: ***Henry C. Cashen II***
Dickstein, Shapiro & Morin
Washington, DC

Charles W. Colson
Chairman of the Board
Prison Fellowship Ministries
Washington, DC

Col. John A. Dramesi U.S.A.F. (Ret.)
Blackwood, NJ

Donald F. Rodgers
Special Coordinator for Seniors
Office of the Secretary of Labor
Washington, DC

Philip K. Straw
Honors Program
University of Maryland/College Park

4:15 p.m.   CONCURRENT PANELS

Panel VIa   DETENTE AND THE SOVIET UNION
John Cranford Adams
Playhouse, South Campus   Moderator: *Frederic A. Bergerson*
                                              Department of Political Science
                                              Whittier College

                                   "The Rise and Stall of Detente, 1969-1974"
                                   Robert D. Schulzinger
                                   Department of History
                                   University of Colorado

                                   Discussants: *The Honorable Aleksandr M. Belonogov*
                                                Permanent Representative of the USSR to the United Nations

                                                Dimitri Simes
                                                Senior Associate and Director
                                                Project on U.S.-Soviet Relations
                                                Carnegie Endowment for International Peace

                                                Hedrick Smith
                                                Washington Correspondent
                                                The New York Times

                                                Helmut Sonnenfeldt
                                                Guest Scholar
                                                The Brookings Institution

Panel VIb   ELECTION CAMPAIGNING
Student Center Theater
North Campus   Moderator *Michael D'Innocenzo*
                                              Department of History
                                              Hofstra University

                                   "Campaign Finance and the Nixon Presidency: End of an Era"
                                   Joel M. Gora
                                   Brooklyn Law School

                                   "Richard Nixon: The Southern Strategy and the 1968 Presidential Election"
                                   Glen Moore
                                   Department of History
                                   Auburn University

                                   Discussants: *David M. Dorsen*
                                                Sachs, Greenebaum & Tayler
                                                Washington, DC

                                                Thomas W. Evans
                                                Mudge, Rose, Guthrie, Alexander & Ferdon
                                                New York, NY

                                                John Herbers
                                                The Council of the Humanities
                                                Princeton University

                                                John Kessel
                                                Department of Political Science
                                                Ohio State University

                                                Maurice H. Stans
                                                Pasadena, CA

7:00 p.m.	Joan and Donald E. Axinn Library, South Campus
Exhibits	***Richard Nixon*** Book, Manuscript, Photograph and Memorabilia Exhibit David Filderman Gallery, Ninth Floor
	Mother and Child: The Art of Henry Moore Art Exhibit Hofstra Cultural Center, Tenth Floor
	Reception
8:00 p.m.	RICHARD NIXON PRESIDENTIAL CONFERENCE BANQUET
	Dining Room, Student Center, North Campus
Presiding	***James M. Shuart*** President Hofstra University
Introductions	***Leon Friedman*** Conference Co-Director Hofstra University School of Law
	William F. Levantrosser Conference Co-Director Department of Political Science
Introduction of Banquet Speaker	***James M. Shuart***
Banquet Address	***Tom Wicker*** Political Columnist, "In the Nation," *The New York Times* New York, NY

8:00 a.m. - 2:00 p.m.	Registration Multi-Purpose Room, North Campus
8:00 a.m.	Complimentary Continental Breakfast Multi-Purpose Room, North Campus

9:00 a.m. CONCURRENT PANELS

Panel VIIa
John Cranford Adams
Playhouse, South Campus

THE ENDING OF THE VIETNAM WAR

Moderator: ***Richard Sobel***
Department of Political Science
University of Connecticut

"Military and Political Considerations Leading to the End of the Vietnam War"
William M. Hammond
Historian
U.S. Army Center of Military History
Washington, DC

"Secret Commitments in President Nixon's Foreign Policy: The National
Security Council and Nixon's Letters to South Vietnam's
President Nguyen Van Thieu"
Nguyen Tien Hung
Department of Economics
Howard University
and
Jerrold L. Schecter
Chairman
Schecter Communications Corp.
Washington, DC

Discussants: ***Frances FitzGerald***
New York, NY

Guenter Lewy
Washington, DC

Robert Miller
Vice President
National Defense University
Washington, DC

Panel VIIb
Dining Rooms ABC
North Campus

SEPARATION OF POWERS: ISSUES AND PROBLEMS

Moderator: ***Linda K. Champlin***
Maurice A. Deane Distinguished
Professor of Constitutional Law
Hofstra University School of Law

"United States v. Nixon Re-Examined: The Supreme Court's
Self-Imposed 'Duty' to Come to Judgment on the Question of
Presidential Confidentiality"
Howard Ball
Dean and Professor of Political Science
College of Social and Behavioral Science
University of Utah

Discussants: ***Robert L. Keuch***
Executive Director & General Counsel
Judicial Inquiry and Review Board
Commonwealth of Pennsylvania
Harrisburg, PA

Arthur Kinoy
Rutgers University School of Law
Newark, NJ

Phillip Lacovara
Hughes, Hubbard & Reed
Washington, DC

Panel VIIc
Student Center Theater
North Campus

APPOINTMENTS TO THE SUPREME COURT

Moderator: ***Bernard E. Jacob***
Hofstra University School of Law

"The Supreme Court Under Siege: The Battle over Nixon's Nominees"
Joseph Calluori
Michael Kennedy, P.C.
New York, NY

Discussants: ***Birch Bayh***
Rivkin, Radler, Dunne & Bayh
Washington, DC

John P. MacKenzie
The New York Times
New York, NY

James McClellan
President
Center for Judicial Studies
Cumberland, VA

11:00 a.m. - 1:00 p.m.	CONCURRENT PANELS
Panel VIIIa **John Cranford Adams** **Playhouse, South Campus**	IMPEACHMENT PROCEEDINGS

Moderator: *Leon Friedman*
        Hofstra University School of Law

"The Nixon Impeachment and Abuse of Presidential Power"
Dagmar S. Hamilton
Associate Dean, Lyndon B. Johnson
School of Public Affairs
University of Texas — Austin

"Normal Legislative Coalitions and Impeachment"
Terry Sullivan
Department of Government
University of Texas—Austin

Discussants: *John Doar*
        New York, NY

        Elizabeth Holtzman
        District Attorney—Kings County
        Brooklyn, NY

        Judge Charles E. Wiggins
        United States Court of Appeals
        Ninth Circuit
        Reno, NV

Panel VIIIb **Student Center Theater** **North Campus**	CIVIL RIGHTS POLICY

Moderator: *John E. Stergis*
        President
        Student Government Association
        Hofstra University

"Richard M. Nixon, Southern Strategies and Desegregation of Public Schools"
Al L. King
Austin, TX

"The Incoherence of the Civil Rights Policy in the Nixon Administration"
Hugh D. Graham
Department of History
University of Maryland—Baltimore County

Discussants: *Robert H. Finch*
        Fleming, Anderson, McClung & Finch
        Pasadena, CA

        Sallyanne F. Payton
        University of Michigan School of Law
        Anne Arbor, MI

        Roger Wilkins
        Senior Fellow
        Institute for Policy Studies and
        Robinson Professor of History
        George Mason University

Panel VIIIc
Dining Rooms ABC
North Campus

RESEARCHING THE NIXON PRESIDENCY:
DOCUMENTS AND EVIDENCE

Moderator: ***Joseph Dmobowski***
Librarian
Whittier College

"Status of the Nixon Presidential Materials"
James J. Hastings
Acting Director
Nixon Presidential Materials Project
National Archives and Records Administration
Washington, DC

Discussants: ***Joan Hoff-Wilson***
Department of History
Indiana University
Executive Secretary
Oganization of American Historians

Harry P. Jeffrey
Department of History
Director, Richard Nixon Oral History Project
California State University—Fullerton

Harry J. Middleton
Director
Lyndon B. Johnson Library
Austin, TX

Mark Weiss
Visiting Professor
Doctoral Program in Speech and Hearing Sciences
The Graduate Center/CUNY

1:00 - 2:00 p.m.

Lunch—See page 27 for Dining Facilities

2:00 p.m.

Plenary Session
John Cranford Adams
Playhouse, South Campus

SECRECY, THE GOVERNMENT AND THE MEDIA

Moderator: ***Victor Navasky***
    Editor
    The Nation
    New York, NY

"Secrecy and Democracy: The Unresolved Legacy of the Pentagon Papers"
John Kincaid
Director of Research
Advisory Commission on Intergovernmental Relations
Washington, DC

"President Nixon's Conception of Executive Privilege: Defining the
Scope and Limits of Governmental Secrecy"
Mark J. Rozell
Department of Political Science
Mary Washington College

Discussants: ***Tom Brokaw***
     NBC News
     New York, NY

     Howard Simons
     Curator, Nieman Fellowships Program
     Harvard University

     Gerald L. Warren
     Editor
     The San Diego Union

     Ronald L. Ziegler
     President
     National Association of Truck Stop Operators
     Alexandria, VA

4:00 p.m.

Plenary Session
John Cranford Adams
Playhouse, South Campus

THE EVOLUTION OF THE NIXON LEGACY

Moderator: *Fred I. Greenstein*
Professor of Politics and Director
Program in Leadership Studies
Woodrow Wilson School of Public
and International Affairs
Princeton University

"Richard Nixon Reconsidered: The Conservative as Liberal?"
Barry D. Riccio
Department of History
University of Illinois at Urbana—Champaign

"Richard Nixon and the Idea of Rehabilitation"
Sherri Cavan
Department of Sociology
San Francisco State University

Discussants: *John Ehrlichman*
Santa Fe, NM

H.R. Haldeman
Santa Barbara, CA

Robert H. Finch
Fleming, Anderson, McClung & Finch
Pasadena, CA

Arthur M. Schlesinger, Jr.
Albert Schweitzer Professor of the Humanities
The Graduate Center/CUNY

C.L. Sulzberger
Author and Former Journalist
Paris, France
Author of
The World and Richard Nixon, (1987)

6:00 p.m.
Dining Rooms ABC
North Campus

Reception

HIGH SCHOOL COLLOQUIUM

Friday, November 20, 1987
9:00 - 10:30 a.m.–Hofstra USA

Presiding and Welcoming Remarks	**James M. Shuart** President, Hofstra University
Introductions	**William F. Levantrosser** Conference Co-Director Department of Political Science
Speakers	**Stephen E. Ambrose** Alumni Distinguished Professor of History University of New Orleans Author of *Nixon: The Education of a Politician,* (1987)
	Robert H. Finch Fleming, Anderson, McClung & Finch Pasadena, CA
	H. R. Haldeman Santa Barbara, CA

Questions/Answers

High School Colloquium Committee

Mark Dion, Vice President for Student Services
David J. Obedzinski, Assistant Dean of Student Services
Edward Carp, Special Assistant for Promotions
Maria Castro, Promotion Assistant
Pam Anthony, Promotion Assistant
Michael DeLuise, Director, Public Relations

PARTICIPATING SCHOOLS

East Islip High School
Islip Terrace, NY

Farmingdale High School
Farmingdale, NY

Harborfields High School
Greenlawn, NY

Hauppauge High School
Hauppauge, NY

Holy Child High School
Westbury, NY

John Glenn High School
East Northport, NY

John F. Kennedy High School
Bellmore, NY

Mepham High School
Bellmore, NY

Merrick Avenue Junior High School
Merrick, NY

North Valley Stream High School
Franklin Square, NY

Saint Agnes High school
Rockville Centre, NY

Saint Hugh of Lincoln School
Huntington Station, NY

Shoreham-Wading River High School
Shoreham, NY

Smithtown High School East
Saint James, NY

Great Neck South High School
Great Neck, NY

South Side High School
Rockville Centre, NY

The Wheatley School
Old Westbury, NY

Woodmere Academy
Woodmere, NY

Index

About the Editors
and Contributors

STEPHEN E. AMBROSE is the Boyd Professor of History at the University of New Orleans and director of the Eisenhower Center. He is the author of biographies of Eisenhower and Nixon.

HOWARD BALL is professor of political science and dean of the College of Arts and Sciences at the University of Vermont. He is the author of dozens of political science and law review articles and has authored or co-authored sixteen books on the Supreme Court and the judicial process, including *Justice Downwind*, *Compromised Compliance* (Greenwood Press, 1982), *"We Have a Duty": The Supreme Court and the Watergate Litigation* (Greenwood Press, 1990), and *Of Powers and Rights: Justices Black and Douglas*.

TOM BROKAW is the anchor, managing editor, and chief of correspondents of "NBC Nightly News with Tom Brokaw." Before joining "Nightly News," he had been anchor of NBC News' "Today" program from 1976 to 1981. He has played a major role in NBC News' coverage of every presidential election since 1976.

SHERRI CAVAN is professor of sociology at San Francisco State University. Her area of specialization is deviance and conformity. She has conducted several studies of rule breaking activity both at the top of the social system and at the bottom. She is author of *Liquor License: An Ethnography of Bar Behavior*, *Hippies of the Haight*, and *Twentieth Century Gothic: America's Nixon*, along with numerous articles and reviews.

CHARLES W. COLSON, former special council to President Richard M. Nixon, founded Prison Fellowship in 1976 after serving several months in prison for a Watergate-related offense. An international outreach to prisoners, ex-prisoners, and victims and their families, Prison Fellowship has over 40,000 volunteers. Colson is a well-known speaker and author. Some of his books include *Born Again*, *Kingdoms in Conflict*, *Against the Night*, and *Why America Doesn't Work*.

JOHN DOAR is currently a partner in the law firm of Doar Devorkin & Rieck in New York City. He has been practicing law since 1950 and served as special counsel, Committee on the Judiciary, U.S. House of Representatives, Impeachment of Richard M. Nixon, President of the United States.

ROBERT H. FINCH is an attorney in California. He served in the Eisenhower, Nixon, and Ford administrations. From 1969 to 1972, he was Secretary of Health, Education, and Welfare.

MONROE H. FREEDMAN is the Howard Lichtenstein Distinguished Professor of Legal Ethics at Hofstra University Law School. His latest book is *Understanding Lawyers' Ethics*.

LEON FRIEDMAN is the Joseph Kushner Professor of Civil Liberties Law at the Hofstra University Law School. He is the author or editor of many books on politics and law including *The Justices of the United States Supreme Court, 1789–1990*. As an ACLU lawyer, he handled a number of law suits against members of the Nixon Administration.

DAVID J. GARROW is a Fellow of The Twentieth Century Fund. He is the author of many books, including *Bearing the Cross: Martin Luther King, Jr., and the Southern Christian Leadership Conference*, which won the 1987 Pulitzer Prize in biography. He is the editor of *The Montgomery Bus Boycott and the Women Who Started It: The Memoir of Jo Ann Gibson Robinson* and co-editor of *The Eyes on the Prize Civil Rights Reader*. Garrow served as senior advisor to "Eyes on the Prize," the award-winning PBS television history of the civil rights struggle.

MICHAEL A. GENOVESE is associate professor of political science and director of the Peace Studies Program at Loyola Marymount University in Los Angeles, California. He is the author of *The Nixon Presidency: Power and Politics in Turbulent Times* (Greenwood Press, 1990), *Politics and the Cinema: An Introduction to Political Films*, and *The Supreme Court, the Constitution, and the Presidential Power*. He has contributed articles and reviews to a variety of journals including *Presidential Studies Quarterly*, *The American Political Science Review*, *Congress & the Presidency*, *Governance*, *Political Science Quar-*

terly, *Western Political Quarterly*, *The Journal of Politics*, and the *International Journal on World Peace*.

SANFORD GOTTLIEB is senior producer of "America's Defense Monitor," a weekly television series sponsored by the Center for Defense Information, Washington, D.C. Since 1960 he has worked full time in the peace and arms control community, serving successively as executive director of Sane, New Directions, and United Campuses to Prevent Nuclear War. He is the author of many articles on foreign policy and military developments.

FRED I. GREENSTEIN is professor of politics at Princeton University and has been involved in academia since 1958. He is also currently a Distinguished Visitor at the University of Melbourne in Australia. He has published numerous books, monographs, and edited works.

H. R. HALDEMAN, a California businessman, was assistant to the president and White House chief of staff in the Nixon Administration. He is the author of *The Ends of Power*, a former Regent of the University of California, and former chairman of the Board of Trustees of the California Institute of the Arts.

DAGMAR S. HAMILTON is professor and former associate dean for academic affairs at the University of Texas at Austin, Lyndon B. Johnson School of Public Affairs. She is a lawyer whose public service includes work for the Civil Rights Division, U.S. Department of Justice, in the mid-1960s and for the Judiciary Committee, U.S. House of Representatives, 1973–74. She is the co-author of *People, Positions, and Power*, and various reviews and essays. She has taught as a visitor at the University of Arizona Law School, Washington University (St. Louis) Law School, and Queen Mary College of Laws, the University of London.

JAMES J. HASTINGS is the director of the Nixon Presidential Materials Project Staff, a part of the National Archives and Records Administration's Office of Presidential Libraries. The Nixon Project has in its custody all of the official records of the Nixon Administration and is responsible for preservation of and access to them. Hastings has been an archivist with the National Archives for eighteen years and has had a wide variety of responsibilities with political, military, and diplomatic records.

TOM HAYDEN is a state assemblyman in California. In 1969 he was prosecuted by the Nixon Justice Department for the antiwar disruptions during the 1968 Democratic convention. Following a widely publicized trial, Hayden was cleared of the charges.

JOAN HOFF-WILSON is professor of history at Indiana University, Bloomington, and is former executive secretary of the Organization of American Historians. Her principal research interests are twentieth-century U.S. foreign policy and politics and the legal status of U.S. women. She is the author of books and articles about Herbert Hoover, Eleanor Roosevelt, and Richard Nixon. Her most recent work is *Unequal Before the Law: A Legal History of U.S. Women.*

ELIZABETH HOLTZMAN was the first woman elected to the position of comptroller in New York City and has been serving in that capacity since 1990. She has been active in fighting waste and corruption in government for many years. She served as a U.S. congresswoman from 1973 to 1981.

HARRY P. JEFFREY is professor of history at California State University, Fullerton, and director of the University's Richard Nixon Oral History Program. He directed the publication by the Nixon Program of the volumes of almost 200 interviews about the early years of Richard and Pat Nixon. His research and writing efforts concentrate on twentieth-century American history.

NANCY KASSOP is assistant professor of political science at The State University of New York—College of New Paltz where she teaches courses in constitutional law, American government and politics, and the presidency. Her principal research efforts have been on the subjects of presidential prerogative power and separation of power conflicts. Her paper, "President Johnson and the Gulf of Tonkin Incident: An Example of Presidential Prerogative Power," received the Pennsylvania Political Science Association Best Paper Award for 1987. She has presented many conference papers on such issues as war powers, treaty termination, and special prosecutors.

JOHN KINCAID is executive director of the Advisory Commission on Intergovernmental Relations, Washington, D.C., and associate professor of political science (on leave) at the University of North Texas, Denton. He is editor of *Publius: The Journal of Federalism* and author and editor of books and articles on political science.

LOUIS W. KOENIG is professor emeritus of political science at New York University and visiting distinguished professor at C. W. Post. His books on the presidency include *The Chief Executive* and *The Invisible Presidency*, and he co-authored *The Presidency Today.*

STANLEY I. KUTLER is the E. Gordon Fox Professor of American Institutions and professor of law at the University of Wisconsin–Madison. His work has covered a broad range of issues and periods in the development of American law and constitutionalism. He is the author of *The Wars of Watergate: The Last Crisis of Richard Nixon, The American Inquisition: Justice and Injustice in the*

Cold War, and *Privilege and Creative Destruction*. He is the founder and editor of *Reviews in American History*.

PHILIP LACOVARA is managing director and general counsel at Morgan Stanley & Company in New York City.

WILLIAM F. LEVANTROSSER is a professor of political science and director of the Colloquium on the American Presidency at Hofstra University. He is the author of *Congress and the Citizen-Soldier* and *Harry S. Truman: The Man from Independence* (Greenwood Press, 1986). Levantrosser has also published numerous articles on national security issues, including "Tonkin Gulf Revisited," in *Lyndon Baines Johnson and the Uses of Power*, edited by Bernard J. Firestone and Robert C. Vogt (Greenwood Press, 1988).

J. ANTHONY LUKAS is an author and journalist. From 1962 to 1972 he was a foreign and domestic correspondent for the *New York Times*. In 1968, he won a Pulitzer Prize for local investigative reporting. In 1986, he won a second Pulitzer Prize for his book, *Common Ground: A Turbulent Decade in the Lives of Three American Families*. He is the author of three other books, including *Nightmare: The Underside of the Nixon Years*.

REVEREND JEB STUART MAGRUDER is senior minister of the First Presbyterian Church in Lexington, Kentucky. Before entering the ministry, he held numerous positions in business and government, including the role of deputy campaign director for the Committee to Re-Elect the President in 1972.

ROGER MORRIS is the author of *Richard Milhous Nixon: The Rise of an American Politician*, the first of a projected three-volume biography. His earlier books include *Uncertain Greatness: Henry Kissinger and American Foreign Policy* and *Haig: The General's Progress*. A former senior member of the National Security Council staff under both Presidents Johnson and Nixon, he has also been a Senate aide and Foreign Service Officer as well as a prize-winning investigative journalist. He now devotes full time to writing both books and syndicated columns for the *Los Angeles Times* and other publications.

VICTOR NAVASKY is editor of *The Nation* and author of *Naming Names* and *Kennedy Justice*.

HERBERT S. PARMET, distinguished professor of history at the City University of New York, has been a prolific writer and scholar in the fields of political history and biography. He is the author of seven books, most recently *Richard Nixon and His America*.

RAYMOND K. PRICE, JR., headed the writing and research team in the Nixon

White House. Before joining the 1968 Nixon campaign he was editorial page editor of the *New York Herald Tribune*. The author of *With Nixon*, an interpretive retrospective on the Nixon years, he has since been assistant to CBS founder William S. Paley, a nationally syndicated columnist, and, since 1985, president of The Economic Club of New York.

BARRY D. RICCIO teaches American history at the University of Illinois at Urbana–Champaign. He has written a number of conference papers and essays on presidential politics and recent American political and social thought. His book on the intellectual odyssey of Walter Lippmann will be published shortly. Currently he is working on a book about New York literary and social critics of the post–World War II period.

MARK J. ROZELL is associate professor of political science at Mary Washington College, Fredericksburg, Virginia. He is author of *The Press and the Ford Presidency* and *The Press and the Carter Presidency*.

ARTHUR M. SCHLESINGER, JR., is Schweitzer Professor in the Humanities at the Graduate School of the City University of New York. He has written extensively on American political, diplomatic, constitutional, and intellectual history, winning Pulitzer Prizes for *The Age of Jackson* and for *A Thousand Days: John F. Kennedy in the White House*. He served as a special assistant to the president in 1961–63.

JOHN SHATTUCK is vice-president of Harvard University (government, community, and public affairs). He served eight years as Washington director of the American Civil Liberties Union before going to Harvard in 1984. He has authored, edited, or contributed to *Government Information Controls*, *Freedom at Risk*, and *Privacy: Cases, Material and Questions*.

EARL J. SILBERT is with Schwalb, Donnenfeld, Bray & Silbert in Washington, D.C.

DAVID R. SIMON is associate professor of criminal justice administration and sociology at San Diego State University. He is senior author of *Elite Deviance* (with D. Stanley Eitzen) and has published in communications, political science, criminal justice, and sociology journals. His principal research interests are in the areas of social structure and personality, white-collar crime and corruption, and alienation. His current research involves the operationalization of C. Wright Mills's sociological paradigm.

HOWARD SIMONS was managing editor of *The Washington Post* during Watergate and was curator of the Nieman Foundation at Harvard University until his death in 1989. He was the author or co-author of several books.

TERRY SULLIVAN is associate professor of political science at the University of North Carolina at Chapel Hill. His research focuses on congressional coalition building and presidential leadership. His books include *Congress: Structure and Policy*, and his most recent articles include "The *Bank Account Presidency*: A New Measure and Evidence on the Temporal Path to Presidential Influence," and "Bargaining with the President: A Simple Game and New Evidence."

GERALD L. WARREN has been the editor of *The San Diego Union* since 1975. From 1969 to 1975 he served as deputy press secretary to the president in both the Nixon and Ford administrations. During the last year of the Nixon Administration, Warren operated as the principal spokesperson.

MARK R. WEISS is professor of speech and hearing sciences at the Graduate Center of the City University of New York and was formerly professor of computer science at Queens College. His research is concerned with improving the intelligibility of speech that is obscured by noise, and he is a recognized authority in this field. He is also recognized as an expert in the authentication and enhancement of tape recordings used in judicial proceedings.

ALAN F. WESTIN is professor of political law and government in the political science department at Columbia University. His writing and research has focused on constitutional law and the impact of information technology on individuals, organizations, and society. He is one of the nation's leading experts on privacy. His books include *Privacy and Freedom*, *Databanks in a Free Society*, and *Computers, Personnel Administration and Citizens' Rights*.

JUDGE CHARLES E. WIGGINS was appointed to the Ninth Circuit of the United States Court of Appeals in 1984. In 1966 he was elected to the U.S. House of Representatives, where he served six terms as a member of the Judiciary Committee.

RONALD L. ZIEGLER is president and chief executive officer of the National Association of Chain Drug Stores, the national trade association of the chain drug store industry. Ziegler began working for President Nixon as a press aide during the president's 1962 California gubernatorial campaign. Ziegler served the president from 1969–74 as press secretary and assistant to the president, after which he supervised the transition with the Ford Administration and established President Nixon's San Clemente office.

Hofstra University's
Cultural and Intercultural Studies
Coordinating Editor, Alexej Ugrinsky

Franklin D. Roosevelt: The Man, the Myth, the Era, 1882–1945
(Editors: Herbert D. Rosenbaum and Elizabeth Bartelme)

The Stendhal Bicentennial Papers
(Editor: Avriel Goldberger)

Faith of a (Woman) Writer
(Editors: Alice Kessler-Harris and William McBrien)

José Ortega y Gasset: Proceedings of the *Espectador universal* International
Interdisciplinary Conference
(Editor: Nora de Marval-McNair)

George Orwell
(Editors: Courtney T. Wemyss and Alexej Ugrinsky)

John F. Kennedy: The Promise Revisited
(Editors: Paul Harper and Joann P. Krieg)

Lyndon Baines Johnson and the Uses of Power
(Editors: Bernard J. Firestone and Robert C. Vogt)

Eighteenth-Century Women and the Arts
(Editors: Frederick M. Keener and Susan E. Lorsch)

Suburbia Re-examined
(Editor: Barbara M. Kelly)

James Joyce and His Contemporaries
(Editors: Diana A. Ben-Merre and Maureen Murphy)

The World of George Sand
(Editors: Natalie Datlof, Jeanne Fuchs, and David A. Powell)

Richard M. Nixon: Politician, President, Administrator
(Editors: Leon Friedman and William F. Levantrosser)